Decisive Factors in Twenty Great Battles of the World

Also by William Seymour

Battles in Britain
Ordeal by Ambition
Lands of Spice and Treasure
Sovereign Legacy
Yours to Reason Why

Decisive Factors in Twenty Great Battles of the World

WILLIAM SEYMOUR
Maps drawn by W. F. N. Watson

St. Martin's Press
New York

DECISIVE FACTORS IN TWENTY GREAT BATTLES OF THE WORLD. Copyright © 1988 by William Seymour. All rights reserved. Printed in the United States of America. No part of this book may be used or reproduced in any manner whatsoever without written permission except in the case of brief quotations embodied in critical articles or reviews. For information, address St. Martin's Press, 175 Fifth Avenue, New York, N.Y. 10010.

Library of Congress Cataloging-in-Publication Data

Seymour, William.
        Decisive factors in twenty great battles of the world / William
Seymour.
                p.   cm.
        ISBN 0-312-03324-9
        1. Battles.   2. Military history.   I. Title.   II. Title: Decisive
factors in 20 great battles of the world.
        D25.S46   1989
        904'.7—dc20   89-34856
                                                                        CIP

First published in Great Britain by Sidgwick & Jackson Limited.

First U.S. Edition
10 9 8 7 6 5 4 3 2 1

To Arabella

Contents

Introduction

IN this book I have selected twenty great battles in which there were one or more easily recognizable factors that had a definite bearing on the outcome of the battle. The battle itself is given only in outline, with more detail reserved for a description of these decisive factors in the second part of the chapter. Some of the battles selected are well known, others perhaps rather less so, and in these I have paid particular attention to the political and military background.

The most important task of evaluating actions of long ago is to assess as accurately as possible the prevailing conditions, and to avoid the trap of judging the merits of a commander's decision with the advantage of hindsight, or his character by the standards of our own time. There are often as many reasons to be given for as against most human decisions, and sometimes this applies to strategical and tactical manoeuvres.

I certainly do not claim to be right in all my pronouncements as to how the battle might have ended had such and such an action taken place or been avoided. Correct solutions to these distant events cannot easily be summoned from the shades, even after the most diligent research. The reader is at liberty to make his own assessment, but I hope I have presented the factors fairly, and that in my reconstruction of them I have not let imagination add too much flesh to the bones of fact.

The principal purpose of the book is to provide a convincing insight into the anatomy of victory and defeat. A battle is won or lost in the first instance by the courage and resolution of the soldiers fighting in it, without these victory is seldom possible. Courage in the face of extreme danger comes naturally only to a few, to find that extra ounce most soldiers fall back on discipline, particularly self-discipline. The good unit – be it regiment, battalion, battery – is a school of virtue teaching its soldiers self-discipline, comradeship, pride, devotion to duty and sacrifice. It is this training that gives a soldier a new flood of strength welling from depths unplumbed; makes him see a battle through to the bitter end without flagging or failing; and impresses on his subconscious that in the last resort death is preferable to the taunt of cowardice.

This theme runs through every battle described in these pages, for there is no example of a battle lost through poltroonery. Indeed on two occasions described the courage and tenacity of the regimental officers and troops gained the victory, when the higher command was sadly lacking in direction. But it is more usual for other factors to play a decisive part. The most obvious being the personal performance and skill, or the incompetence, of the rival commanders. In every battle so much depends upon leadership. In the early ones the general had to be something of a hero, to lead his troops from the front, to be instinctively at the point of danger, and to be all and more of what they themselves were required to be. In later wars the role of the commander became more difficult; the good general did not court danger, but only exposed himself to it when a crisis arose and his presence in the killing zone was necessary. But always he needed to be seen and known by the troops, and if not loved at least admired and trusted for his moral and physical courage and military competence.

There are many other factors that influence victory or defeat, not least the human element – what might be called the psychology of battle. Battles from early days to recent times have been lost through commanders being below par physically – men who were worn and wearied, or fevered and ill. Jealousy leading to deliberate lack of co-operation, the malice of an opposing faction or an army riddled with intrigue have caused plans to miscarry and battles to be lost, and so have obstinacy and pride; cases of treachery and disloyalty are fortunately infrequent among senior generals in modern times, and victory or defeat would seldom turn upon a single instance, but in bygone years they certainly occurred and often with disastrous results.

Then there are those factors beyond the control of the commander. A general may go into battle with a sound plan, an accurate appreciation of courses open to his enemy, and possessed of a steady confidence in his own judgement, only to find that the hand he has to play is dealt him by fate. There is always the unexpected – and not always the luck or opportunity to control it. It may be man-made such as an important order misunderstood, a message never received, or over enthusiastic excitement leading to unscheduled and uncontrolled action. Or nature can deal a cruel card in the shape of a flash storm that turns roads into quagmires paralysing movement, and rivers into impassable torrents. Of course none of these unforeseen misfortunes need be decisive, but there are many instances where something of this sort has seriously upset calculations, and sometimes changed the whole course of the battle.

In the battles selected there are examples of all these vital truths about war, and they are emphasized briefly at the end of each account. There is a short concluding chapter on the nature and pattern of war, which discusses principles and stratagems and relates these to the battles described.

In a work of this sort good, clear maps are essential and, as on previous occasions, Colonel Watson has produced excellent ones. We have worked closely together in an attempt to superimpose the factors on to each of the battle maps and, as far as possible, to include the place names mentioned in the text.

The imaginative idea for the book came from William Armstrong, managing director of my publishers who, as always, gave me every assistance and encouragement. Many others have offered advice or suggestions, and in particular I would like to thank Sir Charles Rowley for putting at my disposal his immense research on the battle of Naseby; Dr Harry W. Pfanz, late of the United States National Park Service, who kindly read the Gettysburg chapter and made useful suggestions in the light of his forthcoming book on General Ewell; Mr Michael Harrison, Director of Property and Land Agent to Leicestershire County Council, who spent many hours conducting me round Bosworth Field; and Mr Richard Lamb who allowed me to use his article on Ligny. I am most grateful to the staffs of the London and Ministry of Defence libraries who took immense trouble whenever I needed assistance in my research, and to my sorely tried secretary I do, as ever, owe a special debt of gratitude for her cheerful diligence.

1   The Battle of Zama

202 BC

ZAMA was the last battle of the Second Punic War, in which Publius Cornelius Scipio (later styled Africanus) defeated the Carthaginian general, Hannibal. By the middle of the sixth century BC Carthage had become a major power in the western Mediterranean, and in the course of much fighting during the following centuries she had expanded her commercial empire in North Africa, Spain, Sicily, and Sardinia. But in the middle of the third century BC she found herself in conflict with Rome, with whom she had been in alliance for almost 300 years. Rome, by then in control of the whole Italian peninsula, felt uneasy at the Carthaginian presence so close, and anyway was desirous of possessing Sicily. She therefore, in 264 BC, brought about the First Punic War.

In the course of this war, which lasted until 241 BC, the Carthaginian commanders in the field and at sea (for it was mostly a naval war) were ill-supported by their politicians. The result was the destruction of their fleet and the loss of Sicily and Sardinia. In the years that followed, Hamilcar Barca worked hard to strengthen Carthaginian power in Spain, and it was from that country that his son, Hannibal, launched an overland attack on Rome when the latter had started the Second Punic War in 218 BC.

Hannibal was to remain in Italy for sixteen years, constantly fighting and – especially in the early years – with great success, winning such battles as Trebia, Trasimene, and Cannae. But he did not get much support from Carthage, and when in 207 BC his brother Hasdrubal marched to his aid with reinforcements, Hasdrubal was defeated and killed on the Metaurus in northern Italy. By the time Hannibal was recalled to Carthage he was virtually penned up in the south of Italy.

Meanwhile, Carthage was fighting on other fronts, foremost of which was Spain. Soon after the outbreak of war Rome had sent the two elder Scipios (Publius and Gnaeus, father and uncle respectively of Africanus) to Spain to destroy Carthaginian power, and to prevent supplies reaching Hannibal. At first they met with considerable success, but when Carthage reinforced the Peninsula with three armies under Hasdrubal, his brother Mago, and another Hasdrubal, the son of Gisgo,

1

the Scipios were defeated in battle and killed. Soon after this disaster for Rome the senate took the bold, but wise, decision to send the twenty-four-year-old Publius Cornelius Scipio to take command in Spain, where he was to win a number of notable victories.

Scipio had fought with his father against Hannibal in northern Italy, and was again in action at Cannae, but little was known of his military prowess when he went to Spain. He was soon to prove himself to be one of the great generals of all time. He had a ready grasp of the principles of war, in particular maintenance of the objective, mobility, and economy of force, he was a brave commander, a natural leader of men, and always entered a battle as fully prepared as possible. Hannibal, his distinguished opponent at Zama, was little, if any, behind him in talent. His strategy has sometimes been decried, but there is little evidence to support this from most of his Italian fighting, and at Zama Scipio got first run and was therefore able to call the tune.

By 205 BC, after victories at Baecula, Ilipa, and the Ebro, Scipio had driven the Carthaginians out of Spain and was able to return home. He knew very well that before final victory Carthage itself would have to be invaded, and Hannibal defeated there, not in Italy. While still in Spain he took the extremely dangerous and courageous step of visiting North Africa in an attempt to win over the powerful Numidian king, Syphax. In this he was successful, and another Numidian prince, Masinissa, who had fought for the Carthaginians in Spain, now came to an agreement with Rome. The way forward in Africa had now become clear from the military standpoint, but politically Scipio had many rivals. He was, however, in 205 BC elected a Consul and given the province of Sicily, from where it was understood the invasion of Africa would be launched.

While in Sicily, trying to iron out the difficulties that littered the political path, Scipio received a Numidian embassy that informed him that Syphax, having married Hasdrubal Gisgo's daughter, Sophonisba, would have to abrogate his treaty with Rome, and in any fighting align himself with the Carthaginians. This decided Scipio to act at once, and in the spring of 204 BC he set sail for Africa. He landed at the promontory called Pulchrum (Cape Farina) with probably about 28,000 men, which would have included 2,000 cavalry. The city of Carthage lay in the Gulf of Tunis, roughly halfway between the two promontories Cape Farina and Cape Bon, and the ensuing campaign took place in what is now Tunisia, north of a line El Kef–Sousse. The climate was equitable, although in the summer months water could be a problem.

Scipio was quickly joined by Masinissa with 200 Numidian horsemen who, in a battle some three miles south-west of Utica, acted as decoy for Scipio's ambush in which he utterly defeated a Carthaginian army sent against him under their general, Hanno. He then attempted to reduce Utica, but although he had ample siege engines the defence proved too

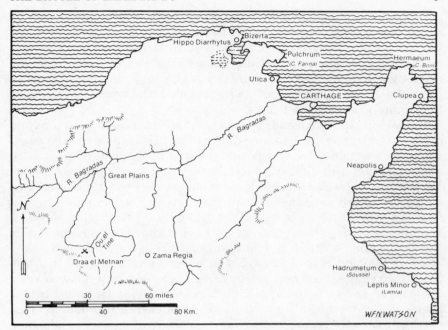

The Battle of Zama. 202 BC

stubborn and, with the approach of a large Carthaginian army (perhaps of 35,000 soldiers) under Hasdrubal Gisgo and Syphax threatening his rear, Scipio decided to take up winter quarters some two miles east of the town.

However, in the spring of 203 BC he won two great victories. Leaving the fleet and 2,000 of his men to blockade Utica he struck southwards, and by a piece of somewhat underhand deception, and considerably helped by Masinissa, he completely surprised first Syphax's camp then Hasdrubal's, destroying both by fire and cutting down thousands of the enemy as they bolted from the flames. Hasdrubal and Syphax escaped the slaughter, only to be soundly defeated a month later at a place called the Great Plains, about eighty miles south-west of Carthage in the Bagradas Valley. Once again the two Carthaginian commanders escaped unharmed, but while Scipio occupied himself reducing towns in the area of Tunis he sent his lieutenant, Laelius, and Masinissa in pursuit of Syphax whom they captured after some severe fighting.

At first the Carthaginian senate remained unexpectedly calm after this further grave setback, and took the offensive against Scipio's fleet, which they narrowly missed destroying. At the same time they recalled Hannibal and Mago from Italy. But it was not long before the peace party in the senate gained the upper hand, and a decision was taken to seek terms from Scipio. These were harsh, in that they aimed to reduce Carthage to an ineffectual African power, independent in name but scarcely in fact. The Carthaginian senate approved the terms, and an embassy was sent to Rome to ratify the treaty, but before it could report back the Carthaginians had twice violated the truce, and Scipio immediately renewed hostilities.

Meanwhile, Hannibal had landed at Leptis Minor (Lamta) in the Gulf of Hammamat, and had marched up the coast to Hadrumetum (Sousse), where he was joined by Mago's soldiers who had sailed from Liguria, although Mago himself had died on the voyage from wounds received in his last battle. Hannibal must have stayed at Hadrumetum for a little while, because he needed to await the arrival of a Numidian prince named Tychaeus whom he had asked to join him. The number of troops Hannibal and Mago brought from Italy is not known for certain, but in the forthcoming battle it is said that his 'Old Guard' from Italy numbered 12,000 and Mago's force may have been around 10,000 (most of them mercenaries). Hannibal was certainly joined by Tychaeus with 2,000 horse, and a good number of Carthaginian levies. He probably had about 40,000 men in all, which would have been a formidable force operating from the secure base of Carthage. But events were to take him farther afield.

Scipio had taken a calculated risk in exposing his line of communications to his base at Utica by marching up the Bagradas Valley and heading west while Hannibal was still at Hadrumetum. He had previously sent urgent messages to Masinissa, who after the peace had gone to sort out the affairs of his kingdom and grab what he could of Syphax's, to join him with as many troops (particularly cavalry) as possible. Scipio did not wish to face Hannibal without Masinissa's force, and by marching into the interior he was going towards his ally, and at the same time by his ruthless destruction of all the Carthaginian towns he came upon he cut off the city of Carthage from a major source of supply.

The result was inevitable: the Carthaginians clamoured for Hannibal to go in pursuit and bring Scipio to battle. He answered their call within a few days, setting off by forced marches for Zama, although he probably left his base before he was absolutely ready. The site of Hannibal's Zama is not precisely known, but it is generally thought to have been eighty miles due west of Hadrumetum.

Some of the events, and their chronology, that led up to the battle are open to question, and are not made easier to follow by the accounts of Polybius and Livy differing in one important respect. But it is usually accepted that Hannibal sent three spies to reconnoitre Scipio's camp, which lay some thirty miles west of Zama. These men were captured, but Scipio permitted them to see much of his camp before returning them – presumably this act of generosity was to impress upon them the moral and physical superiority of his army. At any rate it had the effect of prompting Hannibal to meet Scipio, and a herald was despatched for that purpose. The meeting took place at a rendezvous suggested by Scipio, which necessitated Hannibal moving his camp to a waterless hill feature that caused his troops to suffer from thirst. In the course of the meeting Hannibal proposed quite unacceptable peace terms, and the generals parted to deploy their armies for battle. The plain of Draa el Metnan, where the battle probably took place, lay between the two opposing camps near the Qued et Tine.

Obviously there is substance in this story, but it leaves many questions unanswered, such as had Masinissa, with his 6,000 foot and 4,000 horse, arrived in Scipio's camp before or after the spies departed? Polybius says before, Livy after. Why did Hannibal advance from his original and better position? Did he think he could win the battle by a surprise attack before Masinissa joined Scipio? If so, why waste time on a meeting? Or did he know of Masinissa's arrival, and feel sufficiently uncertain of victory as to make a last attempt at peace before risking the fate of the empire? These are questions that could be debated at length, but the full truth will never be known. However, the outcome of these strange manoeuvres and indeterminate colloquy was the battle of Zama.

It was the month of October in the year 202 BC, and the armies were fairly evenly matched. Hannibal had the most infantry (36,000 to 29,000), but Scipio had the edge in cavalry (6,000 to 4,000). Hannibal had also mustered eighty elephants, a larger number than in any of his previous battles, but probably not all were battle trained.

Scipio adopted his customary order of battle with the legionaries drawn up in three lines: the *hastati** in the first line then the *principes* and finally the *triarii*. But he had had experience of Carthaginian elephants in Spain, and decided against staggering the *maniples* in the usual chequerboard formation, but placed them in column directly behind those in front, thereby allowing a fairly wide passage down the whole breadth of the army for Hannibal's elephants to pass through should they be stampeded. And in order to make this funnelling more effective he narrowed the interval between the *hastati* and *principes* to avoid the beasts charging laterally. The gaps between the *maniples* of

---

*Briefly the Roman appellations are: *velites*, skirmishers armed with javelin, sword, shield, and buckler; *hastati* were front-line troops similarly armed and wearing armour; *principes* were heavy infantry whose duty it was to support the *hastati*; *triarii* were the third line of picked veterans – usually there were 600 in a legion, or half the number of the *hastati* and *principes*. They were armed with a thrusting spear, shield and cuirass; *maniples* were the sub-unit of the legion, and varied between 100 and 160 men.

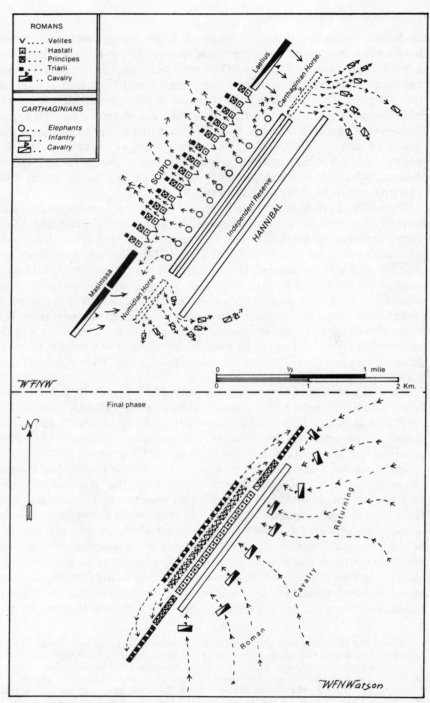

ROMANS
V .... Velites
▢ ... Hastati
▨ ... Principes
■ ... Triarii
▰ .. Cavalry

CARTHAGINIANS
○ ... Elephants
▭ .. Infantry
▱ .. Cavalry

Laelius

Carthaginian Horse

Independent Reserve

SCIPIO

HANNIBAL

Masinissa

Numidian Horse

WFNW

0 .... ½ .... 1 mile
0 .... 1 .... 2 Km.

Final phase

N

Returning

Cavalry

Roman

WFNWatson.

Battle of Zama. 202 BC

6

the *hastati* were filled by the *velites*, and these spearmen would open the battle, and if need be retire along the lines. On the left wing of his army Scipio positioned the Italian horse under Laelius, and on the right wing Masinissa with his Numidian horse and foot mixed. He probably had a total of 23,000 Roman infantry and 1,500 Roman cavalry as well as Masinissa's 6,000 infantry and 4,000 cavalry. He may also have had 600 horse under another Numidian prince called Dacamus.

Hannibal had a heterogeneous force, which was a much more difficult army to handle than Scipio's. He placed his elephants in the forefront of the army with the intention of obtaining a quick breakthrough of which his first line of infantry would take immediate advantage. Polybius makes no mention of any light infantry, but Hannibal's first line consisted of Ligurian and Gallic mercenaries, Balearic slingers and Moors, and the last two were usually light troops who may well have fought in the van directly behind the elephants. The second line comprised native Libyans and Carthaginians who were to fight a separate battle after the first line was done with. In rear, and some 200 yards behind the second line, were the veterans of Italy, mostly Bruttians, who were to act as an independent reserve. On the right flank of the army were the Carthaginian cavalry, and on the left Tychaeus's Numidians – in all probably no more than 4,000 horse.

The reason for the independent reserve, held back some distance behind the second division of Hannibal's army, may well have been the result of an appreciation by Hannibal of Scipio's probable plan of attack, learnt from a careful study of his opponent's tactics in previous battles. Scipio liked to clear the two flanks of an opposing army, then hold the centre with the *hastati* sending out the two rear divisions to envelop the enemy – a manoeuvre that he in his turn may have learnt originally from Hannibal at Cannae. By keeping his best troops in reserve Hannibal was ready for any pincer movement, and equally should the first two lines have a successful fight the reserve was at hand to administer the final hammer blow against the *triarii*.

In the first phase of the battle there may have been some initial skirmishing, but this does not seem very likely, for Hannibal planned to open the proceedings with an elephant charge. This went badly wrong. The Roman trumpeters, buglers, and cornet men put up such a barrage of cacophonous martial music that many of the elephants – presumably those not properly battle trained – took fright. The worst damage they did was to Hannibal's Numidian cavalry, who were simultaneously charged and put to flight by Masinissa's horse. Those elephants that did face the enemy line caused some consternation among the *velites* who had advanced to meet them, but before they could achieve a breakthrough they were driven off by constant javelin jabs. Some rumbled down the gaps Scipio had left for them and disappeared in the rear, while others broke out to the right. Laelius, taking advantage of the confusion they had caused, attacked the Carthaginian horse on the right wing of Hannibal's army and drove them off the field. Thus at the end of this phase Hannibal's elephants and cavalry had gone, and both his flanks were exposed.

In the second phase there was some very confused fighting. Once the elephants and cavalry were clear of the ground both sides advanced, with the exception of Hannibal's third line which stood firm, thus increasing still farther the distance from the main body. The comparative quietness was suddenly broken by the eldritch battle cries of many different races as the mercenaries clashed with the *hastati*. At first the latter were driven back by their more mobile opponents, but the line was never broken, and soon the very weight of the Roman mass prevailed as the *hastati*, with much vocal encouragement from the *principes* in their rear, literally pressed the Gauls and Ligurians back with the bosses of their shields.

The mercenaries, unlike the *hastati*, had no encouragement from their second line. Indeed these Libyans and Carthaginians held back and allowed their comrades to take the full brunt unsupported. This would appear to have been by Hannibal's orders, and not poltroonery, for it is generally admitted that the Africans fought very bravely. But whatever the reason the mercenaries did not appreciate it, and when they had had enough they turned for protection to the second line, who refused to admit them. There was then some in-fighting between the first two Carthaginian lines, until the Africans, having eventually disentangled themselves from the mercenaries, were in their turn forced back upon the third line. But Hannibal was insistent that they should not be permitted to crowd in on his Old Guard, who had orders to lower their spears and push them aside. But having been driven off it seems likely that the best of them may have rallied in the rear, and during the ensuing pause in hostilities been admitted into the ranks alongside the Italian veterans.

The crisis of the battle was now at hand. The *hastati*, bruised and battered, prepared to consolidate their victory over the mercenaries and Africans, but Scipio called them back. The carnage of the field was appalling; swaths of broken men, dead and dying, were lapped around by pools of slippery blood. Scipio needed a pause to reorganize, and Hannibal allowed him to have it. The Romans extended their line by bringing up the *principes* and *triarii* on either side of the considerably diminished *hastati*. Little is heard of Masinissa's infantry during the battle, but if they were still on the field (not having followed their cavalry) then Scipio would have had the advantage of numbers; if they were absent the two sides were almost equally matched. Certainly they were equal in all other respects – weapons, courage, leadership, and determination.

It was the Romans who began the final attack, advancing over the bloodstained field in a thin line (the precursor of Peninsular tactics), and no doubt Scipio had every hope of enveloping his enemy. But he was now up against the hard core of Hannibal's army, and they gave him little chance to manoeuvre, engaging his whole line in fighting of the utmost savagery. The fate of the battle was still in the balance when the Roman cavalry, returning from pursuit of the Carthaginian horse, swept into the rear of Hannibal's sternly engaged troops. These turned and fought with great fury but, crushed between the upper and nether millstones, they were without hope. Most of them died in their ranks, and the few who attempted to escape were ridden down by the Roman cavalry which quartered the field unmercifully. It is said that in the battle of Zama the Carthaginians lost 20,000 dead, and 1,500 men were captured, while the Roman losses were only 1,500 killed and about 4,000 wounded.

When all was lost Hannibal fled to Hadrumetum from whence he was summoned to Carthage, which had capitulated to Scipio without resistance, to partake in the peace negotiations. He urged the senate to accept the terms. Indeed there was not much choice and Scipio, who had recently suffered considerably from Punic perfidy, was pleasingly magnanimous in victory.

Fifty-five years later, long after both the two heroes of Zama had gone into exile – one voluntarily, the other compulsorily – lesser men were more vengeful, and Carthage was razed to the ground. Her empire had existed for almost 400 years, but the Carthaginians were not people with the qualities to confer benefits upon a wider sphere. Their empire was forged on commerce of a cruel and grasping kind. Its demise made way for the higher civilization of Rome. It could be said that the destiny of the Mediterranean world flowed with the blood from the battlefield of Zama.

The decisive event of Zama was the return of the Roman cavalry. Like so many of the ifs and buts of history one can only guess what the result would have been had not Laelius and Masinissa appeared upon the scene when they did. Two of the greatest captains of war were locked in a life-and-death struggle for the future of their world. The outcome must have been very close, and while it seems more likely that the discipline and training of the Roman army would have prevailed, it is entirely possible that Hannibal could have won.

What therefore were the factors that had a bearing on this crucial phase of the battle? Hannibal had only two-thirds of Scipio's cavalry (perhaps a little less if Scipio had the second Numidian contingent under Dacamas), but he started the battle considerably superior in foot soldiers. Even allowing for the fact that the elephants got hopelessly entangled with them, Hannibal's cavalry on both flanks appear to have put up little fight. This is not really surprising, because on the Carthaginian left flank Tychaeus had half the number of horse that Masinissa had, and although on the right the numbers were equal the Roman cavalry was almost certainly superior to the Carthaginian. This is a fact worth noting, for it has often been suggested that Hannibal ordered his cavalry to put up little resistance so that they could draw the opposing horse as far from the field as possible, to allow him to win the battle with his numerically superior infantry.

This he may have done, although a feigned retreat even with well-disciplined troops is a very difficult manoeuvre, and to order your entire cavalry to quit the field after offering only token resistance is taking a tremendous chance with infantry morale. It is possible, although not very easy, to order cavalry to disengage and disappear, but once they are in full flight it is quite impossible to tell what the outcome will be. Unfortunately, the fate of the Carthaginian cavalry is not recorded. Were they caught and cut down or did the Romans, under orders not to leave the field for too long, abandon the chase? The answer to that question would be helpful. More likely Hannibal issued no specific order, for he had a very good idea as to what would happen, and he always planned to win the battle with infantry alone.

Very much bound up with the cavalry action is the question of the pause that took place before the final phase of the infantry battle, and the role that Hannibal intended his third line to play. It seems most unlikely that they were intended to resist a cavalry attack from the rear, as has been suggested by the German writer, Lehmann,* for these were Hannibal's battle-winning troops, and they would surely have an offensive role. Almost certainly their allotted task, had the battle gone according to Hannibal's plan, was to roll up the *triarii* and what was left of the *principes* in the final stages of the battle. The fact that the *principes* were hardly affected during the early fighting meant that Hannibal was as much in need of the pause as Scipio.

Time was the essence of Hannibal's plan. He had no idea for how long the Roman cavalry would be off the field. It was therefore most certainly not in his interest to allow Scipio to call a halt, remove his wounded to the rear and re-dress his battle line. But to advance against the *hastati*, before Scipio had recalled them, would have invited the Roman general to carry out his favourite tactics of envelopment with the *principes* and *triarii*, and that would have been fatal. And when Scipio withdrew the *hastati* Hannibal would have seen that the *principes*, although engaged,

*Scullard p. 242.

had not been seriously weakened. The Roman infantry about to attack were, therefore, nearly twice as strong as his Old Guard. As a result he had no alternative but to accept the pause, and strengthen his ranks with survivors from his first and second lines. This suited Scipio well, for whatever may have been Hannibal's orders to his cavalry, Scipio's would have known better than to be off the field for too long.

And so by the end of the second phase Hannibal's battle had gone wrong. For him all now depended on how much time he had before the inevitable reappearance of the Roman cavalry. Polybius says they 'arrived providentially in the very nick of time', and there is no reason to doubt him. Their return was the one decisive event of the battle, and neither Scipio nor (even less) Hannibal had the ordering of it. No matter how great the general, he sometimes needs to have luck. In Hannibal's last battle it deserted him – for at Zama Fortune frolicked with Destiny.

Zama is the perfect example of a battle being won and lost through a factor outside the control certainly of the losing commander, and almost certainly of the victorious one. In the fierce infantry battle the Romans may just have had the edge, but what put the issue beyond any doubt was the fortuitous reappearance of the Roman cavalry.

2   The Battle of Hastings
14 October 1066

WHEN Edward the Confessor died on 5 January 1066, the Witan, or Great Council, elected Harold Godwinson, Earl of Wessex, to be their king. But his claim to the throne was weak. He had scarcely a drop of royal blood in his veins, and the powerful Earls of Mercia and Northumbria had no love for him. Moreover, there were two foreign princes each of whom believed he had an indefeasible right to the English crown, and were not prepared to stand aside.

With the death of King Hardicanute in 1042 the Danish line came to an end, but Magnus, King of Norway, declared a right to the throne by reason of an agreement made between him and Hardicanute. Had he lived he would undoubtedly have attempted to wrest the crown from Edward the Confessor. As it was, his successor, Harald Hardrada, was waiting a favourable opportunity to invade.

Duke William of Normandy's claim had slightly more substance. He was first cousin once removed to Edward through his great-aunt Emma, and there is good reason to believe that Edward, while in exile in Normandy, had promised him the succession, although he had no right to do so. Furthermore, when Harold had been shipwrecked on the French coast and made prisoner by the unscrupulous Count of Ponthieu, William rescued him and, after treating him with great respect and courtesy, had induced him to swear an oath that he would not oppose his accession to the English throne on the death of the Confessor.

The first of these two claimants to arrive on English soil was the Scandinavian giant, King Harald Hardrada. The English King had considered the threat from Normandy the more dangerous, and had kept his house-carls and the southern fyrd* under arms in the south during the summer. But by early September their pay and rations were

---

*The house-carls were of Danish origin, having been raised by Canute as a royal bodyguard. They were Harold's corps d'élite and numbered about 3,000 men. The fyrd was a levy of free men raised from the districts, known as hundreds, of each English shire. It was possible to assemble about 12,000 of these irregulars at any one time, and they were armed with a wide and curious assortment of weapons ranging from spears to slings and pitchforks.

running out, and being mostly subsistence farmers they were needed at home for the harvest. And so Harold was forced to disband them and sail his fleet to London. This was unfortunate, although it could not be said to have been decisive to the battle. However, William's task was made considerably easier through being able to retain his feudal host under arms during the long period of waiting, and because losses suffered to the English navy on its way back to London gave him temporary command of the narrow seas.

A few days after he had disbanded the fyrd Harold learnt that Harald Hardrada, accompanied by Harold's renegade brother, Tostig, having plundered and burnt Scarborough, had sailed his long-ships up the Ouse and landed an army, of about 10,000 men, at Riccall. He then marched on York, and was met on 20 September at Fulford by the Earls Morcar and Edwin whom he defeated in a desperate battle that lasted for a whole day. The almost total destruction of their army was to have a very serious bearing on the outcome of the battle of Hastings.

The arrival of Harald Hardrada placed Harold in a cleft stick. He knew full well that William was only awaiting a favourable wind, and yet he could not disregard the formidable host in the north. He did not even have time to communicate with the northern earls. In one of the great marches of history Harold raced his house-carls up the Ermine Street, calling out the shire levies as he went, and sprang a surprise upon the Norsemen, who thinking him to be still in the south were taking their ease on the east bank of the river Derwent. Here on 25 September, at the battle of Stamford Bridge, the weary but indomitable Saxons routed the Vikings in the space of six hours of bitter fighting, leaving their leaders, Harald Hardrada and Tostig, dead upon the field. It had been a decisive victory, but not won without cost, for both the house-carls and the levies had been sadly depleted. Two days later the wind moved into the south, and on 28 September the Norman army disembarked, unopposed, at Pevensey.

On learning of Edward the Confessor's death, and that Harold had been proclaimed king, William was exceedingly angry, and when Harold disregarded messages sent to him reminding him of his oath, William made ready for war. The Norman army, unlike the Saxon, was a feudal army, and each baron, or bishop, held his land on the understanding that he raised and equipped a prescribed number of mounted knights for the ducal service; and on this occasion William had prevailed upon the barons to bring twice the numbers of men prescribed for their particular holdings. Furthermore, soon word got around that this was a holy mission blessed by the Pope, with rich rewards for the victors, and volunteers flocked to Normandy from all parts of France. But most of these, and the conscripted men, would be infantry soldiers, for problems of transport restricted the number of horses that could be brought across the Channel. Probably somewhere around 8,000 fighting men had been landed at Pevensey, of which perhaps 2,000 were mounted knights.

Harold received the news of William's landing either in York, or as he was returning to London, and rode on ahead of his army to put in motion the summoning of fresh levies. William had no intention of marching on London, for until a battle was fought he must stay near his ships. He moved his army from Pevensey to Hastings, devastated the surrounding countryside, and waited for Harold to come to him. He had not long to wait, and Harold's impetuosity at this point was to be one of the causes of his downfall.

The English king would not have had more than 5,000 men as he marched to meet William, but orders had gone out for others to join him en route, or proceed direct to the appointed rendezvous. The exact site of the rendezvous is not known: it may have been on Caldbec Hill (just north of the present town of Battle) or it may have been on the ridge known to history as Senlac, where he took up a defensive position. In either case the distance from London was some sixty miles, and Harold – if as seems probable he set off on 12 October – would have reached it on the evening of the 13th. His army, well strung out and very exhausted from trudging miles over rough tracks, would trickle in throughout the night, and indeed during the following morning.

Harold was fighting on his own ground, and knew the countryside well. He had selected a good defensive position on which to await the oncoming Normans. He was facing an enemy strong in infantry, archers and above all cavalry, while his army had no cavalry and virtually no archers. His house-carls, armed principally with shields, and long double-handed battle-axes, were perhaps the finest infantry at that time in Europe; but the fyrd, although often well led by their thegns and capable of fighting very stoutly, were ill-disciplined and had neither the training nor the weapons for repelling cavalry. Therefore the Normans must be invited to attack a strongly held position, and when the cavalry weapon had been blunted their army might be rolled back by a well timed counterattack.

The position that Harold selected lay across a ridge that formed part of a narrow neck of land (now occupied largely by Battle High Street) from which the ground drops away steeply on both sides. The slopes from Senlac ridge were not as steep as those from the neck of land connecting it with Caldbec Hill, but troops attacking the centre and east of the ridge would be handicapped by the climb, while the lower ground to the west (the right of the Saxon line) would, even in October, have been boggy, for the valley between the Senlac ridge and Telham Hill was intersected with streams and the Asten brook. Along the ridge, in a line that extended to a little over 600 yards, Harold drew up his troops for battle with at least a portion of the levies (those armed with missiles and

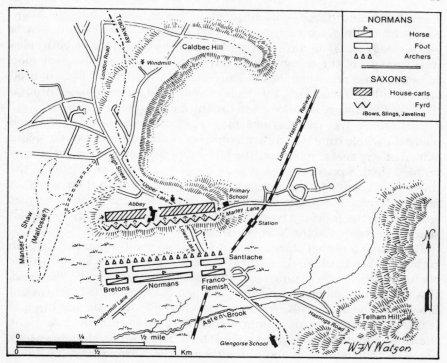

Battle of Hastings 14 October 1066. Battle Positions (superimposed on the modern town of Battle)

javelins) in front of the house-carls, with orders to withdraw through the latter after they had discharged their missiles. The line would have been thickened to a fairly dense formation as reinforcements continued to come in during the early part of the day.

The Norman army left their Hastings camp about 5.30 a.m. on Saturday 14 October, and the long column (stretching for about three miles) was probably deployed into line and ready for battle around 9.30 a.m. William planned to attack in line on a three-division front. The right wing was given to the Franco–Flemish mercenary contingent; the Normans, under the personal command of the Duke, occupied the centre – which was larger than both the two wings put together; and the Bretons formed the left wing. There were to be four distinct phases in the battle, and probably pauses in between, for no troops wearing chain mail and attacking uphill could maintain a sustained effort over a period of almost nine hours. In the first phase, which lasted for about an hour, William used his archers, who made no impression on the Saxon shield-wall, and as Harold had few archers the Normans were soon left without arrows.

In the second phase William sent in his infantry, tough, battle-hardened soldiers, whose cut-and-thrust struggle with the house-carls was a bloody one. The clash was savage, and the casualties on both sides were heavy, but the Saxon phalanx, if dented here and there, was soon reinforced and remained intact. The Norman infantry fell back in good order to allow the cavalry, the pride of William's army, to pass through them and to engage the Saxons in the third phase of the battle.

This attack, like the previous ones, was not a success. The approach along the whole front was difficult, and prevented the horses from being ridden at any speed; moreover the latter, being unarmoured, were very vulnerable to Saxon missiles. A near disaster occurred on the left of the line where the Breton knights, either less staunch than their allies, or faced by a more determined opposition, gave way and in their retreat rolled back the infantry marching close behind them ready to exploit success, and exposed the Norman centre.

There was a period of complete chaos when the fyrd on the English right counterattacked. The whole Norman line fell back, and in the confusion William was unhorsed, and a shout went up that he was dead. It was a crucial moment, and one on which the fate of the battle might have been decided. But William now showed the true qualities of leadership: removing his helmet so that all could see him, he rode along the lines rallying his soldiers to greater efforts. Much slaughter took place on that marshy flank, and although the Norman cavalry floundered in the mud, and many riders were unseated, not a single man who had taken part in the counterattack got back to the Saxon line. This for Harold was serious although not fatal, for by the time this incident took

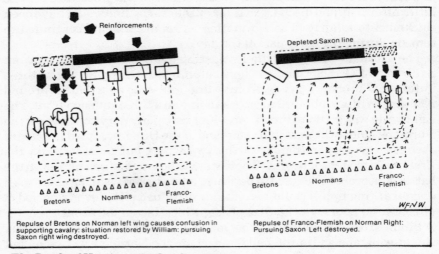

Reinforcements	Depleted Saxon line
Bretons Normans Franco-Flemish	Bretons Normans Franco-Flemish
Repulse of Bretons on Norman left wing causes confusion in supporting cavalry: situation restored by William: pursuing Saxon right wing destroyed.	Repulse of Franco-Flemish on Norman Right: Pursuing Saxon Left destroyed.

The Battle of Hastings: 14 October 1066

place his army would have reached its full strength and he would have had men to fill the gap.

By now the day would have been half spent, and no doubt there was a pause in the fighting, for both sides had taken a severe battering, and reorganization and replenishment of weapons would be necessary. But soon William continued to press with his cavalry, and once again the English played into his hands with a repetition of the Breton incident, this time on the left of their line, and once again they were in due course cut to pieces.

Somewhere around 4 p.m. the last, most crucial and bloodiest phase of the battle began. In spite of severe losses the Saxon line remained defiant. William decided to launch a combined attack of each of his three arms. The archers were ordered to increase the trajectory of their arrows, which might not cause many casualties but would have the effect of raising the shield-wall, and under cover of this fire what was left of the cavalry and the still plentiful infantry were to come to grips with the enemy. Once more the house-carls fought valiantly, but the solid phalanx of Saxon soldiers, which had been dangerously weakened by the second counterattack, now began to crack, and there were no reinforcements available. At last the Normans gained a footing on the plateau, and once upon the level ground the knights were able to drive wedges into the Saxon ranks.

A little after sunset the English king was cut down by a body of four knights before the house-carls could close around the standard.* His two brothers had been killed earlier in the day; the leadership had gone and the fyrd had had enough. They broke and fled, hoping that night and the great Andredsweald forest would cast a concealing cloak upon them. William the Bastard, Duke of Normandy, had won the battle, and the Norman dynasty was born. But it had been a great day for England as the few remaining house-carls closed their ranks and died with their king under the golden Dragon of Wessex and the banner of the Fighting Man.

Apart from the obvious fact that he was severely handicapped through having to fight on two fronts, there were four principal causes for Harold's defeat at Hastings. The first was the almost total loss of the northern earls' army at Fulford. The second was Harold's impatience and impetuosity in leaving London before he was ready. The third – which is the most debatable – concerned the action on the right of the Saxon line, when the Breton knights retreated. The fourth was the similar and ultimately decisive event on the left of their line.

*The legend of the arrow piercing the king's eye may be true, but from the detail depicted in the Bayeux Tapestry it would appear to be a house-carl who was thus wounded.

Until the autumn of 1065 the house of Godwin virtually ruled England. Harold was the powerful Earl of Wessex, his brothers Tostig and Gyrth were Earls of Northumbria and East Anglia respectively, while another brother, Leofwine, had an earldom that stretched from Buckinghamshire into Kent. Only the young Edwin, Earl of Mercia, broke the Godwin stranglehold. But as a result of a serious northern rebellion, King Edward was forced to exile Tostig and appoint Morcar – Edwin's younger brother – Earl of Northumbria. These two young men now controlled half the kingdom with the northern fyrd at their command, and they had been brought up by their troublesome father, Earl Aelfgar, to resent most strongly the political ascendancy of Harold and his brothers.

There is some indication that Morcar may not at first have recognized Harold as king, and certainly disaffection broke out in the north, which required Harold's presence in York to suppress opposition. Furthermore, in order to win their allegiance more surely he married the Earls' sister, Edith, the widow of Griffith ap Llywelyn, King of Gwynedd and Powys. However, there is no shred of evidence that when the crisis came these two men were disloyal or unpatriotic. Indeed, they had nothing to gain from victorious Norsemen or Normans.

The gravamen against them is the handling of their large and powerful army. They have been criticized for not taking offensive action against the northern invaders before they had penetrated far inland, but this would have been difficult and unwise; the farther from the sea the Vikings could be lured the more dangerous became their situation. York formed a splendid base from which to operate, but were they wise to leave this base to offer battle in the open? Communications in those days were more rapid than is sometimes realized; the excellent network of Roman roads, although by now grassed over, still provided serviceable tracks. However, there is no reason to believe that the northern earls had any news of Harold's approach, and quite likely supposed him to be still watching the south coast.

York was no longer the strong fortress of Roman times, and it may well have been that the earls did not consider its defences adequate to resist the Norsemen. More probably they did not believe that Harold could possibly reach them in time, if at all, and that their best hope of survival was to offer battle on ground that was marginally more favourable for their smaller army. The fact that they positioned their ships at Tadcaster, from where they could have cut off Harald Hardrada had the latter been foolish enough to sail beyond the junction of the Ouse and the Wharfe, lends strength to this intended offensive strategy.

Assuming they were without any positive information it is difficult to censure Edwin and Morcar, but as it happened had they stood on the defensive for three days the combined armies of the north and south would have crushed the Norsemen with far fewer Saxon casualties. Both armies would then have been available to march against William, and quite likely would have defeated him. As it was, the northern earls succeeded in gathering some semblance of an army, but almost certainly it would have been short of mounts, and with Harold in such a hurry it had no chance of reaching Sussex in time to be of any use.*

This directly leads into and is closely linked to the second factor that had such an important bearing on the result of the battle. Should Harold have waited longer in London before marching south, and in his turn devastated the country between him and William, leaving the Normans short of provisions and an occupation that was at risk?

It seems fairly certain that it was on 1 October that Harold received news of William's landing, and Guy of Amiens is probably right in saying that he was on his way south, for it would be uncharacteristic of Harold to have dallied for six days in the north when he knew William had got the wind he wanted. But his actual whereabouts is unimportant, for wherever he was summonses would have been despatched at once ordering the thegns of the shires to assemble their levies, and most of them could not have accomplished this in time to march with their king on his chosen date of 12 October.

Harold, no doubt accompanied by his house-carls, probably arrived in London on 5 October, and those men of the fyrd who had survived Stamford Bridge would trickle in during the next few days – a straggling, moiling host much in need of the rest they were not to be given. On arrival in London, if not earlier, the king would have learned of the devastation of the countryside around Hastings, for William knew Harold's impetuous and impatient nature and was gambling on his reluctance to play a waiting game while part of his own earldom was burning. Moreover, William himself simply could not afford to wait, nor could he venture far from his ships before fighting a decisive battle.

Harold had everything to gain by waiting, and much to lose by not doing so. He left London short of archers and infantry, and with only his own and his brothers' house-carls. He was to be joined by the thegns and mounted freemen from those shires along his route, but they were a small percentage of the nation's fyrd; others were to join him later, exhausted from their efforts to reach the battle on time, and still others – including the northern earls – had no chance to be present.

It could not have helped Harold's cause to let William devastate country inhabited by his most loyal supporters, but by leaving the capital with a tired and incomplete army he was playing into William's

*Ramsay, quoting from Chronicle C translated by Florence, says that the Earls remained aloof after Fulford – p. 22 – but this opinion is not generally held.

hands. It is improbable, as is sometimes suggested, that he underestimated his enemy – an unforgivable sin in any commander – and thought that he could defeat William with what troops he had mustered. More likely this was one of those battles in which the chances of victory were sensibly diminished by the temperament of the commanding general.

Having decided to accept battle with an army that was neither as physically fit nor as strong in seasoned troops as it might have been, could Harold, with his undoubted clear judgement and quickness of perception in military matters, have yet snatched victory during the fighting? The opportunity, if opportunity it was, came at that period in the battle when the Breton knights, fighting on the Norman left, gave way and in their retreat not only rolled back their own infantry, but by exposing the Norman left flank forced that division to retreat precipitately.

Harold's strategy was to fight a defensive battle until such time as the Norman cavalry had blunted itself on the shield-wall, and then to go over to the offensive. William's strategy was to dislodge the Saxon phalanx by assault and stratagem. The Norman cavalry, therefore, were the key to the whole battle, and until they had been severely mauled the Saxon line had to remain intact, and Harold had given strict instructions that no man was to quit his position without orders.

The primary authorities for the battle of Hastings are William of Poitiers (who was the Duke's chaplain), William of Jumièges, the Bayeux Tapestry and the Anglo-Saxon Chronicle. The latter might be expected to give the most reliable account from the English side, but it is weak in incidental detail and we do not know exactly what occurred on the right of the Saxon line at this time. What is certain is that the Bretons received a severe pummelling, and there was no question of a feigned retreat; but whether any orders to counterattack were given to the fyrd either by their thegns, or perhaps by one of Harold's brothers,* has never been disclosed. The only indisputable fact is that they broke the line and raced after the fleeing Bretons, and it is reasonable to suppose from what is known of their habitual indiscipline that this was an unpremeditated charge.

For a short while, until the immense personal force of the Duke rallied them, there was chaos in the Norman ranks. There was, therefore, for a brief period the opportunity for Harold to order the Saxon line forward. This massive onset of the whole English army might have overwhelmed the Norman archers and infantrymen, but the slaughter would have been heavy on both sides. There are those, among them General Fuller,†

---

*Burne thinks it was quite likely an organized local counterattack – p. 35.
†p. 379.

who think that Harold by such a move would have gained the victory, but the situation may have appeared very different to the English king on that desperate day than to later generations who have had the benefit of 900 years in which to think it over. Very likely he judged the time was not ripe to take the ultimate gamble, reinforcements were still coming in, and more importantly the Norman cavalry remained a potent force. Once they had regained their balance they would have struck hard and swiftly at the fyrd which, as was soon to be demonstrated, presented a very easy target for mounted troops.

It was certainly a decisive moment in the battle, but for the Normans not the Saxons. Had William not risen to the occasion the invaders might have been in real trouble, for in medieval battles once the cry goes up that the king (or in this case the duke) is down, and the royal insignia vanishes from sight, the mood ceases to be valiant, and is quickly followed by a panic not easily quelled. Harold was probably right to maintain the shield-wall at this stage of the battle, but he was unfortunate in that an important sequel – indeed a very similar event – was to ensure that he was given no second chance to launch his counterattack.

The second occasion on which a considerable part of the English fyrd were lured to swift and exemplary chastisement was an even more decisive occasion than the first, for it occurred when the day was more than half spent, and there were no reinforcements this time with which to shore up the line, which was already beginning to lose shape and cohesion.

There had probably been a fairly substantial pause in the battle after the Breton incident before William again sent his cavalry up the ridge. William of Poitiers declares emphatically that William, now realizing that he could not overcome the shield-wall, and having in mind the fortuitous success that came eventually from the fracas on the left, decided to win the battle by two carefully planned feigned retreats. Assuming there had been a significant pause in the battle there was perhaps time for William to have organized this most difficult of all operations of war. But his chaplain was not present on the day, and writing a few years later for the benefit of his king might – understandably – have been disinclined to asseverate that the Norman cavalry had, like their Breton colleagues, been worsted. Although his account has been almost universally accepted there must be considerable doubt that this was a planned operation, bearing in mind the extreme difficulty of passing the order to hundreds of men to reverse direction during a committed attack.

However, whether feigned or fortuitous this second retreat was the turning point of the battle. Undoubtedly profiting from what had occurred before, the Norman cavalry of the centre, far from taking alarm at the plight of the right wing, were quick to turn upon those of the levies who had so foolishly left the Saxon line. Hack and cut, turn and trample, it was soon over. Not a man got back to the now depleted shield-wall, and the way was made that much easier for the last phase of the battle.

Thus the four factors that lost Harold the battle of Hastings and changed the destiny of England. It is difficult to specify which of them was the most crucial, but if it could be assumed that any one of these factors had operated in isolation without the assistance of the others, then the loss of the northern fyrd was the one most likely to have given William the victory.

Like Zama, Hastings is also a battle where a commander was almost certainly defeated by a chance happening beyond his control. However, this battle also illustrates how that factor of chance can be put to advantage by the presence of mind of a strong personality who dominates the battle.

Harold was in no way to blame for the unauthorized breaking of his defensive line by the fyrd on two occasions. He was powerless to stop them, and their action most probably cost him the battle. Duke William, on the other hand, when his men were unexpectedly thrown into confusion, and he himself unhorsed, saved a very dangerous, perhaps fatal, situation by remounting and riding to the points of danger where all could see him, thereby saving a reverse from becoming a rout.

3   The Battle of Manzikert
August 1071

MANZIKERT is immortal as a battle because it was ultimately responsible for changing the political axis of the western world. It is true there was to be a partial recovery of Anatolian territory, and there were to be other disasters – notably the battle of Myriocephalum in 1176 and the merciless exploitation by the Fourth Crusaders in 1204 – but Manzikert sounded the death knell of the Byzantine Empire, which was for centuries the strongest and most civilized polity in Europe. It was indeed a decisive battle.

Since Constantine the Great founded his city on the site of old Byzantium in AD 330, the Byzantine Empire, as it became known, had undergone many changes of fortune. There had been periods of greatness, expansion and consolidation as well as dark interludes of internal strife and external struggles for existence, for during the empire's centuries-long span there was hardly a day when it was not fighting on at least one front.

The half century preceding Manzikert was mainly a period of extreme decadence. Basil II had been a strong ruler and competent commander, who had successfully hammered the Bulgars (earning the accurate but unattractive epithet of Bulgar-Slayer). When he died in 1025, the void was grievous, and soon afterwards the Normans in southern Italy were taking advantage of the empire's moral and military decline, and in the east a more dangerous and immediate threat came from the Seljuk Turks, a fierce, independent people, proud and predatory.

A cloud of uncertainty hangs over their origins, but they probably came from an area north of the Aral Sea in the late ninth century, and their eponymous leader was the son of an Oghuz prince, and towards the end of his very long life was converted to Islam. At first they were little more than an irritation, carrying out from early in the eleventh century raids into Byzantine territory, which had the limited objectives of plunder and loot. However, by the middle of the century the Byzantines were hard pressed to hold back the storm of Seljuk inroad and foray, for finding the opposition minimal and the grazing excellent, their incursions were becoming more frequent and much deeper. Most serious was

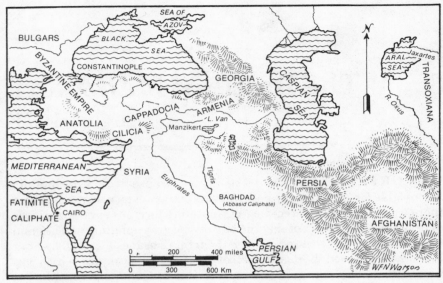

Manzikert

the situation in Armenia, an important buffer state which by 1045, after a lengthy succession of military ventures and tedious negotiations, had been annexed by the empire. But with the fall of Ani, the capital and last stronghold, in 1064 the Seljuks were virtually in complete possession of the country. Its loss was undoubtedly a contributory factor to the defeat at Manzikert.

The victor of Manzikert was Alp Arslan (meaning courageous lion), who was the great-grandson of Seljuk, the founder of the dynasty. He was born in 1029, and became sultan in 1063, ruling over – with considerable help from his distinguished vizier Nizam al-Mulk – an empire that stretched from Transoxania into Mesopotamia. Little is known of his character, but it is clear from his record that he was a great warrior, and a very able general. Obviously he was a hardy and masterful man who could be ruthless, but he was probably neither more nor less cruel than his contemporaries. Ironically, although he was to deal a mortal blow to the Byzantine Empire his ambitions (as were those of his predecessors) were directed towards Cairo, the seat of the Fatimid caliphs, for the Seljuks were Sunnis and determined to promote the Abbasid caliphate. It is a strange and important fact that at no time did Byzantium appear to take advantage of the considerable internal Islamic differences.

At the time of Manzikert in a straight battle, fought in the open, the Seljuks were no match for the Byzantine army which, in spite of the folly of latter-day emperors, could still give a good account of itself if properly and loyally handled. But the Turks were superb horsemen, individually better bowmen, much more mobile and masters of ambuscade and deception. It was their practice to avoid open battle in the plains, and fight a sort of guerrilla warfare in broken and mountainous country. In the first half of the eleventh century the Seljuk army was made up mostly of Turkomans,* but as the empire grew in extent so the army became more professional, and by no means ethnically exclusive. Recruits were drawn from conquered territories and a slave (*gulam*, and later Mamluk) element outnumbered the Turkomans. 'Slave' is a slightly misleading term, for although these men were bought and sold they were paid a wage, shared in the loot and could rise by merit to the rank of emir.

The death of Basil II was followed by some of the most troublesome and treacherous years in Byzantine history. A succession of weak, incompetent emperors, empresses, and their paramours, ruling separately or jointly, were chiefly notable for the measure of their libido, lust, cruelty, and greed. But in 1068, in the person of Romanus Diogenes, there came upon the scene a man who at least did his best to repair the damage done to Byzantium by the lotus-eaters, who had consistently allowed civil bureaucracy to triumph over military necessity.

The Emperor Constantine X Ducas died in 1067, after seven disastrous years on the throne, and left his young son and heir, Michael VII, in the charge of his wife, the Empress Eudocia Macrembolitissa, and his brother, the deputy-emperor or caesar, John Ducas. But in January 1068, despite a promise to her dying husband to remain celibate, Eudocia married Romanus, who then ascended the throne as Romanus IV, and co-emperor with Michael. He came from a distinguished Cappadocian military family, and although impetuous he was a capable commander, and he saw very clearly the need to revive the morale and confidence of the army. This was not easy for him, because he was mistrusted by certain sections of it, notably the mercenaries and the Varangian Guard, who resented the fact that he favoured the native-born troops. He was also heartily disliked by certain members of the ruling class, and in particular the Ducas family. The first mistake Romanus made was not to liquidate John Ducas. He had considered doing so, but foolishly – as it turned out – he discarded the idea.

Romanus quickly saw the military necessity for retaking Armenia, and early in 1068 he set out at the head of a large army for this purpose, but ill news from the Syrian frontier caused him to divert his march to the south-east. In a year of marching and counter-marching there were some undoubted successes, but nothing spectacular was achieved, and indeed in some of his engagements with the Turks the performance of both his officers and men left much to be desired. There were to be other

---

*Turkoman was a generic term applied in the late ninth century to the nomadic peoples of Transoxania who had by then become Moslems.

expeditions before the fatal one of 1071, and in two years of almost continual campaigning in Anatolia, Cappadocia, Mesopotamia, and Armenia, whenever he was able to bring the Turks to battle the results were usually satisfactory, and a certain amount of territory was regained.

The events leading up to the Manzikert campaign are complicated, and can be only briefly related here. In the late summer of 1070 the Emperor had entered into a truce with Alp Arslan which enabled the latter to prepare a major offensive against the Fatimid Caliphate in the belief that his north-eastern quarter was safe. But Romanus considered the truce to have been broken when the Sultan's brother-in-law (who as it happens was in rebellion against the Sultan) raided deep into Anatolia. There was a battle in which the Byzantines, under Manuel Comnenus, were defeated, and later a further laying waste of more territory by another of the Sultan's emirs. Meanwhile, presumably unaware of much of this and still thinking, or at least hoping, the truce held, Alp Arslan was laying siege to Edessa on his way south. But as a sensible military precaution to protect his rear he captured certain strongpoints in Armenia, including Manzikert. This necessitated Romanus's fourth and last expedition.

He left Constantinople in March 1071, and called in the levies as he marched. By the time he reached Sebastea he was in command of a very considerable force of infantrymen, archers and – the mainstay of the army – the heavy cavalry or cataphracts. Many oxen drew a formidable artillery train, and there was a long tail of stores and baggage wagons. There are widely differing accounts as to the numbers of this army; figures of 200,000–300,000 (certain Moslem writers) are definitely exaggerations, and 80,000–100,000 might be nearer the mark. They were a polyglot collection of mercenaries and native troops drawn from the *themes* (provinces governed by a general – the *strategos* – who was also in command of the garrison, usually a corps), and included Franks, Germans, Armenians, Bulgars, Scythians, and Patzinaks, who were non-Moslem Turks. Romanus's principal object was the recovery of the Armenian strongpoints. To reclaim lost territory and re-create the buffer state was essential, but beyond that Byzantine policy at this time was defensive, not aggressive.

The long approach march to the objective was not without its troubles. A minor rebellion of the German mercenaries, who formed part of the Emperor's bodyguard, was quickly quelled, but we are told by Michael Attaleiates – the only contemporary reporter of events – that Romanus was distancing himself from his troops through his arrogant and over-bearing behaviour. This accusation is strengthened by the drastic action he took shortly after crossing the Sangarius river (about 200 miles east of Constantinople). Here he dismissed a number of officers

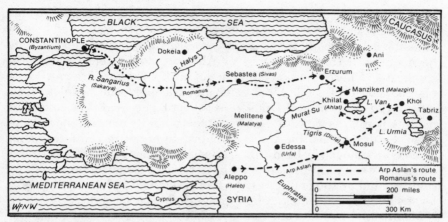

The Battle of Manzikert: 1071 The Approach Marches

and men with whom he was dissatisfied, or considered their loyalty to be in doubt. Among those returned to the capital was Nicephorus Botaniates, who had been a rival claimant for Eudocia's hand and may therefore have been jealous, but Andronicus Ducas, whose loyalty above all others must have been open to question, was retained in a senior command. This was to prove a fatal error.

When Erzurum was reached in July 1071, a council of war was held in order to decide whether to remain on the defensive in this last border town, laying waste the land to the east thereby depriving the Seljuks of food and fodder, or to advance into enemy territory. The discussion is reported (no doubt correctly) in the works of Nicephorus Bryennius, grandson and namesake of one of Romanus's senior generals, but its necessity can only have stemmed from the fact that Romanus seems to have been without any information as to Alp Arslan's whereabouts, or the numbers he had in the field. This was to be one of the deciding factors bearing upon the Byzantine defeat.

In fact at the time Romanus was leaving Constantinople, Alp Arslan was somewhere between Edessa and Aleppo, still pursuing his cherished ambition of destroying the Fatimid caliphate. Not until May did

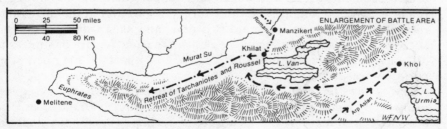

The Battle of Manzikert: August 1071

he learn that Romanus was heading for Armenia, when he at once doubled back to defend his conquered territory. His route and how he assembled his troops is not known for certain, but it appears that he abandoned the local levies at Aleppo, and hastened across the Euphrates (where it is said a number of his horses were drowned) with his bodyguard of some 4,000 men, and travelled via Mosul to Khoi (about 120 miles east of Lake Van) collecting several thousand men, notably Kurds, as he want. At some stage, possibly not until he reached Khoi, he despatched his vizier to Tabriz to organize reinforcements, already summoned by hard-riding imperial messengers. In the course of about six weeks Alp Arslan must have covered some 700 miles of arid country, and by the end of July he had assembled at Khoi a force of at least 40,000 fighting men. A fairly remarkable performance.

Meanwhile, in Erzurum Romanus had wisely overruled those who advised him to remain on the defensive, for he saw little point in laying waste land that he hoped soon to possess, and although unaware of Alp Arslan's position of strength decided to advance into Armenia. This lack of information prompted him to despatch a reconnaissance in force under Roussel of Bailleul, the leader of the Frankish mercenaries, with orders to forage and spy out the land in the area of Khilat on the western shore of Lake Van. Romanus himself, having well provisioned the army for its march south-east across barren land, intended to attack Manzikert.

His two primary objectives were Manzikert and Khilat, and either through intuition or because his local intelligence was an improvement on his long-range service, he believed that while Khilat might be strongly held, Manzikert could prove to be a soft option. Still without news of his enemy's whereabouts, but suspecting him to be somewhere east of Lake Urmia mobilizing an army, Romanus took the always risky step of dividing his army. He sent Joseph Tarchaniotes – a Georgian general who had strongly advocated the waiting policy in Erzurum, and now opposed the division of the army – with a large force, including almost all the infantry, to join with Roussel and to take and hold Khilat.

Romanus had been right in that Manzikert, although a place of considerable strategic importance, was weakly garrisoned, and it surrendered without a fight. The Emperor put a garrison in the town, and retired to his camp to celebrate this first (and as it turned out, last) success of the campaign, firmly convinced that in the circumstances a distance of some thirty miles between the two parts of his army was perfectly acceptable.

It was now the middle of August, and Alp Arslan was hurrying his army from Khoi, probably along the south shore of Lake Van. In advance of the main body was a force of perhaps 10,000 men under a battle-experienced commander named Sundak. On or about 16 August (which would have been the time Romanus entered Manzikert) this Seljuk advance guard encountered the combined troops of Tarchaniotes and Roussel in the area of Khilat.

The exact strength of the two armies is not known, but it is almost certain that Alp Arslan's was the smaller, perhaps not more than 40–50,000 men. In which case Sundak's advance guard would have contained considerably less men than the combined troops of Tarchaniotes and Roussel, and yet the latter on being confronted (and probably surprised) by the Seljuks scattered and fled precipitately, not back towards Romanus but westward in the direction of Melitene. Furthermore, no word of this débâcle was ever sent to the Emperor from his defeated generals. Indeed it is not certain whether they were defeated – reports differ – but it seems that if there was any resistance by the Byzantines it was minimal.

The battle of Manzikert is known to have been fought on a Friday, and the consensus is that it was more likely to have been Friday 19 August than the 26th. In this case it would have been the 17th (the day after the capture of Manzikert) that the Emperor received news that his vedettes were being attacked by what he assumed were no more than enemy detachments. He therefore despatched Bryennius with a comparatively small force to drive these troublemakers away. However, Bryennius, whose men were picked off by fairly intense, accurate long-distance archery and were then engaged in hand-to-hand grapple, quickly realized that he was confronted by something much more dangerous than a few fighting patrols. These Turks were in fact the troops (by now probably reinforced) that had driven Tarchaniotes and Roussel from the field. But this Romanus refused to believe, and at first turned down Bryennius's call for reinforcements. Later, perhaps after the receipt of further and more drastic reports, he sent an Armenian commander called Basiliacus, an impulsive, foolish time-server, at the head of a regiment of cavalry to repair what at that time he considered to be the incompetence, and even cowardice, of Bryennius.

The exact place where the battle of Manzikert was fought is no longer known, but from existing accounts it obviously took place on a plain which stretched back to mountainous country. To march from Khilat to Manzikert, Alp Arslan would have to cross a mountain range, descending to the steppe some eight miles to the south-east of Manzikert. Here there is a large expanse of plain backed and flanked by broken mountainous country, which is most probably the site of the main battle. At the edge of this plain Basiliacus fell into a typical Seljuk trap; disobeying one of the strictest Byzantine rules of war he allowed himself to be lured into good ambush country by a feigned retreat, there to have his force almost entirely eliminated, and himself made captive.

On learning of this disaster from returning wounded, but not aware of its extent and still without precise information, Romanus ordered Bryennius, with a considerably increased force, to push forward and cover Basiliacus's withdrawal. As he rode towards the foothills the scene of battle told its grisly tale, and before long Bryennius's men were hotly engaged by what was now quite clearly an important element of the Sultan's main army. In a running fight Bryennius extracted most of his troops, receiving three wounds himself while covering their withdrawal.

That night the Byzantine camp was attacked by hordes of wild Turks intent to kill and destroy. Attaleiates has left a vivid account of the corybantic din arising from the screams of wounded men and horses, meaningless shouting as mercenary tribes failed to recognize friend from foe, and the clatter of local traders caught plying their wares outside the camp. But the defences held, and on the next day Romanus sent what infantry he still had to drive the enemy from the camp and the banks of the nearby river (the Murat Su).

Romanus remained indecisive. He was still groping in the dark, and before he would commit himself to a major battle he sent out messengers to recall Tarchaniotes and Roussel. What became of the messengers we do not know – presumably they were chopped – for those two stalwarts were by this time in the vicinity of Melitene and heading west. But Alp Arslan, operating in friendly country, had been from the start well aware of his adversary's every movement, and it seems probable that he was behind the strange and quite unexpected appearance in the Byzantine camp on Thursday 18 August of the Caliph of Baghdad's representatives. They came with the offer of a truce, which Romanus spurned, and so battle became inevitable. He was probably quite right, for he must return to Constantinople as a conqueror or not at all.

The next day the Byzantine Emperor drew up what was left of his army for battle. The right wing was commanded by Alyattes, *strategos* of the Cappadocian theme, Romanus was in the centre with his guards, Byrennius had command of the left wing, and the strong reserve of mercenary cavalry, which included the Germans – now demoted from bodyguard duties – formed the rearguard under Andronicus Ducas. The latter was a proven general of some worth, but a shadowy and malign figure.

Oman infers that on the day of the battle the Seljuks heavily outnumbered the Byzantines,* but it is generally believed that Romanus started the campaign with a much greater army than Alp Arslan was ever able to muster. However, with a large portion of the Byzantine army having defected, and many slain, the numbers at Manzikert may not have been too disparate. Alp Arslan is said to have left the ordering of his host to his eunuch general, Taraug, who adopted the usual

*A History of the Art of War in the Middle Ages, p. 219.

Turkish formation of a crescent, which allowed for a covered withdrawal of the centre if necessary – and a withdrawal to broken country was their favourite tactics. The Sultan directed the battle from a command post. The preliminary precautions he took in making his emirs swear allegiance to his son, Malik-Shah, should he be killed; his battle dress of white, and his substitution of sword and mace for bow, indicating his determination to fight to the last; are sometimes construed as lack of confidence in victory. This may have been so, but it is unlikely that he would wish to lower morale, and more probably they were the normal and expected precautions that any monarch in the Middle Ages would take.

During the course of the day Romanus was to ensure his undoing by disregarding the precepts for fighting the Turks laid down by Leo the Wise in his *Tactica*. Admittedly he did his best to obey the first rule which was to engage the enemy frontally as speedily as possible, but the Seljuks on their faster mounts withdrew before him across many miles of plain, while running rings round his flanks with infuriatingly harassing tactics. Most of his infantry had gone with Tarchaniotes, so his flanks were unprotected. Eventually, many of the sorely tried horsemen, maddened by the hail of stinging arrows, detached themselves in pursuit and were ambushed.

Meanwhile, the bulk of the army drew steadily on, over the Sultan's abandoned camp and on towards the broken country, where no doubt a similar fate to that suffered by men from the wings awaited them. So intent was Romanus on coming to grips with the foe that it was almost dark before he realized that unless he turned back quickly his unguarded and fully provisioned camp would be plundered. And so there was nothing for it but to give the order to retire. On the whole the advance had been well and steadily conducted, but the withdrawal was another matter. This is always a difficult manoeuvre to execute, and if not properly controlled its purpose can be easily misconstrued. On this occasion there was a lack of communication with the wings, and gaps began to appear. This was the opportunity the Turks had waited for, and their light horse galloped in to cause maximum confusion. Romanus then ordered another about turn to beat off the attacking horsemen. This might have saved the situation had not Andronicus Ducas, in charge of the rearguard, refused to obey the order and marched his men back to the camp, leaving the rear of the army exposed to a whirlwind of hostile cavalry.

As darkness set in, the wings, losing hope and cohesion, began to disintegrate, and the centre became isolated, but Romanus fought on with the utmost gallantry, until his horse was killed under him, and he was wounded and taken. For the first time in history the Turks had captured a Byzantine emperor. The slaughter went on far into the night, the emperor's camp was plundered, and by the next day the entire magnificent Byzantine army had been torn apart in utter rout and ruin.

Romanus was brought before the Sultan, who treated him with magnanimity. It was in his interest to keep this emperor, whom he had humbled, on the throne and so the peace treaty was a sensible one which included the payment of a large ransom, a pact of non-aggression, and a return to the Turks of certain key places then in Byzantine hands. He then released Romanus and sent him back, as a mark of respect, with a small escort.

But no Byzantine emperor could be allowed to survive a disgrace such as Manzikert. The Ducas faction in Romanus's absence had despatched the Empress Eudocia to a convent, and proclaimed the feeble Michael VII sole emperor. Romanus somehow managed to raise another army, but in an attempt to regain his throne was defeated by Constantine Ducas at Dokeia, on the road to Constantinople, in the autumn of 1071. He escaped from the battlefield, and made his way south to Cilicia, and with another army was defeated again, this time by the traitor Andronicus Ducas. Soon afterwards, with the usual coldblooded ferocity of the times, his eyes were gouged out so 'pitilessly and inhumanely' that he died.

The Seljuks now became masters of much of the Anatolian plateau, where their tents and flocks supplanted the farmsteads of the empire, although many of the cities held out for some time longer. The flourishing *themes* which had provided the empire with some of its best recruiting grounds had disappeared, and never again would a Byzantine army march with impunity across Anatolia. The Emperor Alexius I achieved a partial recovery, but Manzikert and its aftermath heralded the loss of Christian rule in Asia Minor, as well as the rapid demoralization of the Byzantine Empire with the consequent need, or supposed need, of the long series of troublemaking Crusades. The Battle had lasted only a few hours, but its effect upon Europe was felt for many years.

There were four factors of importance that had a direct bearing on the almost unbelievable destruction at Manzikert of the once superb Byzantine army. They were the state of that army when Romanus succeeded; the loss of Armenia in the second half of the eleventh century; the almost complete lack of intelligence during the campaign; and the treachery of the generals.

It has been argued that the battle was lost before the army left Constantinople, but this would be stretching the truth. On the other hand Oman says, 'Though the internal condition and administration of the empire had been steadily deteriorating since the death of Basil II (1024), it cannot be said that its army showed any decline till the very day of Manzikert.'* Undoubtedly this is going too far the other way. Perhaps Fuller is nearest to the mark when he writes, 'There can be little doubt that in the year 1071 this organization [the order of battle and method of attack] was nearly as perfect as it had been under Basil II; but the army, though still virile, was rotten, for forty years of court mismanagement and parsimony had undermined it morally. It was not courage, organization, and tactical skill that was lacking, but discipline, morale and confidence.'† To the three prerequisites that Fuller lists as lacking could be added loyalty among the senior officers.

The foundations of the Byzantine army were laid between the late sixth and middle seventh centuries with the creation of the *theme* armies, each under its *strategos*. In each *theme* were settled bands of professional soldiers, who were given a sufficient holding of land to enable them to subsist comfortably and equip themselves for battle, when called out by their *strategos*. These free yeoman smallholders, who were exempted from all fiscal impositions save land tax, formed the rank and file of the emperors' armies (although there were always some mercenaries and the emperors' bodyguard), and they were officered mainly from the noble families.

The army was not strictly a feudal one, although the benefits of land holding were tied to military obligation. However, the *strategi* had to take into consideration the need to retain, both in peace and war, a sound economy, good husbandry and a satisfactory relationship between the soldier-peasantry and the aristocracy. So in practice the call-up was by selection, not conscription. The organization of the army and its training for war were based upon two military manuals *par excellence*. The first, compiled by the Emperor Maurice, probably in 579 when he was still only a general, was called the *Strategicon*, and 300 years later Leo VI the Wise wrote his *Tactica*. The sound military canons contained in these manuals, which stood the test of time so admirably, together with well-chosen recruits, a high standard of training and discipline, ensured that the army was both professional and scientific.

Unfortunately, in the fifty years before Manzikert a succession of deplorable rulers totally disregarded the vital importance of the military establishment to the welfare of the empire. The principal trouble was the gradual undermining – and eventual elimination – of the free soldier-peasantry, the very backbone of the army, through the greed of the large landowner. This had been going on since the ninth century, despite the wiser emperors' attempts to halt it, and was fatal not only to the military organization but to the agrarian and fiscal policy as well.

The plight of the army reached its nadir with the accession to the

---

A History of the Art of War in the Middle Ages, p. 218.
† p. 397.

throne of Constantine X Ducas in 1057. This pleasure-seeking, dissolute monarch had been his predecessor's finance minister, and was closely allied to the Church and civil bureaucracy rather than to the militarists. He was soon in deep financial trouble, and in order to bolster the treasury, offices were sold and extortionate tax-gatherers caused the break-up of the small military estates with the subsequent depopulation of the principal recruiting grounds. This meant an inevitable reduction in the strength of the native troops and consequent reliance upon the *foederati*,* and a mélange of mercenaries from different nations, many of whom were of low quality. By 1067, when Constantine died, the army was short of everything, and was no longer an attractive career for the patrician families. Indeed with the civil element in control, the generals in great disfavour and the army estimates slashed, the whole military machine, upon which the safety of the realm depended, was being systematically broken.

Such was Romanus's inheritance when he came to the throne in January 1068. He did his best to lift the affairs of the army out of the catalepsy by which it was so sorely afflicted, but the obstacles were considerable and the time too short. Undoubtedly the searing of the army's spirit that had been in process for many years was one of the main causes of its destruction at Manzikert.

Closely linked to the run-down of the army, and an important contributory cause of defeat, was the loss of Armenia to the Turks in the second half of the eleventh century. Almost since the days of Heraclius (610 –41), himself an Armenian, these people had played a most important role in the military might of the Byzantine Empire. Its finest cavalry was Armenian, many of its generals and emperors were of Armenian stock, the safety of the empire's eastern frontier was in Armenian hands, and latterly the military magnates who swallowed up the small peasant-estates were mostly Armenian.

The trouble throughout history has been that no one is prepared to leave Armenia alone, and the Byzantines were no exception. This Christian country, elevated to 5,000 feet and almost encompassed by high mountains, formed an admirable buffer state against Islamic invasion. Through it the great trade routes crossed from east to west and north to south, and as a barrier for defence and a springboard for attack it was a country of great strategic importance. The Byzantines could gain access only by a steep mountain track rising to some 3,000 feet, but for the Seljuks it was downhill all the way to Anatolia. The country was also in parts extremely fertile. Two centuries before Manzikert Byzantium had cast covetous eyes on Armenia and, not content with

*Barbarian tribes who took service with the empire under the leadership of their own prince.

suzerainty, and its limited degree of autonomy, little by little had completely annexed the country.

At the time this policy was begun, and even at the time of its conclusion in the mid eleventh century, there was no direct threat to the empire from the east. Allowing for the fact that internal strife had weakened the Armenian potential to act as a buffer state, the paramount claim of military necessity (although it was more probably a desire for territorial expansion) might just have held had it not been for the subsequent treatment meted out to the country by a succession of incredibly foolish emperors.

Large emigrations of the tough native peoples, which had begun much earlier, continued either voluntarily or by persuasion, the noble families were offered large grants of land in other parts of the empire to assist in the general undermining of the Armenian state and Church (where there existed deep theological differences), and in furtherance of this objective the long-standing system of local government was abolished. This process was extended into the military sphere when Constantine IX disbanded the 50,000-strong native forces vital for the country's defence and replaced them with weak garrison troops, leaving the Armenians virtually defenceless against the rapidly increasing Seljuk raids.

It is little wonder that they resented the treatment which had brought them to this lamentable pit of degradation, and that they became bitter and resentful with no desire to resist the invaders. Had Armenia been left to play its proper role as a buffer state it is entirely possible that Manzikert might never have been fought, and Romanus IV Diogenes have had sufficient time to revitalize the army. The humiliation imposed upon the Armenians, the complete crumbling of the country's means of defence, leading to its loss in 1064, had a direct bearing on the defeat at Manzikert in 1071. And that defeat, entailing as it did the permanent loss of Armenia, was decisive to the future fortunes of the Byzantine Empire.

Historians throughout the ages have given many reasons for Romanus's defeat in 1071, and pinpointed a number of decisive factors, but very few – if any – have concentrated on his complete lack of information, which (apart from the betrayal) was the most decisive factor of all.

It is often taken for granted that because he was, unlike Alp Arslan, operating for the most part in unfriendly country Romanus could not be expected to know what was going on. But this is nonsense; the simple fact is that he must have possessed a remarkably bad intelligence service, if indeed he had one at all. Admittedly the distances were vast, but swift horses were plentiful and in regions of great ethnic diversity carefully chosen men could pass anywhere, setting up an efficient spy net and intelligence system. But nothing of the sort was attempted, and this led to hesitation and wrong decisions both before and during the battle.

Indecision at Erzurum was due to this lack of intelligence; Roussel was sent off on a reconnaissance, but for some reason he never reported back, perhaps because his orders were not to do so until his return, which was inexplicably delayed. This led to Romanus's decision to divide his army, against the advice of a senior general. It was done because he thought Alp Arslan to be somewhere around Lake Urmia at this time; had this been so the risk was perhaps permissible, but as it turned out it was a wrong decision – and would still have been a wrong decision had Tarchaniotes stayed to fight. At no time during the preliminary engagements does Romanus appear to have received information from the front – other than from the evacuated wounded, and in such circumstances it is difficult for a general to make battle-winning decisions. There is no doubt that throughout the campaign he was fighting with one hand tied behind his back on account of his total lack of information.

The most decisive events of the actual battle were undoubtedly the actions of the two senior commanders, Joseph Tarchaniotes and Andronicus Ducas, and the mercenary leader Roussel. Tarchaniotes had command of a substantial part of the army (his exact numbers are not known), and he appears to have left the battlefield at the head of his men without ever having loosed an arrow. Had he fought and been worsted (as some Moslem writers assert) surely he would have fallen back on the main army, or at least sent messengers with an explanation.

Although Roussel was a mercenary to whom bloodshed was a profession, once Tarchaniotes had left the field he probably reckoned that he would be well advised to do so too and sell his services elsewhere, but the reason for Tarchaniotes's behaviour is much more difficult to explain. It is usually attributed to treachery, and indeed the facts support this.

There are three possible reasons for his apparent defection, and one of them excludes treachery, but no evidence survives to support any of them. Twice Tarchaniotes had been in confrontation with Romanus, first over leaving Erzurum and then on the wisdom of dividing the army, and on both occasions he had been overruled. Could he have become disgruntled at this cavalier treatment of a senior commander? To endanger an army in order to salve hurt feelings would seem to be carrying resentment too far. Was he a member of the Ducas faction in opposition to Romanus, and could he and Andronicus Ducas have planned a joint defection when opportunity arose? Nothing is now known of his political leanings, but he was said (by Bryennius) to have been 'an excellent man', and the fact that he argued against dividing the army does not lend strength to premeditated defection. It is a fact that the morale of the troops was low, and indeed at times they were mutinous. Faced with a dangerous situation, and a chance to run, could they have mutinied and forced Tarchaniotes's hand? It is a possible solution, for in the circumstances he would have had little desire to return to his emperor, even if the troops had permitted it. Too little information has survived for the mystery to be solved, but his behaviour played a major part in Romanus's defeat.

So far as is known Romanus could have had no cause for suspecting treachery from Tarchaniotes – if indeed it was treachery – but with Andronicus it was another matter. John Ducas was a bitter enemy and a dangerous man to leave behind, even though he had been exiled to Anatolia. Oaths of loyalty extracted from that family were meaningless and, as already said, it would have been better for Romanus had he liquidated the caesar. But taking his son, Andronicus, on the campaign proved a fatal blunder. He may have been included as a hostage for the good behaviour of his father, and although known to be one of the empire's best generals he was given command of the rearguard, which may perhaps indicate that Romanus preferred to have him reasonably close throughout.

The moment came for him to carry out, in the words of Attaleiates, 'the plot he had already hatched for the emperor's destruction' when after the initial withdrawal the order was given to face about and beat off the close attack of the Turks. Gaps had already appeared in the host, and the Turks had begun to infiltrate between the corps. A reversal of the standards was the customary signal for withdrawal, and in a confused situation this order could be (and in this case was) misunderstood. Instead of attacking the infiltrating enemy, Andronicus added fuel to any doubts by spreading the word that the Emperor was defeated, and marched the rearguard back to camp, leaving the army unprotected. It was a deliberate, premeditated act of treason, and it ensured that swift destruction would rush upon the army.

Such were the key events that led directly to the defeat at Manzikert, and indirectly to the eventual dissolution of the Byzantine Empire.

Romanus was defeated in battle by treachery. Very often treachery is a factor outside the control of the commander, and if it leads to defeat the commander can be said to be unlucky. But what is interesting here is that Romanus in giving Andronicus Ducas a command (Tarchaniotes may have been a traitor, but it is not proven), knew that he could be exposing his army to treachery. He must have had a reason for this, and it must have been a gamble. Romanus was not defeated by a factor outside his control, but he was an unlucky general, and they are a genre that often get defeated.

4

The Kingdom of Jerusalem
Prelude to Hattin

IN 1081 Alexius I Comnenus won the Byzantine throne, and set about putting life into an empire that was suffering from the deadness of despair. Realizing he had not the strength to defeat the encircling Turkish menace with his own military resources, he appealed to Pope Urban II for mercenaries. The Pope was willing to oblige, but on a very much larger scale than Alexius had wanted. Instead of a few thousand tough battle-hardened mercenaries there arrived in Constantinople, between the summer of 1096 and the spring of 1097, substantial armies of combatants and non-combatants each with their own leader and all demanding food and accommodation, and very ready to go on the rampage to get it.

At the time of their arrival the political situation was very favourable to the First Crusaders. The threat of a united Moslem empire under a Seljuk sultan had not materialized. The Sultanate of Rum had become independent, a new dynasty – the Danishmends – had taken control in north-western Anatolia; Mesopotamia and the Levant were ruled by a number of emirs, while Palestine was governed from Cairo by the powerful Fatimid caliphs. The Crusaders were therefore confronted by a deeply divided, and mutually suspicious, enemy. In this they were fortunate, for their accomplishments could never have been achieved against a united foe.

The relationship between the Byzantines and the Crusaders underwent many changes. There were alternating times of co-operation, neutrality, and opposition, and when it suited them both sides would weave webs of intrigue with their Moslem neighbours. In the early days co-operation was readily forthcoming – Alexius was quite keen to see them out of his domains – and during the summer and autumn of 1097 remarkable progress was made. Two battles (Nicaea and Dorylaeum) were fought and won in Asia Minor, albeit at heavy cost to the Christians, and by the end of October Baldwin of Boulogne had carved out for himself the county of Edessa and the main army lay before Antioch.

But the inhabitants of that great fortified city of northern Syria offered stubborn resistance, and even worse the first – of what were to be continuing – dissensions broke out among the leaders. The principal momentum of those early Crusaders was undoubtedly faith in their mission and a genuine desire to make their pilgrimage to Jerusalem and to free that city from the infidel. Unfortunately these worthy ideals were shortly to be overshadowed by the lure of territorial gain, and the strife required to satisfy earthly glory took precedence over supernal vows.

After suffering tremendous hardships in a siege that lasted for over seven months Antioch was eventually taken by treachery in June 1098. After some argument Bohemond of Taranto was confirmed as Prince of Antioch and remained in his principality, while the rest of the army, under Raymond of Toulouse, marched on Jerusalem. That city proved an even stronger fortress than Antioch, and the Crusaders were desperately short of siege machines and timber. However, by chance a Christian squadron had put into unoccupied Jaffa with materials that were hastened, under guard, to Jerusalem. The burning heat and shortage of water made conditions almost unbearable, and not until 15 July 1099 was the last assault successful. The appalling massacre that followed sent frissons of horror coursing through the civilized world, for the unbridled and indiscriminate killing of men, women, and children irrespective of colour, creed or race far exceeded the normal coldblooded ferocity of those times.

Even before the city had been taken there were fierce arguments as to how it should be governed, by whom and with what powers. The choice of lay rulers was narrowed down to Raymond of Toulouse and Godfrey of Bouillon. Both refused the title of king in the city where Christ had been crowned, but eventually Godfrey accepted election as Defender of the Holy Sepulchre (*Advocatus Sancti Sepulchri*), and Arnold of Chocques became Patriarch.

Godfrey was to prove himself a good fighter and a man of courage, but a somewhat weak character. He gained an impressive victory over the Egyptians at Ramle, but through jealousy and mistrust of Raymond he lost the chance of capturing the important town of Ascalon. He lived for only a year, and immediately a further dispute followed over the succession. Raymond – one of the few leaders of the First Crusade who remained loyal to Alexius – was away in Constantinople, Bohemond of Antioch had been captured by the Turks, and so the choice fell on Baldwin of Edessa. He seems to have had no qualms about wearing the crown, which was placed on his head by the new Patriarch (Daimbert of Pisa) in the Church of the Nativity on Christmas Day 1100. Thus four and a half years after the armies of the First Crusade had arrived in Byzantium they had achieved their ambition of founding the Kingdom of Jerusalem.

Ever since Nicaea the Franks (a name, together with Latins, commonly given the Crusaders) had had to fight their way for almost every mile of the road to Jerusalem, and the pattern was to continue during the next four decades. Moreover, these attempts to recover the Holy Places for Christendom, and the desire for permanent settlement, required diplomacy as well as fighting. Moslem had to be played off against Moslem, and occasionally against Byzantine, and the Franks had to be prepared to take sides with whichever party offered the best opportunities at the time.

The four principal states of the kingdom became Jerusalem, Antioch, Tripoli, and Edessa. Tripoli had surrendered to the Franks in June 1109. After the usual arguments as to the division of the spoils the greater part was allotted to Bertram,* the son of Count Raymond of Toulouse who after leading a somewhat unsuccessful fresh crusade in 1101 (mostly comprised of Lombards) had been foremost in attempting to wrest Tripoli from the Moslems before he died in 1105. The Counts of Tripoli and Edessa were nominally vassals of the king, although they often acted independently. The princes of Antioch were never vassals. However, all four states would usually – but not always – combine in times of danger to the realm.

In order to expand their territory, and retain that which they had conquered, the Franks were in a constant state of warfare, and their principal enemies in the first half of the twelfth century were the emirs of the Seljuk sultans of Baghdad, and the Egyptian forces of the Fatimid caliphs. Their strategy was aimed at keeping these powerful foes from uniting, and to be sure of this they needed to take the important central cities of Aleppo, Homs, and Damascus. This they failed to do, but through skilful diplomacy and hard fighting they succeeded for many years in forestalling any united effort against them.

Meanwhile to survive at all it was necessary to gain possession of the seaports on the coastal plain in order to receive fresh supplies of men and materials from Europe, and for their own communication purposes. Ascalon did not fall until 1153, but Jaffa was taken in 1099, Arsuf and Caesarea in 1101, Acre in 1104, and Sidon in 1110, but Tyre held out until 1124. While the Latin armies accomplished these conquests, lands east of the Jordan (Oultrejourdain) and parts of the Hauran were mainly acquired through large raids instigated by the holders of fiefs in Samaria and Galilee.

There occurred in 1118 three events of importance for the Kingdom of Jerusalem. On 7 April King Baldwin died while on campaign against

*The Genoese claimed, and were given, a share in the state for their naval assistance. Back in 1087 they had annihilated the Moslem fleet in the western Mediterranean, and gained command of the sea, thus enabling them and other fleets from Italy to render immense help to the Crusaders.

the Egyptians. He had been a most successful ruler, who despite great difficulties had established a viable kingdom reaching from Beirut to the Dead Sea. He was childless, and after some hesitation the High Court elected his cousin, Baldwin of Le Bourg, Count of Edessa, to succeed him. Four months later the Emperor Alexius died. He had been for the most part extremely patient with the Crusaders under considerable provocation, but he had never completely come to terms with the principality of Antioch. This same year saw the establishment of the Military Orders.

There had been in Jerusalem since 1070 a hostel for poor pilgrims, whose monks owed allegiance to the Benedictines, but in 1118 they were given permission to form their own Order under the Pope with the title of Hospitallers. Their Master decided that while some brothers should continue to minister to the hungry and sick pilgrims, the Order's main task should be the creation of a well-trained and disciplined army of knights, whose distinctive emblem was to be a white cross on their tunics. At the same time a knight called Hugh of Payens persuaded King Baldwin to allow him to form another military and religious order, which took the name of Knights Templar from their original headquarters in a wing of the royal palace close to Solomon's Temple. They too became an independent Order and were divided into three classes: knights, sergeants, and clerics. Their badge was a red cross worn, in the case of the knights, on a white tunic and by the sergeants on a black tunic.

The original task of these two Orders, to keep open the pilgrim routes, was soon expanded to that of an élite very professional fighting force, capable of taking on the enemy anywhere. They recruited men and money intensively in Europe, and in due course became both rich and powerful. Whereas in the early years the feudal knights provided the backbone of the Latin armies, their numbers soon proved inadequate to cope with the many calls upon their service, and mercenaries – although used extensively – were extremely expensive. Therefore the Military Orders came to form the most important element in the Latin armies. The value of their high-quality performance was, however, somewhat offset by their insistence on independence. They fought as partners and not subordinates, so that the Latin princes did not have complete control of military operations.

The First Crusaders had to face many very capable adversaries among the Syrian and Iraqi emirs, but their three greatest opponents were undoubtedly Imad ed-Din Zengi, his son Nur ed-Din, and the greatest of the three, Salah ed-Din Yusuf, known to history as Saladin. Zengi first became prominent in 1127, but did not immediately worry the Franks, for he concentrated upon subduing his Moslem rivals; but in 1129, by which time he was in virtual control of inland Syria, he met the

Frankish army outside the walls of Damascus (which city they had nearly obtained through a doubtful piece of chicanery) and thrashed it.

However, his most serious blow against the kingdom – the taking of Edessa – did not come until 1144, by which time King Baldwin II, and his son-in-law Fulk, who had succeeded him, were dead, and the kingdom was ruled by Queen Melisend, mother of the boy Baldwin III. Moreover, Joscelin of Courtenay, the capable Count of Edessa, had also died and been succeeded by a son who was a weak and dissolute man.

But even a strong ruler would have found it hard to save Edessa. The county was ripe for plucking, for it was weak in natural defences and military resources, and being somewhat out on a limb with hostile neighbours it was dependent on co-operation from other states, and in particular Antioch. The ruler of that state was now Raymond of Poitiers, who had for some time been in armed disagreement with the Byzantine Emperor John and, when he died, with his successor Manuel. And so when the Count of Edessa appealed for help Raymond refused it, and although Queen Melisend sent troops they arrived too late.

The news of Edessa was received in Europe with dismay and foreboding, and prompted the launching of the Second Crusade. The Crusaders who came to the Holy Land in 1148 were led by King Louis VII of France and the Emperor Conrad of Germany. Circumstances had changed considerably in the fifty years since the First Crusade. The Turkish opposition was stronger and better organized (and took fearful toll of the Germans and French on their way across Asia Minor), the Byzantine Emperor was far less enthusiastic, and the eastern Franks had shed much of their religious fervour and had settled down to a *modus vivendi* with their Moslem neighbours, which the new pilgrims could neither understand nor completely condone.

Louis and his Frenchmen sailed from Attalia on the Aegean coast, and landed at Antioch. He was almost immediately in disagreement with Count Raymond, who had plans to use the newcomers for regaining Edessa and taking Aleppo, thereby strengthening the northern section of the kingdom – which after all was the underlying purpose of the Crusade. But the new men, while perfectly willing to kill infidels later, had come primarily as pilgrims to purge their souls, and Louis certainly, and probably many of his followers, first looked forward to the privilege of walking barefoot into the Church of the Holy Sepulchre. Therefore it was to Jerusalem that he led his troops, where he joined Conrad who had landed at Acre and reached the Holy City before him.

Shortly afterwards (in June 1148) the decision was taken, at a council in Acre attended by all the magnates of east and west Franks, to abandon any attempt to recapture Edessa in favour of an attack on Damascus. It was a disastrous decision, for not only was Damascus one of the most strongly defended cities in Syria, but its rulers had been

inclined over the years to friendship with the Franks. The largest
Christian army yet to take the field was before the city on 24 July, and
five days later it was withdrawing to Galilee. Divided and inept leadership, internal dissension and a suspicion of treachery had played their
part in the débâcle. Conrad and many Crusaders left immediately
afterwards, Louis followed a few months later. The Latin kingdom had
been left structurally weakened, and with its Moslem and Byzantine
relationships seriously impaired.

Great warriors, like lesser men, come to dust and silence, and few of
them leave great or greater sons behind them. Zengi, who was assassin-
ated in 1146, was an exception, for his son Nur ed-Din proved equally
zealous and proficient in carrying out his father's task of uniting the
emirates and worsting the Franks. It is possible he could have been
stopped in his tracks had Raymond of Antioch had his way with Louis,
for in early 1148 he was scarcely strong enough to withstand an
offensive by two armies. Raymond did in fact have a minor success
against Nur ed-Din towards the end of that year, but in June 1149 Nur
ed-Din got his revenge when he defeated and killed Raymond and the
leader of the Assassins* who was assisting him. Antioch itself was
saved, but Nur ed-Din captured most of the fortresses in the Orontes
valley, and considerably reduced the principality.

The death of Raymond of Antioch, followed two years later by the
assassination of Raymond II of Tripoli, created serious regency problems for King Baldwin III. He was only twenty, but wise for his years,
and he not only found time to guide the fortunes of these two states, but
in 1153 to gain by battle the important town of Ascalon. In 1154 Nur
ed-Din completed his task of bringing the dissident emirs of Syria to heel
when through a change of dynasty he was able to enter Damascus
unopposed. He now ruled the whole of the eastern flank of the Latin
kingdom, and what had previously been a loose confederation of
emirates, beneficial to Latin strategy, became a united command.

In 1155 Baldwin thought it wise to make a pact with Nur ed-Din, but
foolishly broke it two years later, and paid the penalty by being severely
defeated in a battle just north of Lake Tiberias. Pressure was further
exerted on the kingdom when in 1159 Nur ed-Din found the Emperor
Manuel eager to make a truce with him, for he regarded the Saracens as
a useful political pawn in his relationship with the Franks. Such were
the complications of Latin and Greek affairs at this time.

Baldwin III died in 1162 aged only thirty-two. He was succeeded by
his brother, Amalric, whose reign was chiefly notable for his five

*The sect was founded in 1090 by the Persian Hasan as-Sabah, a devout Shia and
dedicated enemy of the Abbasid caliphs and their servants. As Grand Master of the Order
he founded he demanded of his followers that they should, if necessary, immolate
themselves in the perpetration of their many political killings.

invasions of Egypt in the space of six years, the last in 1169 being a large-scale amphibious operation in conjunction with Manuel's imperial army. There was much to be said for an Egyptian conquest both commercially and strategically, for Nur ed-Din was also interested in possessing the Fatimid kingdom thereby completing the encirclement of the Latins. And Nur ed-Din had the advantage, for while he sent troops south under his able general, Asad ed-Din Shirkuh, he was able to carry out diversionary operations against the Frankish northern border, which sent Amalric scurrying back to defend his kingdom.

Inevitably there were some successes and once, when in league with the Fatimid vizier, Shavar, Latin troops occupied Cairo; but the whole project was too ambitious, and early in 1169 Shirkuh finally established himself in Cairo on behalf of Nur ed-Din. In the spring of that year Shirkuh died and was succeeded by his nephew Saladin, who lost no time in consolidating his position and becoming master of all Egypt.

Saladin was the greatest warrior the Christians had to fight. He dedicated himself to their extirpation, and from 1170 until the treaty he made with King Richard I in 1192 it was the leitmotif of his life. Born in 1138 at Tekrit in Armenia, he spent much of his youth in Baalbek and Damascus, where his father was in service first with Zengi and then with Nur ed-Din. In Damascus he might have remained in comparative obscurity had his uncle, Shirkuh, not taken him on his Egyptian campaign in 1160 and turned him into a conqueror for Islam. However, it is not only for his military prowess that he is remembered, but as much for his breadth of view, generosity, and moral integrity. He could be utterly ruthless when time and occasion demanded, but so often it seemed that justice, truth, and honour were the wellsprings of his actions.

Fortunately for the Latin kingdom there were to be a few frustrating years for Saladin before he could muster his full strength. While Nur ed-Din lived he found himself on a leash, for his suzerain was deeply suspicious of his acts of aggrandizement in Egypt, where after the abolition of the Fatimid caliphate he ruled supreme. But in 1174 Nur ed-Din died, and Saladin immediately set out to win Syrian suzerainty. However, for more than ten years he had to fight and negotiate with the Zengi dynasty, who somewhat naturally championed their heir against the son of their former master's servant.

In between his attempts to establish his position in Syria and Iraq, Saladin had fairly frequent engagements with the Franks. In 1177 he met with a serious defeat near Ramle, although he gained his revenge a year later; but for the most part he made little headway against the Latin kingdom, whose policy was to avoid major engagement except in defence of their castles and towns.

Meanwhile, that kingdom was entering its most dangerous period.

Amalric, the last really effective king, had died in 1174 and was succeeded by his son, Baldwin IV, who was only thirteen and a leper. There was the usual scramble for the regency, although Baldwin was soon to show considerable intelligence, and unbounded courage in coping with his distressing disease and with Saladin's almost constant challenges. But whereas the Moslems were becoming every year more united, the Latin realm was becoming almost daily more divided.

Through battle, treaty, and negotiation Saladin was gradually imposing his authority on the Zengids, whose attempts to enlist Frankish assistance did not endear them to the rank and file of their supporters. In the summer of 1183 he gained Aleppo by treaty, and this left only Nur ed-Din's nephew, Izz ed-Din, obdurate in Mosul. Two years later the gallant but unhappy leper king was released from his misery. Count Raymond III of Tripoli had been regent for the past two years, and with the agreement of the barons he negotiated a four-year treaty of peace with Saladin.

With his rear thus protected Saladin was able to give his full attention to subduing Izz ed-Din, who at the beginning of 1186 agreed to acknowledge him as his suzerain. The empire was now complete and stretched from Cyrenaica to Mesopotamia, with a grand coalition of emirs whose services he could call upon. In the north the Byzantine Empire lay helpless after the annihilation of its army at Myriocephalum in 1176, and the victorious Seljuk Sultan sought Saladin's friendship. Only the Franks, and a peace treaty, stood between him and the recapture of Jerusalem. Soon these obstacles would be removed.

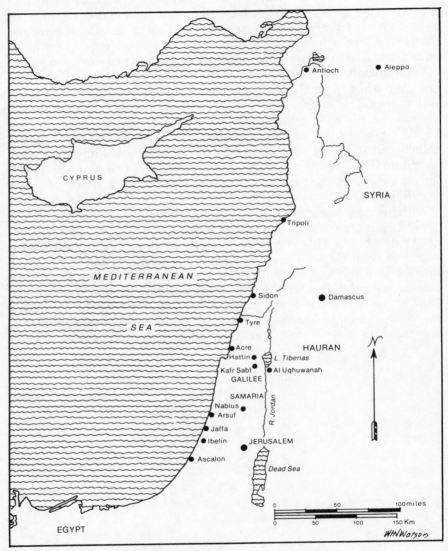

The following labels appear on the map:

- Aleppo
- Antioch
- CYPRUS
- Tripoli
- SYRIA
- MEDITERRANEAN
- Sidon
- Damascus
- SEA
- Tyre
- HAURAN
- Acre
- Hattin
- L. Tiberias
- Kafr Sabt
- Al Uqhuwanah
- GALILEE
- SAMARIA
- Nablus
- R. Jordan
- Arsuf
- Jaffa
- Ibelin
- JERUSALEM
- Ascalon
- Dead Sea
- EGYPT
- *N*
- WinWatson

Scale: 0 — 50 — 100 miles / 0 — 50 — 100 — 150 Km

The Battle of Hattin: 4 July 1187 Palestine

5 　The Battle of Hattin
4 July 1187

KING BALDWIN IV nominated his nephew (yet another Baldwin), the son of his sister, Sibylla, by William of Montferrat, Count of Ascalon and Jaffa, as his successor. William died in 1177, and three years later Sibylla married Guy of Lusignan, who had been brought to the east by his brother Amalric, the Constable, for that very purpose. The marriage was strongly opposed by the King (Baldwin IV) and his barons, for Guy was not much more than a boy, and patently a weak and inexperienced one. He was marrying into the royal house, and this untried younger son of a minor French nobleman could conceivably gain the throne.

Guy was one of the four principals on the Latin side in the drama of Hattin. The other three were Raymond III Count of Tripoli, Reynald (sometimes called Reginald or Renaud) of Châtillon, and Gerard of Ridefort, Grand Master of the Templars. Raymond was without any love for Guy, and Reynald and Gerard were bitterly antagonistic to Raymond.

In 1185, when Saladin began to forge the last link in his chain of conquests and Baldwin IV lay dying, Raymond was regent of the realm. This was his second regency, for he had acted in that capacity during Baldwin's minority. He had succeeded to Tripoli as a boy in 1152, and through his wife, Eschiva, he held Galilee as a vassal of the king. He was a veteran of many battles, and had been Nur ed-Din's prisoner for eight years. Now aged forty-five, Raymond was a man of action and ambition, a good soldier and wise administrator and counsellor. He was arguably the man best fitted to cope with the contentions of these dangerous times, but he had many enemies in high places.

Reynald of Châtillon had come to Palestine with King Louis in the Second Crusade, and had remained in the country. Unpleasant, unstable, and unprincipled, he was the man most responsible for the disaster at Hattin. His redeeming features were his gallantry and his good looks, which captivated Constance of Antioch whom he married and through whom he became the prince of that state. Before long he had antagonized the Byzantine emperor and his own king through a marauding expedition to Cyprus. In 1160 Nur ed-Din's soldiers obliged the Crusaders by removing him for sixteen years, but on his release he married Stephanie of Milly (Constance having died during his captivity), and through her became lord of Kerak and Montréale. From his castle of Kerak (at the south-east end of the Dead Sea) he caused untold trouble by violating two truces with Saladin in order to carry out raids on harmless caravans and Red Sea ports. For these and other misdemeanours Saladin twice (unsuccessfully) besieged his castle, and vowed one day to kill him with his own hands.

Gerard of Ridefort had arrived at Tripoli in 1173, and become one of Count Raymond's knights, with whom he very soon quarrelled over the matter of a broken promise for the hand of a rich heiress. Gerard thought himself ill-used by this tergiversation of his lord and never forgave Raymond. Shortly afterwards he joined the Templars and quickly rose to be their seneschal. When the Grand Master, Arnold of Toroge, died in 1148 during a recruiting tour in Europe, Gerard was elected to succeed him, and thus became virtually the kingdom's leading soldier.

When Baldwin IV died in 1185 Raymond continued his regency amid considerable hostility from the court party, but the wheel of fortune was not spinning kindly for the Franks. Exactly a year later the boy King, Baldwin V, died. Provision had been made for this contingency by Baldwin IV, and the barons had sworn that Raymond should continue to administer the kingdom until a committee consisting of the Pope, the Emperor and the Kings of England and France had decided between Sibylla (mother of Baldwin V by William of Montferrat) and her half-sister Isabella. But a camarilla of Guy's friends managed to trick Raymond, and in violation of their oaths pre-empted any committee by sending for Sibylla and Guy from Ascalon, and having them jointly crowned.

When Raymond discovered he had been outwitted he summoned those barons loyal to him to Nablus, where they agreed to his suggestion that the crown be offered to Isabella and her husband Humphrey of Toron, who were with them at Nablus, and that they should march to Jerusalem. This *coup de main* might have succeeded for, with the exception of the Templars and Reynald, Raymond had the support of almost all the magnates and the tenants-in-chief of the crown. However, they reckoned without Humphrey who was so alarmed at the prospect of kingship that he slinked off to Jerusalem and made his peace with Sibylla. Thus without their nominal head the opposition party dissolved; the barons mostly made their submission to Guy, but this Raymond would not do, and he retired to his wife's fief in Tiberias.

Saladin was watching these events with interest, but he was a man of honour and would probably have kept the truce even though with the Latin kingdom split down the middle he must have felt that now was his opportunity to wrench the linchpin from the wheel of state. But Reynald of Châtillon did it for him. At the beginning of 1187 he carried out the third of his plundering raids on a caravan proceeding peaceably from Cairo to Damascus, killing or imprisoning the military escort and carrying the considerable booty to his castle. Saladin demanded restitution and release of the prisoners, first from Reynald who refused, and then from Guy who, thoroughly alarmed, ordered Reynald to comply. Reynald again refused, making the outrageous claim that his was an independent state, and had no truce with Saladin.

War was now inevitable, although the Prince of Antioch and Raymond of Tripoli, acting independently, sought to renew the truce. But Raymond went further, for he had now convinced himself (not without reason) that he alone could save the kingdom, and should be its king. He therefore enlisted Saladin's active help in assisting him to attain his objective which, when one considers that Saladin's own objective was the destruction of the kingdom, shows how convoluted was the Saracen–Frank relationship. Guy was dissuaded only with difficulty from besieging Tiberias for this act of treason, and starting a civil war. Instead he sent a mission to mediate, which included Balian of Ibelin, the Archbishop of Tyre and the Grand Masters of the Military Orders.

The details of what occurred next are confused and contradictory, but the outcome is indisputable. It appears that Saladin wished to send a strong raiding party into Galilee across Count Raymond's territory, but for what purpose has never been satisfactorily explained.* Saladin is said to have asked Raymond's permission and he, not wishing to offend his ally, gave it on condition the party left at sunrise and returned at sundown the same day, and did no damage to property. Raymond then sent warning messages to all Christian posts in the neighbourhood, including the negotiating mission then on its way to Tiberias. The raiders duly returned at sundown having done no damage to property, but proudly displaying the heads of many of the mission at the end of their swords.

The party, less Balian who had stayed in Nablus to conduct some business, had reached al-Fulah on the night of 30 April where they received Raymond's message. Gerard of Ridefort determined to give battle to the raiders (which was quite contrary to Raymond's stated wishes), and hastily summoned what Templars there were in the neighbourhood. The clash occurred the next day at a place generally called the Springs of Cresson, which may have been about ten miles north of Nazareth. Even with Gerard's reinforcements the numbers

* Beha ed-Din, who was Saladin's contemporary and biographer, asserts that there was no raiding party, and that the force which annihilated the negotiating mission was a part of the main army under Saladin's son, el-Afdal, advancing to battle positions. This could be the correct version.

were hopelessly uneven, for the Moslems were said to have 7,000 men. The result was a massacre from which only Gerard (wounded) and two or three knights escaped. The Archbishop of Tyre, who had wisely broken his journey in Nazareth, Balian and Reginald of Sidon, who seems to have been one of the survivors, eventually reached Tiberias. Guy had suffered a grievous loss of good soldiers, and the Raymond–Gerard feud had been fuelled.

The whole business had so ashamed Raymond that he returned to his duty, and having broken his pact with Saladin accompanied the envoys to meet Guy. Back in Jerusalem he made his submission to Guy and Sibylla, who behaved towards him with considerable magnanimity. On the surface Christian unity now prevailed, but beneath it resentment and distrust still smouldered.

Both sides now busily prepared for the forthcoming trial of strength. The numbers of fighting men given by the various authorities, contemporary and later, vary considerably, and mostly err on the high side. The Latin army that assembled at Acre at the end of June 1187 probably contained about 1,200 knights. 10,000 infantrymen and a good many (perhaps 2,000) Turcopoles. These were troops recruited from the local population, and used mainly as cavalry. They were bowmen less heavily equipped than the knights, but except on special occasions had the same role in battle. They formed a considerable part of the troops of the Military Orders, who themselves formed the professional core of the army. Each of these two Orders could, on the occasion of a *levée en masse* such as Guy had now ordered, muster about 400 knights. However, this would mean leaving the castle garrisons dangerously reduced, and the castles formed the strategic defence of the realm.

Saladin had proclaimed a jihad immediately following Reynald's last raid, and he now drew on troops from the Hauran, Aleppo, and all other parts of his empire. Even Izz ed-Din sent him a formidable contingent from Mosul. His numbers are not known, but almost certainly exceeded those of the Franks and may have amounted to as many as 20,000 in all. Most of the warriors would be mounted on those small, fleet country-breds, and their principal weapon was the bow, although there would have been a fair number of mailed horsemen who, like the Turkish knights, would fight with lance and sword.

In view of what happened at Hattin it is interesting to recall the knights' clothing. This consisted of a mail hauberk that reached down to the knees and was often extended to give protection to the legs, arms and hands; it was usually worn over some form of leather jerkin and under a cloth surcoat. This latter was intended to deflect some of the sun's scorching rays from the chain mail. The neck and face were protected by a mail coif, and the head was covered by a pot or conical-shaped helmet with nose guard. The sergeants when mounted would not be so heavily

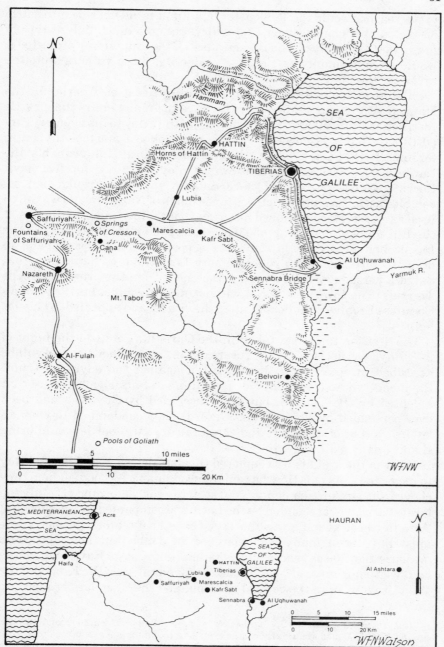

The Battle of Hattin: 4 July 1187

protected, nor would the Turcopoles. The knights did not ride into battle on the cumbersome destrier of chivalry, but on a much lighter type of horse, quite possibly of Andalusian stock. If the animal was protected it would have been only partially so, and it was more vulnerable to the arrows of the infidel than was its rider.

Saladin assembled his host at al-Ashtara, east of Tiberias in the Hauran, at the end of May. Here he gave the many emirs their battle instructions, and allotted the right wing of the army to his nephew, Taqi ed-Din, the left to his most able lieutenant, Gökböri, and took the centre for himself. On Friday 26 June the army moved to al-Uqhuwanah at the southern tip of Lake Tiberias, where they remained for five days. Reconnaissance patrols informed Saladin that the Franks had assembled at Saffuriyah, which lies to the north of Nazareth and was often used as a base.* He positioned his army about fifteen miles to the east in the hill country just north of Tiberias. In 1183 and again in 1184 the Franks had refused battle from a strong position, and it was probably in order to lure them into country more favourable to his tactics that Saladin personally led a strong detachment from the army to besiege Tiberias. The town was taken without much trouble, but Raymond's Countess Eschiva shut herself up in the citadel and appealed to Guy for help.

The decision to march, taken in the Christian camp on the night of 2–3 July, was decisive for the future of the Latin Kingdom, and will be described in detail later. It was taken against the advice of Count Raymond, whose arguments for remaining at Saffuriyah were at first accepted by the Council, but later discarded by Guy who had been over-persuaded by Reynald and Gerard. They condemned Raymond's advice as that of a traitor, and said that to refuse battle would bring shame on them all.

Many of the knights had deplored this last decision, and begged Guy to reconsider, but this time he remained adamant. As good soldiers they obeyed without further demur, and so in the early morning of 3 July the largest army yet assembled by the Latins, accompanied by the Bishop of Acre in whose keeping was the True Cross,† set off for Tiberias. There must have been many who marched in doubt, but few who could measure the consequences of this fateful enterprise. Raymond, whose land was being crossed, was by custom given the van, the King and the True Cross were in the central division, and the Templars brought up the rear.

---

*It is just possible that the Springs of Cresson raiders had been sent to reconnoitre this ground, but 7,000 men seems rather large even for a reconnaissance in force.

†This precious small piece of the Cross was kept in a bejewelled case encrusted with pearls and precious stones. It was taken into battle and displayed on other important occasions as a sacred emblem, much as the colour or standard was in later armies. The Arabic biographer Imad ed-Din describes it as the supreme object of Christian faith.

The position of the Templars – and no doubt the Hospitallers as well – was a wise and normal precaution, for Saladin's tactics of attempted encirclement, and bringing pressure to bear on the rearguard so as to separate it from the main body, were well known. And this is precisely what occurred during that bone-searing hot day on the road to Tiberias. The seemingly limitless, straw-coloured arid plateau the Christian army had to cross was completely waterless, and soon men (some heavily encumbered with chain mail) and horses were being tortured by thirst. They had covered some seven miles when the enemy light horse attacked them with a cloudburst of arrows. From then on relays of fresh Turks kept up a relentless pressure as Guy's soldiers, their lips parched and crusted, their tongues like tags of leather, strove to fight them off. So great was the pressure on the rearguard that it began to lose contact with the centre, and Gerard asked the King to call a halt.

The main body was by this time somewhere near the small deserted village of Marescalcia, about halfway between Saffuriyah and Tiberias. A few miles to the east lay a range of hills rising to 1,100 feet with three passes that led, down steeply falling ground, to Tiberias which is over 600 feet below sea level. At the northern point of this range of hills are two rocky outcrops known as the Horns of Hattin, which stand guardian to the village of that name some 600 feet below. Count Raymond and the vanguard had pushed on ahead of the army, and may perhaps have seen the disposition of Saladin's men on the Tiberias Hills; at any rate he sent back a message strongly advising Guy to hasten forward so as to reach water by nightfall. But Guy felt the men were too weary, and pitched camp. It was a controversial and crucial decision.

Few of the survivors were likely to forget that night. The wounded continually cried out for water, but not a drop was available to moisten withered tongues. All night long enemy patrols prowled the perimeter loudly praising Allah for having delivered the Christians into their hands. Some authorities say that to add to the army's discomfiture they set fire to the nearby scrub, but this seems more likely to have happened during the battle next day.

On the morning of Saturday 4 July the army set off in the same order, marching through Lubia with the intention of breaking through the enemy at the northern pass by Hattin. Initially the vanguard made some slight progress, with the enemy giving way in places; but Saladin had made his dispositions with care and cunning. The battle was fought just south of the Horns of Hattin, and he had his army drawn up in the form of a crescent with the wings forward of the centre, so that very soon the whole Latin army would be encircled so closely that in the words of Imad ed-Din 'not an ant could have got out'. The Saracens were fresh and their morale was high, which was much more than could be said of the

Christians, and again we are told by Imad ed-Din that Saladin had a fleet of camels standing by with large reserves of arrows and other weapons.

The tactics of both sides were expected to be straightforward, and in accordance with their respective 'manuals'. The Franks had their heavy cavalry protected by the crossbows of the infantry, who were themselves somewhat protected by their thick gambesons. They would open their ranks for the knights to charge, and form a rallying point for their return. The Saracen horsemen would worry the flanks and rear of Guy's army, and would be prepared to retreat before a charge, turning in pursuit when their enemy retired. But at Hattin lack of morale among the Christian infantry made a nonsense of tactics, and lost the battle. These weary, dispirited soldiers maddened by thirst had had enough. Before the battle was very old they left the road and dragged themselves up a nearby hill, from where no amount of entreaty by their king would make them move. Soon the Saracens were among them; many prisoners were taken, but many more were left dead upon the ground, their tongues swollen and lolling out.

Take away the infantry and the knights are at too serious a disadvantage to win a battle on this scale. Guy, realizing the hopelessness of the situation, brought them together in a solid phalanx with the Cross in the centre. Here they fought with tremendous courage against heavy odds. As horses and men sank down in tangled heaps those who were left fighting were suddenly engulfed in drifting thick smoke, for Saladin had ordered the grass to be fired to add to their discomfiture. The last stand was made upon the slopes of Hattin hill. Here about 200 knights rallied round the king until Saladin called a halt to the slaughter. Almost the entire Christian chivalry had been lost, the Bishop of Acre was dead and the True Cross was in the hands of the infidels.

Towards the end of the battle, either under orders or on his own initiative, Count Raymond led Balian of Ibelin, Reginald of Sidon, and a handful of followers on a forlorn charge in which they managed to break through, and seeing that the battle was virtually lost they galloped from the field to safety. Some chroniclers, without much conviction, assert that Taqi ed-Din opened ranks to let them through, presumably with the idea of trapping them, rather than to aid their escape; the latter reason was useful to blacken Raymond's character still further, but soon he was beyond caring, for within three months death would release him from the odium of military treachery, a crime he was convinced had been committed out of loyalty to the common cause.

When the killing had ceased and the prisoners had all been rounded up Saladin dispensed rough justice to those Christians who had survived. Towards King Guy he behaved magnanimously, as he did towards the other knights* who were all, with one exception, honourably treated and later released. The exception was Reynald of Châtillon whom he killed with his own hand as he had promised. The lower ranks, sergeants and infantry fared less well, being for the most part sold into slavery, and the Military Orders fared worst of all. These Saladin regarded as villains of the deepest dye, and a danger to his faith. At least 200 of them were put to the sword in cold blood. These were fierce times, and what may be considered an act of savage barbarism perpetrated by a Moslem sultan was far surpassed fourteen years later at Acre when a Christian king (and an English one at that) ordered the massacre of more than 2,000 prisoners.

In mobilizing the great Christian army most of the castles had been denuded of troops, and the victor of Hattin had little difficulty in mopping these up. The few that did resist could be bargained for with promises to release important prisoners – such as Guy and Gerard for Ascalon. Only a very few such as Kerak held out for more than a year. Indeed within eighteen months the Crusaders were left with only Tyre, Antioch, and Tripoli in Syria. Jerusalem surrendered in October 1187, when Saladin's treatment of the inhabitants was in marked contrast to the shameful behaviour of the First Crusaders in 1099.

The effect of the battle of Hattin upon the crusading movement was very similar to that of the battle of Manzikert upon the Byzantine Empire. In both cases the vanquished lived on for a period of time – the Third Crusade and the death of Saladin enabled the enfeebled and sadly attenuated Latin kingdom to survive for a further hundred years – but in both cases the defeat was the turning point in their history. Hattin was the triumph of Islam over Christendom, of the Crescent over the Cross, under whose banner the battle was fought. The Crusaders lost control of Jerusalem and the strategically important inner areas of Syria and Palestine, and the papacy lost control of the Crusaders, whose movement henceforth became increasingly secular.

It might be said that the battle of Hattin was lost seven years before it was fought when, in 1180, Baldwin IV's sister, Sibylla, married Guy of Lusignan and the kingdom split into two factions. Some of the complicated details of the clash of personalities, and the constant intriguing for power that went on for much of Baldwin IV's reign, and all of his son's, have been touched upon. The kingdom was morally weakened through long periods of baronial rule, and the sinister machinations of a court cabal headed by Agnes of Courtenay (the mother of Baldwin IV and Queen Sibylla), her relations and certain magnates of the realm. It was

*Including, strangely enough, the Grand Master of the Templars, Gerard of Ridefort. The Grand Master of the Hospitallers had been killed in the battle.

a very important contributory factor, but the kingdom's fate was sealed on the Horns of Hattin.

The deep cleavage that had done such harm was papered over when Raymond came from Tiberias to make his submission to Guy and Sibylla, but the paper was very thin. One cannot help feeling a trifle sorry for Guy on the eve of battle. The man who wore the Latin crown stood, at the best of times, on a windy pinnacle, and at Saffuriyah the King was beset by bickering barons and by a personal lack of confidence and resolution. On the decision of this weak man depended the fate of the army and the kingdom.

The army's camp at the beginning of July was at a place called the Fountains of Saffuriyah, which lay a mile to the south of the small unwalled town. The surrounding area was fertile arable land, and there was an abundant supply of stream water available even in summer. As has been noted, between Saffuriyah and Tiberias was almost fifteen miles of broken ground, parched and arid with probably no water, and certainly insufficient for an army of 20,000 men.

The bare facts, already recounted, that preceded Guy's decision to march from Saffuriyah were Saladin's attack on Tiberias, probably to lure the Franks from their base; Countess Eschiva's appeal to her suzerain for help; her husband's sound military reasons for ignoring her plea and for remaining at Saffuriyah; and Guy's agreement, until being over-persuaded by Reynald and Gerard. But of course there was much more to it than that.

To what extent the contemporary and near-contemporary accounts of all that Raymond is alleged to have said when called upon to speak at the council of Saffuriyah (and possibly at one in Acre previously) are correct, and not written with the advantage of hindsight, is not known. But what he had to say on the folly of an advance to contact are almost certainly correctly reported. He began by reminding the council that it was his wife and his land that were endangered, although he did not believe that any harm would come to Eschiva, and that Tiberias could be easily recovered later. He forcefully pointed out the incredible foolishness of advancing fifteen miles over waterless country, harassed all the way by the enemy, in order to give Saladin the chance he wanted of engaging a tired and thirsty army on ground of his own choosing. And finally he is alleged to have drawn the attention of the council to the fact that it had always been Latin military strategy to avoid endangering the army in any large-scale battle in unfavourable conditions, for if the Moslems were denied a victorious campaign for any length of time they invariably despaired. He therefore advocated standing on the defensive,* for he felt certain that Saladin would attack or have to disperse his army.

*Some accounts say he even suggested withdrawing to the coast to be certain of avoiding battle, but this seems unlikely.

All this was sound reasoning, and the council appears to have endorsed it. But Raymond was by no means the only experienced soldier present, and one wonders why two others, Reynald of Châtillon and Gerard of Ridefort, were later to put strong objections before the king. Surely they would not hazard their own lives and the safety of the whole army purely out of animosity to Raymond? Did they really believe he was a traitor, and was trying to lead the army into a trap? It seems most unlikely, although no doubt they wished Guy to believe it to be true. One is left with the possibility that they really thought the Christians could win the battle, or at least win through to water before having to fight.

It is an interesting aspect hitherto not greatly considered. But by starting before dawn, with four hours of cool marching, the army could have gained contact by soon after midday, and not have been too afflicted by thirst. That they did not succeed was due in part to their having struck camp too late, but principally to the action of the Saracen light horse. Here Guy's tactics may have been at fault, because he should have had enough infantry with their deadly crossbows to keep the hit-and-run Turks at a distance from the main body and rearguard, as indeed they had done under his leadership in 1183. There are no reports of shortage of bolts and arrows, which presumably were carried on pack animals. It looks very much as though Gerard, perhaps the most professional soldier there, was definitely of the opinion that Raymond was wrong and that to advance was a justifiable risk. And just conceivably he could have been right in that thinking.

But Guy had other, more personal, reasons for the decision he eventually took. He had assembled the entire chivalry of the kingdom for the purpose of eliminating Saladin and his army. To refuse battle (especially in defiance of the Grand Master of the Templars) might severely shake his somewhat tenuous hold upon the throne. He must have remembered that in 1183, when he was regent, he had assembled nearly as large an army at Saffuriyah and marched it to the Pools of Goliath. There he had taken up a strong position facing Saladin's army, and despite the urgings of almost all his knights he did nothing for five days, save diffuse ceaseless defeatism and uncertainty, until the Moslems dispersed. Baldwin was so furious at what he deemed was Guy's caitiff conduct that he dismissed him from the regency.

There was also the appeal of the Countess Eschiva to be considered. Raymond could have been wrong in his asseveration that no harm would come to her, and anyway it had long been recognized that there was an obligation on the sovereign to march to the assistance of any of his fiefs in times of great danger. It had not always been honoured, and ironically the last occasion on which it was, the supplicant had been the egregious Reynald at Kerak – he who a few years later was to give as an excuse for violating the truce that his was an independent state.

Finally there was Guy's personal relationship with Raymond. Until quite recently they had been bitter enemies. When Guy first became king Raymond had threatened armed intervention, and he had refused to pay homage at the coronation. Could he now in this, Guy's first battle as King, be leading him to destruction? It seems very far fetched, but Guy might not have needed much persuasion from those ruthless manipulators of the truth, Reynald and Gerard, to believe it to be so.

With the benefit of hindsight we can say with confidence that by ordering the army to march on the morning of Friday 3 July 1187 Guy of Lusignan lost the most decisive battle the Crusaders ever fought. He broke with tradition in hazarding the army unnecessarily, especially when there were no reserves to fall back upon, and for this he stands condemned. But it is unfair to censure him too severely, for he was under extreme pressure and he was not a strong character. Moreover, in the opinion of the present writer he had some grounds for thinking he might succeed, provided he handled his army properly – which in the event he does not seem to have done.

The decision to march was obviously the dominating factor of the battle, but once they were committed to action there was another crucial decision to be taken. It presents a fascinating problem, but one that is not easy to unravel with the differing and vague accounts of the Saracen dispositions that have come down over the centuries. Conjecture is at liberty to roam, but there are too few hard facts upon which to build a conclusive case.

If one takes a consensus of the contemporary, or near contemporary, reports it seems fairly certain that at that time there were two roads to Tiberias from Saffuriyah. One lay to the south-east via Kafr Sabt, from there to the south end of the lake and thence north along its shore, and the other branched off to the north between the villages of Marescalcia and Lubia, thence through Hattin to the Wadi Hammam which emptied into the lake north of Tiberias. In both cases the distance to the town was about twenty miles. There may even have been a third, more direct, route branching from Kafr Sabt.

What chroniclers of the battle do not make absolutely clear is the exact position of Saladin's troops. He undoubtedly held the Horns of Hattin area and the northern range of the Tiberias hills, but did he on the day before the battle still have troops at Kafr Sabt, which is a little over four miles to the south of his main concentration? He probably did leave a detachment there, and another guarding the Sennabra bridge at the south end of the lake, but both places would be lightly held. It is an important point, because originally we are told Guy intended to take the southern route.

The main part of Guy's army reached the area between Marescalcia and Lubia soon after midday, and were – particularly the rearguard – already battle weary. Raymond, who commanded the vanguard, does not seem to have been seriously troubled by the enemy, and he sent back anxious messages to the King to press on, for the springs in that area had proved to be dry and he clearly understood the immediate need for water. For some reason he advised Guy to turn north, which meant fighting his way through Hattin to the water beyond; he may have made contact with the enemy at Kafr Sabt, and believed that route to be impassable. From what little evidence there is the northern route seemed to offer the least hope, and Raymond's choice comes under suspicion if one believes the story that some of his knights betrayed the army's route to Saladin – but that was probably a later fabrication to impugn further his alleged treachery.

But choice of route soon became a secondary consideration. The unfortunate Guy again found himself the unwilling arbiter between two fiercely opposed parties, who used powerful arguments in support of their convictions. The Grand Master of the Temple was determined the army should make camp and not advance any farther that day: his men, he said, had borne the brunt of the fighting, and were in no condition to engage the enemy's main army. Raymond was equally adamant that without water for another fifteen hours none of the men would be in a condition to fight with any hope of success. Guy for the second time overruled Raymond, and ordered the army to encamp for the night.

Once again events proved Raymond to have been right, and historians have mostly condemned Guy for making a fatally wrong decision. In fact he probably took the only course open to him, for had he ordered the march to continue towards Hattin it is very doubtful if the Military Orders, who were a law unto themselves, would have obeyed. The infantry, as so often, were the key to the battle. On the next day thirst brought them to the end of their tether. Would it have done so some hours earlier? It is a question that cannot be answered, nor for that matter will it ever be known why Raymond advised what seems to have been the most difficult route. It is possible that the lake might have been reached and disaster avoided by continuing the march through Kafr Sabt.

King Guy decided to stake his kingdom on the hazards of war. It was a brave decision, and perhaps not quite such a foolish one as is usually made out. Had he been a luckier and more able general the chance of victory was quite possibly there, and the Saracens were very well aware of it. Battles are often won and lost on narrow and impalpable margins; successes are woven into the pattern of history, and are sometimes unremarked, but posterity seldom condones failures. At least in the hour of his undoing the King behaved with fortitude.

Saladin was undoubtedly a fine general, but at Hattin he had the victory handed to him when the Christian army left their well supplied base to cross a parched desert. Theirs was an army seamed with envy, mistrust and downright malevolence. In such a situation the only hope lies in a strong and ruthless commander, who knows what he wants and overrules the warring factions. Guy of Lusignan was not such a man. He was weak and indecisive. Of all the battles described this is the only one to be lost through a combination of almost every human failure, save only courage.

6   The Battle of Bosworth
22 August 1485

EDWARD IV died on 9 April 1483, leaving the kingdom to his twelve-year-old son, Edward, but he had designated his brother, Richard, Duke of Gloucester, as Protector during the King's minority. At the time of Edward's death his son was at Ludlow with his uncle Anthony, Earl Rivers, while Gloucester was in the north of England. Edward had married Elizabeth Woodville, whose unpopular family now had a slender control of the council in London. Clearly they could not prevent the protectorship, but they hoped to establish a regency council to whom the Protector would be responsible. They lost no time in fetching the new king from Ludlow.

Richard set out from Yorkshire at about the same time as the King left Ludlow, and met his cavalcade at Nottingham on 29 April. The tendentious writings of Tudor historians have portrayed Richard as a wicked monster, but in fact he was nothing of the kind, nor was he deformed. He had served his brother most loyally, and was a good commander and courageous fighter. He was intelligent and able, but too impulsive for his own good. He was also a typical product of his time in that he was intensely ambitious, and sufficiently ruthless to deal drastically with any obstacle to his ambition. This was clearly demonstrated when he met his nephew in the Midlands. He dismissed the King's Welsh escort, arrested his uncle, Rivers, his half-brother, Sir Richard Grey, and his chamberlain, Sir Thomas Vaughan (all of whom he later had executed), and with many protestations of loyalty accompanied the bewildered boy to London, where they arrived on 4 May.

Richard may not have had designs on the crown at this early stage, but he was determined to brook no interference with his rule during the minority, and to this end he took steps to secure the loyalty of a number of peers who were hostile to the Woodville faction. One of these was the Duke of Buckingham, a lineal descendant of Edward III's fifth son, and a man scarcely less ambitious than Richard. At first Buckingham was of considerable assistance, for when in the middle of June Richard began thinking in terms of the throne Buckingham arranged for the young King to be 'more comfortably lodged' in the Tower, and accompanied

Richard and the Archbishop of Canterbury to Westminster, where Edward's queen and her family had sought sanctuary. As a result of this embassy the Queen was reluctantly persuaded to surrender her second son, Richard Duke of York, who joined his brother in the Tower. Both boys were murdered there, probably in the autumn of 1483.

Meanwhile, Buckingham worked most skilfully in promoting Richard's cause among the citizens of London, and on 23 June he was able to head a deputation that waited upon Richard to swear allegiance to him as King Richard III. The new King was duly crowned on 6 July. But some three months later Buckingham, for a reason not properly known although presumably underscored by intense ambition, veered over to the Woodvilles. They had been in touch with Margaret Beaufort (then married to Lord Stanley), and through her had arranged for her exiled son, Henry Tudor,* to invade England with troops supplied by the Duke of Brittany. The invasion was to coincide with an insurrection in the west country headed by Buckingham. Henry did sail – somewhat belatedly – but by the time he was off Poole he had only two ships left, and the insurrection had collapsed and Buckingham had been executed. But it showed Richard that he had an active rival for the throne.

As time went on Richard's position became less secure. He was surrounded by treachery, and in April 1484 his son, the Prince of Wales, died and it was known that his wife could have no more children. There were many who looked favourably on the proposed marriage of Elizabeth of York and Henry Tudor as a means of ending the wearisome York and Lancaster strife. When an attempt to kidnap Henry in France and deliver him to Richard failed, the Tudor's following in England was, if anything, strengthened. It probably came as something of a relief to Richard to learn that the long-threatened Lancastrian invasion was definitely planned for the summer of 1485. In June of that year he took up residence in Nottingham Castle, from where he could be kept in close touch with events through relays of couriers posted at twenty-mile intervals along the principal highways.

Henry sailed from Harfleur on 1 August. He had with him his uncle Jasper Tudor, Lord Oxford, and some knights who had shared his exile, and his ships were filled with about 2,000 French mercenaries. He landed at Mill Bay, close to Milford Haven, on 7 August. It was an area he knew well from childhood, and as good as any from which to start his great adventure. He marched unopposed to Haverfordwest and on to Aberystwyth, which place he reached on 10 August. From there he

---

*Henry's claim to the throne was exceedingly slender, his lineage being studded with the bar sinister. His mother was the great-granddaughter of Edward III's son, John of Gaunt (the Beauforts having been legitimized by Richard II), and his father, Edmund Tudor, was the son of Owen Tudor and Catherine, widow of Henry V.

struck east and north-east to Welshpool, and on 15 August Shrewsbury opened its gates to the invader. After Shrewsbury his route was Newport, Stafford, Lichfield, Tamworth, and Atherstone, where he spent the night of 20 August.

The date of Henry's departure from France, his landing in Wales and his progress through the principality into England are well authenticated, but thereafter a veil descends upon the preparations of both armies, their exact dispositions for battle, and the precise course the battle took. Even the site of the battlefield has recently – but not very convincingly – been contested. This veil has been only partially penetrated: so much remains conjecture based upon a careful study of what evidence there is, and a close examination of the field.

The two accounts most generally accepted are those of the Croyland Chronicle and Polydore Vergil's. The continuator of the Croyland Chronicle (whose identity is not known) was probably present at the battle, but judging from his very brief description he could not have seen much of it. The account written by Polydore Vergil (an Italian scholar, naturalized in 1510) is the most plausible still extant, but it was written some time after 1506 at the request of Henry VII, and so there was a time lag and perhaps a bias, although within the bounds of understandable discretion Vergil did his best to present facts truthfully.

In his march through Wales Henry undoubtedly collected a substantial number of armed followers. Neither Sir Walter Herbert in the south nor Sir William Stanley in the north made any attempt to hinder him. But his most useful attachment came from Rhys ap Thomas of the House of Dinefwr, who was a powerful landowner in Carmarthenshire, Pembrokeshire, and Cardiganshire. A known Lancastrian sympathizer, Rhys was almost certainly in touch with Henry before the expedition, and he planned the Tudor's route so as to be able to protect the southern flank, although he did not bring his 'great bande of soldiers' to join Henry until the latter had reached Welshpool on 13 August. In Shrewsbury Sir Gilbert Talbot joined Henry with 500 soldiers, and thereafter his route was largely dictated by the need to win over the Stanleys – Thomas, Lord Stanley, and his brother Sir William.

Meanwhile, what of Richard? The King was at Nottingham, or more precisely Beskwood Lodge nearby, when on 11 August he learnt of Henry's landing. At least some in Wales had remained loyal, for even with well-posted couriers – and that was probably not the case in the heart of Wales – to ride 200 miles in four days was a fine feat. He soon learnt that William Stanley, among others, had betrayed him, but he retained slender hopes of his brother Thomas.

Richard was both surprised and angered at the ease and rapidity with which Henry had marched through Wales, and by the time the latter reached Shrewsbury he had still not mustered all his troops. Lord

Stanley had been visiting his estates in Lancashire, and the Earl of Northumberland – Commissioner of Array for the East Riding – was travelling far too slowly. But when Richard's scurryers (mounted scouts) informed him that Henry was at Lichfield he realized he could wait at Nottingham no longer, because the rebels might decide to take the road for London. Accordingly, on 19 August the royalist army (which included Northumberland who had arrived with his men that day) left Nottingham for Leicester.

From Shrewsbury Henry marched to Stafford, then turned south-east through Lichfield and Tamworth to Atherstone. At either Lichfield or Tamworth he collected some pieces of ordnance, which put a brake on the rapid progress his army had been making hitherto, and at Atherstone he met both the Stanleys, but the meeting was inconclusive. On 21 August the two armies closed the gap between them. Henry marched from Atherstone to a place called White Moors, which lies five miles from Atherstone up the Roman road through Fenny Drayton, while Richard marched west from Leicester to the high ground immediately north-west of Sutton Cheyney.

The probable site of the King's camp was on the north-eastern end of a ridge that extends for about a mile in the direction of Shenton. Here the ridge, at 417 feet, reaches its highest point and would have given Richard a good view over much of the surrounding country. The land below and to the south of Ambion Hill, the commanding feature, was called Redmore Plain (Redmore was the first name given to the battle) and at the time of the battle it was rough, uncultivated ground with a large marshy area to the south and east of the hill. Much has been written over the years about the extent of this marsh, and it is important for two reasons – the distance to which Henry had to sidestep it in order to come square to Richard's line, and the position of Lord Stanley and his retainers. The consensus is that it covered an east-west line from not far to the south of Sutton Cheyney to the south-west of Ambion Hill, and its average depth to its southern limit was six hundred yards. And so it was a very formidable obstacle guarding what was to be Richard's left flank.

The western end of Ambion Hill, which was a mile from the King's eve of battle camp, offered the best battle position in the neighbourhood. On the morning of 22 August the royalist camp was early astir, and the men set off for this position. The army probably marched and fought in column of battles, with the Duke of Norfolk commanding the van, the king at the head of the main battle marching behind him, and the reluctant Northumberland bringing up the rear. There is disagreement among historians as to Richard's numbers, the top figure being around 12,000. This is probably on the high side, for with defections and deserters the total may not have reached 10,000. Norfolk with the vanguard had about 1,200 bowmen flanked with 200 cuirassiers under

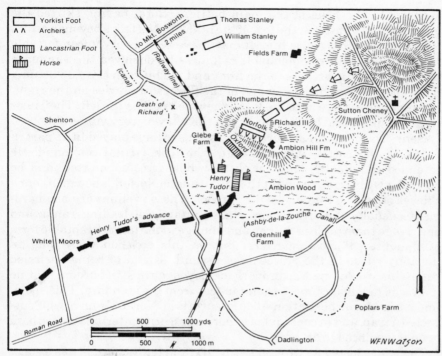

The Battle of Bosworth: 22 August 1485

his son Lord Surrey; the main battle was made up of billmen and pikemen with heavy cavalry on the wings, and Northumberland probably commanded about 2,000 billmen. Richard's guns may have been sited on the left flank of the army to the south of Norfolk's troops.

By the time Henry Tudor reached White Moors his original 2,000 Frenchmen, and the small number of fellow exiles who had sailed with him, had been more than doubled, and were further increased shortly before the battle by the arrival of Sir John Savage (William Stanley's son-in-law) and other important defectors. Even so he could not have had more than 5,000 soldiers but the Stanleys, who he had reason to hope would join him, probably commanded about 4,000 men between them. Therefore if Henry had any hope of success the Stanleys had to co-operate. But after Atherstone there was to be no meeting with them until the battle had been won, and to every plea for co-operation they returned an evasive answer. Up to the eleventh hour they were to remain an infuriating enigma.

Henry's advance to Ambion Hill would have been, like Richard's, in column of battles with the cavalry on the wings. Lord Oxford commanded the van, and Henry with Lord Pembroke (Jasper Tudor) marched at the head of the main battle. Oxford, having skirted the marsh, found himself at the foot of the hill with Norfolk's bowmen only a few hundred yards above him. It must have been a very uncomfortable moment, but with commendable calmness he deployed the vanguard into line with the archers to the front and the billmen close up behind. Sir Gilbert Talbot had command of the Shropshire levies on the right, and Sir John Savage with the Welshmen took post on the left. The Tudor right was protected by the marsh, but the left was very vulnerable.

Henry was not a great warrior and seems to have played little part in directing the battle. It was Oxford who took virtual command. He intended to fight the battle with his whole force committed, and he opened it with a cannonade at the same time as Norfolk's bowmen sent a shower of arrows into his leading troops. These preliminary bombardments usually did little more than irritate the leading ranks and encourage them to close the gap and indulge in the more acceptable form of slaughter at close quarters. But on this occasion there was an uncanny pause in the proceedings. Oxford, fearful of being encircled before his whole line was properly deployed, gave strict orders that no man was to advance more than ten feet from his standard. This seemingly unnatural hesitation at first surprised Norfolk's men who suspected a trap, and in consequence there was a brief interlude before both armies advanced to attack.

The battle lasted for around two hours, and for Richard it was a sorry tale of treachery and tribulation. As the leading ranks of Norfolk's and Oxford's battles became locked in hand-to-hand combat, and men started falling under the steel flail of sword, pike, and bill, they were quickly reinforced by men from the main columns. Norfolk was the first casualty of importance. He was a veteran of many fights, and his loss was a severe blow to Richard. Soon wide gaps began to appear in both armies, and all depended on three men – two watching from the sidelines, and a third closer at hand.

Northumberland was the first to display his treachery. He had been most dilatory in bringing his troops to Leicester, and once there had behaved as though he had little intention of partaking in the battle if he could possibly avoid it. When Richard sent urgent messages to him, at a critical stage of the battle, to bring his troops forward he failed to obey, saying that he had better hold back in order to guard against any Stanley intervention – in fact he was waiting to see what the Stanleys would do.

But he was not the only man waiting to see what they would do; both Richard and Henry knew that the Stanleys now held the key to victory or defeat. Neither commander could afford a battle of attrition, for without the Stanleys Henry was hopelessly outnumbered, and Richard was fearful that as time went on others might follow Northumberland's example and hold back or desert. Henry appears to have taken positive steps to draw the Stanleys into the battle. He rode out to the left flank of his army accompanied by his bodyguard and with standards unfurled so that William Stanley, whose troops were not far distant, might be more likely to rally to his cause.

The sight of this cavalcade, prominent and vulnerable on the flank, is said to have determined King Richard to scorn the entreaties of his entourage to seek safety through flight, but rather to seize the chance of ending the battle by a decisive blow against the man who had caused him so much trouble. And so the proud, impulsive Plantagenet, mounted on his great white courser, quickly gathered what men of his household and bodyguard he could muster (perhaps no more than 100), and rode down the north-west slope of Ambion Hill, right across the front of William Stanley's men, to cut down the Welsh usurper.

In the first few seconds of this conflict of truly majestic splendour Richard felled Sir William Brandon, Henry's standard-bearer, and then unhorsed Sir John Cheyney – a warrior renowned for his courage and his poundage. For a few minutes it looked as though this sudden and unexpected onslaught would achieve its purpose; but just in time Henry's supporters, now quite possibly supplemented by William Stanley's men, closed round their leader. The Red Dragon fluttered again, and King Richard was dragged from his horse and hacked to death.

This is the most usually accepted account of how the second and last English king to die in battle did so in the best traditions of medieval chivalry. There are some who say it makes a good, but quite implausible, story and that the King was unhorsed in the bog on the left flank of his army – now the site of King Richard's well – while trying to repay Lord Stanley for his infidelity. Whichever is right the result was the same: with the King dead his followers had no reason, or wish, to continue the fight. They appear to have dispersed in all directions, and if the royalist casualty figures of 1,000 are correct many must have perished in the bog or in the limited pursuit, for it is too high a figure for a brief two-hour battle. The victors lost no more than 200 men.

Lord Stanley, who seems to have taken no part in the battle, was at hand to place the golden circlet worn by Richard upon the new King's head. The body of its previous wearer was stripped naked, slung over a horse and taken to Leicester in the wake of the victorious army. Here it was exposed to the public view for two days, and after this shameful treatment the last Plantagenet king was buried in the church of the Greyfriars. But even there it did not find a permanent rest, for when the son of the victor of Bosworth dissolved the monasteries the Greyfriars was plundered, Richard's tomb destroyed, and his body thrown into the river Soar.

The Wars of the Roses were not quite done with, for two years after

Bosworth the imposter Lambert Simnel was made the figurehead of a revolt in which the Earl of Lincoln, whom Richard had nominated as his heir and who may have been present at Bosworth, played a prominent part. Henry was obliged to crush this uprising at the battle of Stoke on 16 June 1487, and then at last the Wars of the Roses ended. But it was the battle of Bosworth which introduced the Tudor dynasty, one of the most splendid in the history of the British monarchy.

At Bosworth the deciding factor was betrayal. It is possible that Richard missed the opportunity of delivering a decisive tactical blow in the very early stages of the battle. A quick victory might have been obtained had the King ordered an all-out attack with his main battle as Oxford was off balance deploying the vanguard into line, and bringing up his artillery. It was a cumbersome manoeuvre to perform with an enemy poised only a few hundred yards away with the advantage of a hill. But the moment soon passed, and our knowledge of the actual fighting is so slender as to rule out any particular action, or lack of it, as being decisive.

It was the behaviour of the Stanleys, even more than that of Northumberland, which in the end gave Henry the victory, for whichever way the Stanleys went Percy would follow. Thomas Stanley had married as his second wife Margaret Beaufort, who had been first married to Edmund Tydier, or Tudor, Earl of Richmond, and she was the mother of Henry Tudor. Her marriage to Stanley was purely one of convenience between two people who led quite separate lives, and although Margaret was involved in clandestine negotiations with Henry in France, there is no record that Thomas was in any way party to them. On the contrary, after a somewhat shaky start which involved a brief visit to the Tower, he became firmly attached to Richard and as Lord High Constable and Lord Steward of the Household he was always in attendance on the King. Nor did his loyalty waver for a moment at the time of the Buckingham revolt, although Margaret was deeply involved.

After his coronation in 1483 it must have appeared to Richard, with so much outward approval from almost all the nobility of the land, that his position was quite secure, and this was confirmed in a triumphant progress through the Midlands to the north. Stanley, too, had reason to congratulate himself on being firmly entrenched in the royal favour. But by the spring of 1485 Richard's power base was beginning to crack. In March he lost the support of his devoted wife, Anne Neville, and the previous year their only son had died, thus leaving the future of the dynasty in doubt. In Wales there was considerable sympathy for the claim of Henry Tudor, and there were many there who were active in the Lancastrian cause.

It was not unnatural that Richard should be ever ready to suspect treachery from those whose track record was not particularly auspicious. He must have known that chief among these was Thomas Stanley. True, ever since Edward IV won at Tewkesbury he had been, unlike his brother William, solid for the Yorkist cause both in peace and war. But he was a trimmer *par excellence*, and from Blore Heath to Barnet he had procrastinated, prevaricated and generally displayed exemplary caution, favouring first one side and then the other. Indeed caution was Thomas's hallmark, just as impetuosity was William's. Until this time – and in the case of Thomas for some time afterwards – the Stanley brothers had survived and thrived through carefully blending caution, cunning, and sufficient disloyalty to enable them to be generally on the winning side, but to escape the stigma of treason if things went slightly wrong.

As Richard was undoubtedly well aware of the unreliability of the Stanleys – William even more so than Thomas – it may seem strange that in January 1485 he commissioned Thomas to raise an army. But he did not have much choice, for without the Stanleys – who after Norfolk and Northumberland were the most powerful families in the land – he could never be sure of the north-west. Lord Stanley delegated this task to his son, George Lord Strange, for the county of Lancashire, and his brother William for Cheshire. Thus at the time of growing unrest William Stanley was charged with the defence of one of the most sensitive parts of the kingdom against a possible Tudor invasion. He was almost certainly aware of the detailed planning for that invasion some while before Henry landed, and he had no intention of taking any steps to prevent it.

However, for the present Richard was unaware of William's intended treachery, and Thomas was still seemingly very much the King's man. But in July, when the court was at Nottingham, he sought Richard's permission to visit his estates in the north, where he had not been for almost two years. It was a fairly ominous request and no doubt Richard was urged to refuse it, for with Thomas closely confined there could be no question of his disloyalty. But that would never have done, for his son would command his troops, and it was important that Richard should show some degree of trust. That it was a fairly slight degree was evident when permission was only given for Thomas to leave on the understanding that he sent his son to Richard in his stead. This Stanley did, and Lord Strange arrived at Northampton about a week before Richard marched.

At the time Thomas asked permission to leave the King it is probable that they both knew about the forthcoming invasion, but it was William who was the most closely concerned with Henry's progress to Bosworth. He was not among those to whom Richard sent orders, on hearing of Henry's landing, to join him at Leicester (although Thomas was), for the

King knew that he was fully aware of what was required of him in North Wales. But William, having lamentably failed in his duty to stop Henry, brought his troops to the neighbourhood of Shrewsbury. Here his force was close to Henry's, although the two men did not meet until 17 August at Stafford. The meeting was brief, and so far as Henry was concerned unsatisfactory, for even William was not prepared to commit himself thus far ahead.

Meanwhile, Thomas on receiving the King's command to come to Leicester (he was probably marching towards Shrewsbury at the time) made the feeble excuse that he was suffering from the sweating sickness – those who contracted this dreaded disease usually had little chance of sending apologies for absence. It was about this time that Lord Strange was apprehended trying to escape from Nottingham Castle; on being questioned he implicated his uncle and Sir John Savage, but refused to admit that his father had traitorous designs. Richard was now at least certain of one brother, whom he at once branded as a traitor, but he may still have entertained slender hopes that the other would persevere in his duty, for his son was in mortal peril.

We have it from Polydore Vergil that at Atherstone on 20 August Henry met both William and Thomas Stanley and that 'they enteryd in cownsaylle in what sort to darraigne battayll with King Rycherd yf the matter showld coome to strokes . . .' This amicable meeting may not have been concluded to the entire satisfaction of Henry, for both Stanley brothers continued to prevaricate. For Thomas this was perhaps understandable, but William could now have no reason for holding back.

At the conclusion of the meeting Henry remained in Atherstone until his troops arrived, and on the next day he continued his march to White Moors. The position of the Stanleys before and during the battle is not easy to assess. It seems fairly certain that William made his camp on the eve of the battle a mile or so slightly west of north of Ambion Hill in the vicinity of a small village called Near Coton, but where Thomas encamped is not known. Among historians the most popular place is south of the battlefield in the Stoke Golding–Dadlington area, but if this was so and he had any intention of joining the battle the marsh would have made it difficult for him. It is quite likely that he, too, was north of the battlefield and in close touch with his brother. His exact position is not very important, for it is almost certain he took no part in the actual fighting.

William Stanley's troops, and Thomas's if they were close by, would have been plainly visible from Richard's position and not far distant from Henry's. On the morning of the battle, before he left camp, Richard sent a final message to Lord Stanley to join him at once, or else his son would die; Stanley is said to have replied that he had other sons and he would not join the King. It may be true that he had at last shown his colours, but certainly Lord Strange did not die.

Henry, too, sent an urgent message to his stepfather shortly before battle was joined, and is believed to have received the slightly more encouraging reply that he would make his own dispositions and join when the time was ripe. But Polydore Vergil says Henry 'wer no lyttle vexyd'. For Thomas the time was never ripe, but William's men undoubtedly joined the fight at about the time, or very shortly after, that Richard was striving to reach Henry.

Thomas Stanley may have played no part in the battle to put his stepson on the throne, but his masterly inactivity was sufficient for him to reap rich rewards, not least of which was his elevation to the dignity of an earl. At Henry's coronation the Earl of Derby in his 'riche gowne furred with Sables' carried the Sword of State from the Tower to Westminster Abbey. But William, who had done much more for Henry, was not so well rewarded, and in the end his impetuosity was his downfall when he foolishly meddled in the Perkin Warbeck affair. He was executed in February 1495.

The sorry tale of Henry Percy, Earl of Northumberland's treachery has already been briefly told, and there is little to add. The Croyland Chronicler puts it very nicely and succinctly: 'But where the Earl of Northumberland stood, with a troop of a size and quality befitting his rank, no opposition force was visible and no blows were exchanged in anger.'

The family record was not one to encourage any Yorkist to put much faith in the Earl's reliability, for both his father and his grandfather were killed fighting for the Lancastrians, at St Albans and Towton respectively. Richard knew well before the battle that Northumberland's loyalty was gravely suspect and his co-operation a matter of doubt. He had made a specious excuse of the plague to avoid calling up men from the East Riding (who would undoubtedly have fought loyally for Richard) at the time of the King's summons, and he may well have been in traitorous communication with Henry Tudor. The Percys were powerful in the north-east, but it should have been possible, and certainly it would have been wiser, for Richard to have eliminated Northumberland before Henry landed. As it was he was probably happy to allow his 2,000 men to take the rearguard and, as Northumberland naïvely put it, keep the Stanleys from attacking the royalist flank, for treachery in the front could have been much more damaging.

To what extent did the treachery of the Earl of Northumberland and the Stanley brothers affect the issue at Bosworth? If Polydore Vergil is right and William Stanley's troops joined in time to save Henry from being cut down by Richard and the men who accompanied him on his wild dash to the flank, then there can be no doubt that William's active, and Thomas's passive, support won Henry the battle. Had Richard been killed before William's men could reach the fight then, of course, his intervention was of little account, because in medieval battles once the king, or figurehead, was down the troops usually gave up, and that is what Richard's did at Bosworth. But if Richard was triumphant William's chances of survival were slender in the extreme, and so it seems certain that when he saw the issue was in doubt he struck hard and decisively.

All along the Stanleys held the key to the battle, for had they fought with Richard Henry must surely have been defeated. If this is accepted it raises the interesting question as to what degree of assurance, if any, Henry had from them before he embarked on what would have been a most hazardous adventure without their co-operation and that of Rhys ap Thomas. The general opinion is that they had given no pledge in advance, although Rhys probably had. Maybe, but it is tempting to think that through Margaret Beaufort, and other supporters, Henry had been made aware that his passage through Wales would be in the nature of a triumph, and that the Stanleys were well disposed towards him, and in accordance with their principles ready and eager to reinforce success.

Northumberland's treachery must have been more galling for Richard, for it completely undermined his command of the battle. Had he brought his men into action when called upon by Richard after the first difficult half hour or so, when the struggle still hung in equipoise, there was every prospect that Henry's army could have been swept away while the Stanleys still hesitated. The royalist army had the better generalship, the greater numbers and the advantage of ground. Only treachery within the assembled ranks could deprive them of victory, and Northumberland supplied it.

King Richard may have missed a tactical chance to defeat Henry Tudor, but it was a fleeting one, and Bosworth is a classic example of a general being forced to give battle when victory was dependent upon loyalty. Battles have been lost through circumstances that occurred before the battle was fought – badly trained troops, inefficient organization, loss of confidence in the higher command and, in early battles, hostility to the ruling house from within. It might be said that Bosworth was lost through the last of these causes. But Richard had not ruled badly and while he obviously feared treachery there was little he could do about it, and the victory went to Henry through circumstances beyond Richard's control – and indeed beyond Henry's.

7   The Naseby Campaign
April–June 1645

THE tortuous path that led to the outbreak of the Civil War stretched back to the end of the Tudor era, when the Stuarts inherited an economy moving rapidly towards inflation, and an unfinished Reformation. This was not, of course, the fault of Charles, but by his extravagance and obstinacy he considerably exacerbated the situation. For eleven years, from 1629, he ruled without a parliament, and when he eventually summoned one he consistently refused to yield to his opponents within the Chamber.

Matters came to a head in November 1641 with Parliament passing, by the narrowest of margins, the Grand Remonstrance – a most damaging indictment of Charles – which was shortly followed by the Militia Bill that removed control of the armed forces from the King. Gradually the two parties – Royalist and Parliamentarian or, pejoratively, Cavalier and Roundhead – took shape. Nevertheless, war was still not inevitable, although in January 1642 Charles did his best to make it so. Accompanied by some 300 troopers he came to Westminster to arrest five members of the Commons who were the ringleaders in a move to impeach the Queen but, warned of trouble, the Members had escaped by river, leaving Charles looking extremely foolish and his opponents greatly strengthened. On 10 January he and the Queen slipped furtively out of London.

During the summer John Pym was able to pass through a greatly reduced, and now pliant, Parliament nineteen propositions, which made religious as well as secular demands upon the King and which would have the effect of making Charles little better than a puppet of Parliament. His uncompromising belief in the absolute rule of kings would never allow him to surrender to such demands, and the only alternative was to fight. On 22 August 1642 the King unfurled his standard at Nottingham, and the country clattered into civil war with the utmost repugnance.

In 1642 there was no standing army as such. The defence of the kingdom rested in the first instance with the navy (on the outbreak of hostilities most of its officers and men sided with Parliament), and in the event of invasion there were fortress garrisons and the county militia, known as the trained bands, who came directly under the lieutenant of their county. These men were mostly infantrymen – musketeers and pikemen – and the name indicated that they were available for training rather than that they had been trained. In fact most of them, with the notable exception of those in London and Cornwall, were almost entirely untrained. The 8,000 or so London men were easily the best organized and trained, and they constituted a formidable ready-made force for Parliament, which also possessed the Tower's large arsenal. To counteract this loss the Royalists needed to take possession of the ordnance in the major ports and garrison towns, which they did not find easy – Hull was taken for Parliament by the navy, Dover Castle was also wrested from the Royalists, and Bristol and Plymouth declared for Parliament.

The main build-up of the armies in the first instance was from Volunteers, and both sides had a ready supply, albeit of men mostly without any military experience. The King was shortly joined by his nephews, the Princes Rupert and Maurice, who came from Holland with some men, arms and ammunition. Rupert quickly established himself as a fearless, and impetuous, cavalry leader. He was a young man with immense pride and panache, somewhat inclined to treat with contempt Charles's older advisers and commanders. He was very sure of himself, and by no means unskilled in military matters; throughout the war he was often a catalyst in the shaping of strategy.

The King's army was at first too weak to undertake any military enterprise, and the Earl of Essex, who was initially in command of Parliament's army, did not march out of London until almost three weeks after Charles had laid down the gage. Essex was a slow, indecisive general, and he was lamentably served by his intelligence – although later Parliament's scouting was way ahead of the Royalists'. As a result of this he failed in his principal task of putting his army between London and the King, who left Shrewsbury on 12 October and slipped past Essex while he was at Worcester trying to keep the south and west midlands protected. The first engagement of the Civil War was a minor cavalry skirmish at Powick Bridge, south of Worcester, where Prince Rupert defeated an advanced cavalry force from Essex's main army.

The first major battle was fought at Edgehill on 23 October 1642. After some three hours of very hard fighting (during which Prince Rupert demonstrated for the first, but not the last, time the power and the danger of the uncontrolled cavalry charge) both armies had had enough with neither gaining a decisive victory. However, the Royalists had forced the Parliamentarians to withdraw, leaving the road to London open.

Charles now, characteristically, showed a sad lack of resolution. Rupert pleaded to be allowed to lead a flying column of 3,000 men on London, which might conceivably have succeeded in its task, but the King hesitated between quick military action and the possibility of a settlement with Parliament. His decision to march was not taken until after Lord Essex had got his army back to the capital. In November, at Turnham Green, the Royalists found the road to London decisively blocked by 24,000 troops, and Charles withdrew the army to Reading. As a free man he would never again come so close to London.

During 1643 there were a number of comparatively minor engagements in the south-west of the country and the midlands. In the south-west the Royalists did particularly well, winning the battles of Braddock Down in Cornwall in January, and Stratton in May. Two months later the victorious generals, Sir Ralph Hopton and Sir Bevil Grenvile, defeated Sir William Waller, one of Parliament's foremost generals, at Lansdown near Bath. But in this battle their casualties were very heavy, and the gallant Sir Bevil was killed in the hour of victory. He was a man the King could ill afford to lose. Not long after this battle Hopton was seriously injured in an explosion, but Royalist successes continued under Prince Maurice and Lord Wilmot. The battle of Roundway Down was won on 13 July, and by the end of that month Prince Rupert had captured Bristol, and Exeter surrendered to Prince Maurice in September.

There were successes in the midlands and farther north as well, notably Lord Newcastle's defeat of Lord Fairfax and his son, Sir Thomas, at Adwalton Moor in June, which gave the Royalists possession of the whole of the West Riding. There was confidence, therefore, in their ranks as they squared up to meet Lord Essex at Newbury in the biggest battle fought in 1643. Could they but annihilate Essex's army it would seem that total victory might be theirs. But it was not to be. In a confused affair fought to the west of the town, in which artillery played a more important part than in any other Civil War battle, there was no clear-cut victory, and the laurels went chiefly to Essex who forced the King from the field and had an open road to London.

The year 1644 began with a Royalist defeat at Nantwich, and this was followed in March by the Roundheads' first significant victory, when Waller defeated an army commanded jointly by Lords Forth and Hopton at Cheriton, near Winchester. But the most important engagement of 1644 was Marston Moor. On the evening of 2 July Prince Rupert gave battle to the combined Parliamentarian and Scottish army, under the Earls of Manchester and Leven, that had been besieging York. The battle, which was fought partly in a thunderstorm and partly under a harvest moon, resulted in a decisive defeat for the Royalist army, and the north was lost to the King.

Marston Moor was a grave setback for the Royalists, but they had some satisfaction that September when the King and Sir Richard Grenvile outmanoeuvred Lord Essex at Lostwithiel in Cornwall, and inflicted a very severe defeat on his army. On his way back to Oxford the King found his way barred at Newbury by an army, considerably larger than his own, under Lord Manchester. The Second Battle of Newbury ended indecisively, but the Royalists got through to Oxford.

Until June, when the battle of Naseby was fought, the year 1645 was mainly notable for the splendid victories achieved by the Earl of Montrose in Scotland, and for the formation of the New Model Army in England. By the end of 1644 Montrose had disabled two of the three Covenanter armies, and having worsted the Clan Campbell at Inverlochy in February 1645 he went on to win two battles (Auldern 9 May and Alford 2 July) that were tactical gems. The New Model Army was the precursor of our regular army, and the first successful attempt to weld together an efficient fighting machine. It also won the battle of Naseby and for that reason, if for no other, it warrants a special mention here.

The establishment eventually decided upon was to be eleven regiments of horse, each of 600 men, twelve infantry regiments of 1,200 men each and 1,000 dragoons. In addition there was to be a formidable train of artillery provided mainly with demi-culverins and sakers. Originally it was intended to form the army from existing units in the armies of Essex, Waller, and Manchester, but these armies were not strong enough to provide the necessary numbers. The cavalry did not present too great a problem, for volunteers were plentiful, but the infantry were some 7,000 men short. Conscription in London and the south-eastern counties failed to raise the required quotas, and the army took the field in April 4,000 infantrymen short of establishment, although within a month or two the deficiency had been made good, but with untrained and undisciplined troops.

There was also argument in both Houses of Parliament as to who should command this élite force. The Lords were inclined to favour Essex or Manchester, while the Commons put forward the name of Sir Thomas Fairfax, a professional soldier, who had distinguished himself in the field and who was not involved in politics. Fairfax was eventually appointed commander-in-chief on 21 January 1645 – but it was to be almost six months before the Committee of Both Kingdoms allowed him to exercise untrammelled command in the field. Philip Skippon was appointed major-general of the foot and chief-of-staff.

The post of lieutenant-general of the horse was left open when other appointments were made, and by the time the army took the field the

Self-Denying Ordinance* caused complications over the appointment of Oliver Cromwell, who was the obvious choice. However, Parliament quickly found a means to release their foremost soldier from its ensnaring coils, although Cromwell was not officially appointed lieutenant-general of the horse until June.

The New Model Army was considered ready to move by the end of April, although it was well short of establishment. Parliament also had General Massey's army in the west, General Poyntz's in the north, and the Earl of Leven's on the borders. The Scots, however, were fearful of coming too far south while Montrose was causing the Covenanters such trouble in their homeland. The King had an army at Oxford, where he was himself until the beginning of May, another under Lords Goring and Hopton in the south-west, and Sir Charles Gerard commanded a considerable force of Welsh levies that could be called upon. Thus was the scene set for the decisive campaign of the First Civil War, and the fighting of what Lord Digby called 'a battle of all for all'.

While the New Model Army was still short of establishment, and by no means fully trained, Fairfax was sent with 11,000 men to the relief of Taunton. But on 7 May the King, greatly strengthened by the arrival from the west of Lord Goring's cavalry, left Oxford and this so alarmed the Committee of Both Kingdoms that they ordered Fairfax – then at Blandford – to detach five regiments for Taunton, and return with the rest of his force. The Royalists, therefore, were presented with a chance to cut off Fairfax's withdrawal before he could join Cromwell, whose troops were in the Oxford area, and defeat both forces in detail.

The King held a council at Stow-on-the-Wold on 8 May at which two propositions were discussed. To march west and attack Fairfax, or to attempt the relief of Chester (besieged by Sir William Brereton), and then to defeat the Scots, thereby regaining the whole of the north. At the time of this council it could not be known that Fairfax had been ordered to split his army, and so it would have involved a large-scale incursion into the west country; on the other hand it was known that all was not well with the Scots' army, and Chester, with its sea route to Ireland, was of great importance. Prince Rupert and Sir Marmaduke Langdale (for quite different reasons) argued strongly for marching north, the rest of the council favoured attacking Fairfax before his new army was ready. In the end the King reached a disastrous compromise. The army would march north, but Goring – greatly to his satisfaction, for he relished an independent command – would return with his cavalry to the west.

The departure of Goring left the King with only some 3,000 horse and

*A measure, which disallowed a member of either House to execute any office or command, military or civil, passed by Parliament in April 1645 and designed to exclude certain senior officers, no longer considered competent, from command.

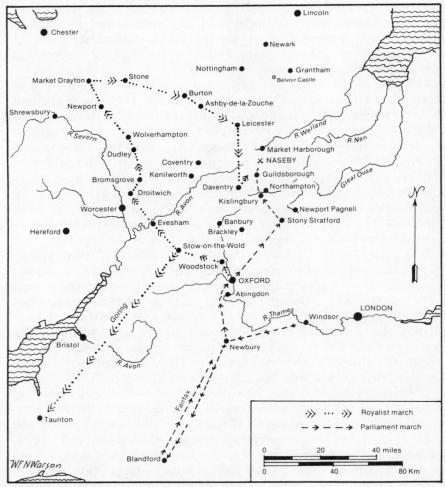

The Naseby Campaign: April–June 1645

5,000 foot, but as he marched north he drew off all available garrisons to swell this meagre force. Parliament decided to besiege Oxford, but this did not – as they had expected – bring Charles back, for he considered the city well fortified and provisioned. He had, however, come to regret the loss of Goring and to realize that without him he had little chance of defeating Fairfax. Goring was, therefore, summoned to march at once 'with all the strength you can make' to Market Harborough. It was a summons he had no intention of obeying; instead he sent a number of specious excuses. Sir Charles Gerard was also ordered to bring his troops to Market Harborough.

When the Royalists reached Market Drayton they recieved the welcome news that Brereton had removed his troops from besieging Chester. The immediate urgency to march north had now receded, and it was therefore decided to turn east, and while awaiting reinforcements to take Leicester. Prince Rupert achieved this after a short, ferocious night battle, and there followed a quite unwarranted and disgraceful massacre of the inhabitants. After Leicester there was again divided counsel in the Royalist camp. Lord Digby, and certain others, advocated a march on Oxford to defeat Fairfax, but Rupert felt that until reinforcements had been received the army was not strong enough, and that anyway Fairfax would now come after them – and on both counts he was right.

Eventually it was decided to make for Daventry, which place was reached on 7 June. Here the army stayed for six days, for the quite unnecessary purpose of rounding up and sending to Oxford, under a cavalry escort of 1,200 men, huge herds of sheep and cattle. The King and Rupert must have known by then that the siege had been raised, and they could not afford either the time nor the men for this venture. These wasted days allowed the initiative to pass to Fairfax who was able to close on the Royalists before Gerard's Welshmen and other reinforcements could arrive.

Fairfax left Oxford on 5 June, and after an unsuccessful attack on Boarstall House marched north of Newport Pagnell to Stony Stratford. On the way he was joined by Vermuyden's regiment, which brought his strength to about 13,000. He was, therefore, considerably superior to the King in numbers. Fairfax paused at Stony Stratford until 11 June in order to organize regiments into brigades, and familiarize commanders with the order of battle. He also sent urgently to Cromwell (who was busy raising men for the Eastern Association) to join him with what horse he could muster. He then advanced almost to Northampton before turning west to Kislingbury, for he was aware that the Royalist army was in the Daventry area.

Throughout the days leading up to the battle of Naseby it was noticeable how much superior were Parliament's intelligence reports to those of the Royalists. The army commander, and the Committee of Both Kingdoms in London, were quickly appraised of Royalist movements (although they did not always interpret them correctly), while Charles and Rupert often had little idea of Fairfax's position. A dangerous illustration of this occurred when they were surprised on Borough Hill. Charles was hunting in Fawsley Park and Rupert had no idea how near the enemy were when their patrols clashed with his outposts. Luckily it was too late in the day for Fairfax to mount an attack, for the Royalist army was scattered and quite unprepared.

The King shared Prince Rupert's desire to avoid battle until reinforcements arrived, and so when they marched from Borough Hill they took what precautions they could to conceal their direction, and made for Market Harborough en route for Belvoir Castle. But they were not successful, for in the early hours of 13 June Scoutmaster-General Watson brought news of their withdrawal, and moreover a letter from Goring had been intercepted which clearly established that Fairfax had no need to worry about his army, for it was still before Taunton. Fairfax camped the night of 13–14 June at Guildsborough, and patrols sent forward to maintain touch with the enemy captured men of the rearguard in Naseby.

At a midnight conference in Market Harborough the King's council, fearing that a further withdrawal with the enemy so close would be bad for morale, decided to fight. Accordingly Rupert, with some reluctance, for he still maintained it was too soon to accept battle, had the army deployed by the early hours of the 14th along the commanding high ground that runs from East Farndon to Great Oxendon. It was an excellent defensive position on which to await the attack of an enemy possessing superior numbers.

By sunrise that same morning the Roundhead army had reached the Naseby ridge, and Fairfax with Cromwell rode forward at about 8 a.m. to reconnoitre the ground for the most suitable position. There could be no certainty that the Royalists would stand and fight, and so it was uppermost in the two generals' minds to select ground that might encourage them to risk an assault. This prompted Cromwell to suggest the high ground in the Mill Hill area as seeming more suitable than the broken marshy land ahead of their present vantage point north-east of Naseby, and Fairfax agreed. When the army had been moved to this position it was at first deployed on the forward slope, but probably in the belief that raw recruits would be steadier out of sight of the enemy initially, the troops were withdrawn to a reverse slope position until the Royalist advance.

On the East Farndon ridge at about 7.30 a.m. Rupert sent forward his scoutmaster, Ruce, to discover the enemy's position. For some reason that is difficult to understand (although it may throw some light on the Royalists' inferior scouting) this man returned with negative information, and so Rupert went forward himself. It was not long before he sighted the enemy's army just at the time they were on the move to their final position. He was too experienced an officer to think they were withdrawing, but he was also the very embodiment of the offensive spirit and could not resist the chance of catching them off balance. He therefore sent a galloper back to the King requesting that the army should be brought forward at once, while he rode on to reconnoitre a position. It was a grave strategic error.

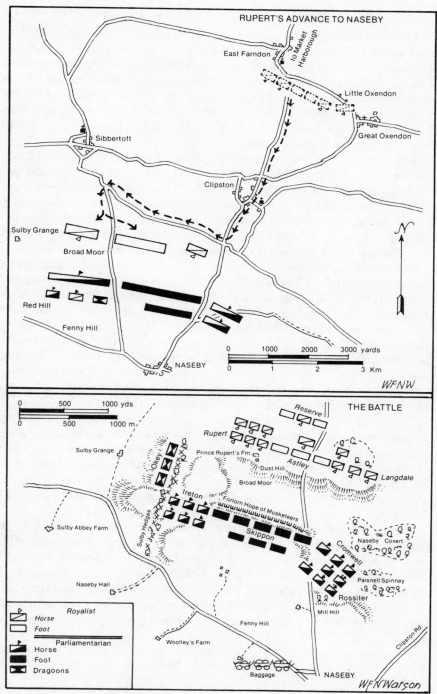

RUPERT'S ADVANCE TO NASEBY

To Market Harborough

East Farndon

Little Oxendon

Great Oxendon

Sibbertoft

Clipston

Sulby Grange

Broad Moor

Red Hill

Fenny Hill

NASEBY

0	1000	2000	3000 yards
0	1	2	3 Km

WFNW

THE BATTLE

0	500	1000 yds
0	500	1000 m

Reserve

Rupert

Sulby Grange

Okey

Prince Rupert's Fm

Astley

Langdale

Dust Hill

Broad Moor

Ireton

Forlorn Hope of Musketeers

Sulby Abbey Farm

Sulby Hedges

Naseby Covert

Skippon

Cromwell

Naseby Hall

Paisnell Spinney

Rossiter

Mill Hill

Fenny Hill

Woolley's Farm

Clipston Rd

	Royalist	
◿	*Horse*	
▭	*Foot*	
	Parliamentarian	
◤	Horse	
▬	Foot	
✕	Dragoons	

Baggage

NASEBY

WFN Watson

The Battle of Naseby: 14 June 1645

81

The position that Rupert selected was on a ridge known as Dust Hill, and when the army arrived he drew it up in three lines. That distinguished veteran Jacob Astley commanded the infantry in the centre, Prince Rupert's cavalry was on the right and Langdale's on the left. In the second line was Colonel Howard's infantry with squadrons of horse between regiments, and the reserve of 1,300 men consisted of the King's Lifeguard, Prince Rupert's infantry and the King's Horseguards. There were in all some 4,280 horse and 3,900 foot.

About half a mile to the south in parallel order Fairfax had 14,600 troops – the cavalry numbered 7,200, the infantry 6,400 and Colonel Okey commanded 1,000 dragoons* – drawn up in two lines. Sergeant-Major-General Skippon's infantry held the centre, Cromwell's cavalry was on the right, Colonel Ireton's on the left, and Cromwell had selected the thick hedgerow called Sulby Hedges, on the army's extreme left flank, along which to line Okey's dragoons dismounted.

The battle began about 11 a.m.† with the Royalist line advancing at a steady pace, and contact was made almost simultaneously along the whole front. On the eastern flank Cromwell moved forward to meet Langdale's charge. The Northern Horse with only 1,700 men were outnumbered and proved no match for Cromwell's Ironsides, who also had the advantage of slope, and it was not long before they were routed and driven back on Rupert's regiment in reserve. When their defeat was accomplished Cromwell sensibly, and in contrast to Rupert's action, ordered two regiments to hold Langdale's men from rallying and kept the remainder of his wing for the final phase of the battle.

In the centre Astley's seasoned troops proved greatly superior to the Roundhead infantry with their large number of raw recruits, and after some hard hand-to-hand fighting drove the enemy's first line back upon the second but, short of numbers and later without cavalry support, they became an easy prey. The action on the Royalist right flank was perhaps the most interesting; it may well have been decisive to the result of the battle, and it was certainly so to the fate of Astley's infantry.

Prince Rupert was nominally commander-in-chief of the Royalist armies, although he was finding the King increasingly convinced of his own military ability and much inclined to take control in the field. Nevertheless, it is arguable that as commander-in-chief he should not have led the cavalry in person, but allowed Prince Maurice to do so while he remained in general control of the battle. But that was not in Rupert's nature, and if there was a cavalry charge in the offing he needs must be

---

*Figures for both armies from *Naseby 1645* by Peter Young. As in so many battles, numbers given vary considerably. For example, Markham gives the Royalist horse as 5,520 and the foot as 5,300. But most agree that Fairfax had about 14,000 men in all.

†*Calendar of State Papers Domestic – Charles, I, Vol VII*. Other accounts say 10 a.m. and 10.30, but in view of the Royalist movements that morning 11 a.m. seems to be about right.

in it. And so he led his two lines of cavalry to meet and merge with Ireton's troopers, and to ride on out of the battle.

Rupert's advance to contact may have been slightly quickened by having to run the gauntlet of Okey's cross-fire from the Sulby Hedges, but that does not appear to have emptied many saddles. For some reason on this wing the cavalry of both sides halted for a minute or two within a short distance of each other. Rupert was the first to move and when battle was joined there was a fierce fight for perhaps half an hour. Ireton had some initial success when his two right-hand squadrons broke the Royalists to their immediate front, but the centre squadron failed to press its charge, and on the extreme left the Roundhead horse was put to flight.

Meanwhile, Rupert was away at the gallop with all the troopers he could muster from the fray, and did not draw rein until he met the Roundhead baggage train more than a mile away near Naseby, where he was rudely repulsed by the guard. His men became scattered, and by the time he had collected those he could and returned to his duty on the field of battle his horses were in no state to fight, and in any event it was too late. The infantry, left on their own, had fought with extreme courage but, hopelessly outnumbered and beset by Cromwell's cavalry on their left flank and the remains of Ireton's on their right, together with Okey's dragoons now remounted, had eventually laid down their arms and formed the greater part of the large haul of prisoners.

Rupert rejoined the King and the reserves – most of which had not been committed, but would have been had Rupert remained in overall charge of the battle – where an attempt was made to face the enemy now re-formed for a final thrust to victory. But the thrust was never made, for one volley from Okey's dragoons was sufficient. The Royalist troops, despite all that their officers could do, had had enough, and the field was soon deserted. The pursuit was for the most part controlled, but continued for twelve miles and was attended by considerable slaughter. Parliament's casualties in the battle were not heavy, probably around 180 men killed; the Royalists lost about 450 in the battle, and a further 350 in the pursuit. The entire Royalist commissariat fell to the victors, including the King's cabinet in which were his private papers with some damning correspondence between himself and the Queen.

The First Civil War was to drag on for a further year, but Naseby had sounded the death knell of the King's military machine, for although only a small number of men were killed, 5,000 prisoners had been taken and that figure included a great many experienced officers. The King could never again collect an army to match the New Model in the field. To be defeated by an army nearly twice your size – and not easily defeated at that – can be no disgrace, but there must have been many

Royalists who pondered at length and in sadness over the important factors that had contributed so decisively to their defeat.

Naseby was one of those battles that need never have been fought; but a sorry tale of compromise, lack of resolution, dilatoriness and muddle over a period of six weeks inexorably led to disaster.* In April 1645 the Royalists probably had their last chance – and it was a very good one – of forcing Parliament to offer Charles acceptable terms. Goring was the key to immediate success; once he had joined the King at Oxford the New Model Army might have been decisively defeated while half of it was marching and countermarching in the west, and while it was still not completely ready. Alternatively, also with Goring's troops under command, and later with the prospect of Gerard's, the whole north could almost certainly have been retaken, and the Royalist cause would have assumed a very much healthier aspect. But the decision taken at Stow-on-the-Wold, and the wasteful meandering round the midlands, eventually made it necessary for Charles to accept battle on most disadvantageous terms.

Once battle had been joined it seemed likely that the side with the greatest numbers and better leadership would win. Fairfax was a very good commander; Cromwell (whose presence alone was worth double the 600 troopers he brought to the field) handled his cavalry superbly; and although Astley's infantry fought magnificently, without cavalry support they could not compete with Skippon's men. Nevertheless, Prince Rupert committed serious strategical and tactical errors, both of which considerably contributed to the King's defeat, and could be said to have caused it. His was the decision to abandon the very good East Farndon–Great Oxendon defensive position, and he was responsible for the absence of his cavalry from the field at a critical time of the battle.

On the night of 13 June the Royalist army was at Market Harborough. Charles was again vacillating on the wisdom of going north (although Rupert still favoured this), and the immediate plan was to march to Belvoir and draw in troops from Newark. But that night news was received that Fairfax and his army were only six miles away. Charles was immediately summoned from nearby Lubenham, where he was sleeping, and a council was held at which Digby and certain others strongly urged the King to stand and fight. Now that the enemy was so close, these men argued, any further withdrawal would smack of retreat and be damaging to morale. Rupert held to his view that to give battle with such inferior numbers would be most unwise, but he was overruled.

---

*For a detailed account of Royalist indexterity prior to the battle of Naseby see the author's *Battles in Britain*, Vol. 2, Sidgwick & Jackson, 1975.

The country around Market Harborough was undulating, mainly unenclosed with little woodland, but with a series of ridges separated by ground that in places was marshy even in summer. Some two miles south of Market Harborough, and just to the south of East Farndon, there was one such ridge running south-east through Little Oxendon. It was a good natural defensive position, and greatly favoured by Jacob Astley for his infantry. Here the army was drawn up to await an attack over difficult ground that would go some way to compensate the defenders for the disparity in numbers. It is true the flanks were unprotected by natural obstacles, but any attempt to turn the position would still entail a fairly steep uphill assault.

As previously related, somewhere around 8 a.m. on the morning of 14 June Rupert, having ridden forward to reconnoitre, saw the enemy in the process of moving to their finally selected battle position. Like some old war horse pawing the ground at the scent of battle, he appears to have thrown off the qualms he had about fighting with inferior numbers, and sent back orders for the army to come up to a new position he selected, which conformed with the one being adopted by the Roundheads in the Mill Hill area.

We can only guess at Rupert's thoughts when making this decision. He never cared much for a defensive battle, and perhaps having been manoeuvred by the council into fighting at what he considered was an inappropriate time he felt that the best chance was to mount an attack before the enemy was ready – for he would never have thought they were withdrawing. If so he must have known that he would not have been in a position to engage for at least two hours, and Fairfax did not need that amount of time in which to be ready.

The decision to risk all on a difficult assault against a greatly superior enemy is not easy to understand. Rupert might not have won a defensive battle, but he would almost certainly have been able to leave the field with an army that was sufficiently intact to fight again. Worse was to follow, for once committed to the attack his heavily outnumbered infantry could yet have won the day had they been properly supported by their cavalry. But the steadiness of Cromwell's horse, and the impetuosity of Rupert's, were to nullify the courage, superior training and discipline of the Royalist foot.

The Royalist advance across Broad Moor was at a steady pace, with the cavalry of the right wing slightly in advance, but battle was joined almost simultaneously along the whole front. Rupert's two principal subordinate commanders were his brother, Prince Maurice, and the Earl of Northampton. In his front line there were some 850 troopers with a further 880 in the second line, or reserve, under Sir William Vaughan, and formed in five troops of between 100 to 200 men in each.* His total of 1,730 sabres was considerably less than the five regiments of horse with which Henry Ireton opposed him.

Some accounts of the opening stages of the cavalry fight have Rupert's men advancing at a fast canter which quickly developed into a gallop as his troopers swept all before them. But in fact, after an initial pause during which there were brief signs of irresolution among some of Ireton's regiments, the fight was stubbornly contested at close quarters. Ireton was a brave, but not a brilliant, soldier and as a cavalry commander he was outmatched by Rupert. Nevertheless, his own regiment fought well against the heavy punches of the two princes, until he made the mistake of swinging it in to assist the infantry. This left Colonel Butler, on the Roundhead left, exposed and his regiment broke when Rupert ordered Lord Northampton to bring up the second line. They, and others of Ireton's horse, were driven from the field with virtually all of Rupert's men in hot pursuit. Moreover, according to the report despatched to the Speaker from the battlefield, they took with them on their flight about 1,000 infantrymen.

The infantry battle is important to Rupert's performance on the right wing. Fairfax had withdrawn his troops (other than the forlorn hope) to a reverse-slope position before the battle had begun, and when they advanced over the brow, as the Royalist army approached, there was time only for one musket volley before Skippon's and Astley's men came to push of pike. The Parliamentarians had the advantage in numbers and ground, but their regiments – particularly some of Skippon's – lacked training and discipline. Fairfax's regiment on the Roundhead right stood firm, and indeed was not so heavily engaged, but Skippon's men were soon in trouble. What was left of Ireton's cavalry shored them up temporarily, but when Skippon, in the thick of the battle trying to steady the ranks, was seen to be hit, they became discouraged. It was not long before the Royalists pushed them back on to the reserves, and many of the less stalwart – despite the efforts and example of their officers – sought safety in flight. The situation had now become desperate. Ireton had been wounded – and for a short time was a prisoner – Fairfax's left flank was open, and his centre in disarray. Men of both sides have put it on record that had Rupert's cavalry been present at this moment the King would have had the victory.

On the Roundhead right Oliver Cromwell was engaged in a beautifully controlled cavalry fight against the Royalist horse under Sir Marmaduke Langdale. Cromwell's men had an unpleasant rabbit-hole-infested slope to ride down, and the first to engage the enemy was Whalley's regiment on the left. After a short-range pistol volley the fight became one of swords, and because Cromwell had the advantage of numbers he

*Markham, pp. 214, 215.

was able to detach troops to strike Langdale's left flank. Hard pressed in the centre and right, and outflanked on the left, the Royalist horse gave way, and the whole wing was soon in flight. But Cromwell had his men well in hand, and leaving four bodies of horse to pursue, he turned his other troops on Astley's now open flank. At much the same time Okey emerged from Sulby Hedges, and mounting his dragoons attacked the embattled Royalist infantry from the other flank.

There was but one chance left, and a slender one at that. The reserves were still in hand and the King, gallant as ever, made ready to lead them into battle at the head of his Lifeguard. But the Scottish Earl of Carnworth pulled his charger back, exclaiming, 'Will you go upon your death?' and a moment of glory was lost. Meanwhile, the Royalist infantry, by now completely overpowered, had mostly laid down their arms, although some – like Sir George Lisle's regiment of Bluecoats – died in their ranks.

What had become of Rupert's men while all this was happening is not precisely known, nor is it germane to the damage that his disappearance from the field had done. Some of his troopers may have pursued Ireton's men into Naseby and beyond, undoubtedly there was plundering with consequent delay in rallying, and there was a brief affray with the guard on the Roundhead wagon train. The crucial factor, however, is that by the time he eventually returned to the battle it was virtually all over, and he could do nothing but join the King in defeat.

It is not a very fruitful exercise to compare Cromwell's performance with Rupert's, for in the first place two more contradictory characters would be difficult to find. But Cromwell was the greater cavalry commander. He, like his near-contemporary and other great cavalryman, Gustavus Adolphus, knew the value of a coldly calculated well-controlled approach to battle, rather than one of Rupert's – or later Cardigan's – uncontrolled charges which have invested war with glamour, but seldom with victory.

It is also, perhaps, a little unfair to compare Rupert's handling of his men with that of Cromwell's, for the latter had a superiority in numbers (3,600 to 1,700) and could afford to detach troops, whereas Rupert was heavily outnumbered. Nevertheless, having broken the Parliamentarian left, he still might have been able (had he not lost control) to leave two regiments for the pursuit and swing the rest against the hard-pressed, and at that time uncovered and nearly broken, Roundhead foot. It could very well have won him the battle.

In this battle there were many factors – the decision taken in council at Stow-on-the-Wold, Goring's subsequent disobedience, Rupert's abandonment of a good defensive line, and his long absence from the field of battle – which, had the principles acted differently, could have altered the course of history.

Naseby, unlike Bosworth where there is some doubt, was a battle quite definitely lost before it was fought; indeed it should never have been fought. Nevertheless, once the two sides engaged it was leadership that won the victory. The Royalists had no one to compare with Fairfax and Cromwell, and their leadership was divided. Prince Rupert virtually took over command from the King, but the latter was the Commander-in-Chief, and by no means merely a nominal one. Split leadership is often disastrous, and on this occasion it may have been responsible for Rupert trying to command half the cavalry as well as the battle. He was not a good general and at Naseby, more perhaps than in his other battles, he showed it.

8 The Battle of Leuthen
5 December 1757

FREDERICK II ascended the Prussian throne on 31 May 1740. His father, Frederick William I, had raised the House of Hohenzollern above all the other German princes, and left his son an army of 80,000 men drilled and disciplined on the parade grounds of Potsdam under the strict supervision of his devoted servant and close companion, Field Marshal Prince Leopold of Anhalt Dessau (The Old Dessauer). But it was Frederick II, known to history as the Great, who infused a living, and immortal spirit into the Prussian army. His courage in adversity, his fiery dynamism, and his mastership of manoeuvre and strategy, forged an army which, trained to perfection and close-knit by active service, was to achieve the professional primacy of Europe.

A large part of Frederick's many successes in battle can be traced to his willingness to learn from his mistakes, and above all to the fact that he was one of the most offensively minded generals of all time. He placed great reliance on artillery, and the importance he attached to mobility led him to be the first in the field with horse artillery. His intention was that by the rapid movement of guns the artillery would be on hand to neutralize enemy batteries and with close supporting fire pave the way for the charge. It did not, of course, always work according to plan, but at Leuthen the mobile batteries were able to give powerful support to the Prussian infantry as they began their attack on the village.

However, it was as a cavalry commander that Frederick stood pre-eminent, not only among the generals of his time, but of all time. And it was to his cavalry that he made the most far-reaching and important improvements in equipment, tactics, and horsemanship. He inherited a cavalry arm that comprised large men on large horses (trained to approach the enemy at a ponderous trot), discharging their weapons in line. All this he quickly changed.

After his first battle (Mollwitz, 1741) in which his infantry saved the army from defeat, he clearly saw that cavalry and infantry intimately mixed was no good, and he forbade the use of firearms mounted – other than for flankers and videttes – and relied upon the controlled charge with the sword. He expected his cavalry to be able to charge for one mile over rough ground, and the last 800 yards to be at the gallop. Strict discipline and rigorous training of individuals and formations were the secrets of Frederick's success, and he was well served by some excellent cavalry commanders, in particular Generals Seydlitz and Driesen. Out of the twenty-two major battles fought by Frederick, or his generals, it would be true to say that in fifteen of them cavalry played the decisive part.

There were a number of important factors that imposed a limitation on Frederick's strategy and tactics. Although he considerably expanded his father's army he went into battle with an army that was almost always numerically inferior to that of his opponents. Moreover, in many cases much of his manpower was foreign (in 1750 there were 50,000 foreigners out of 132,000) and inevitably there were desertions. However, he was often able to overcome lack of numbers by superior tactics. One of Frederick's famous maxims in his *Military Instructions* reads: 'It

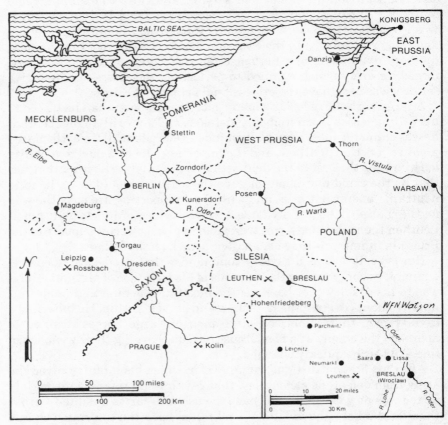

The Battle of Leuthen: 5 December 1757: Eastern Europe

is an invariable axiom of war to secure your own flanks and rear, and endeavour to turn those of your enemy.' Frequently his tactics were shaped to that end, and in endeavouring to evolve new methods of turning the flank of a large force there developed his impressive Oblique Order (*Schräge Stellung*), which Frederick used to perfection at the battle of Leuthen.

Other restrictions the Prussian king had to contend with were weak finances which would not permit him to keep an army in the field for any length of time; poor intelligence, until the cavalry arm had been properly organized; serious logistic problems, caused partly by the amount of baggage that the élite Prussian officer corps was wont to take on campaign, and the transportation difficulties of food and fodder – this latter inhibited him from moving too far from a base. Consequently it was rare for the Prussian army to pursue a foe for any distance, and Frederick's strategy was usually short forays into enemy territory, a knock-out blow and the disruption of communications.

Frederick invaded Silesia, on the slenderest of pretexts, in December 1740, and at the Treaty of Dresden five years later it seemed that he had got what he wanted. But he had involved himself in a lifelong struggle with the House of Austria, and gained the reputation of an unscrupulous intriguer and ruthless aggressor. Maria Theresa brooded deeply over the loss of Silesia, and all Europe regarded with considerable awe this lightning-charged being from Berlin. His ambitions only awaited time and occasion, and when in 1756 the Seven Years War engulfed most of Europe, Frederick was ready. With an army of 60,000 he violated Saxon neutrality (a pre-emptive strike that was militarily understandable) and soon crushed the Elector Augustus's troops, putting the defeated soldiers into Prussian uniforms to fight for him.

During 1757 – the year of Leuthen – the Prussian army was continually at bay; apart from the doubtful assistance of the Duke of Cumberland, commanding Hanoverian troops, Frederick had to contend alone against armies from the Empire, Russia, France, and Sweden. It is true he could operate on interior lines but, with only some 200,000 men at most facing this ring of steel buttressed by more than 500,000, it required all the military genius that Frederick undoubtedly possessed if Prussia was not to be wiped from the map. But Frederick could not be everywhere, and seldom could he, or his commanders, concentrate more than 40,000 men against an enemy nearly always numerically superior.

Inevitably there were reverses: at the bloody battle of Prague Frederick narrowly avoided defeat, Kolin was a disaster, the Duke of Bevern failed to relieve Schweidnitz, whose garrison surrendered with 6,000 men and 180 pieces of cannon, and he then lost Breslau. But at Rossbach on 5 November Frederick won a crushing victory over the

French under the Prince of Subise. He paused here only to refit his army and then marched, at the head of 14,000 men, from Leipzig to Parchwitz, a distance of 170 miles which the army covered in fifteen days.

On the march to Parchwitz, where Frederick arrived on 28 November, tidings of Bevern's defeat at Breslau reached the King, and he at once ordered the remnants of that army to join him at Parchwitz, giving the command to General Zieten. But even with the junction of the two armies Frederick could only muster 24,000 infantry in 48 battalions, 12,000 cavalry in 128 squadrons and 167 cannon, of which 71 were heavy pieces. The Austrian enemy, Frederick knew, was likely to be double that size, but he was to fight the battle of Leuthen with hardly any mercenaries, and in his Prussians he had behind him a race of men as stern and resolute as any to be found in Europe. Despite the victory at Rossbach the tide was running strongly against the Prussians, but Frederick was never one to despair; assembling his generals he proceeded to animate them with a stirring address before continuing his march, on 4 December, to Neumarkt.

At this small town Frederick found 1,000 Croat soldiers who barred the gate to his advance guard and then attempted to escape by the Breslau side of the town; but the Prussian Cavalry got among them and in the cut and thrust killed 300 and took 600 prisoners. More importantly a whole field bakery, which the Austrians could ill afford to lose, fell into Prussian hands. From this the troops got some much needed sustenance, while from the prisoners Frederick got important information of the enemy position.

The Austrian army comprised 84 battalions of infantry, 144 squadrons and 210 guns; their exact number of men is not definitely known, but it was not far short of 80,000. Prince Charles of Lorraine, Maria Theresa's brother-in-law, was in command. His record in the field did not inspire confidence; defeated at Chotusitz in 1742, Hohenfriedberg and Soor in 1745, and Prague in 1757, he had only partially redeemed himself against a weak opponent at Breslau. He had with him Field-Marshal Daun, the victor of Kolin, but he preferred the flattery of General Lucchese to the sound advice of the Field-Marshal, and advanced from a secure base to take up a position which although strong made Frederick's task considerably easier. When, a little later, Frederick had viewed the Austrian position he remarked to Francis of Brunswick, 'The Fox has crept out of his hole, now I will punish his impertinence', and despite the inequality of numbers, and the qualms of some of his generals, he decided to attack.

The Austrians had advanced from behind the river Lohe, which runs just west of Breslau, and crossed the Schweidnitzer-Wasser to take up a position astride the one major road in the area, which ran from Neumarkt to Breslau. Their right rested on the village of Nippern some

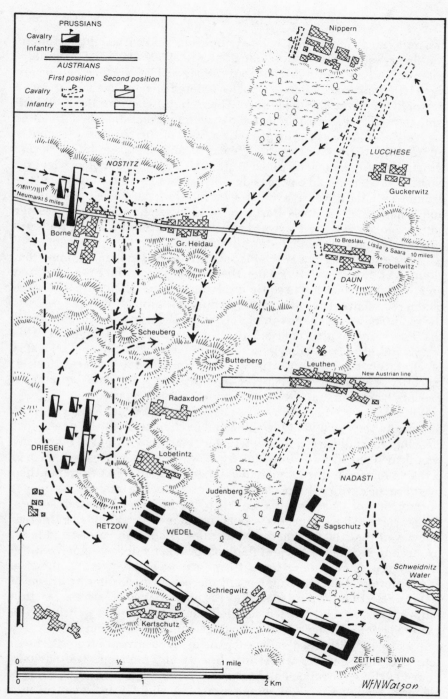

PRUSSIANS
Cavalry
Infantry

AUSTRIANS
First position Second position
Cavalry
Infantry

Nippern

LUCCHESE

Guckerwitz

NOSTITZ

Neumarkt 5 miles

Borne

Gr. Heidau

to Breslau, Lissa & Saara 10 miles

Frobelwitz

DAUN

Scheuberg

Butterberg

Leuthen

New Austrian line

Radaxdorf

DRIESEN

Lobetintz

Judenberg

NADASTI

N

RETZOW

WEDEL

Sagschutz

Schweidnitz
Water

Schriegwitz

Kertschutz

ZEITHEN'S WING

0   ½   1 mile
0   1   2 Km

WFNWatson

The Battle of Leuthen: 5 December 1757

93

two miles north of the road, where Count Lucchese with eight battalions was firmly established behind impassable peat bogs; their left originally extended only to Leuthen some four miles south of Nippern, but before the battle commenced Prince Charles ordered General Nadasti to move his corps southwards to the village of Sagschutz, where his flank – which was 'refused' – was also protected by swampy ground, although not as securely as Lucchese's. The ground in front of the position was gently undulating with one or two small features, and one larger hill at Borne, which the Austrians occupied with five regiments under General Nostitz. Frederick had one considerable advantage in that he knew the ground well, for it was a favourite place for his peacetime manoeuvres, and when later he took Borne he had a second and even greater advantage, for with that forward position lost to the enemy the contours effectively masked the Prussian approach.

At 5 a.m. on 5 December the Prussians marched in four columns from Neumarkt. It was still dark when they reached the village of Borne, and an icy mist further obscured their advance. General Nostitz had three Saxon regiments of dragoons and two hussar regiments drawn up across the road. They were taken completely by surprise. In the cold, pale dawn the Prussian cavalry charged the line frontally and in flank; this whirlwind of hostile horsemen quite unnerved the Saxons, who fled precipitately back to Nippern with their commander, General Nostitz, mortally wounded, and leaving 600 prisoners in Prussian hands. Frederick ordered his cavalry to carry out a limited pursuit.

While the rest of his army was closing up on Borne, Frederick rode forward to the main vantage point and from here, with the dawn mist clearing, he could see the complete Austrian dispositions. Their army was drawn up in two lines, for by now Nadasti's corps, which had hitherto formed a third line, had extended the left flank from Leuthen to where the cavalry was posted near Sagschutz. The infantry regiments in support of the cavalry on this flank were Württembergers, Hungarians, and Bavarians – none of them very reliable. Frederick knew well that the treacherous quagmire, profuse in rushes and laced by streamlets, made the right flank of the enemy unassailable, but the left offered some chance for a turning movement, even though the enemy line rested on an unpleasant morass formed from the drains of Gohlau. He therefore decided that his only chance of success lay in a flank attack against the left and left centre, packing a punch on the extreme left and at points between Sagschutz and Leuthen.

For this purpose the plan was for the army to advance from Borne in four columns ready to wheel into line at any moment. The advance guard of three battalions and a battery of ten 12-pounders was under General Wedel; the right wing (marching slightly in advance) was commanded by Zieten and had forty-three squadrons and six battalions led by Prince Maurice of Dessau; the left wing with the remainder of the infantry, and flanked by forty squadrons under General Driesen, was commanded by General Retzow, and the rearguard was commanded (curiously enough) by Prince Eugene of Württemberg.

As the army marched south their progress was obscured from the enemy, even from such vantage points as windmills. Daun, apparently unable to grasp the significance of the contours, was convinced that Frederick had slipped away intent on cutting their lines of communication in Bohemia. But Lucchese, on the right flank, had no such illusions, for he could see part of Frederick's cavalry left on the Borne Hills in a deception role. Not only certain of an attack, but that the attack would develop against him, he urgently called for reinforcements. At first these were refused, but Charles at last succumbed to his importunities and sent the reserves from the centre of the line, and some cavalry from the left. Hence, just as Frederick was preparing to develop what was a textbook example of the Oblique Order against Prince Charles's left flank, a part of that flank and much of his reserve were four miles away.

The Prussian army had been able to get sufficiently close to the point of attack before their intention was realized, and when shortly after noon Wedel's battalions, moving in echelon and supported by cavalry and the ten 12-pounders, were observed between Lobetintz and Sagschutz it was Nadasti's turn to clamour for reinforcements. But it was too late, for at 1 p.m. Wedel's men were tearing the entrails out of his left flank. Wedel's leading battalions, placed *en potence* to the main thrust, kept edging to the right of Nadasti's line. Making their way through bog and wood they not only turned his flank but got behind the 'refused' angle of the line, where they charged a battery position and put the Bavarian and Württemberg troops to flight all the way to Leuthen, leaving 2,000 prisoners on the field.

Meanwhile Prince Maurice stormed the rising ground beyond Sagschutz, and drove the enemy towards the Prussian advance guard, while Zieten, managing somehow to get his cavalry through the morass, charged Nadasti and scattered his troopers back to Rathener Wood, nearly two miles behind the line. The broken left line, well served by artillery, tried to rally behind Gothlau, supported by reinforcements arriving from the right flank; but Charles could only throw these in piecemeal, and quickly lapped about by the enemy – and at this point considerably outnumbered – the whole line was again forced to give ground. The guns were safely withdrawn to Leuthen, but the few German troops who still bravely attempted to stem the avalanche of steel and shot were soon engulfed in the smoke and carnage of the field.

More by accident than design, for the Austrian left and centre was chaotic by now, making the giving and receiving of orders a matter of extreme chance, the whole line traversed an angle of 75° and a new position was taken up. The line pivoted on the centre of Leuthen; Lucchese swung round in a south-westerly direction, while Nadasti was forced northwards. Leuthen offered a strong natural defence and the Austrian artillery was well positioned. Here the battle hung in the balance for more than half an hour.

It was now that Frederick brought in his left wing, which had hitherto been only lightly engaged. As these men marched upon Leuthen they were met by a murderous fire of grape- and case-shot from the Austrian batteries, and the village itself, although hopelessly congested and corpse-strewn, was powerfully defended. But the combination of Frederick's heavy cannon − firing with deadly effect from the Butterberg Hill eminence − and the steady advance of the Prussian Guards, who stormed the village with great élan, slaughtering the defenders with parade-ground precision, proved decisive at this point. However, the battle was not yet won.

Lucchese's men, who had so far not been engaged, outflanked the Prussian line and could have enveloped it. At about 4 p.m. he swung his troops into the attack, but once again the contours deceived the Austrians, for the higher ground between Radaxdorf and Leuthen concealed forty squadrons of cavalry under General Driesen, which Frederick had detached from the left flank of his army to guard against just such a manoeuvre by the enemy. Driesen swept into the attack under cover of the Butterberg guns: charged in front and flank by the Bayreuth Dragoons and in rear by the Puttkammer Hussars, Lucchese's force was massacred, and he himself was killed. Driesen then wheeled round and took the enemy infantry in rear.

As night approached, the Austrian army, crippled and crumbling, but still not completely broken, tried to form a third line on the axis Saara−Lissa, in a last desperate attempt to stem the storm of Prussian foray. But the line was scarcely formed before it bent and broke, and the whole army streamed back in headlong flight across the four bridges that spanned the Schweidnitzer-Wasser, with the Prussian cavalry in close pursuit. The Austrians lost some 10,000 men killed and wounded, and 21,000 men and 116 cannon were taken. The Prussian losses were 6,250 of which 1,141 were killed. It was a magnificent victory: Frederick was to say later that with two more hours of daylight it would have been the most decisive of the century.

Although there were to be other victories in this long and melancholy struggle − notably at Liegnitz and Torgau in 1760 − Leuthen was undoubtedly Frederick's finest stratagem and manoeuvre of the war. Napoleon said of it: 'This battle is a masterpiece of movements, of manoeuvres, and of resolution; enough to immortalize Frederick, and rank him among the greatest generals.' Well might he say that, for the

victory of Leuthen ensured Prussian survival, and laid the foundations
of a national unity that gave strength to its people in the dark days of
Napoleonic invasion, when the land was encompassed with fear and
foreboding.

The most decisive factor in this very important battle was undoubtedly
the brilliant use Frederick made of the Oblique Order, but success was
made easier for him by the ineptitude of Prince Charles, who made a
series of strategical and tactical blunders.

Before he defeated the Duke of Bevern at Breslau Charles had known
that the Prussian king was coming into Silesia with a force of about
14,000 men. It would have been a comparatively simple matter for him
to have intercepted Frederick (whose army he outnumbered at least six
to one) on a line between Parchwitz and Liegnitz, and fought a battle on
ground of his own choosing with an overwhelming superiority not only
in men but in cannon.

Having failed to do this and allowed Frederick to join forces with
Bevern's army, why cross the Schweidnitzer-Wasser? It was a small
stream, but its banks were steep in parts and the surrounding fields in
December were boggy. It was a natural defensive barrier, and with such
superior numbers Charles could have afforded to despatch a corps to
cross the water higher up and pose a great threat to Frederick's flank as
his troops attempted to cross the river.

Having neglected these two obvious choices, either of which might
have given him the victory, if indeed Frederick decided to risk battle in
such unfavourable circumstances, why did he not at least go farther
forward and occupy in strength all the rising ground in the Lobetintz,
Scheuberg, Borne area, thus denying Frederick the ample room he
needed for manoeuvre under cover? Finally, after neglecting all these
sensible stratagems, and allowing Frederick to develop his flank attack,
the only remaining hope would have been to have swung the whole of his
right wing against the Prussian left at the outset of the battle. If done
with promptitude and resolution this might well have spoiled the
perfect execution of the Oblique Order.

In a *Military Instruction* of March 1742, relating to the cavalry, it is
possible to see the genesis of the Oblique Order, but it is not known when
Frederick first put it into practice, nor indeed whether the idea orig-
inated with the Prussian king. Some say it was a favourite tactic of
Epominondas in the fourth century BC, and had been copied down the
ages by other great commanders, but certainly Frederick brought
eighteenth-century linear tactics to their zenith by this manoeuvre. He
had used the Oblique Order in at least three battles before Leuthen

(perhaps Hohenfriedberg, 1745, was the first one), but only there was it to be seen to perfection.

The principle is simple enough, but it can only work with soldiers who are sternly disciplined and well drilled, under a commander of the highest calibre. Even the plan must be flexible, and the commander prepared to improvise at the last moment. Frederick's two objectives in devising this manoeuvre were first to concentrate an overwhelming force on the vulnerable flank or rear of the enemy, thus giving his smaller army local superiority, and secondly to be able to exert the greatest possible control throughout the battle. This latter was not easily achieved in eighteenth-century warfare, and with the Oblique Order direct control of the attacking force was lost once that force was committed, but the cavalry of the 'refused' wing (the infantry lacking mobility was a different matter) remained responsive to any alterations in command that might become necessary.

The Prussian army, because it was invariably smaller than its enemy, and therefore deployed along a shorter front, was vulnerable to a flank attack, and at the same time found it difficult to execute one of its own. The Oblique Order aimed at overcoming this, but for success the intention had to be concealed by a night march, or by elaborate deception, or by use of a covered approach – and then carried out with speed and vigour – otherwise the enemy had time to reinforce the threatened flank, and the whole operation could go wrong.

In order to make the maximum impression on the point assailed it was necessary to reinforce the attacking wing (the right in the case of Leuthen), but the difficulty comes with the left wing which is at first 'refused', reaching back from the attacking wing in a staggered formation of echelons. It was usually a long thin line with the principal task of keeping the enemy in a fixed position. If this wing takes no part in the battle the enemy is able to withdraw troops to the threatened flank, but if on the other hand it becomes too heavily engaged the whole object of the exercise is lost.

It is easy to appreciate that the correct degree of the angle of attack, and the exact timing and phasing of the operation, call for considerable skill and are hard to gauge. Minor adjustments at the points of attack can be made by the local commanders – and indeed are often necessary – once the attack has gone in, but if the main thrust is not successful at the first attempt it is usually impossible to re-form and start again. Several modifications were possible – for example at Leuthen the line of attack was diagonal to the enemy, whereas at Kunersdorf (two years later, and a disaster) it was perpendicular – the principle of 'refusing' one wing to the enemy and strengthening the one which is to attack remained inviolate.

Simple though it may appear, the Oblique Order was a manoeuvre that could easily go wrong if the principles were disregarded, as they were at the battle of Kolin six months before Leuthen. On that occasion the approach was made in full view of the enemy, the commander of the attacking wing was not reinforced sufficiently, and the commander of the 'refused' wing engaged the enemy in too great a strength. The result was failure at the point of attack. But at Leuthen the recipe for success – rapid movement, concentration, surprise, and a decisively delivered hammer blow – were strictly adhered to, and the whole operation brilliantly executed gave Frederick a resounding victory.

The Oblique Order fell upon hard times, but in Prussian military circles Leuthen was to become an heroic apologue. When Hitler was overrunning the Netherlands and France the last, and least attractive, of the Hohenzollern monarchs telegraphed the Fuehrer from Doorn: 'The Anthem of Leuthen is resounding in every German heart.'

Leuthen is the only battle described in this book in which military skill and incompetence were the sole reasons for victory and defeat respectively. Frederick could well have been defeated by a competent adversary – not necessarily a brilliant one – but once out of danger his undoubted military genius won a great victory.

9 Saratoga Campaign: The Battles of Freeman's Farm and Bemis Heights
19 September and 7 October 1777

THE conclusion of the Seven Years War in 1763 meant for Britain an expansion of empire commercially and territorially, but her American colonists were not content to be merely a source of overseas investment, and were beginning to aspire to some form of home rule. This was an aspiration that found neither sympathy nor understanding from George III and his parliaments, whose concept of empire was based on allegiance and obedience. And for the next twelve years the colonists were at the receiving end of a good deal of ill-informed and muddled thinking by successive First Lords of the Treasury, misplaced fiscal legislation, some good intentions misconstrued by the colonists, and eventually the crowning folly of trying to put back the colonial clock by coercion.

General Gage, who had been appointed Governor of Massachusetts, had warned the home government that coercion would lead to war, but his warning was ignored, and when the New Englanders were driven to a state of rebellion Gage was ordered, in April 1775, to move against the insurgents in Massachusetts, Connecticut, and Rhode Island. At Lexington the rebels – as the colonists were now being called – took heavy toll of his force, and although he gained a technical victory at Bunker Hill in June he achieved nothing and lost over 1,000 men (from a total force that numbered only 6,000), while the Americans lost fewer than 500. In March 1776 the British, finding their position untenable, had to evacuate Boston. On 4 July of that year the colonists, despairing of achieving any form of home rule, declared their independence.

As early as May 1775 a handful of Americans, under the inspiring leadership of Benedict Arnold and Ethan Allen, had surprised the British garrison at Ticonderoga and taken the fort with its useful store of heavy cannon. And during the following winter Generals Schuyler and Montgomery, with Benedict Arnold, came very close to taking Quebec when they mounted an offensive against General Carleton's troops in Canada. In May 1776 General John Burgoyne arrived in Canada with English and German reinforcements, and with a plan to advance down the Hudson river in conjunction with an advance up it by

General William Howe, who had by then succeeded Gage. This was attempted by Carleton that autumn, but he got no farther than Crown Point on Lake Champlain, and did not consider himself strong enough to take Ticonderoga.

Burgoyne, who had returned to England in December 1776, disapproved of what he considered to be Carleton's pusillanimity, and in the following February he presented a paper to Lord George Germain, Secretary of State for the Colonies, entitled 'Thoughts for Conducting the War from the Side of Canada'. In brief this recommended the assembling of 8,000 men at Crown Point to be joined by 2,000 Canadians and 1,000 or more 'savages' – Red Indians – together with an artillery train and a corps of watermen. This force was to move on Ticonderoga and then down the Hudson to Albany, while Howe sent an army up that river. Simultaneously a diversionary force was to move from Oswego down the Mohawk river and join up with the main armies at Albany.

In his 'Thoughts' Burgoyne made it perfectly clear that the only object of the Canada army was to make a junction with Howe's force, so that after Albany had been taken and communications opened up to New York, Howe would be free to take his whole force southwards. It is important to stress this in view of Howe's failure to co-operate. This plan, which had the approval of the King and Germain, was sound strategically. To occupy the Ticonderoga–Hudson line would effectively cut off the New England states, which could be held in check and then conquered before dealing with the southern states should they still remain in arms. The plan also had the advantage of providing an almost continuous (there was a short break at Fort George) waterway for transport from Ticonderoga to Albany.

Complications, however, quickly arose. Howe was also submitting plans to Germain from America. His first, which Germain received on 30 November 1776, proposed a three-pronged thrust from Canada, New York, and Rhode Island, for which he required 15,000 more troops. But three weeks later, realizing he was unlikely to get the required troops, he altered the plan to giving what assistance he could to the northern army, but making the main thrust against Philadelphia. Germain received this alteration on 23 February 1777. Later Howe changed the plan again, saying that he had abandoned the idea of all expeditions 'except that to the Southward, and a diversion occasionally upon Hudson's River', and that he would take his army by sea, and advance on Philadelphia from the south.

This last alteration was not received in London until 8 May, by which time Burgoyne (who had been appointed to command the northern army) had arrived in Canada with his own plan approved. It was the worst possible choice, for it meant Howe removing his army from between Washington and the lower Hudson. Nevertheless, it was

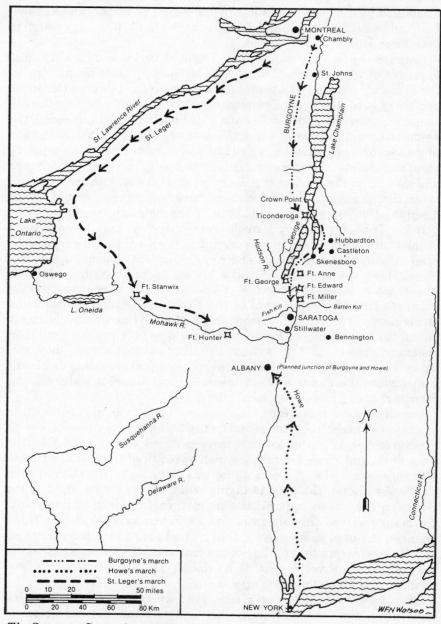

The Saratoga Campaign: 1777

approved by the King and Germain with the proviso that whatever Howe might meditate 'will be executed in time to co-operate with the army ordered to proceed from Canada'. This was the nearest Howe came to receiving definite orders to assist the northern army, and he did not get the letter until 25 August; by then Burgoyne was encamped on the Hudson near Saratoga still hoping Howe would support him.

Burgoyne assembled his army at Montreal. A debonair, amusing, and ambitious man, he was brave to a fault. He had served with distinction in comparatively high rank in Europe for seven years, and was always a popular commander who paid much attention to the proper training of officers and men. He had under his command at the start of the campaign seven British and eight German regiments, the latter being commanded by Major-General Baron von Riedesel. The total British force, which included 411 artillery men, was 4,488, while the Germans numbered 4,699. At Skenesboro the army was joined by 148 Canadians, 500 Indians and 682 Tories (loyalists).* There were also a large number of non-combatants. As was usual at the time the grenadier and light companies were detached from their regiments to form an élite corps, and to this corps were added the light companies of the three regiments which were to remain as garrison troops in Canada. The Indians were a constant source of trouble, otherwise it was a useful army of some 9,000 combatants, which included tough, well-trained and disciplined regular soldiers. There was also a fleet of thirty powerfully armed boats, and carts for overland transport.

On 20 June, a few days after the diversionary force under the command of Colonel St Leger had set out for the Mohawk valley, Burgoyne's army and his fleet moved towards Ticonderoga. The fort was commanded by General St Clair who had for its defence a totally inadequate force of about 2,500 men. Burgoyne was expecting to be faced with a formidable siege, and it was principally for this reason that he had brought a large artillery train – many of the guns were left behind after Ticonderoga† – but resistance was not great, and by 6 July the fort was in British hands.

The capture of Ticonderoga was not a significant victory, but it could not be left occupied in Burgoyne's rear. He lost no time in ordering the pursuit. St Clair in his withdrawal had, for some strange reason, left two regiments at Hubbardton to await his rearguard, and these were surprised by the speedy march of General Simon Fraser's grenadiers and light infantry battalions, and Riedesel's Germans following at a

---

*Figures compiled by Charles W. Small, United States Park Historian.

† Burgoyne has been criticized for having marched with too great a weight of cannon, but there is ample evidence from those who took part in the campaign that both in numbers and calibres the guns taken were very necessary.

more ponderous pace. A short and very sharp engagement followed in which Burgoyne's forces suffered 174 casualties and the Americans 166, but the latter also lost 228 men made prisoner. The Americans had been defeated, but they had fought with a skill and valour that must have impressed Burgoyne, who hitherto had been guilty of underestimating their worth.

This was more forcibly brought home to him in the next serious engagement, which was fought at Bennington, a small place in the newly created state of Vermont, on 16 August. After Hubbardton, St Clair's force was in a state of disarray, and he had fallen back to join General Schuyler (commanding the Northern Department) at Fort Edward. Burgoyne had had to dally at Skenesboro for a fortnight to await the arrival of provisions – his whole campaign was bedevilled by supply problems – but on 24 July he set off to march the twenty-three miles to Fort Edward over a quite appalling track that had been thoroughly blocked by the Americans. His heavy artillery and stores went back to Ticonderoga and rejoined him by way of boat down Lake George to Fort George.* The army reached Fort Edward on 30 July, by which time Schuyler had abandoned the place and fallen back to a defensive position at Stillwater. Burgoyne still held the advantage in both numbers and morale, but time was running out and he was desperately short of supplies, and so the disastrous raid into Vermont was conceived.

For some time past General von Riedesel had been urging Burgoyne to procure horses for his dragoons, whose fighting prowess was diminished through having to flounder about in jackboots. And so when the ever optimistic Philip Skene – the loyalist leader who lived at Skenesboro and acted as Burgoyne's political officer – assured Burgoyne that there were loyalists, horses, and supplies to be collected in the Connecticut river valley against a virtually negligible opposition, a small force – too small for a hazardous operation of this kind – was despatched under the German, Lieutenant-Colonel Baum.

Baum soon learnt that Bennington (where it was said the horses would be found) was held not by 400 militia as he was led to believe but by 1,500 well-armed troops under an extremely able New Englander called John Stark. He at once sent back this information and Burgoyne despatched Lieutenant-Colonel Breymann with reinforcements on 15 August. But before they could arrive Baum's troops had been defeated, and he himself killed. Stark next defeated Breymann, whose soldiers had made very slow time in admittedly very heavy going, and in a chaotic withdrawal they were saved from annihilation by oncoming

---

*Burgoyne has often been criticized for not taking the whole army by this route, but he had very good reasons for deciding to march.

darkness. Bennington had cost Burgoyne 527 of his German troops (28 of whom were officers) and 37 rangers. The Americans, whose casualties were no more than 30 killed and 40 wounded, had also taken four guns. It was a defeat from which Burgoyne's army never really recovered.

Burgoyne's position by the end of August had become most unenviable. He had heard from Howe that he was intending to go to Pennsylvania; his army had been reduced to 6,074 men fit for duty, of which 4,646 were regular soldiers; to advance would mean severing his line of communications, and therefore he had to assemble a large quantity of stores, which would take time; he was unaware of what St Leger was doing,* and due to an unfortunate incident in which his unruly Indians had scalped the daughter of a local clergyman he and his troops were subjected to a campaign of intense and unwarranted vilification throughout America. There was still a chance to go back, and in the circumstances no one could have blamed Burgoyne for doing so. But he decided to continue the advance, and on 13 September the British troops crossed the Hudson by a bridge of boats placed just above Saratoga. The Germans crossed the following day. The army, now augmented to 7,702 by some recruits who had joined just before the crossing, marched in three columns down the west bank of the river.

Meanwhile, the American troops of the Northern Department had had a change of command: Major-General Horatio Gates had replaced Schuyler. Gates had served in the British army as an infantry officer, but not possessing the means to purchase command of a regiment he had resigned his commission and, at loggerheads with the Establishment, had returned to America where he had served in his youth. He was a cautious and somewhat unimaginative commander, who was inclined to lead from behind. Shortly after taking over the army he moved it from the mouth of the Mohawk to a place farther up the Hudson known as Bemis Heights. This was a naturally strong defensive position, which through the prowess of a Polish engineer called Koscinszko was made even stronger. Gates had under command 28 regiments of foot, 200 light cavalry, and 22 cannon. His Continental† troops and Colonel Daniel Morgan's 500 marksmen were first class, but the militiamen recently joined from New England were very raw. He was numerically superior in troops to Burgoyne, he was soundly barricaded and time was on his side.

The American defensive position was in the region of one and a quarter miles in length, and three-quarters of a mile in depth.

*St Leger had in fact been outwitted by Arnold and let down by his Indians; by 22 August he was on his way back to Oswego.

†On declaring their independence on 4 July 1776 the Continental Congress, sitting in Philadelphia, set about raising a Continental army. These were to be federal troops, who were to serve for two or three years. The short-service (month or two) militia remained under the control of the colonies.

Earthworks and breastworks stretched from the high ground overlooking the river to Neilson's (a local farmer) house on the left flank, and the position was further strengthened by a deep ravine to its immediate front. The line was held principally by Continental brigades; on the right artillery dominated the road and river, in the centre the fortifications ran north-westward to Neilson's barn, and here another battery

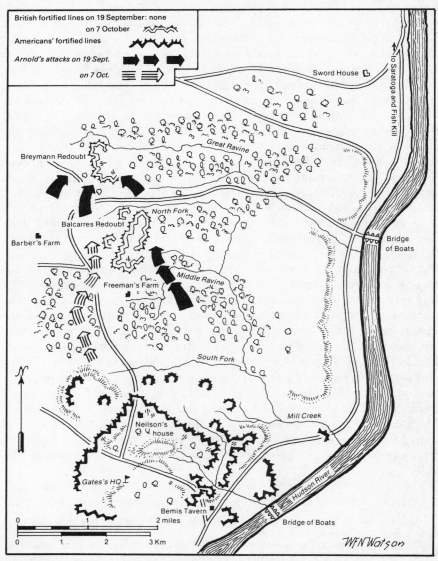

The Battles of Freeman's Farm (19 September) and Bemis Heights (7 October 1777)

was in position. To the west of the barn was a hill that had been only partly fortified, but the main position ran south-west to Gates's head-quarters.

Burgoyne's first contact with the enemy was on 17 September in the area of the Sword House, some five miles north of Gates's position. He was advancing through fairly dense wooded country, and with very few reliable scouts, for by now his best Indians had gone. Gates, on the other hand, had plenty of information on what was happening in Burgoyne's camp, for Lieutenant-Colonel James Wilkinson – his deputy adjutant-general – had reconnoitred almost up to it, and some Germans had deserted to the enemy. Burgoyne was, however, aware that the Albany road was blocked, and he had received a report that on the left of the enemy position there was an unoccupied hill. He decided, therefore, not to continue down the Albany track and engage Gates frontally, but to feel for the left of the position and try to turn it, and roll the line off the bluff towards the river.

The army left the Sword House at 8 a.m. on 19 September in thick mist and drizzling rain. They marched in three groups: Fraser was on the right, General Hamilton commanded the centre, and General Phillips, with Riedesel in support, commanded the left wing on the river road. Fraser's column took a wide sweep to the west, while Burgoyne at the head of the centre column followed a wagon track which crossed the Great Ravine and then continued westwards to just north of Freeman's Farm – Freeman, a loyalist who was to give his name to the battle, had abandoned his holding some time before. The three columns were well separated; particularly was this so with the centre and left ones. The mist had cleared, and by 9 a.m. the sun shone brilliantly on the red coats and gleaming bayonets of Burgoyne's heavily accoutred soldiers, as they weaved their way through the unaccustomed conditions of bush and forest.

At Freeman's farm Burgoyne halted to allow Fraser's column, which had the longest approach march, to reach its starting position. Shortly after 1 p.m., when Fraser was adjudged to be ready, a prearranged minute-gun signal indicated the time for the columns to advance to contact. At about the same time an advanced picquet came under a withering fire. Gates, characteristically, was not in favour of offensive action; he had planned to remain behind his defences and let the British attack him. But under pressure from Major-General Arnold, commanding the left wing, he relented so far as to allow Morgan's riflemen, supported by Dearborn's light infantry, to go forward. It was these men who engaged the forward troops of the centre column under Major Forbes, and virtually wiped them out.

The battle now joined was to be a savage pounding match that lasted until nightfall. Morgan's riflemen were reinforced by two regiments from General Poor's brigade, but attempts to work round the British right were unsuccessful due to some devastating flanking fire from Fraser's advanced column. The brunt of the fighting was borne by Hamilton's centre column, and of the four British regiments that held the line here the 62nd took tremendous punishment. They had fought magnificently and earned Burgoyne's special commendation, 'Well done, my brave Springers' shouted above the roar of the battle. At the end of the day they had only some 70 all ranks still standing from the 250 with whom they had started the day.

Fraser gave Hamilton what help he could, but Morgan's men were keeping his troops fully occupied. In this close-quarter fighting there was little to be gained by the British through their superiority in cannon, for there were high casualties among the gunners. However, the Americans failed to use the guns they overran because those gunners who survived always removed the linstocks. A serious handicap to Burgoyne was the loss of many officers, so easily picked off in their gorgeous plumage by American sharpshooters. He himself was always in the thick of the battle, but he could not do very much to influence events; it is strange, however, that he delayed so long in contacting Riedesel away to his left, and in the end it was men from his column who were to save the day for the British.

Arnold's troops of the left wing had suffered heavy casualties, but they were still full of fight. One final push and they might well have broken through to victory, but Gates feared Arnold's impetuosity and grudged him further troops, and Riedesel's men arrived just in time. It was General Phillips who, riding up from the river and seeing how desperate was the situation, ordered up four of Riedesel's guns, and personally led a charge to relieve the pressure on the 62nd. While Riedesel himself, acting upon orders he at last received from Burgoyne (as late as 5 p.m.), swung into the battle at the head of his own regiment, two companies of the Brunswick von Rhetz Regiment, and two 6-pounders. The charge of the German troops, and the grape-shot their gunners fired at almost point-blank range, together with fast-falling darkness, undoubtedly saved Burgoyne's centre. Arnold's men withdrew to their entrenchments, and the combatants of both sides had had as much punishment as they could take. Burgoyne had suffered 600 casualties (including 35 officers), which was about a third of the troops actually engaged. The Americans lost 283 all ranks with a further 33 reported missing.

It was a battle in which neither side could claim a victory, although the British remained masters of the battlefield and their morale was still high. But for Burgoyne there was little comfort. He was carrying a heavy load of responsibility not only for the still hoped for success of the campaign, but for his many wounded and for the ladies who were administering to their need so tirelessly. Supplies – and soldiers – were running short, the way back was dark and doubtful, and the way forward perilous.

Although Burgoyne was not aware of it until a day or two later, by the time the battle of Freeman's Farm was fought his back door had been virtually closed by John Stark and General Lincoln taking Fort Edward, and Colonel John Brown who, although repulsed at Ticonderoga, had taken Fort George and captured many of Burgoyne's supply ships on Lake Champlain. But Burgoyne had ruled out any retreat, and had it not been for a communication received from General Clinton in New York he would have renewed the offensive on 21 September. As it was he decided to await definite news of the advance towards Albany that Clinton promised, and meanwhile he would strengthen his line, which now ran from the Hudson to the high ground north-west of Freeman's Farm, by a series of redoubts and strongpoints.

During the closing days of September and early ones of October messengers winged their way most perilously between Burgoyne at Saratoga and Clinton in New York. Clinton strongly disapproved of Howe's decision to go to Philadelphia, and in compliance with the latter's directive did what he could to assist Burgoyne once he had received reinforcements. On 3 October he embarked 3,000 troops in 60 vessels and sent them up river to carry out what proved to be a very successful military operation. They captured the two forts, Montgomery and Clinton, that barred the way up the Hudson just above Peekshill, inflicting heavy casualties on the Americans, and they came to within forty-four miles of Albany before the river pilots refused to take the vessels farther. It was a brave attempt, but it came too late to be of assistance to Burgoyne, who had anyway been told by Clinton, through one of the messengers, that he lacked sufficient numbers to fight his way through.

Meanwhile, with the knowledge that another battle was inevitable, the British worked strenuously to construct the best line of defence that time and the country would permit. The redoubts, protected by long palisades and earthworks, formed the principal pivot points of the line. The strongest was named Balcarres Redoubt after the commander of the light and grenadier troops who held the position, and echeloned back from this was the Breymann Redoubt, a small square earthwork with sally ports. The third strongpoint was called the Great Redoubt, which overlooked the Hudson and the river road. Along the whole line as much use as possible was made of natural obstacles. By 4 October the soldiers had created a strong defence, but the ground was so uneven and densely wooded that a good field of fire could not always be obtained. Furthermore, by now almost all the Indians, who acted as the eyes of the army, had deserted.

On 4 and 5 October Burgoyne held councils of war. Undoubtedly he was a very worried man; his supplies could not last beyond the end of the month, and while his numbers were at best static, Gates's were increasing almost daily. Gates was to fight the coming battle with 6,444 Continentals and 6,621 militia, which was more than double what Burgoyne could muster. At these councils Generals Riedesel and Fraser were in favour of a withdrawal, either back to the line occupied briefly at Fish Kill, where the army crossed the Hudson, which could be turned into a strong defensive position, or across the river to Batten Kill, and attempt to restore the lines of communication.

Burgoyne would have none of this and advocated leaving a small force of 800 men to guard the base camp, and to march the remainder of the army to attack the left flank and rear of the American position. To send the army blundering around the American left flank over ground that had not been reconnoitred against defences whose strength was unknown was too daring a proposition for the generals to accept. Moreover, they thought that while the flank march was in progress it would not be difficult for Gates to swamp the 800 men, and in destroying the bridges over the two riverside creeks imperil the army's line of retreat.

In the end a compromise was reached whereby a reconnaissance in force of some 1,500 men should be sent round the enemy's left flank to observe the strength of the position, with a view to a full-scale attack on the following day. Should the reconnaissance find the position too strongly held then the army would withdraw to Fish Kill.* It was certainly a more sensible plan than Burgoyne's original suggestion, but if it was really to be just a reconnaissance it should have been carried out by far fewer troops. A large force advancing towards the enemy's flank is liable to be misconstrued by them as a major attack to be dealt with by a similar, or preferably larger, body of troops. And this is exactly what happened in what became known as the battle of Bemis Heights.

The force that left the defensive position shortly before midday on 7 October had been carefully chosen for mobility and fire power, and included the light infantry and grenadier companies, the rangers and the German jaegers, as well as Canadians and loyalists. Two 12-pounders, six 6-pounders and two 8-inch howitzers were in support. In the end the total was nearer 2,000 than 1,500, and the force was divided into two wings and a centre, with Burgoyne and his staff riding with the latter. Fraser commanded the right wing, Riedesel the centre, and Major John Acland of the 20th Regiment had command of the left with the British grenadier companies.

After marching for about three-quarters of an hour the advance guard was to the west of the Barber farm, beyond the redoubts and north of the

---

* From the evidence Burgoyne gave later to Parliament it looks very much as though he always meant to attack with these 1,500 if circumstances were favourable (*A State of the Expedition from Canada*, p. 17).

Middle Ravine. Here, in two small clearings, the force halted, while 150 irregulars were despatched to reconnoitre Gates's extreme left. Wilkinson, who observed the force at this halt, told Gates that in his opinion an attack was imminent. On this occasion Gates was content to give battle – although he did little to influence it once it was joined – and he ordered Morgan and Dearborn to outflank the British right, Poor to attack the left, and Learned was to be ready to thrust at the centre. Like all good plans it was simple, and with odds of about four to one it was fairly certain to succeed.

The British had just ended their halt at Barber's farm when Poor's men, who had the shortest route from the American lines, fell upon their left. Major Acland's grenadiers fought with tremendous zest, but were hopelessly outnumbered and had to give ground, losing as a prisoner their seriously wounded commander. Shortly after Acland had been attacked, Morgan and Dearborn opened up a devastating fire on the right of Fraser's wing, who were as hotly engaged as Acland's men. They too had to fall back despite Fraser's valiant efforts to rally them. Always prominent on his white horse, he was an obvious target for an American marksman, and in the course of this fierce action he fell mortally wounded. His death later that evening was a terrible blow for Burgoyne, for not only was Fraser a great friend but he was also undoubtedly his finest officer.

The withdrawal on both flanks left the centre very exposed. Here not many more than 300 Germans faced some 3,000 Americans from Learned's brigade and General Ten Broeck's militia. They fought with great gallantry, supported for as long as possible by the Hesse-Hanau artillery, and inflicted grievous casualties on the Americans, but by the middle of the afternoon it was clear to Burgoyne (whose bullet-ridden coat testified to his front-line courage) that the whole line must withdraw behind the fortifications. By now he had had some 400 casualties and lost 8 cannon. Morale, understandably, was becoming shaky, but Burgoyne could reasonably have hoped to hold the defences, and later to extricate the army safely.

This he might well have done but for one man – Benedict Arnold. This unpredictable soldier but brilliant leader had quarrelled with Gates and been deprived of his command, but once battle was joined he was not the man to stay quietly in the camp. Before anyone could stop him he was out and, acting like one possessed, he roared around the field rallying the scattered units and taking charge first of one brigade and then another. But he acted with sense as well as zest and courage. He quickly realized that the Balcarres Redoubt (into which most of the British had withdrawn) was too strongly held to be stormed, and so he bypassed that to the rear and mopped up a few Canadians in isolated log cabins, before tackling the Breymann Redoubt.

Breymann was a most unpopular officer, who drove his men beyond any reasonable endurance. While he lived terror of their commander increased their customary courage, but when he died (by whose hand is uncertain) they abandoned the position. In this assault Arnold's horse was shot under him, pinning his leg and breaking it, but the battle was almost over. With the remnants of the army now threatened in flank and rear Burgoyne broke off the fight, and just before sunset the British withdrew to the Great Redoubt. Out of about 2,000 men actually engaged 176 had been killed, more than 200 wounded and 240 captured.

General Burgoyne did not surrender until ten days after the battle of Bemis Heights. Gates bombarded the British out of the Great Redoubt encampment, and the weary and depressed army, with their supplies almost exhausted, marched – together with the ladies, although the wounded had to be left behind – to their old positions at the Fish Kill Creek. Gates pursued in a leisurely fashion; he had no need to hurry, for the trap was virtually closed. Surprisingly, he took the initiative and launched an attack on the British position. He thought he had only a rear-guard to deal with, but luckily learnt his error just in time to call off what would have been a very costly operation. Thereafter he contented himself with starvation tactics and a constant pounding of the British position.

After enduring four days of this punishment Burgoyne called a council, and a decision was taken to abandon the position – less the guns and transport – stealthily by night. But before darkness set in scouts reported that the route back was totally closed. On 14 October, with the full agreement of his senior officers, Burgoyne asked Gates for terms. To these he at first objected, but Gates, unsure of Clinton's whereabouts and anxious to be done with Burgoyne, was inclined to be lenient. The Convention of Saratoga was signed on 16 October, and the surrender took place the next day.

The war was to drag on for another four years, but Saratoga was the turning point. Ticonderoga, the Highlands and indeed all the land from New York to the Canadian border – save only Rhode Island – was now in American hands. In February 1778 France signed a treaty recognizing American independence, and became her active ally. But above all American soldiers had defeated a British army and forced it to surrender. In doing this they had gained confidence in their officers, in themselves and in their cause.

The Saratoga campaign got off to a bad start in London through conflicting plans, breakdown in communications and Lord George Germain's failure to appreciate that there were insufficient troops in America for simultaneous expeditions to Pennsylvania and Albany. And then when Howe insisted on going to Philadelphia, leaving Clinton with too small a force to do more than take the Highlands on the lower Hudson, Burgoyne's task had become wellnigh impossible.

A close examination of the many accounts of the campaign, once it had got under way, and the detailed evidence given by Burgoyne and some of his officers to a committee of the House of Commons, makes it very difficult to prove – despite asseverations to the contrary by some historians – that, during the long march, there was any decisive action or decision (except the one to retreat) which, if acted upon differently by Burgoyne, would have saved him from defeat. But once battle was joined on that thickly wooded, broken piece of ground near Saratoga there were two factors which contributed very greatly to Burgoyne's ultimate failure. The presence in Gates's camp of Benedict Arnold, and a wrong decision by Burgoyne after the battle of Freeman's Farm.

The United States, in the 200 years of its military history, has produced more than one soldier of quality who has combined panache and élan with a combative and confident spirit – Jeb Stuart, Custer, and Patton come readily to mind – and the first of these *beaux sabreurs* was Benedict Arnold. Unfortunately Arnold was to ruin a legendary record of courage and leadership by committing treason of the deepest dye, and on account of this contemporaries and near contemporaries writing about him have tended to play down, and in some cases totally distort, the services he rendered his country in the War of Independence.

In the Saratoga campaign Arnold's principal contribution to Burgoyne's downfall was in the two final battles, but he had played a decisive part in raising the siege of Fort Stanwix and compelling St Leger to leave the Mohawk valley. He was a proud, sensitive man who pulsed with dynamic confidence. No one could impugn his courage or powers of leadership, but his impetuous nature constantly got him into trouble. Moreover, a hasty temper often gave too much rein to too sharp a tongue. There was more of the quicksand than the rock in Benedict Arnold.

On 1 September he joined Gates's army, which was then at the mouth of the Mohawk river, with 1,200 men, and took command of the left wing. He never held Gates in the same degree of respect as he did Schuyler, but they had campaigned together in 1776 and, despite the fact that at Valcour Island Arnold had disobeyed Gates's order and lost the American fleet, they had remained on perfectly friendly terms. According to his biographer, Arnold was detailed by Gates to reconnoitre the Bemis Heights position, and to assist the Polish engineer, Kosciuszko, in the construction of its defences, and he was also active at the head of a skirmishing force in harassing the British advance from the Fish Kill.*

Arnold's left wing consisted of two brigades: Brigadier-General Enoch

* Arnold, pp. 166, 167.

Poor's 2,116 men from the 1st, 2nd and 3rd New Hampshire regiments, and the 2nd and 4th New York regiments with two regiments of the Connecticut Militia; and Brigadier-General Ebenezer Learned's brigade of 1,243 men from the 2nd, 8th and 9th Massachusetts regiments and a New York regiment. It is not certain whether Colonel Daniel Morgan's riflemen and Major Henry Dearborn's light infantry (together totalling 674 men) were under command, but they probably were, and Arnold also had 200 horsemen of the Connecticut Light Horse and 22 cannon. The ground to Arnold's immediate front was more open than some, and the left wing lacked the protection of the ravine which fronted the right and centre of the position. It was against the left wing that Burgoyne directed his attack.

Gates had decided to await the British in his entrenchments, and this he would have done had not Arnold argued hotly against such tactics. He rightly pointed out that the British were well versed in siege warfare and if allowed to come within artillery range their guns could do great damage; on the other hand they were neither trained nor equipped for jungle fighting. To go forward, Arnold stressed, must be right, for if needs be they could always fall back on their defences, whereas to wait and possibly be pushed out of them might end in a rout. This battle-winning advice was accepted – if only to a limited degree – and Morgan's and Dearborn's riflemen were sent forward to engage the enemy. The first phase of the battle, in which they alone of the Americans took part, lasted from about 9 a.m. until 12.30 p.m. by which time Colonel Wilkinson had reported back to Gates and urged him to send in further troops. As a result two regiments of Poor's brigade were despatched immediately, and they were followed a little later by the whole of Learned's brigade. Thus by 4 p.m. most of Arnold's division was committed.

Arnold's personal performance at the battle of Freeman's Farm has been the subject of a great deal of contradictory writing. There are accounts by those who fought that make no mention of his presence on the field, while there are others who assert positively that he was in the forefront of the fighting. The personal accounts of any battle by most individuals are bounded by their own participation, and it is therefore not surprising that some officers may have failed to notice what senior commanders were fighting. On the other hand there is no reason for such as Captain Wakefield of Dearborn's Light Infantry to invent the fact that he saw Arnold participating in the opening engagement, or of Marshall – a colonel in Learned's brigade – saying that 'about 4 o'clock, Arnold, with nine Continental regiments and Morgan's corps, was completely engaged with the whole right wing of the British army'.* Colonel Wilkinson in his memoirs says that no general officer was in

* Furneaux, p. 168.

action until Learned was ordered out, although he admits that he was sent by Gates to recall Arnold, who had galloped, without orders, to the sound of the guns. Wilkinson, who was Gates's deputy adjutant-general, had a wider view of the battle than most participants, but his recollections are slightly suspect, for he greatly disliked Arnold even before his treason.

Anyone who has studied Arnold's character must find it difficult to believe that he would be content to stay in camp while his division was in action, and although Wakefield may have been mistaken in his timing the weight of evidence is that Benedict Arnold was on the field of battle at least by the early afternoon. Personally in action or not, his contribution to the outcome of the battle was decisive. His advice to go forward may well have saved Gates from defeat, and had he been reinforced (and in the end the battle hinged on who could produce reinforcements – Gates could, Burgoyne could not) the Americans would have gained a clear-cut victory.

Arnold's action in the battle of Bemis Heights is again controversial. All are agreed that he had a blinding row with Gates on 22 September, sparked off by the latter's official dispatch in which he greatly played down the undoubtedly very fine performance of Arnold's division at Freeman's Farm. Arnold's hasty temper was given full vent, and his tongue and pen got out of control. Gates remained quite calm under all the vituperation, but dismissed him from his command. Arnold made numerous threats to leave the Northern Department, and Gates was only too ready to give him a pass, but Arnold probably never had much intention of leaving, and on the days before the battle remained sulking in his tent.

No one denies that when the battle was at its height Arnold could be restrained no longer, and pursuing glory through all hazards took command wherever he found the leadership lacked fire and spirit. What is open to question is how much his personal performance contributed to winkling Burgoyne out of his redoubts and driving him from the field. Certainly Gates had sufficient troops to push the British into the Hudson, but superior numbers can often be of no avail if the leadership is supine. Burgoyne in his evidence to Parliament was to say that but for Arnold's intervention he should 'in a few hours have gained a position, that in spite of the enemy's numbers, would have put them in my power'.* This was one of Burgoyne's more spectacular hyperboles. Albany by then was a vanished dream, and the army's future was no better than a forlorn hope. Arnold's part in the battle of Bemis Heights was certainly decisive, but only in preventing Burgoyne from extricating his army and avoiding a severe disaster.

*

*Burgoyne, p. 17.

Arnold might well have been called upon to make a greater contribution at Bemis Heights if Burgoyne had decided to strike at once after Freeman's Farm, when there would seem to have been a fair chance of breaking through. At the close of the fight on 19 September both armies were, understandably, totally exhausted, for the battle had been one of hard pounding. However, British morale was high, for they had remained masters of the field having seen the Americans recoil back to their entrenchments. On the other hand Gates had battle-fresh troops to call upon, whereas virtually all of Burgoyne's army had been committed. Both sides stood to their arms on the night of 19–20 September expecting to be attacked.

The most informative evidence on the state of the American position on the morning of the 20th comes from Colonel Wilkinson, and he paints a very dark picture of turmoil and tribulation in their camp.* Early that morning a British deserter from the 62nd Regiment gave the Americans what appeared to be authentic information of an immediate British attack. Wilkinson says they were in no position to resist this renewed offensive; the troops were exhausted, very short of ammunition, and they 'could not boast of more than a bayonet for every three muskets'. Nevertheless, full credit was given to the deserter's story, and in the fog and mist the lines were manned with everyone passing 'an hour of awful expectation and suspense'.

In the event, as is known, there was no attack. But Wilkinson asserts that the deserter's information was not incorrect, for after the surrender he had the chance to discuss the occasion with Major-General Phillips, who told him that Burgoyne had determined to attack the left of the American line in great strength, with a holding operation on their right and centre, on the morning of the 20th. He was only deterred from this, according to Phillips, by Fraser who requested a twenty-four-hour postponement because his grenadiers and light infantry were not fully recovered from the exertions of the previous day. This latter is very suspect, for in the first instance Fraser's men had not been so pressed as some in the previous battle, and we have it from Lieutenant Digby that, 'It was Gen Phillips and Fraziers opinion we should follow the stroke by attacking their camp that morning'†, i.e. the morning of the 20th. It seems that Wilkinson's memory of his conversation with Phillips was partly at fault, but it is unlikely that he would have forgotten, or exaggerated, the plight of the American camp at that time.

Burgoyne in his statement to Parliament makes no mention of having issued orders for an immediate attack. Indeed, he is emphatic that any thought of attack would have been most foolish. 'I do not believe that

* Wilkinson, p. 250.
† Digby, p. 275.

with an army exhausted by a long and severe action, and deprived of an uncommon portion of officers, the question of attacking the enemy next morning would have occurred to any man of professional judgment.'* In their evidence the Earls of Balcarres and Harrington, Colonel Kingston, Major Forbes and Captain Money all supported (quite rightly) their commanding general in varying degrees of emphasis. Colonel Kingston reinforced a point made by Burgoyne that prisoners and deserters reported the American position to be strongly held with four times the number of men available to the British.

There are many discrepancies between Burgoyne's statement and the evidence of witnesses to Parliament, and contemporary accounts of the battle and subsequent events. This is not surprising, for no doubt in some instances the former had been adjusted with the benefit of hindsight and the need to put as favourable a slant as possible on actions under critical review. Despite what he said to Parliament Burgoyne almost certainly contemplated an attack on the morning of 20 September (if not he certainly should have done), but either on advice of his commanders or, more likely, from his own observations, he decided the men needed a twenty-four-hour respite and he therefore postponed the attack until the following day.

However, on that day (21 September) Burgoyne received a message from General Clinton in New York. In this Clinton offered to send 2,000 men (all he could spare) against Fort Montgomery in the Highlands, some 40 miles up river from New York, but warning him that he might have to abandon the enterprise if attacked in flank. Burgoyne at once despatched a messenger accepting this offer of a diversion. In his statement to Parliament touching on Clinton's projected attack on Fort Montgomery, Burgoyne said: 'I should have thought it the part of madness to have risked an attack upon the enemy, in the weak state of my army, for some time after the late action, and under the expectation of a powerful diversion.'† He also wanted to await the return to duty of his many lightly wounded men, and there was still the chance, or so he thought, of reinforcement from St Leger. He therefore decided to strengthen his position with redoubts and wait upon events.

In the course of the Saratoga campaign Burgoyne was called upon to make a number of difficult decisions. One of the hazards in trying to reconstruct remote actions lies in speculating the motives behind them, and it is easy to be led astray by what has been written later in defence of these actions. So often certain facts are clear-cut, while it is not possible to be sure of others. At Skenesboro and Bennington, Burgoyne's judgements may well have been sure-footed, and almost certainly his refusal to go back was correct for, as Fortescue says, 'other operations depended

*Burgoyne, p. 122.
†Burgoyne, p. 123.

upon his advance'.* But at Saratoga, where it is possible to get a clearer picture of Burgoyne's problems, it can be said that he undoubtedly missed the last chance – albeit a slender one – of accomplishing his mission.

If Burgoyne had put into action, on the morning of 20 September, the plan he obviously had in mind, and which General Phillips later outlined to Wilkinson, and delivered a body punch to the American left flank and a holding operation against the centre and right, he would have found the Americans totally disorganized. But it is true his army was not really ready that day for another major engagement; it was therefore marginally correct to postpone the attack for twenty-four hours, even though the chances of success were sensibly diminished through allowing the Americans more time to recover.

However, there was no excuse for a further postponement on the 21st. Burgoyne was well aware that all Clinton had offered was nothing more than a diversion, there was no certainty he could carry it out, and anyway with the delay in communications Clinton could not hope to mount his attack for about a fortnight. Gates was gathering strength daily, and would soon have an army many times the size the British could bring against him, and Burgoyne's supplies were fast running out. To remain inactive, struggling with the spectre of unfulfilled expectation, must have been wrong; to hazard a thrust at the heart before the road was barred for ever offered a slender alternative to disaster. It would have been a gambler's desperate throw, which Burgoyne, a dedicated gamester, might have been expected to make.

These two battles were a climax to a campaign which began almost three months before the first one was fought, and for the purpose of analysing victory and defeat the campaign must be looked at as a whole. It is an interesting example, and although the only one given in this book by no means the only one to have occurred, of defeat made almost certain through political ineptitude and interference. Burgoyne had a perfectly good plan, but its success was entirely dependent on full co-operation from Howe. The Colonial Secretary, Lord George Germain, attempted to control operations 3,000 miles away in a country about which he knew nothing. He had given inflexible orders to Burgoyne while at the same time approving a plan of Howe's that made it impossible for these orders to have anything but a disastrous conclusion.

---

*Fortescue, p. 241.

10   The Battle of Borodino
7 September* 1812

IN June 1807 Napoleon and the young Emperor Alexander of Russia met on a raft moored in the river Niemen, where a treaty was signed and a frail, short-lived friendship established. It was a brittle alliance that was easily fragmented by subsequent events. In 1809 Napoleon's offer of marriage with the Tsar's sister met with a frigid reception; no doubt it would have been turned down (the Romanovs were too proud to blend their blood with a parvenu Corsican, however gifted he might be), but it was tactless, to say the least, of Napoleon to announce his engagement to an Austrian archduchess while negotiations were still in progress with the Russians.

The cooling-off period thus begun was exacerbated by Russian fears of Napoleon's action in creating the Grand Duchy of Warsaw (any movement towards the liberation of Poland immediately alarmed the Russians), and his various annexations of territory, some of which were in violation of the Tilsit treaty. But the breaking point came when Russia took steps to mitigate the severities imposed upon her by the so-called Continental System, which by the Berlin decree of 1806 banned all commercial dealings – imports and exports – with Britain. If Russia – or indeed any of the signatories to the decree – were to relax her enforcement of the provisions the whole system foundered.

The fact that by 1811 the Continental System was becoming threadbare, with even France occasionally trading with England, did not prevent Napoleon from seizing the opportunity of Russian defection to launch a major offensive to subdue that country once and for all. Whether it was his original intention to occupy Moscow seems doubtful, for he had every hope of bringing the Russian armies to bay well west of Smolensk, and although enormous care was taken over the supply system, it could only be sustained for a short, sharp campaign. On the night of 23–24 June 1812 the leading troops of the invading armies crossed the Niemen.

*The Russians give the date of the battle as 26 August, for they still held to the old Julian calendar, not adopting the Gregorian until the turn of this century.

A little more than four months later the terrible disaster that befell the French in their retreat from Moscow has tended to overshadow the battle which in a large measure was responsible for that disaster. Borodino was fought on 7 September 1812, and although the French were technically the victors, for the Russians withdrew from the field, the Russian army had not been destroyed, which was the sole object of Napoleon's invasion. Both sides had suffered enormous casualties, but the Russians had replacements readily available and a supply situation which was not perilous, while Napoleon was then operating on lines of communication that were far too long to sustain what troops he had left. In consequence a few weeks later it was the French not the Russian army that was destroyed.

Including those held in reserve east of the Oder, Napoleon had mustered more than 600,000 men and some 1,400 guns. These troops had been drawn from nearly all of Europe, and only about 270,000 of them were Frenchmen, and that number included men who were only French by virtue of living in places that were French by conquest. Austria and Prussia, who had little choice in the matter, sent armies, Italy supplied 45,000 soldiers under the Viceroy Prince Eugène, and Napoleon withdrew 27,000 from the 243,000 soldiers (again many of whom were not French) who were tied down in the Iberian peninsula. Only Napoleon's former marshal, Crown Prince Bernadotte of Sweden, refused to send troops to join the host. Nearly all these foreign soldiers fought most valiantly under good junior leadership.

This splendid array, which marched east with such high hopes of victory, was divided into five principal groups. In the centre there was the main striking force commanded by Napoleon himself, and this was supported by Prince Eugène's Army of Italy, and an army commanded by Napoleon's brother, King Jerome (who on being censured for dilatoriness was to depart before Borodino). These centre armies numbered some 380,000 men. In addition there were two flanking armies. Marshal Macdonald's away to the north covering the Baltic coast, and Field-Marshal Schwartzenberg's Austrians protecting Napoleon's southern flank. Each of these armies had about 34,000 troops. Although the call-up was now netting young recruits the morale and efficiency of the *Grande Armée* was of a very high order.

Napoleon's strategic plan for the invasion was, as might be expected, brilliantly conceived. But unfortunately it was not so well executed, because he had miscalculated the problem of supplying such a vast host operating over very difficult country. Once across the Niemen progress was not as fast as expected and the divided Russian armies were able to escape the trap. Napoleon crossed the river at Kovno with the main striking force, and Jerome crossed some sixty miles to the south of Grodno. The pincer movement was designed to defeat the two widely

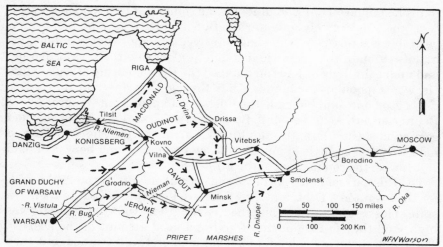

Borodino: Approaches to Western Russia

separated Russian armies in detail, and Prince Bagration's Second West
Army might well have been caught had Jerome moved more quickly.
Barclay de Tolly, commanding the First West Army, hastily withdrew
in front of Napoleon and made for the fortified camp at Drissa where,
under a plan worked out by the Tsar's Prussian adviser, Colonel Ernst
von Phull, he was meant to stand and hold Napoleon while Bagration
struck the enemy in flank.

But all Phull's plan did was to divide the armies still farther. Barclay
quickly realized this danger and headed south-east for Vitebsk, where
he fought a delaying action, but on learning that Bagration (with whom
he was on the worst possible terms) could not join him there he withdrew
to Smolensk. Here the two armies were at last united in the first week of
August and Barclay, who was the Tsar's commander-in-chief, assumed
overall command.

Almost everyone in the army, except the cautious Barclay, was
anxious to engage the French, but he, finding his left flank in danger,
ordered a further withdrawal. Napoleon attacked his strong rearguard,
and a very bitter battle ensued in the suburbs of Smolensk and on a
plateau just to its east in which both sides suffered very heavy casualties, but the action enabled Barclay to make a clean break and withdraw
his army down the Moscow road. Such was the outcry against Barclay's
continued evading tactics that the Tsar was prevailed upon to replace
him as commander-in-chief (although he retained command of the First
West Army) by Prince Kutuzov.

Kutuzov was sixty-seven years old, and because of his life-long
addiction to champagne and rich food (both of which were in good supply

in his headquarters at Borodino) he had somewhat fallen upon decrepitude and was scarcely able to ride. But in earlier days he had been a veritable salamander, who had survived among other wounds two bullets through the head. He had fought alongside the great Suvorov, and under the Tsar he had commanded the Russian army at Austerlitz. He was a popular commander, but through his age and infirmities not a good one, and he made the mistake of appointing General Levin Bennigsen as his chief-of-staff. Bennigsen was a senior general who had commanded (indifferently) the Russian army in 1807; he was a proud man who recked little of any but his own opinions, and he was on bad terms with the commander of the First West Army.

The Russian soldiers welcomed the arrival of Kutuzov on 29 August, for they wanted a fight, and they felt sure he would give it to them. In spite of losses at Smolensk and the weary withdrawals their morale was high, and they felt confident of giving a good account of themselves. Their infantry were splendid fighting men and well trained, but they were at a disadvantage in fire power through being badly armed with many different calibres of musket. They still adhered to Suvorov's dictum that the bayonet was better than the bullet.

The Russian cavalry, which consisted of the usual heavy and light regiments and dragoons, was much better mounted than the French by the time the latter got to Borodino. In addition they had thousands of those superb horsemen the Cossacks, unsurpassed in pursuit, outpost work and ambush, although of less value in an open fight. Russian artillery had been recently reorganized with a new range of weapons, and was on a massive scale with forty-four heavy batteries and fifty-eight field batteries. The army possessed a useful corps of pioneers, but their medical services – like those of the French – were exceedingly primitive and quite unable to cope with the heavy casualties.

While Barclay – as yet not superseded by Kutuzov – was withdrawing towards Moscow and examining possible positions on which to make a stand, Napoleon was pondering the wisdom of calling a halt in Smolensk and continuing the campaign in 1813. There were considerable advantages in this, not least of which was the question of supply, which despite the enormous losses of men remained critical. But the object of the campaign had yet to be achieved, and Alexander with his huge militia potential had time on his side. Napoleon therefore decided to tempt the Fates, and on 29 August marched out of Smolensk along the stony path of burning villages that led to Moscow and ultimate destruction.

It is said that Bennigsen selected the Borodino position on his way to join the army, and that earlier sites reconnoitred by Barclay's staff were discarded. This may be so, for Kutuzov was not anxious to engage before the arrival of General Milaradivitch with 18,000 militia, and there were certainly as good, if not better, positions farther west of the one that the

Russians now chose and hastily strengthened. The village of Borodino lies on the north bank of the river Kolocha, at the confluence of that river and the small Voina stream, on the new road to Smolensk. There were two other tributary streams in the area, the Stonitz that ran parallel to the road and south of it, and the Semenovka which joined the Kolocha a little upstream of the Voina. The Kolocha flowed north from Borodino to join the large Moskva river, and along this stretch its banks were precipitous.

The extreme right of the Russian position was in the loop formed between the Kolocha and Moskva rivers, and the left rested on the wooded area around Utitsa on the old Smolensk road. In the angle between the Stonitz and Semenovka streams there was a low ridge, and at its northern end a fair-sized mound which offered an excellent field of fire. This was strengthened and became known as the Raevsky Redoubt after the corps commander whose troops defended it.* South of the redoubt the ground was mainly flat, marshy, and in places wooded. There were a few hamlets, and at least one, Semenovskaya, proved a liability to the defence and had to be demolished, but three small fortifications, called the Bagration Flèches, formed the central pivot of the left centre. On the extreme left, where the ground was wooded, there was another prominent mound near Utitsa village. Almost in the centre of the main defensive position, but nearly a mile to the west, was the Shevardino Redoubt which Kutuzov strengthened and defended with a division supported by cavalry and artillery.

The right of the Russian line was given to Barclay's First West Army, and because Kutuzov thought that the French would make their main advance down the new Smolensk road this sector was heavily defended at the expense of the centre and left, where Bagration's Second West Army troops were overextended and very vulnerable. Kutuzov did not occupy the Utitsa mound, but he had prepared a large, and what promised to be successful, ambush with Bagration's IIIrd Corps in the wooded area on the extreme left of the line. But unfortunately Bennigsen, in his tour of the position, gave the corps commander contrary orders and brought his troops into the open. For the most part the Russians occupied a strong natural position, made stronger as far as was possible in the time available, but the left could be turned and here, as it happened, Kutuzov was lucky.

While the Russians were busy preparing their defensive positions, Napoleon was slowly concentrating his army for a massive punch against the enemy's left wing. Riding forward to observe the ground he saw at once that the Shevardino Redoubt would have to be cleared before

---

*General Nikolas Raevsky was one of Tsar Alexander's most distinguished generals, who in this battle personally led an assault against a French battery accompanied by two sons – aged sixteen and eleven.

he could develop his attack against the Russian main position. This task was given to the 5th Division (General Compans) of Marshall Davout's I Corps, supported by two cavalry corps. The battle began not long before sunset on the evening of 5 September, and was not broken off until almost midnight, by which time the Russians had lost some 5,000 men, and the French only slightly less.

The Russians, commanded by Prince Gorchakov, had fought with great courage (as indeed had the French), but Kutuzov should never have agreed to Bennigsen's plan to defend the Shevardino Redoubt. It was outside effective artillery range, and had no strategic value to the defence. The left wing, whose main hope lay in the Bagration Flèches, was just as vulnerable as it had been before the battle, in which the Russians lost a lot of good men and three guns. The next day, 6 September, was surprisingly peaceful. Both sides were getting ready for the big battle; the Russians were fully occupied in improving their position, and Napoleon was anxious to examine the ground more closely and prepare his plan.

He now moved his headquarters to the flat ground north of Shevardino, from where he carried out more than one reconnaissance of the Russian position. He was not well, suffering from a heavy cold and cystitis, and he could not have been cheered by the state of his army which, except in numbers where he had a slight advantage (about 130,000 to 122,000), did not compare too favourably with that of the Russians. The heavy losses (some 250,000 since the army had crossed the Niemen less than three months ago) and the shortage of food had not improved French morale, and the cavalry in particular were at a disadvantage, for they had lost a large proportion of their horses, and those that survived were in poor shape. The Russians, on the other hand, were still very well mounted and they also had the advantage in gun numbers, and in calibre.

In the course of this day Davout approached Napoleon, while he was on one of his reconnaissances, with a request that he be allowed to lead his corps and Prince Poniatowski's Vth Polish Corps on a flanking attack against the Russian left wing and rear. He felt that with 40,000 men he could roll up this weak sector of the Russian defence and gain a quick and decisive result. It was just the type of manoeuvre that should have appealed to Napoleon, but after considering it for a moment or two he turned it down in favour of a massive frontal offensive. Longstreet was to have the same idea at Gettysburg, and met with the same rebuff — and with less reason.

The plan eventually formulated was for Davout's Ist Corps to advance against the Bagration Flèches (Napoleon was under the impression that there were only two, not three, fortified positions there), and immediately to his left Ney's IIIrd Corps would attack the enemy line from

Semenovskaya north to the Raevsky Redoubt, closely supported by Junot's VIIIth Corps, with the Guard in rear. The whole weight of the attack was therefore to be against the Russian left and centre on a front of about one and a half miles. Eugène's IVth Corps, with the 3rd Division of I Corps, was to operate north of the Kolocha with the task of clearing the village of Borodino before crossing the river by the three specially constructed pontoon bridges and make for the Raevsky Redoubt. Murat, in overall command of the cavalry, had three corps (I, II and IV) massed to the rear of Davout. The only concession made towards a right hook was the despatch of Poniatowski's V Corps along the old Smolensk road to outflank the Russian left.

The artillery (which totalled 587 guns, but was somewhat short of battery pieces) was to open the battle with a massive cannonade. Two batteries, each of twenty-four guns, were brought up on the night before the battle and positioned on the plateau north-east of Shevardino to pound the Bagration Flèches, and these were augmented by sixty-two pieces under General Pernety, commanding I Corps artillery, and taken from the Guard artillery and the divisions of Desaix, Compans, and Friant. They were to be used in a counter-battery role, while General Sorbier (commanding reserve artillery of the Guard) was to make available all the Guard howitzers to blast the enemy entrenchments. As soon as contact with the enemy had been made on the French right a further forty guns from III Corps would open up on the Raevsky Redoubt. Artillery was to play a major part in the forthcoming fight.

At 6 a.m. on 7 September the rumbling thunder of Pernety's guns signalled the beginning of the battle. An earlier start was planned, but it was found that the two batteries brought up in the dark had been positioned out of range and had to be moved. The Russian gunners were quick to respond, and the cannonade thus begun was to last off and on for many hours filling the field with clouds of smoke, which reduced visibility and increased the confusion of close-quarter fighting.

No sooner had the guns of I and III Corps hurled their shot at the Russian positions than the leading divisions went into the attack. Eugène was quickly into his stride against Barclay's troops in Borodino, who were driven back across the bridge, which they failed to destroy; but they soon retook the village before being ordered to withdraw on to the main position, and this time they did destroy the bridge. Eugène left one division and some cavalry in the village, and by about 9.30 a.m. he had brought the remainder of his troops across the pontoon bridges for his attack on the Raevsky Redoubt.

Meanwhile, Compans's 5th Division of I Corps, closely supported by Desaix's 4th Division, was advancing against the Bagration Flèches in what Napoleon hoped was irresistible strength, but the Russian guns were cleverly sited and their iron mouths belched discharge after

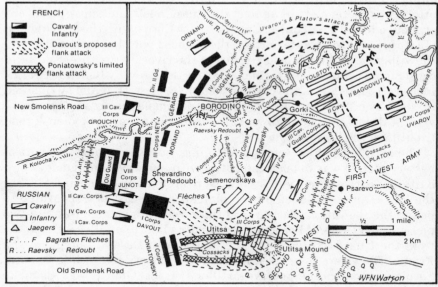

MORNING

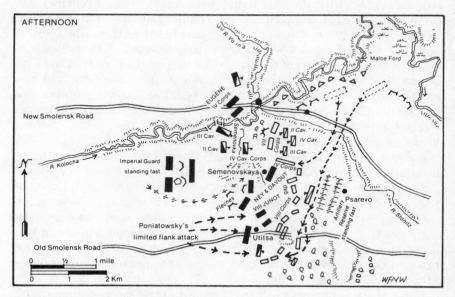

The Battle of Borodino 7 September 1812

discharge of canister, which quickly ploughed swaths of dead and dying Frenchmen. And to add to their discomfort the Russian jaegers poured relentless volleys of musket ball into the advancing troops. Compans was wounded, and Davout so shaken when his horse was shot under him that he had to be carried from the field, and Desaix took over the corps. The fighting here was exceptionally bitter with great numbers of troops involved in deadly grapple. The French gained possession of the fortifications, but Bagration ordered up two brigades from General Tuchkov's III Corps to counterattack, and at the point of the bayonet they drove the French out. The time was about 8.30.

Kutuzov, who had not stirred too much from his headquarters, now realized that his dispositions favoured the right too heavily and he ordered General Baggovut to march his II Corps across the rear of the Russian position to give support to the left centre. But before his troops could come into action the French once more assaulted the Bagration Flèches. The fighting was again of the very heaviest; the French gained two of the fortifications, but in attacking the third they were repulsed. At this juncture the flamboyant and very courageous Murat took personal command and attempted, with some degree of success, to stabilize the situation.

The fight for the flèches was to go on for a further two hours, and by now it had become a battle of all arms. The artillery of both sides continued to sweep away thousands of men; opposing cavalry met and merged in a mêlée of flailing hooves and barking carbines; while the infantry, their faces varnished in sweat and their uniforms caked in blood and dirt, went in with the bayonet. The Russian casualties were most serious throughout the senior ranks, but worst of all was the loss of the very competent and brave commander of the Second West Army, Prince Bagration, who received a wound from which he died a fortnight later.

Meanwhile, what of the two flanks on this bloodstained morning? On the French right Poniatowski's corps had been slow in coming in to the attack, and it was almost 8 a.m. before it was fully involved with a Russian grenadier division acting as a screen to their IIIrd Corps. Their task was made easier through this corps having sent troops to bolster the defence of the flèches, and the fact that on the previous day the Russian chief-of-staff had overruled his commander-in-chief's ambush plan and placed the troops in a dangerously exposed position.

Poniatowski's men had little difficulty in taking the village of Utitsa, which after a costly fight the Russians abandoned, and it looked as though they would take the tactically important hill behind the village, and seriously endanger the Russian left. But it was partly to defend this that Kutuzov had ordered II Corps to march from the Russian right, and these troops arrived in time to withstand Poniatowski's constant attacks. The battle on this flank then died down, but not before the Russian corps commander, Tuchkov, had been killed.

After the capture of Borodino, as already noted, Eugène crossed the bulk of his corps to the south bank of the Kolocha preparatory to assaulting the Raevsky Redoubt. He had left a number of guns in the Borodino area which were in range of the north side of the redoubt, and these he supplemented with breaching batteries whose remorseless pounding from the south bank were designed to soften up the defenders before the attack went in. The redoubt provided fairly good protection for the Russian gunners within (there was not room for any infantry), but enormous destruction was done to the IIIrd Cavalry Corps which was positioned slightly in rear, and given orders to stand firm throughout.

Eugène's infantry attacked at about 9.30 a.m., and the battle was just as fiercely contested here as anywhere else on the field. Raevsky's VIIth Corps was under strength, having had to provide reinforcements for the left, and was quite inadequate to cover the line stretching south to Semenovskaya. Nevertheless, the first French attack was repulsed with heavy loss, but a second was soon mounted, led by Morand's 1st Division (attached to IV Corps) and General Bonamy's 30th Infantry Brigade. These troops, having fought their way through an intense and destructive fire, managed to get into the redoubt and engage the stalwart Russian gunners in savage hand-to-hand combat. For a short while they held the fortification, but the Russians were soon at them again and forced them out with a bayonet charge.

All round the redoubt the battle raged, and by now the *Chasseurs à Cheval* of Grouchy's IIIrd Reserve Cavalry Corps were in action, vainly trying to penetrate the hastily formed Russian squares and suffering heavily in the process. Once again the casualties among the Russian senior officers were grievous, and included the chief-of-staff of the First West Army (wounded), and the brilliant young commander of the Russian artillery who was killed. But by 11.30 these tough and desperate Russian soldiers still stood at bay around the Raevsky Redoubt, and Napoleon ordered yet another attack to go in, but a diversion on the left flank caused this to be postponed.

Somewhere around 10.30 a.m., on receipt of information that a ford across the Kolocha was unguarded, Kutuzov ordered General Uvarov's Ist Cavalry Corps (about 2,500 sabres) and General Platov, Hetman of the Don Cossacks, to go into action against French troops still on the north bank of the river. In splendid array, the sunlight flashing on their sabre blades and lance tips, some 8,000 horsemen came, at a sedate pace, to press back Count Ornano's squadrons of *cuirassiers* and *chasseurs* screening the left of the *Grande Armée*, but they could not penetrate the squares of the division that had been left at Borodino, and when French cavalry crossed the river from the south the Russians withdrew after some spirited fighting. Kutuzov was extremely critical of the tardy and ineffectual performance put up by the two cavalry commanders, but the very presence of this fresh cavalry force, with its hordes of Cossacks milling around the French flank and rear, had seriously disrupted their plan and progress in front of the Raevsky Redoubt.

Besides the two attacks on the right and left, described above, Napoleon launched a third about an hour after the battle had begun. This was directed at the Russian left centre from a point south of the ruined Semenovskaya village to the area of the Raevsky Redoubt, and was undertaken by elements of Davout's and Ney's corps greatly assisted by the cavalry corps of Latour-Maubourg, operating on the left of the attack, and Nansouty's on the right. In this sector of the field, as in others, all three arms were engaged. There was the usual preliminary bombardment, to which the Russian gunners replied by hurling ball, grape and canister into the advancing infantry columns, which hastily deployed into a long wall of scarlet and blue. But above all, this was to be a cavalry battle with lines of horsemen in brilliant uniforms riding knee to knee in a controlled advance before breaking into the charge with flashing steel and thrusting lance.

In the course of some desperately fierce fighting on foot and on horse, and on both sides of the Semenovka stream, the Russians, who had fought with the utmost courage and steadfastness, were eventually pushed back, and this vital sector began to cave in. There was no question of defeat – all they needed was time to re-form, reorganize and repair the damage. Ney and Murat, who had been in the forefront of the battle (as always), and in Napoleon's absence managing it, sent urgent messages to the Emperor for reinforcements to break through the enemy while he was still off balance, and quite likely win the battle. But Napoleon after some moments of indecision refused to commit his reserves, and the opportunity was lost.

This great battle of Borodino was to rage all through the afternoon and into the evening. There still remained the Raevsky Redoubt to be taken. By midday the Russians had regained it, and the next attack Napoleon had ordered Eugène to mount had to be postponed on account of the threat posed by the cavalry of Uvarov and Platov. This delay was particularly unfortunate for the IVth Cavalry Corps, which had been moved to the Semenovskaya front when Eugène's men had been taken to repel the Cossack threat. Here they had to remain for more than two hours at the mercy of the Russian guns in the redoubt, which caused very severe casualties among them. It was nearly 3 p.m. before Eugène was ready to mount another large-scale attack, which was supported by a great weight of artillery bringing cross-fire to bear on the redoubt from batteries at Semenovskaya and Borodino.

Again it was mainly a cavalry fight with the infantry required, as always, to hold the conquered ground. Squadron after squadron engaged in desperate, milling combat and the sharp, deadly note of clashing blades had hardly been heard before the French lost the commander of their IInd Cavalry Corps, General Montbrun. His place was taken by one of Napoleon's personal aides-de-camp, General Auguste de Caulaincourt, but he was killed as he entered the redoubt at the head of the 5th Cuirassier Regiment. Inside the redoubt the Russian gunners put up a savage resistance before being overwhelmed by the arrival of Brigadier Sivray's 9th Infantry Regiment. The spectacle inside was tragic. Corpses in grotesque shapes lay all around, and wounded men suffering from horrible injuries tried to support themselves on the wrecked guncarriages.

The Raevsky Redoubt was in French hands, but the battle had another two hours or more to run, and much of this time was taken up by a cavalry engagement in which several thousand horsemen were involved. Eugène aimed for a breakthrough, and to achieve it he assembled on the plateau behind the redoubt all the available French cavalry. Line after line of these splendid men advanced against the Russian squadrons drawn up for battle with columns of infantry close behind. Soon Russian and French soldiers were inextricably mixed. Barclay de Tolly was in the thick of the fighting, urging on his hussars and lancers, and narrowly avoiding death when his horse was shot under him. Amid the swirling mass of horsemen, infantry and gunners played their part. The rattle of musket fire signalled the end of many horses, and the thunder of cannon heralded swaths of broken men. It was the last big fight of the day, and it had the quality of an epic.

By 5 p.m. both sides had had just about enough. Poniatowski, on the French right, had put in a strong attack on the Utitsa mound, and General Baggovut (whose II Corps had come across earlier from the Russian right) found himself somewhat out on a limb as the main Russian line began to give ground in the centre and right. He therefore withdrew to comply, leaving the Poles in possession of the feature.

The end was at hand, and compared with the momentous and fiery events of the day it came quietly. The Russians were still at bay, and there were some who thought that if Napoleon would now send in the Guard they would be overwhelmed. Again the Emperor refused, and this time most of his senior generals including Berthier (his chief-of-staff) and Murat agreed. During the night Kutuzov decided to withdraw from the field early in the morning, but he still considered he had won a defensive battle.

The casualties on both sides had been exceptionally heavy, and more particularly was this so in the number of senior officers who had been killed or wounded. It seems probable that around 30 per cent of the troops engaged became casualties, but an exact figure will never be known. General Sir Robert Wilson, who was not present at the battle, but was at the Tsar's headquarters throughout the campaign, states the Russian casualties as 36,000 and the French as 35,000. He may be about right with the French numbers (although his statement that twenty-six of their generals were casualties is too low, the correct figure being thirty-eight), but the Russians probably lost as many as 40,000 men. In this battle neither commander-in-chief distinguished himself, but the courage, fire and spirit of the subordinate commanders extorted many feats of valour and endurance from their men.

Kutuzov fell back from Borodino at a fairly leisurely pace, and Napoleon did not press him. On 13 September, with his army camped on the outskirts of Moscow, the Russian commander considered the prospects of making a stand, but he was persuaded against this. He therefore fell back through and beyond Moscow, and Murat brought the first French troops into the city on the afternoon of 14 September. Shortly afterwards fire broke out, destroying many houses, but even so there was ample accommodation for the 95,000 remaining troops of the *Grande Armée*.

As on the battlefield so in the city, Napoleon's lethargy proved the undoing of his army. He appeared unable to stir himself, or to make any realistic appreciation of his predicament. He sent constant overtures for peace to Alexander, who would not enter into negotiation while a single Frenchman was on Russian soil. While Napoleon dithered and delayed the Russian army prepared to take the offensive. Recruits poured in and soon the 85,000 troops who had entered their camp at Tarutino were increased to 120,000. Not until 19 October did Prince Eugène lead the French van out of Moscow. Napoleon had left it too late. The story of the hardships and horrors of the retreat from Moscow and the destruction of the *Grand Armée* is well known. When Ney led the straggling remnants over the frontier on 14 December, the toughest, the cruellest, and the most costly of Napoleon's campaigns had virtually ended.

At Borodino there were three factors of interest that could have contributed to the result of the battle – Davout's request to launch a large-scale flank attack, the Russian cavalry action on the French left, and Napoleon's refusal to commit the Guard. There were also two other factors that had a wider connotation and affected the course of the whole campaign – the question of supply, and the decision to leave Smolensk.

To take the two wider issues first, the matter of supply is of outstanding importance. It would be true to say that the entire campaign foundered on this problem. This was not due to any lack of foresight, because Napoleon had given immense thought to it, but partly to the enormous length of front (300 miles), partly to the composition of the armies and the difficulty of communication, partly to the terrain, but principally to the fact that everything had to be based on a quick victory which was not obtained.

There was no hasty improvisation or rushed planning, for Napoleon had been considering the need to invade Russia for some months. Nine depots were established west of the frontier, each holding large quantities of rations sufficient for many days. The supply train (26 transport battalions) necessary to bring these rations forward was 5,424 horse-drawn, and 2,400 ox-drawn wagons, which required 200,000 draught animals (this besides 110,000 war horses), and each of them consumed almost twenty pounds of fodder a day.* It was calculated that not far short of a third of the rations carried were required for the draught animals, and this clearly restricted the number of days it was possible to feed an army forward of its depots or supply dumps.

Moreover, once into Russia even this limitation was confounded, for although it was summer the roads and countryside generally proved almost impassable – chiefly because of the deep sand – for all but the few light-cart battalions, and there was no suitable grazing for the animals. Large quantities of rations had to be dumped and wasted. Before the army reached Vilna 20,000 horses had been lost (no doubt they were eaten, but their skinny carcasses could not have made a very nourishing pabulum), and there were no immediate replacements. In the past, once a breakthrough had been achieved it was usually possible to supplement the ration from local supplies, but in 1812 this could not be done. The army passed through villages deserted and burnt, and when the troops were foraging they found nothing, for the people had taken with them what they had not burnt.

In the face of such an indomitable foe, and unco-operative countryside, all the Emperor's well-considered logistic plans were of no avail in supplying the enormous requirements of the *Grande Armée*. And the matter of supply should have been a very important factor when he was faced with his first big decision of the campaign at Smolensk.

Napoleon, having twice failed to trap the Russian armies in his well conceived pincer movements, decided to launch an all-out frontal attack on Smolensk, where the Russian First and Second West Armies were now united. The battle was fought on 16 and 17 August. Thanks to a spirited rearguard action by Raevsky's VII Corps, and some slow manoeuvring on the part of Junot, Barclay de Tolly was able to fight a moderately successful action at Valutino, just east of Smolensk, and the Russian armies were able to disengage along the Moscow road. Napoleon retired to Smolensk to consider the future.

*Figures from Glover, p. 144.

By now he must surely have realized that the whole campaign was heading for disaster. He had hopelessly misjudged Alexander and the Russian people. He had set out to bring the Tsar to heel by a quick and decisive victory, but so far that victory had eluded him, and almost certainly had he gained it the Russians would have fallen still farther back, regained their strength and continued to defy him. There were three possibilities. To go back, which Napoleon would never have considered, to hold the line of the two rivers – Dvina and Dneiper – during the winter and resume the offensive in the spring, or to go forward at once in the hope that the Russians would stand and fight.

There were powerful arguments in favour of wintering in Smolensk. In the course of the long march sickness, desertion, the need to garrison depots, staging points, bridges along the lines of communication, and battle casualties had reduced the army to around 155,000 men. It is true he still had numerical superiority, and replacements were coming in, but many of them were raw recruits who needed time to train. The efficiency of his cavalry was considerably diminished through the heavy loss of horses, and likewise his horse artillery lacked their full complement of animals. Food was becoming scarce, and he had outrun his supply depots. The Russians might be falling back in the centre but on the flanks, in spite of minor victories by his two supporting armies, they were still active and threatening. Moreover his Austrian and Prussian allies were at best only half-hearted.

The compelling need to go forward was to gain a quick and decisive victory before the winter broke. It was a gamble, for Napoleon had no reason for knowing that the Russians would make a stand. They might well continue to fall back and thus even further worsen his supply problems. Moreover, with an army whose fighting efficiency had been diminished through severe losses there was no certainty of a crushing victory (and it had to be crushing) if the Russians did stand and fight. On the other hand if he gave Alexander a six-month respite the Tsar would have time to mobilize and train new armies, and to obtain material assistance from Britain. It is easy with hindsight to say that to go forward was a mistake, but it is also possible to say that had Napoleon been his former self at the battle of Borodino he might well have gained the decisive victory he wanted, and therefore his decision would have been right.

Napoleon went forward, and maybe he had his doubts, for on 28 August when the army was at Viazma it started to rain heavily and continuously. On the 30th the Emperor announced, 'If this rain continues we shall retire tomorrow to Smolensk.' On the 31st the sun shone, and that day the army marched a further fifteen miles along the road to destruction. On the morning of Borodino, as the sun broke through the mist, Napoleon is said to have turned to his staff and exclaimed, 'It is the sun of Austerlitz.' Perhaps it would have been better had he returned to Smolensk on 31 August and been able to say, 'It was the rain of Viazma', for surely all things considered a period of recuperation and reorganization in that city would have been wiser before attempting a hazardous 280 miles to Moscow.

From the crossing of the Niemen to the departure from Moscow, with only a few brief flashes of former brilliance, there was an uncharacteristic lethargy noticeable in Napoleon. The vivid days of action and audacity were sadly missing; confidence and the old sure-footed judgement were lacking. The dusk of his power could be seen approaching. All this was reflected in his failure to have a proper grasp of the battle at Borodino. And it is often said that in particular it was responsible for his refusal to consider, for more than a few moments, Davout's request to combine his corps with that of Poniatowski, and with a force of some 40,000 troops roll up the Russian left from the rear. But in that he may have only partly erred.

The request was made on the afternoon of 6 September – the day before the battle – and Davout's intention was to carry out this wide turning movement by a night march. There were two immediate difficulties that sprang to Napoleon's mind: the always present fear that the Russians, on obtaining information of this encircling manoeuvre, would retire yet again; and there was also the fact that a night march through the thickly wooded country would have serious direction difficulties, and put an unnecessary strain on horses and men, which would blunt their fighting efficiency at the time of the attack. There was a third, although far less likely, factor to be considered. The long flank march would take time and deprive the army of a large body of troops. If the timing went wrong and the Russians were to attack while Davout was still marching, a most awkward situation would develop.

Davout's idea was very much in line with what Napoleon himself had often done on accepting a calculated risk, and it is possible – although unlikely – that he resented being reminded of what could be done by Davout with whom at the time he was not on particularly good terms. It is much more probable that his rapid time-and-movement appreciation was correct, and that Davout's suggested manoeuvre was far too ambitious. Nevertheless, a strong right hook at Bagration's very vulnerable left might easily have had a decisive effect. Poniatowski's V Corps was not strong enough for such a punch, as was apparent from his efforts; reinforced he might well have turned the Russian left in a less spectacular, but much safer, operation than Davout's deep penetrating night march.

*

Kutuzov did very little personally to influence the battle, but one thing he did do – the launching of a cavalry attack on the French left – might have had a very considerable effect on the issue had it been undertaken with a force of all arms, and more resolute commanders. In the event it was a good example of something and nothing, and the fact that this cavalry force caused considerable dislocation of the French battle plan shows what might have been accomplished had the cavalry been supported by infantry.

Generals Uvarov and Platov crossed the Kolocha by a ford at Maloe, and were soon engaged with General Count Ornano's Italian and Bavarian light cavalry screening the French left, which they routed and captured three guns. Platov and his 5,000 Cossacks then crossed the Voina stream and came down in the rear of General Delzon's 13th Division of IV Corps, while Uvarov engaged the division frontally. Delzon's men hastily formed square, and their commander sent urgently for assistance. Soon the 6th Hussars and the 8th *Chasseurs-à-Cheval* of the 3rd Light Cavalry Division crossed the river and joined the battle. The Russian cavalry then withdrew, having lost their captured guns.

Uvarov's attack was unhurried and half-hearted. He had been given no infantry support, although he did have two batteries of horse artillery, which he does not seem to have made much use of. With such a small force there could have been no question of a successful turning movement, and Kutuzov perhaps only intended it to cause a diversion and relieve the pressure on his centre. In this he was entirely successful, for the French attack had to be postponed by some three hours, which gave him time to reorganize his line, and enabled his gunners to do immense damage to large numbers of French cavalry brought in to fill a gap when units of IV Corps were sent across the river.

Even though troops from the Russian right were being thinned to assist the left, it would still have been possible to mount a larger-scale attack of all arms on Eugène's corps, which would have had very serious consequences for the French.

It could never be said with any certainty that if Kutuzov had developed a strong turning movement on Eugène's flank he could have won the battle, but it is entirely possible that had Napoleon sent in the Guard to exploit the breakthrough in the fight around Semenovskaya he could have had a more decisive success than what he did in fact achieve. It is interesting, therefore, that undoubtedly one of the reasons for his refusal to commit his reserves at this time was the uncertainty of what was happening on Eugène's left north of the Kolocha.

When the battle in the centre, on both sides of the Semenovka stream and around the Bagration Flèches, was at its crisis Ney was heavily counterattacked by men of the Second West Army, and he called urgently for reinforcements. Napoleon, after some hesitation, ordered General Claparède, commanding the Polish Legion of the Vistula in the Imperial Guard, to go forward, but almost at once he changed his mind and instead sent General Friant's 2nd Division of I Corps. This was the first occasion that the Emperor held back his reserves. The second, and more important, came shortly afterwards. Friant's division, led by Brigadier Dufour's Light Infantry Regiment, pressed the Russians hard, and eventually opened up a wide breach in this most vital sector of their line.

Napoleon was at his command post near Shevardino watching (usually seated on a chair) the battle through his glass, and surrounded by regiments of his Guard all ready and eager to take a part. When an officer (one of the many who were constantly coming to headquarters to give a situation report) arrived from Murat and Ney, who were masterminding the battle, requesting immediate reinforcements to punch the Russians while they were off balance, permission was given for the Young Guard to go forward. But they had no sooner set off than the Emperor cancelled the order without any explanation, and by the time a second urgent appeal reached him he had been informed that the Russians had brought forward troops to shore up the line. Whereupon he turned to General Belliard, who had brought the request, and said, 'Before I commit my reserves I must be able to see more clearly on my chessboard.' And so the infantry of the Guard remained immobile, and what appeared to be a heaven-sent opportunity to win the battle with an immediate and decisive body blow was lost.

But was the opportunity such a good one? Napoleon might have been expected to take it in his more robust days fighting nearer home. But now age, and perhaps experience, had made him cautious, and he was a very long way from home and no doubt feeling a trifle insecure. The Guard were his devoted house-carls, there could be no unnecessary sacrifice, for the object of the campaign had yet to be achieved. And more immediately the tactical situation was still somewhat obscure. As already mentioned, there was a dangerous situation developing on the French left, and Napoleon was without precise information as to how Poniatowski's Vth Corps was coping. Finally, there was in front of him a still undefeated and resolute foe. There is no sure answer to the question of should the Guard have been committed, but Napoleon was probably right to be cautious at this stage. What is certain is that the Russians were quick to take advantage of the respite to hurry up reinforcements.

In the evening, as this terrible battle was drawing to its close, the Emperor stirred himself and rode forward across the scarred, pitted and corpse-strewn field to examine the Russian line which had fallen back, but still held firm from Gorki on the right to a point on the old Smolensk road about a mile to the east of Utitsa. If there were any victors it was the French, and one last push might (although nothing could be certain) turn a marginal success into a campaign-winning triumph.

It appears that there were some (although who they were is not clear, for those who had earlier clamoured for action now concurred in caution) who wished to see the Guard unleashed to complete the victory. To these Napoleon is said to have exclaimed, 'I will not have my Guard destroyed. When you are eight hundred leagues from France you do not wreck your last reserve.' And surely on this occasion he must have been right. These fresh troops would no doubt have thrown back the Russians in disarray, but not until they had given a good account of themselves, for there was plenty of fight in them yet. Moreover, the French cavalry was in no state to follow up and administer the *coup de grâce*, without which there could be no annihilation. The Guard, therefore, could have suffered grievous casualties for little purpose, and then who would protect the Emperor on the long road to the Beresina?

Both sides were to claim Borodino as a victory, but neither could have claimed the alleged victory to have been won by brilliant generalship. There was plenty of good leadership from corps commanders downwards, and an abundance of courage in both armies, but it was mainly a slogging match with no clear cut direction from either Kutuzov or Napoleon.

This was because Kutuzov was too old and infirm to command effectively, and for Napoleon it was the first major battle in which he showed undoubted signs that his formidable powers were in decline. He was to display occasional flashes of brilliance between Borodino and his abdication, but his former genius was sadly lacking here. And it is interesting to see how the pattern at Borodino was in some respects repeated at Waterloo. In both battles the flank attack was rejected in favour of a frontal pounding, and in both battles Ney's request for reinforcements at a critical time was refused. This uncharacteristic indecisiveness, coupled with a certain lethargy, was to be even more pronounced in the Waterloo campaign. There it was a principal cause of defeat, at Borodino it was to deny him a decisive victory.

11   The Battle of Ligny
16 June 1815

IT is probably true to say that more Englishmen know about the battle of Waterloo than about any other battle that was ever fought. At Waterloo Napoleon, who was a man built upon a far larger scale than the common run, was toppled; so great was the fall that even now, after 180 years, we talk about someone 'meeting his Waterloo'. Moreover, it was as the Duke of Wellington said, 'the nearest run thing you ever saw in your life'. Indeed, had Blücher's Prussians been prevented from joining the Anglo–Dutch army, Napoleon would very likely have won his way to Brussels.

The battle of Ligny, fought two days before Waterloo, was the last of Napoleon's victories. It was a victory that should have won him the campaign, but on the 16th and 17th of June, through dilatoriness and deviation, he lost it.

The period of history known as 'The Hundred Days' began at the end of February 1815, when Napoleon decided to end his exile on the island of Elba and return to France. It was a well-calculated risk which he was driven to take by Louis XVIII's vindictive treatment towards him. The timing was propitious, for that same king's folly was causing considerable unrest throughout France. Napoleon landed near Cannes on 1 March with his permitted military establishment of 1,000 men and 4 cannon. Having survived the only real crisis of the march, when through his coolness and courage he won the hearts of a regiment that blocked his path just south of Grenoble, the Emperor reached Paris on the 20th, and entered the Palace of the Tuileries in triumph.

Napoleon could have been under few illusions that the Allied governments would permit him to retain the throne, but largely to placate the peace party in France he put out friendly feelers. Even without the clumsy and precipitous action of his brother-in-law, Murat, King of Naples, in declaring war on Austria and fighting a losing battle in the north of Italy, these had no chance of succeeding. A treaty of alliance was signed between England, Prussia, Austria, and Russia, and soon the Emperor was to find France almost encircled by vast armies numbering over 660,000 men, which before the end of the year could be considerably increased. To meet this threat France had in 1815 an army of only 149,200 soldiers immediately available for war, but many veterans quickly volunteered to rejoin the colours and the 1813 class of conscripts was recalled, although to equip the men would take time. To guard the long frontier it was necessary to mobilize 200 battalions of the National Guard each of 560 men.*

There were two options open to Napoleon. He could wait to be attacked, and as it was unlikely the Allies would be in sufficient strength to assault the defences of Paris for some three months he would have that time in which to mobilize and train new recruits – but much of France would be occupied. Alternatively he could strike at those of the Allies which were nearest to him. These were the Duke of Wellington's Anglo–Dutch army of 110,000 men (of which 17,000 were employed in garrison duties), and Prince von Blücher's 117,000 Prussians, which as part of the Allies' grand design were advancing to the attack from Brussels and Liège respectively. In May Napoleon decided upon the latter course; to attack clearly offered the best chance, for a quick victory might reap a rich reward. But by the time 20,000 men had been detached to put down a revolt in La Vendée, and various forts and strongholds had been manned, the *Armée du Nord* mustered only 122,721 men and 366 guns.† Napoleon was, therefore, outnumbered unless he could keep his opponents apart and defeat their armies separately.

The prodigious efforts to put France on a war footing in the incredibly short time available showed no signs of that creeping malaise that was so soon to affect the Emperor. By June France had 560,600 men under arms of whom 196,000 were organized into an army of the line. Obtaining recruits was not nearly such a problem as equipping and arming them. Nevertheless, the arsenals were found to be fairly well stocked, and broadly speaking the front-line soldiers were equipped and armed up to European standard. Moreover, although the *Armée du Nord* obviously contained a number of raw recruits (4,000 out of the 18,500 élite troops of the Imperial Guard were newly conscripted) it was largely comprised of veterans, and overall was of a higher quality than either the Anglo–Dutch or Prussian armies in which there were a number of newly formed militia battalions and ethnic problems.

There was one important imperfection in Napoleon's army in that the junior ranks, who were extremely loyal to the Emperor, were seamed with mistrust and suspicion towards many of their seniors who had taken favours of the Bourbon king and flaunted themselves at his court during Napoleon's exile. To what extent this was reflected in Napoleon's choice of generals is not known, but for one reason or

*Figures, Chalfont, p. 25.
†Figures, Glover, p. 153.

another he made some disastrous and battle-losing commissions and omissions.

As his chief-of-staff he appointed Marshal Soult, for he had failed to persuade Berthier, who had served him so well in the past, to rejoin (he committed suicide on 1 June). Soult was a good fighting general, but he had no staff experience and painfully lacked Berthier's clarity of thought and expression. Had Berthier been present the bumbling messages and orders that were despatched to the commanders, and which caused so much uncertainty and indecision, would have been more clear and precise. Marshal Suchet would have made a much better chief-of-staff than Soult, and Soult would have made a much better wing commander than Ney.

In the first instance Grouchy was given command of the cavalry, which was later handed to Kellermann. The most brilliant cavalry commander of the time, not only in France but in all Europe, was Murat, who having displeased the Emperor was left in the cold. Had he been present at Waterloo the cavalry would never have been allowed to perform its act of self-immolation.

Grouchy was removed from the cavalry to take command of the right wing. He had recently been appointed a marshal for his good work in the south of France, and while he was a competent leader of cavalry he had had no experience in command of all arms on a large scale. Davout, whose talent was wasted as Governor of Paris, was far better suited for command of a wing, while Grouchy could have taken over the Army of the Alps, the post first earmarked for him.

Finally, and belatedly, Ney was summoned to take command of the left wing. From a strictly military point of view this appointment was a grave error, although it may have had some political advantages. 'The bravest of the brave' was a brilliant fighting soldier and adored by the rank and file, but he was quick-tempered, unpredictable and lacking in sufficient intelligence for a crucial command. He could have been given the reserve, or perhaps replaced the sick Mortier in command of the Guard, ready to lead into battle the final body blow and thrust to the heart. For whatever reason some appointments had been badly cast, and too many good generals had been selected for extrusion. Napoleon was to pay a heavy forfeit for this.

But before these problems were to arise everything had gone very smoothly. The concentration of the army from forts and garrisons, in some cases more than 1,000 miles from the Belgian frontier, was masterly. Strict precautions had been taken to preserve secrecy, and certain deceptive measures employed to indicate a possible advance through Mons to cut off the Anglo–Dutch army from the sea. Napoleon was very conscious of the need for both speed and surprise. By 4 June the various units were all on the move. Carefully and skilfully the army

made its way towards the river Sambre. On 12 June, when Napoleon left
Paris for Laon, it was closing on the Belgian frontier without the Allies
having any clear idea of what was happening.

On the evening of the 14th the hub of this juggernaut wheel
was around Beaumont where Napoleon and the Guard were centred.
Slightly in advance of the town was VI Corps (Lobau) and III Corps
(Vandamme), and Grouchy's four corps of reserve cavalry were some ten
miles to the east – they had suffered from being forgotten by Soult and
had received no orders. The head of II Corps (Reille) bivouacked at
Thurin, and d'Erlon's I Corps was in its rear near Sohr-sur-Sambre;
Gérard's IV Corps was slightly astern of station (to use a nautical
metaphor) and was assembling at Philippeville. The army, now concentrated on a front of less than twenty miles, was poised to advance to
contact and cross the Sambre on the morning of the 15th.

Napoleon's overall plan was extremely simple, and had it been
properly executed would almost certainly have been successful. A
wedge was to be driven between the two Allied armies and then, holding
them apart, he would defeat them in detail. For this purpose the army
(after crossing the Sambre) would be divided into two wings and a
reserve, which latter Napoleon would bring into action according to
circumstances. The wings were to move up two arms of a triangle from
Charleroi the apex, to make contact with the two Allied armies. The
larger enemy force (which in the event was the Prussian) was to
be brought to battle and decisively defeated by one of the wings
strengthened by the reserve. The other wing was to contain the smaller
Allied force, and might be called upon to send assistance to the main
battle. As soon as the latter had been won the second Allied army would
be attacked in force.

Marshal Ney, who did not arrive until the late afternoon of the 15th,
was to be given command of the left wing consisting of I and II Corps, two
light cavalry divisions and two divisions of the Cavalry Corps, with a
total of about 40–45,000 men. Marshal Grouchy, with about the same
number (III and IV Corps), would command the right wing. The Guard
and Lobau's VI Corps, together with what horse of the Cavalry Corps
were not allotted, would comprise the reserve. A French corps was a
self-contained unit of three arms, for Napoleon believed in allotting his
artillery regiments as an integral part of the corps, but a division was
the smallest unit to have artillery permanently attached.

Meanwhile, what of the Allied armies? Wellington was always fearful
for his right flank, and Napoleon's deception measures strengthened his
belief that an attack might come from the direction of Mons. In the
middle of June the divisions of I Corps (Prince of Orange) were dispersed
in the area covered by Enghien, Nivelles, and Soignies with corps
headquarters at Braine le Comte; those of II Corps (General Hill) were

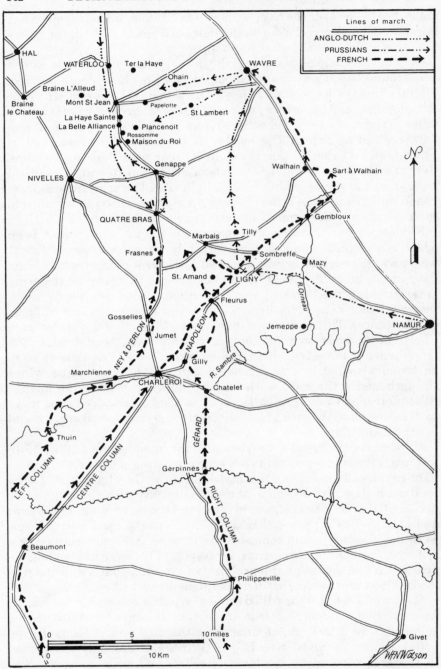

The Battle of Ligny: 16 June 1815: Napoleon's advance into Belgium

at Ath, Grammont, and Oudenarde, with corps headquarters at Ath. The Reserve (two British divisions and the Duke of Brunswick's corps) was quartered around Brussels, and the cavalry (General the Earl of Uxbridge) was mainly based on Grammont, Ninove, and along the river Dendre with the Brunswick contingent at Brussels, and there were three brigades forward around Mons supporting outpost troops. This wide dispersion was somewhat vulnerable to sudden attack, but such an event was not considered likely.

Over the years there has been much discussion as to whether Wellington was taken by surprise by Napoleon's rapid concentration and attack across the Sambre in the area of Charleroi. The opinion of most historians is that he certainly was, and that his dispositions and lack of proper communications made it difficult for him to fulfil the agreement made with Blücher on 3 May that in the event of an attack he would concentrate towards the Prussians at Sombreffe. But it has to be remembered that since the Allies were not officially at war with France they were not permitted to send reconnaissance patrols across the frontier. Wellington has his champions, notably Siborne, who asserts that information from the outposts had prepared him for Napoleon's advance, and that his dispositions and concentration plans were adequate to meet any attack as soon as he knew its line.*

Be that as it may, it seems certain that it was not until 3 p.m. on 15 June that Wellington received definite news that the Prussians had been attacked at Thuin. There had been no communication from Blücher (this lack of liaison between the Allies was nearly disastrous), and Wellington still considered that an approach from the west to cut him off from the sea was likely. Orders were given for a preliminary concentration with the centre of gravity towards the west rather than towards the inner flank. When eventually, at the celebrated ball given by the Duchess of Richmond, various messages came in that at last clarified the situation for the Duke, further orders (the third) were immediately issued, and this time for concentration on Wellington's inner flank towards Quatre Bras. But it was almost too late, and indeed would have been but for an inspired piece of disobedience by General Constant Rebecque (the Prince of Orange's chief-of-staff) who in defiance of orders rushed first one brigade and then a second to stem the advancing French.

However, it was the Prussian army that was the first to be engaged. Full mobilization had been ordered by King Frederick William III at the end of March and, pending the arrival of Field-Marshal Prince von Blücher, the entire organization was in the very capable hands of his chief-of-staff Lieutenant-General Count von Gneisenau. There were

* Siborne, Vol. I, p. 86.

many problems connected with the setting up of seven army corps, and even by June and after prodigious efforts the four that were to fight at Waterloo were not up to full strength; particularly was this so in artillery. This conscripted army, which contained a great many militia regiments and men from the western areas of Germany who had fought at one time under Napoleon, were not nearly so well trained, equipped or so experienced as the men they were going to fight.

Owing to the appalling state of the Prussian economy there were grave financial problems in quartering and supplying the 117,000 men who comprised Blücher's army, and the fighting probably came just in time. In the middle of June 1 Corps (Zieten) had its headquarters at Charleroi, and the brigades were placed along the frontier so as to provide early warning of attack, and to be able to cover the concentration of the other three corps; II Corps (Pirch I) were in the area Namur-Huy; III Corps' (Thielmann) headquarters were at Dinant with brigades at Ciney and Huy; IV Corps (Bülow) was farther back in the Liège area; Reserve Cavalry was at Sombreffe and Reserve Artillery at Gembloux. Army headquarters was at Namur. There were no divisions in a Prussian corps, which was made up of four brigades each of three regiments with three battalions. Each corps had at least two cavalry brigades and twelve artillery batteries totalling ninety-six guns. With pioneers, engineers, and normal services a corps would contain between 25,000 and 30,000 all ranks.

At 3 a.m. on 15 April the *Armée du Nord* began the crossing of the Sambre. The left column was to advance from Thuin to Marchienne, the centre upon Charleroi and the right column by Gerpinnes to Châtelet. The detailed planning cannot be faulted, but in the execution there were one or two mishaps. Through faulty transmission of orders, and in Vandamme's case negligence, I and III Corps were late in starting, and IV Corps (Gérard) did not complete its concentration until 7 a.m., and then the commander of its leading division and five members of his staff defected to the enemy. General de Bourmont's family had suffered in the reprisals following the La Vendée revolt; nevertheless this was – as Blücher made quite clear – a deed of base treachery by an unprincipled, disgruntled general. The consternation this desertion caused was partly responsible for Gérard's corps not being completely across the Sambre that night, and although the information de Bourmont imparted to the enemy was of little value his defection undoubtedly had its effect on morale.

Zieten's I Corps, whose outpost line stretched for almost fifty miles from Dinant westwards to just south of Binche, fought a delaying action with great resolution, which gave Blücher time to effect his concentration in the Fleurus area. In the withdrawal they did not, however, destroy the three important bridges over the Sambre at Marchienne,

Charleroi, and Châtelet. Napoleon had hoped to have the first two by 9 a.m., but owing to the late start of Vandamme's corps Pajol's cavalry (I Corps Cavalry Reserve) was unsupported before Charleroi, and it was midday before the town was taken. There was a similar delay at Marchienne through the fierce resistance of General Steinmetz's brigade, and on the right although the Prussians had been forced to withdraw Gérard had only one division across the river.

Nevertheless, the advance so far had gone well with the line of the Sambre cleared by the early afternoon. The Prussians were now standing before Gosselies and Gilly, where there was to be some fierce fighting. When Marshal Ney arrived with the army Napoleon gave him command of the left wing, with orders to push the enemy out of Gosselies and advance up the Brussels road towards the Anglo–Dutch at Quatre Bras, but there was probably no mention in these verbal orders of taking Quatre Bras on the 15th.

At much the same time Grouchy was given command of the right wing, and the Emperor himself went forward with him to plan the attack which he hoped would drive the Prussians out of Gilly and Fleurus. But unfortunately Vandamme, whose corps formed part of the right wing, was disinclined to take orders from Grouchy whom he considered to be no more than a cavalry commander. The two generals spent two hours arguing the best plan of attack, and not until about 5.30 p.m., when Napoleon had come up, was the attack launched. Gilly was soon cleared, but the hour was considered too late to assault Fleurus.

The left wing also bivouacked that night short of its objective. Steinmetz's troops again put up a stout resistance in defence of Gosselies and the town was not taken until 3 p.m., by which time the Prussians had suffered heavy casualties. The Brussels road was now clear, but by this time General de Perponcher's 2nd Dutch Belgian Division had been fully alerted and two brigades were soon in position in the Quatre Bras–Frasnes area. That evening Frasnes was taken by a division of Reille's corps, but General Piré's light cavalry, which pushed on to reconnoitre Quatre Bras, met strong resistance from Prince Bernhard of Saxe-Weimar's Nassau regiment in the region of Bossu Wood, and was forced to retire. Quatre Bras having now been reinforced, Ney, his troops totally exhausted after nineteen hours' marching and fighting, decided to bivouac in and around Frasnes.

As soon as Blücher received information of the French advance upon the Sambre he had ordered Zieten to fall back fighting so as to cover the concentration of the other corps. This, as has been related, Zieten did with consummate skill and courage, but with a loss of 1,200 men. The corps then withdrew to its selected position at Ligny, and was the only one of the four Prussians corps to reach its proper destination that night.

Pirch I's corps bivouacked at Mazy some six miles from Ligny.

Thielmann's was fifteen miles off at Namur, and most distant of all was Bülow's corps which was ordered to come to Hannut. But Bülow, at Liège, was under the impression that there was no war and therefore no hurry, and so he sent a message announcing his arrival at Hannut by midday on the 16th. The message was delayed in reaching Blücher's headquarters, and a further order from Blücher for Bülow to march to Sombreffe was also misdirected. It was now impossible for IV Corps to fight at Ligny on the 16th, where its presence might have altered the entire situation.

On the morning of 16 June when Napoleon took stock of the recent manoeuvring and fighting he had much to be pleased about. The secrecy and skill with which the advance to contact had been made were a fine example of his former genius. As a result of the fighting to date he had obtained control of the two roads leading to the heart of the Allied armies, and had advanced sufficiently far up them to make it very difficult for those two armies to unite their forces without a withdrawal. He felt he was now in a position to pursue the underlying strategy of the operation (two wings and a reserve), which he expounded in a written directive to Ney.

But it was now that the gods began to withdraw their favours. A physical decline, which had shown some evidence at the time of Borodino, was to affect the clarity and coherence of his thinking; the former restless activity and the incisive mind were lacking. Lethargy crept in. The old Napoleon would have hastened the concentration of his rear formations which were badly scattered, neither would he have indulged in wishful thinking based on no evidence. The Emperor was convinced the Prussians would not stand at Ligny; he hopelessly underestimated Blücher's numbers and his willpower, and he also considered it most likely that Wellington would fall back on Brussels. His first orders on the 16th to Ney and Grouchy were, therefore, ridiculously optimistic, with the former being instructed to take Quatre Bras and advance towards Brussels where the Emperor expected to be that day, while Grouchy was to push the Prussians through and beyond Gembloux.

It was not until about 11 a.m., when he went forward to the leading troops, that Napoleon discovered the Prussians were standing at Ligny. Although he was still not completely convinced he had more than a strong rearguard to deal with, the plan was immediately changed. Ney, who now had Kellermann's 3rd Cavalry Corps under command, was to take Quatre Bras and contain Wellington's troops, while the main thrust would be made by the right wing, where Ney might be called upon to assist. A short while later Napoleon realized that Grouchy's wing of 45,000 men had almost the whole Prussian army before it.

The position taken up by the Prussian army had been previously selected for its strategic importance, for it covered roads into north

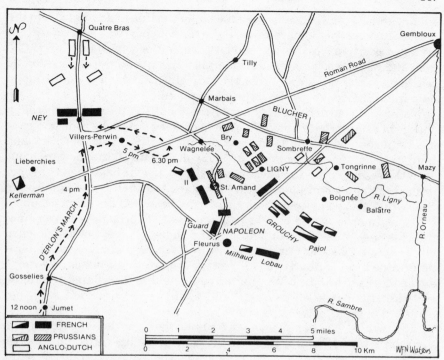

The Battle of Ligny: 16 June 1815

Belgium and Germany. The line was held along and forward of the
Namur–Nivelles road from the junction of the old Roman road north of
Bry to east of the crossroads above the village of Tongrinne. The battle
was mainly fought in and around a number of valley villages – from the
St Amands in the west through Ligny almost to Balatre – which lay in
an amphitheatre of low hills. Ligny itself was divided by a brook; the
streets were narrow, but many of the houses were solidly built with
wall and hedge enclosures, and they made good strongpoints. The
surrounding land was wet, but there were tall crops of rye.

Zieten's corps was the only one available to take up a position on the
early morning of the 16th, and his brigades occupied Bry, St Amand, St
Amand la Haye, and Ligny. The battalions were intermixed in these
villages, which could not have helped control in the street and village
fighting. Pirch II's brigade formed a second line between Bry and Ligny,
and the Corps Reserve Cavalry took post behind and to the left. Pirch I's
corps arrived from Mazy about midday and was held in reserve in front
of the Nivelles–Namur road, extending from the Roman road to Sombreffe. Thielmann's III Corps did not arrive from Namur until almost

3 p.m., and his four brigades held the left of the line at an angle from the crossroads east of Sombreffe to Balatre. Blücher was attempting to occupy a position which stretched for seven miles with a force of 84,000 men and 224 guns. This was considerably lower than the accepted ratio of troops to the mile, and probably indicates that he was counting on help from Bülow's corps or Wellington or both.

Wellington had arrived at Quatre Bras about 10.30, and having taken charge of affairs there and given the necessary orders he rode across to meet Blücher whom he found at the mill of Bussy between Bry and Ligny. One glance at the Prussian army drawn up on the forward slope with the reserve – also on the forward slope – too far back to give proper immediate support, induced him to remark to Blücher and Gneisenau that while everyone knew their own army best, had his army occupied that position he would expect it to get beat. The Prussians were not impressed by this wise admonition, and indeed it may have deepened Gneisenau's existing mistrust of Wellington as a competent general determined to give battle at all costs. Plans were discussed, but none agreed to, as to how best Wellington could aid the Prussians, and in the end the Duke rode off saying, 'Well I will come; provided I am not attacked myself.'

Meanwhile, Napoleon was anxious to hasten the attack on the Prussians while Blücher was still concentrating his corps, but first he had to make certain Ney was engaging the Anglo–Dutch troops at Quatre Bras, and Gérard's corps had to arrive and form up on the right of his attack. The plan was to neutralize the Prussian left, largely by Grouchy's cavalry, while the main attack developed against the centre and right, thus with the expected aid from Ney he would drive the beaten Prussians away from Wellington and ensure that an Allied concentration became impossible. A decisive victory at Ligny, with the Prussians driven off to the north-east, had become the linchpin of the campaign. For this purpose Napoleon had, when Lobau's corps had been belatedly ordered up from Charleroi, 71,203 men (including 13,100 cavalry) and 242 guns, against Blücher's 83,417 men (8,150 cavalry) and 224 guns.* But if he could neutralize Thielmann's corps he could engage the centre and right on equal terms.

Between 11 and 12 o'clock the French light cavalry had advanced on Fleurus, and they soon drove back the 6th Uhlans forming the Prussian outpost. These troops retired and took post on the left of the Brandenburg Dragoons (part of Zieten's Reserve Cavalry) who stood in front of the Tombe de Ligny. At 1 p.m. Gérard's corps arrived and Napoleon completed his dispositions for the battle.

---

*Becke, while agreeing with Siborne and Gardner on the number of Prussians, puts the French at 78,000 men and 242 guns.

Vandamme's corps was to spearhead the attack on the left against the St Amand positions; it was given General Girard's division from Reille's corps, which was fighting with Ney, and that division formed up on the left of the corps with General Domon's 3rd Cavalry Division on its left. As soon as Gérard's corps arrived it was sent up the Fleurus road to occupy ground facing left (therefore at right angles to Vandamme) with a line extending from the Tombe de Ligny to the southern face of Mont Pontriaux. Grouchy's cavalry had the task of containing the Prussian left, and for this purpose he had Pajol's 1st Cavalry Corps and Exelmans' 2nd Cavalry Corps, and two infantry battalions from Gérard's corps. The Guard and Milhaud's 4th Cavalry Corps were around Fleurus. Lobau's VIth Corps was still marching up from Charleroi.

Ney had received a number of communications from Napoleon in the course of the morning, and was becoming somewhat confused, which partly explains his failure to seize the initiative. At 2 p.m. Soult sent another dispatch to him, which he did not receive until 4 p.m., in which he informed the Marshal that the Emperor would begin the battle against the Prussians at 2.30. Ney was to attack whatever force was before him, and having driven his enemy back he was to turn towards the Ligny battle and envelope Blücher's right and rear. A further message, sent an hour later, was intended to impress urgency upon him and to stimulate him to greater effort. These messages left much to be desired, and Ney never properly understood his role.

The battle of Ligny began at last at 2.30 on a very hot afternoon. It was full late in starting if the Prussians were to be decisively defeated and driven off to the north-east that day. There had been too little sense of urgency in the orders and dispatches sent out during the morning, which inevitably resulted in unnecessary tarrying by unit commanders in both wings. This delay greatly diminished, although it did not extinguish, Napoleon's chances of winning the campaign.

The first troops to engage were the leading divisions of Vandamme's corps, which pressed hard on the defenders of St Amand. Throughout the afternoon and evening the fighting around the St Amands and Wagnelée was exceptionally bitter, with the villages changing hands several times. First the Prussians then the French bent and broke before the storm of musket fire that lashed these valiant infantrymen like wind-driven rain. Napoleon was determined to force Blücher to commit his reserves in order to prop up his hard-pressed right and centre. These men, who were standing upon a forward slope and out of proper supporting distance, suffered cruelly as the French batteries performed their remorseless task. Vandamme had ordered Girard's division to move up on the left and take St Amand la Haye, supported by Domon's cavalry on its left. This the division did but Zieten, calling upon his reserves, hit back furiously and four times the hamlet changed hands, with Girard and two of his brigadiers among the fallen. Towards 4.30 Blücher left his command post and personally directed a fresh and shattering offensive against the French left which was vainly trying to take and hold the villages. But at 5 p.m. the Prussians were still in possession of St Amand, St Amand la Haye, and Wagnelée.

Meanwhile, Gérard had committed his corps against the Prussians holding Ligny. Here was perhaps the hardest fighting of this extremely vicious battle, which raged among the houses, the church, the castle, and on both banks of the brook. Men of two armies were locked in deadly grapple, with first one side gaining the advantage then the other. Defences and strongpoints were torn away, dead and wounded lay everywhere, their gaping wounds smothered in flies, and the little stream was reddened by blood.

On the French right Grouchy's men were doing a fine job containing Thielmann's III Corps; they pushed the Prussians out of Boignée, although an attack on Tongrinelle by the two attached battalions of Gérard's corps was unsuccessful. Thielmann's task was made no easier when he was ordered to send Colonel von der Marwitz's cavalry brigade to assist the Prussian right, and at much the same time Blücher ordered General Pirch's comparatively fresh corps to join the fight raging between Ligny and St Amand la Haye.

At about 5.30 the battle took a strange twist. Lobau's VI Corps had still not arrived at Napoleon's headquarters, but he had available some 18,000 men of the Guard and eight regiments of cuirassiers from Milhaud's corps. These he was about to order to march upon the much weakened Prussian right and centre, when he received a distress signal from Vandamme which caused him to postpone the order. Vandamme reported the presence of a large column of all arms heading towards the French left-rear and Fleurus. So grave did he consider the danger that he had withdrawn a division to cover Fleurus. Napoleon was mystified (as indeed was Blücher), for although he expected to be reinforced by Ney these troops would not arrive from the direction of this column, and he feared it might be units sent by Wellington who had managed to master Ney in the fighting at Quatre Bras. Extremely valuable battle time was lost to the French until it was learnt that the column was d'Erlon's corps, which having fought a minor cavalry action north of Mellet then further confused the issue by turning about and disappearing to the west. D'Erlon did leave a division and some cavalry as a connecting link, but failed to notify Soult, and these men took little part in the battle.

By 7 p.m. the men of both armies were becoming desperately weary, but Napoleon still had a large reserve uncommitted. Three-quarters of an hour later, as clouds heavy with rain came closer to the earth and the rumble of thunder vied with the French cannonade, the Guard and cuirassiers were ready to attack. Weary the Prussians may have been, but their courage and resolution was no wit dimmed at the sight of this fresh and formidable onslaught of tall men in bearskin caps. Stoutly they defended the villages and Ligny, beaten back yard by yard in frontal assault and a flank attack by Milhaud's horsemen. Blücher, having sent an aide-de-camp to inform Wellington that he would have to retreat,* put himself at the head of a cavalry charge in a last desperate endeavour to thrust the French back. But it was not to be, and the warrior prince had his horse shot under him. Only by good fortune, and the presence of mind of his aide-de-camp, Count Nostitz, did the French soldiers fail to recognize their prize. The almost senseless Field-Marshal was dragged from the field to the safety of Gentinnes and medical attention.

As the rain poured down and the darkness was lit by bursts of flame from the cannon the Prussians, greatly assisted by Thielmann's corps which took the offensive and held the French at bay round Mont Pontriaux, carried out an unhurried and well-executed withdrawal unhindered by any French pursuit. Napoleon had won his last battle, but in a comparatively confined area of two square miles 27,000 men lay dead; 16,000 of them were Prussians, who also lost 21 guns.

During this stern struggle at Ligny Marshal Ney's left wing was having plenty of fighting against Wellington's troops at Quatre Bras. That battle eventually ended inconclusively at about 9 p.m. with each side suffering some 4,000 casualties. Ney could have won had he launched Reille's corps, supported by d'Erlon's, into the attack earlier than 2 p.m. And even at that time the Anglo–Dutch could only muster around 8,000 men against Reille's 20,000. But owing to the good defensive position in wooded countryside amid high-standing corn, and the excessive caution of the French commander, General Perponcher's troops stubbornly held their ground, while reinforcements poured in during the afternoon. By 6.30 p.m. Ney's chance of victory – excellent in the morning, good in the afternoon – had gone. Wellington with 36,000 men had superiority in numbers and in guns, and when fighting ceased his troops stood fast on their original positions. Ney could have done much better but, harassed and hampered as he was by conflicting orders, the fault was by no means entirely his.

At the end of the fighting on 16 June Napoleon still had a marginal advantage. He had defeated Blücher and held Wellington. All would depend on how well he played his cards on the 17th. But before that there was important work to be done, on the night of the 16–17th, in

---

*Major Winterfeldt was wounded, but reached the Anglo–Dutch lines. However, through a series of misunderstandings his verbal message was not delivered to Wellington.

determining which way the Prussians had gone. However, so confident was Napoleon that they no longer needed to be reckoned with, and that he had the Allied armies irretrievably divided, no orders for pursuit were given until the early hours of the morning. Then Pajol's cavalry went forward, and at 7 a.m. a message was received at army head-quarters (despatched three hours earlier) that large bodies of Prussians were retreating in disorder down the Namur–Liège road. This con-firmed Napoleon's preconceived appreciation of the way Blücher would withdraw. But these men were some 6,000 west Germans who after Ligny thought they had had enough and were deserting. Incidentally, their loss was not a serious one for the Prussians, who would fight better without them.

In fact a snap (and, as it proved, vital) decision had been taken on the battlefield by Gneisenau, in the absence of Blücher, to march via Tilly to Wavre. But in the hustle of giving out orders and rallying the regiments into recognizable formations no word was sent to Wellington, who only discovered that the Prussians had withdrawn when he sent out a patrol the next morning under Colonel Gordon. Gneisenau had grave suspi-cions about Wellington's determination to fight before Brussels (not that that excused his lack of liaison), and it would appear that his decision to make for Wavre was in order to safeguard his communi-cations back through Louvain, for the army had been pushed too far north of the Nivelles–Namur road to make it possible to head direct for Liège.

Fortunately for the Allies Blücher was made of sterner stuff, and when he rejoined the army later that night, at the temporary head-quarters at Mellery, he and his quartermaster-general, Grölmann, made it quite clear that from Wavre the army would march west in support of Wellington. The withdrawal continued during the whole of the 17th (Bülow's IV Corps joining via Corbais and Dion-le-Mont) and by nightfall the whole army was assembled about Wavre.

Virtually nothing was done in the French camp on the morning of the 17th until about 11 a.m. when Napoleon, who still thought the Prussians were decisively defeated, at last realized through Ney's dispatches that by directing Lobau's corps and the Guard to Marbais he could take Wellington's troops in flank while Ney led a direct assault on Quatre Bras. But Ney, who now with a force of 40,000 men had made no attack earlier in the morning, seemed still disinclined to stir himself, and when Napoleon arrived at Marbais at 1 p.m. Ney's men were preparing their lunch. Not until 2 p.m. did the attack go in, and by then a supreme opportunity to maul the Anglo–Dutch army had been lost because Wellington, who at 9 a.m. had eventually received word from Blücher, had begun his withdrawal to Mont St Jean some four hours earlier, and helped by torrential rain he just made good his escape.

Nor were matters going any better on Napoleon's right. Grouchy had been given command of a force of 33,000 all arms with which to chase Blücher, but although Grouchy was anxious to move off fairly early Napoleon had kept him hanging about on the Ligny battlefield. His orders, dictated by Napoleon to General Bertrand (Soult being back at Fleurus), were not entirely clear. But the essence of them was that he should make for Gembloux, from where he could best discover the whereabouts of the Prussians with whom he should keep in close touch, and at the same time maintain contact with the main army and supply Napoleon with information. Grouchy carried out only the first of these instructions, for on reaching Gembloux he camped for the night with no news of the Prussians and no contact with Napoleon.

Thus was the drama of the two days that led up to Waterloo. Battles had been won, lost, and drawn. On the Allied side there was demonstrated a spirit of concord and determination, but with the French success had bred failure. Where resolution and rapid action were needed, uncertainty and lethargy had taken control of the Emperor and his marshals. This was no time for indecision and equivocation. 'If the trumpet give an uncertain sound, who shall prepare himself to the battle?'

In the two decisive days of 16 and 17 June there were many events, some of them minor, some of them important, that had a direct bearing on the result of the campaign. But perhaps the two most important factors were the d'Erlon débâcle on the 16th, and the terribly wasted hours on the morning of the 17th. Had these two events been ordered differently Napoleon must have been in Brussels on the 17th or 18th.

Lieutenant-General Count d'Erlon commanded I Corps of Ney's left wing, and the corps spent the night of 15 June in and around Marchienne. On the morning of the 16th Ney was in no hurry and did not appear to appreciate the need for rapid action, and in consequence the rear units of I Corps were still on the Sambre at 8 a.m. At about midday d'Erlon, whose corps by then was at Jumet, received orders from Ney to move on Frasnes and send one division to Marbais, but there was something of a mingle-mangle with Reille's corps in the confines of Gosselies, and it was almost 4 p.m. before the corps crossed the Roman road. It was around this time and place that the trouble began.

There is no doubt that soon after 4 p.m. d'Erlon, who at that time was forward of his corps on reconnaissance, saw a written note signed by Napoleon and addressed to Ney ordering his corps to march at once to Ligny. And there is not much doubt that this note was carried by General de la Bédoyère (not Colonel Laurent as Siborne states) an ADC of the Emperor. What is disputed is whether the note was actually written by Napoleon or whether (as Becke has it) it was a forged fabrication on the part of de la Bédoyère who, riding to deliver an earlier dispatch and knowing what was in Napoleon's mind, ordered the corps to change direction and then rode on to find d'Erlon to whom he showed the forged authority. Certainly there are pointers (such as Napoleon's surprise at the appearance of the corps on the wrong line) that give credence to Becke's imaginative account, but it would seem more likely that the hastily scribbled note was genuine. Anyway its origin is a matter only of interest: wherever it came from the result was the same.

On seeing the note d'Erlon hastened to rejoin his troops and lead them through Villers-Perwin to appear on the extreme left of the French line. Ney had been sent two orders – timed 2 p.m. and 3.15 – directing him to envelop the Prussian right and fall upon their rear. It was not until after the second one had been despatched that Napoleon learnt that Ney was faced by at least 20,000 Anglo–Dutch troops, and this it is thought prompted him to send the scribbled note asking only for d'Erlon's corps which he believed (correctly) to be still uncommitted. The orders were to attack the Prussian rear, which I Corps marching from Frasnes in a south-easterly direction was certainly not going to do. Hence the uncertainty of the French at Ligny, the subsequent pause in the fighting and the consequent completion of the battle too late for Napoleon to gain a decisive victory.

Just as serious was d'Erlon's subsequent behaviour. When he hurried off to Ligny he had sent his chief-of-staff, General Delcambre, to inform Ney of his action. The Marshal's mercurial temper boiled over on learning that just as he required the corps to take part in a renewed attack he was about to make it had been taken from him. Delcambre was despatched at once with a peremptory order for d'Erlon to return. He reached d'Erlon a little after 6.30 p.m. at which time an order was on its way from Napoleon instructing the corps to head for Wagnelée and assume its intended role of envelopment. Before he could receive this order d'Erlon had started to march back. He did, however, leave Durutte's division and three regiments of cavalry, but their impact on the battle was minimal, for Durutte had been ordered by d'Erlon to 'be prudent', which he was to the extent of being pusillanimous.

D'Erlon had been the recipient of a number of contradictory orders and instructions, and had undoubtedly become a trifle bewildered. But for a senior general he did not show much intelligence or initiative. Even if he did not appreciate that Ligny was the major battle of the day, he had come within two miles of the fighting and had at least double that distance to return, and the hour was late. It would have seemed wiser for him to have taken position on the left of the line pending instructions from the Emperor (which in fact were on their way) instead of marching back to Frasnes, arriving too late to take part in the Quatre Bras battle.

Thus half of the left wing had been unemployed, while its participation at either Quatre Bras or Ligny could have been decisive.

There can be no doubt that on 16 and 17 June Napoleon was badly served by three senior lieutenants whose appointments he may have come to regret. Soult was a liability as chief-of-staff, Ney was unimaginative and unintelligent, while Grouchy was out of his depth in commanding a wing. And on a slightly lower level there was d'Erlon. But a great deal of the blame for missed opportunities lies with Napoleon himself. The campaign had been planned with the Emperor's customary skill, but there was no longer the energy, vitality, and dynamism displayed in former battles. Imprisoned by a nagging illness, Napoleon seems to have found it hard to concentrate.

On the 16th perhaps the greatest mistake was to overlook Lobau's corps, which was not brought up from Charleroi until it was too late for it to join the battle of Ligny, where its presence might have ensured the destruction of the Prussian army. But it is probably true to say that on the morning of 17 June Napoleon's dilatoriness, compounded by that of his left-wing commander, made it impossible for him to win the battle of Waterloo. The usual early morning orders were missing, contact with the Prussians was lost until Pajol's misleading report came in at 7 a.m., and no attempt had been made to find out from Ney the exact position at Quatre Bras. Nor had Ney been informed of the victory at Ligny. At both headquarters the situation was uncertain and obscure.

However, at 8 a.m. General de Flahaut arrived at Imperial head-quarters at Fleurus with information that Wellington's troops were still holding their position at Quatre Bras. This was unexpected but not upsetting, for Napoleon had fresh troops within easy reach for a combined assault with Ney on Wellington should the latter decide to remain in position, which the Emperor thought most unlikely. And so nothing more was done than to order a cavalry patrol to reconnoitre round Quatre Bras, and to dictate a hopelessly indecisive dispatch to Ney. This began by telling the Marshal that the Prussian army had been put to rout ('*mise en deroute*') which showed how out of touch Napoleon was. Then after castigating Ney for various mistakes on the previous day the letter informed him that the Emperor was going to the mill of Bry from where in the unlikely event of the English army '*agir devant vous*' he would march directly on the English from the Quatre Bras road. No urgency in the letter for Ney to attack at once, which of course was so necessary.

At this moment there were three courses open to Napoleon. He could order Ney to hold Wellington in his present position, while he led the rest of the army against Blücher and made certain the Prussians were put completely out of action. Or he could maintain contact with the

Prussians through a light force of cavalry and, say, two infantry divisions, while he led the rest of the right wing and the reserve, in conjunction with Ney, to fight a decisive battle against the Anglo–Dutch on the 17th. Or he could detach the right wing to neutralize Blücher, while he led the fresh troops (Lobau's VI Corps, Drouot's Guard, and Milhaud's cavalry) to smash the Anglo–Dutch whom Ney would already have attacked frontally – the action he had in part hinted at in his letter to Ney. Napoleon chose the third course which, in the prevailing circumstances, was probably the best one, but any one of the three could have brought success had it been executed with speed.

Unfortunately for the French this was not to be. More golden minutes were idled away. Grouchy appeared anxious to get after the Prussians, but Napoleon insisted on his company for a tour of the Ligny battlefield. We are told that the Emperor was far from well, suffering pain that he strove to control through a dose of laudanum. However, the grisly sight of the battlefield appeared to cause him little distress, and wherever he went the troops cheered him. Desultory conversation with Grouchy and other generals on the battle, the latest news from Paris and the plight of the wounded was interrupted when at about 11 a.m. reports from Quatre Bras announced that the Anglo–Dutch were still holding their position in some strength. On receipt of this information the Emperor did at last shed his sloth, and orders were despatched for immediate action.

In accordance with the plan Grouchy was given the IIIrd and IVth Corps, a division of the VIth Corps, 4,350 cavalry and 96 guns – a total force of almost 33,000 men – with which to pursue and neutralize the Prussians. But largely through having no accurate information as to which way they were going, the written orders that were sent after him were unsatisfactory and incomplete. At the same time Ney was sent a short, but urgent, dispatch ordering him to attack at once in concert with the troops Napoleon was sending to Marbais.

All this was very praiseworthy, but it was a great deal too late. Wellington had begun his skilful withdrawal soon after 10 a.m., and when Napoleon reached Marbais at 1 p.m. Ney had still not attacked. Even then, with the Emperor's personal spur, there was a chance that Wellington might have been caught, but the rain, persistent and heavy, turned the countryside into a sodden mass and the roads became too congested. The wheel of history spins upon individual follies: the man who once said 'I may lose a battle, but I shall never lose a minute' had lost a campaign through losing five precious hours.

Napoleon won the battle of Ligny, but to win the campaign he needed to annihilate the Prussian army and this he failed to do. The causes for this important failure were many. His chief-of-staff was not good enough, he himself was physically below par, he underestimated the strength and willpower of his adversary, and through an unnecessary misunderstanding he lost the use of a whole corps. Any one of these misfortunes or mistakes could be a cause for defeat, and it is a measure of their courage and perseverance that despite a combination of them all, and with 12,000 less men, the French managed to force the Prussians from the field.

The Prussian army contained all the ingredients for defeat. There had not been time to train or equip them properly, and they were a heterogeneous force with a large element of unreliable soldiers. Moreover, through an administrative muddle they too had a corps which never reached the battlefield, and Blücher's dispositions were not very cleverly made. These were reasons enough for an army, facing one of the greatest captains of all time, to be defeated.

12 The Battle of Waterloo
18 June 1815

IN the afternoon of 17 June deepening storm clouds blotted out the sun and soon, as the thunder rumbled overhead and the rain lashed down, the dusty tracks became veritable quagmires confining both the withdrawing Anglo–Dutch and the pursuing French to the paved road. The Emperor himself was in the forefront of the pursuit, and Captain Mercer relates how 'in deep and gloomy obscurity' he first saw that 'mighty man of war' appear on a plateau with his lancers and cuirassiers.* Immediately afterwards Mercer was in action with his guns during a fierce skirmish in the single narrow street of Genappe as the Earl of Uxbridge's cavalry covered the withdrawal of the army from Quatre Bras, and the Life Guards and the 7th Hussars did battle with General Jacquinot's 3rd and 4th Lancers.

But the terrible conditions underfoot rendered unavailing all Napoleon's efforts to catch and defeat Wellington's army that day. After the action at Genappe the pace of the pursuit slackened, and the weary Anglo–Dutch went on their way unmolested to the carefully chosen position at Mont St Jean. The French were never far behind, and as dusk approached the leading troops were at the ridge hard by the farm La Belle Alliance. The Emperor, anxious to establish that Wellington meant to stand at Mont St Jean, ordered Milhaud to open up a cannonade with his horse artillery on the Anglo–Dutch position. The response seemed to reassure Napoleon, who then retired to his headquarters at the small farmhouse of Le Caillou.† But in the early hours of the 18th he rode forward again, still worried that his enemy might have slipped away in the night, until with the coming of dawn he could see the bedraggled bivouacs under a murky haze.

Meanwhile, on the 17th the Prussians, marvelling that their withdrawal was unhindered, were making their way towards Wavre. By nightfall the entire army was concentrated round that town, and the

---

*Mercer, Vol. I, pp. 268, 269.

† According to Mercer, whose battery was then positioned close to the famous Wellington tree, Napoleon had ridden forward to witness the firing, and his group was treated to a round of ball from one of Mercer's guns. *ibid.*, pp. 283, 284.

resupply of ammunition that had caused serious concern to the forward troops had been resolved. At 2 a.m. on the 18th Blücher sent a dispatch to General von Müffling, who was his liaison officer at Wellington's headquarters, that IV Corps would be ready to march at daybreak to attack the French right flank, closely followed by II Corps. Thus the two corps that Wellington had asked for were to be available immediately, and I and III Corps were to hold themselves in readiness. This information must have greatly relieved Wellington, but as will be seen later the good intention of early assistance was somewhat nullified by the disposition of the corps on the night of the 17th, and the order of march for the 18th.

At about 6 a.m. on the morning of Sunday 18 June the Duke of Wellington and his staff left the inn at Waterloo, which was his headquarters, to ride the two miles to Mont St Jean. The rain had at last ceased, but the soldiers had spent a wretchedly wet and cold night. As the Duke, plainly but immaculately dressed in a blue civilian coat, white buckskins, hessian boots, a white cravat, and a blue cloak, which he made full use of whenever there was a shower, rode along the line he looked – and was – completely relaxed. The troops forbore to cheer, for they knew he disliked any overt emotional display. Indeed they had no love for him, nor he for them, but there was mutual respect and understanding.

South of the village of Mont St Jean is Mont St Jean Farm, close to which an east–west ridge of low heights crosses the Brussels–Charleroi road at right angles, and almost on the crest of this ridge the fairly wide *chaussée* was crossed by a smaller, unpaved country road leading from the Brussels–Nivelles road in the west to Ohain and Wavre in the east. The greater part of the Anglo–Dutch army was drawn up along and immediately to the north of the country road, as it were in a crescent with the right horn curling forward at Hougoumont and the left on the slightly less protruding farm buildings of Papelotte and Ter La Haye. Immediately to the east of the main *chaussée* the country road was lined by two banked-up holly hedges, and in parts it was deeply sunk. This feature, together with the fairly gentle undulation on the north side of the ridge, gave good protection to troops on the reverse slope and considerably facilitated lateral communication.

The southern slope of the ridge presented in parts a fairly steep glacis, especially where the road leading south towards Charleroi passed through a cutting before reaching La Haye Sainte. This farm abuts the west side of the *chaussée* and is some 200 yards from the crest of the Mont St Jean ridge; from here the road, which bisected the battlefield, continues along an undulating, shallow valley until it reaches another ridge that crosses it from east to west and forms a plateau almost parallel to the one at Mont St Jean. On this ridge, just to the east of the road, stands La Belle Alliance. These two ridges, upon which the rival armies were assembled, are separated by about 1,500 yards of open, undulating plain which at the time of the battle grew tall crops of corn only partly flattened by the rain and marching soldiers.

The two farms of La Haye Sainte and Hougoumont formed vital bastions of the defence. La Haye Sainte was the key to any frontal attack, for so long as it remained untaken its garrison could pour a

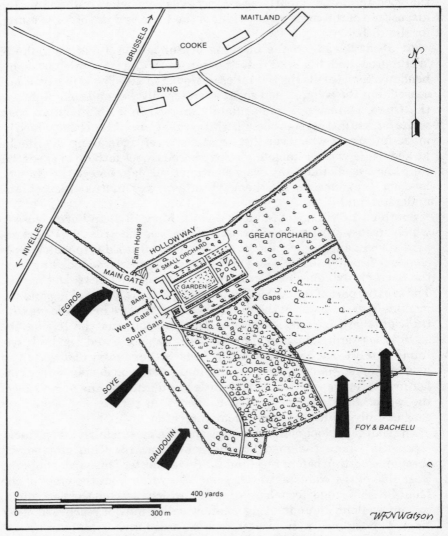

The Battle of Waterloo: French Attack on Hougoumont

destructive enfilading fire on to any advancing column. It is strange, therefore, that Wellington allotted only a small number of troops to defend it. A little to the north of the farm and to the east of the road was a sandpit, which was not so much a pit as a hollowed-out semicircle fronting the road with a hedge and mound on its north side.

Hougoumont was at the time of the battle the pleasant country home of a Monsieur de Luneville. It consisted of a château, a square brick building to which was attached a little chapel, a farmhouse that stood to the north-west of the château, a large and small barn on the west side of the enclosure and a gardener's house to the south. There were two yards; the one opening out from the main north gate was a farmyard with a well in the middle of it, and leading from this was the courtyard. Besides the large and solid wooden gate at the north end of the enclosure, the high-walled buildings could be entered by another gate on the south side and by a small door that opened on to a lane running along the west side.

The garden was bounded on the south and east by a high brick wall, and on the north side by a hedge. There were two orchards; a large one to the east of the garden and a smaller one to the north. The southern boundary of the large orchard was formed by an extremely thick hedge, which had a gap in it at the angle where it was joined by a copse that stretched away to the south for about 300 yards. The hedge completely concealed the garden wall. Immediately to the north of the enclosure there was a 'Hollow Way' formed by a lane and a double hedge, which played an important part in the battle.

There is a valley beginning near La Belle Alliance, which runs round the west of Hougoumont towards Merbe Braine; it is concealed from the Mont St Jean ridge, and so if the Anglo–Dutch army had not held Hougoumont Napoleon would have had a covered approach along which to mount a left hook to outflank their position. Hence the importance of Hougoumont, for the position that Wellington had selected to defend was a strong one so long as the threat to his right flank, which was always uppermost in his mind, could be safeguarded.

The Anglo–Dutch position from flank to flank covered some three and a half miles, but not much more than two miles was held in depth. For this the Duke had present on the field 49,608 infantry, 12,408 cavalry and 5,645 gunners manning 156 guns. A total of 67,661 men.* At this time it was reckoned that to occupy a position strongly 20,000 troops were needed for each mile of front. And so in theory the Duke had enough men even without the 17,000 and 30 guns under Prince Frederick of the Netherlands that were left at Hal, and took no part in the battle.

For convenience of command the line was divided into three principal

*Figures from Siborne, Vol. I, pp. 460, 461.

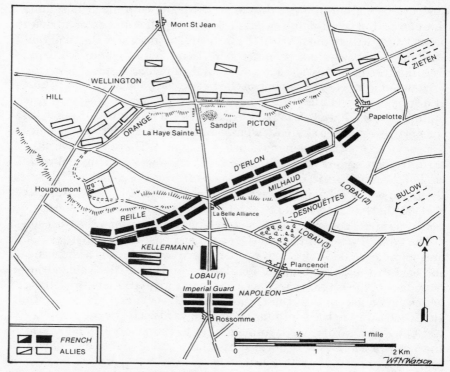

The Battle of Waterloo: 18 June 1815

sectors. Lord Hill had charge of the troops to the west of the Nivelles
road, the Prince of Orange was entrusted with the centre section
between the Nivelles and Charleroi roads, and General Picton was made
responsible for the eastern sector of the line. In doing this Wellington
scrapped his corps organization, and also separated some of the divisional units. This was presumably part of his plan to stiffen the whole
line with a sprinkling of his best troops, and in particular to give
additional strength to the right flank.

On the extreme right of the line, and as it happened outside the battle
area, Wellington put Lieutenant-General Chassé's 3rd Dutch–Belgian
Division to act as bridge between the main army and Prince Frederick's
and General Coville's troops at Hal. At the right end of the actual
battle line, where the Mont St Jean ridge falls away to the valley, was
General Clinton's 2nd British Division, placed *en potence* as a further
safeguard against a flank attack, or should that not develop, as a tactical
reserve. The importance of Hougoumont was immediately apparent to
Wellington's perceptive eye, and he had ordered the light companies of
the 1st and 2nd Guards Brigades to go there on the evening of the 17th.

They were only just in time to drive off a French force which was hoping to gain this good tactical position. On the morning of the 18th, after a visit by the Duke, the garrison was reinforced. Immediately to the north of Hougoumont was the remainder of General Cooke's 1st Guards Division. Most of this wing was under the command of Lord Hill. The sector in which the Guards stood was nominally the responsibility of the Prince of Orange, but Wellington himself was there when the action was most crucial.

The 3rd British Division (General Alten) held the line from the 1st Guards Division up to the crossroads. Immediately to the east of the crossroads came Picton's 5th British Division, which had been severely mauled at Quatre Bras. In front of this division, and overlapping two of its brigades, was General Bylandt's Dutch–Belgian brigade occupying a dangerously exposed forward slope position. The extreme left of the Allied line was entrusted to General Vivian's 6th Cavalry Brigade. Their role was to patrol the left flank until the Prussians came up. In front of them, based on Papelotte and Ter La Haye, was the 2nd Brigade of Nassauers – less a battalion at Hougoumont. Protruding from the centre of the line were the strongpoints of La Haye Sainte and the sandpit. La Haye Sainte was occupied by Major Baring's 2nd Light Battalion of Colonel Ompteda's 2nd King's German Legion (only some 360 men), and in the sandpit were placed two companies of the 95th (Rifles) from Kempt's 8th British Brigade of 5 Division.

The whole of the cavalry, except for those regiments on the extreme flanks, was massed behind the infantry. Of the horse artillery six of the British troops were in theory attached to cavalry brigades, but in the confusion of the night arrival units tucked themselves away as best they could. In the battle Wellington was to use them as mobile reserves, and he positioned most of his field artillery just forward of his infantry, where they could fire on the advancing infantry and cavalry.

The main features of this great defensive position were the weight of fire that could be brought to bear upon the attackers and the disproportionate strength of the right wing. The enemy had to survive accurate marksmanship from the skirmishers and riflemen stationed on the forward slope, and concealed to a great extent by the standing corn, then the grape- and round-shot of the artillery, and finally successive volleys from Brown Bess and two feet of cold steel. The excessive strengthening of the right was partly due to Wellington's expectations of a strong enemy left hook, and partly because he had received information in the early hours of the morning that the Prussians would come up on his left.

Across the plain behind La Belle Alliance ridge, where the *Armée du Nord* was preparing for the battle, Napoleon was (at about 8 a.m.) eating his breakfast and impressing on his staff the simple task ahead. 'We have ninety chances in our favour and not ten against.' He had wanted to start the battle at 9 a.m., but was persuaded by his Guard Artillery General, Drouot, that the ground was far too soft for the guns to operate, and he therefore decided to postpone the main action until 1 p.m. It was a grave error, because every hour gained was golden for the Prussians (whom Napoleon was still discounting) and therefore for Wellington.

When the army was eventually drawn up it was a most impressive and well-orchestrated array with drums beating, bands playing and the echoing acclaim of 'Vive l'Empereur' as Napoleon rode down the lines. But if it was intended to frighten it plainly failed in its purpose. In the front line was d'Erlon's corps, positioned to the right of the Brussels road, and Reille's on the left of that road, with light cavalry on their outer flanks. In the second line, some 200 yards behind Reille's troops, were Kellermann's corps (24 squadrons) and General Guyot's reserve cavalry of the Guard. Behind d'Erlon's corps, but only a hundred yards in rear, were Milhaud's 24 squadrons and the Light Horse of the Guard (Lefebvre-Desnouëttes). In the centre, astride the road, were 10,000 men of Lobau's VI Corps, and in the rear – another 200 yards back – were the divisions of the Imperial Guard. The horse artillery batteries were with their respective cavalry formations, and the field artillery formed up in front of their divisions. In all Napoleon had 48,950 infantry, 15,765 cavalry and 7,232 gunners manning 246 cannon – a total of 71,947 men.* These massed troops were to attack on a comparatively narrow front of a little over two miles, for Napoleon rejected the seemingly more advantageous flank attack on Wellington's left in favour of a Borodino-style massive frontal assault.

At about 11.30 a.m. he ordered Reille to begin what he intended to be a diversionary attack on Hougoumont in the hope that Wellington would withdraw troops from his centre, which was to bear the main thrust an hour or so later. Reille having opened up a heavy artillery barrage ordered Prince Jerome's division, supported by General Piré's 2nd Cavalry Division, to advance upon the small wood that lay to the south of the château. The need to hold Hougoumont was of vital importance to the outcome of the battle, and the fighting there will be described in detail later. It lasted throughout the day (although the crisis was passed by 2 p.m.), for Jerome despite the urging of his chief-of-staff was hell-bent in pursuit of glory, and refused to pull back when matters went seriously wrong, but summoned reinforcements. It is true Wellington had to reinforce the garrison, and that in one glorious moment of heroism (that could have had a decisive effect on the battle) the château was nearly lost. But it proved a costly diversion, for a large part of

---

*Figures, Siborne, Vol. I, p. 461. They did not include Grouchy's detached force of 33,000 men, which as the battle opened were unsuccessfully attempting to intercept the Prussians.

Reille's corps was committed for most of the battle without greatly affecting Wellington's overall plan of defence.

While Jerome's men were pounding themselves against the unyielding bastion of Hougoumont, and shortly before he gave orders for the main attack to start, Napoleon received information from a patrol sent to reconnoitre towards Frischermont which at last brought home to him the truth about the Prussians. He now knew that at least one corps was on its way to launch itself against his vulnerable right. The odds in his favour were sensibly diminished, but he remained seemingly unmoved and still convinced he could defeat Wellington before the Prussians arrived. He did, however, send an urgent message to Grouchy giving him this information and urging him to hurry to the support of the army. But it was too late, Grouchy was too far away to take any effective part in the main battle. Napoleon also ordered Subervie and Domon to take their cavalry towards this new threat, and they were shortly followed by Lobau's divisions.

Soon after 1 p.m. 78 guns that had been ordered forward to support d'Erlon's attack unlimbered along a spur some 250 yards from La Haye Sainte and thundered into action. Three-quarters of an hour later Ney led forward d'Erlon's corps to storm the farm and the sandpit. The four divisions crossed the 1,300 yards of smoke-shrouded plain echeloned from just west of the Brussels road to the far left of the Anglo–Dutch line. For some reason, with the exception of the right division which marched in column of battalions each with a two-company front, the troops advanced on a deployed battalion frontage with 200 men in the front rank and successive battalions marching close up in rear. This made it impossible to form square against cavalry attack, and enabled the Anglo–Dutch gunners to mow down rank upon closely packed rank. Furthermore, contrary to normal procedure, the troops were given only limited cavalry support by Milhaud's cuirassiers (Dubois and Travers).

Nevertheless, vulnerable though it may have been, this formidable phalanx of fierce-featured men devoted to their Emperor and to the Eagles and Standards they proudly carried, must have been an awe-inspiring sight. But the Anglo–Dutch soldiers were ready and had, through Wellington's reverse-slope dispositions and the wetness of the ground which impeded the cannonballs, escaped the worst of the bombardment. Only Bylandt's brigade on the forward slope had taken severe punishment.

D'Erlon's splendid battalions were sadly shaken as the canister ripped through their ranks. But any check was hardly noticeable, and soon La Haye Sainte and the sandpit were encased by hordes of fiercely determined men. La Haye Sainte had not been properly prepared, and even worse one of its massive gates had been broken down and used for firewood. The men of the King's German Legion (KGL) were great fighters, but they were driven out of the orchard and forced back into the farm buildings. Although the sandpit was reinforced by a KGL battalion, the weight of the attack had become too great for this unprotected position, and the men of the 95th (Rifles) withdrew through the hedge on to their battalion.

At about this time Bylandt's sorely tried Dutch–Belgians beat a hasty retreat, but although the situation on this part of the front had become very critical their disappearance had no moral or physical repercussions on Picton's thin line. In some of the fiercest fighting of the day his two brigades (Kempt's and Pack's) were almost overwhelmed by 8,000 Frenchmen, but arrayed in line two deep the British soldiers opened up at less than 50 yards, pouring a hail of lead into the oncoming French. The gallant Picton fell with a bullet through the head, and the fight developed into a desperate affair of thrusting and parrying with the bayonet. Every bit as critical was the action on the west side of the Brussels road. Here the left brigade of General Alix's division, closely supported by cuirassiers, had broken through, and Wellington ordered the German brigades in front of the oncoming horsemen to form square, for all along the line his infantry was only just holding and cavalry could have ridden through it. But help was at hand.

At this most critical moment Lord Uxbridge, either on his own initiative (as he later claimed) or on orders from Wellington, launched the heavy cavalry. Sir William Ponsonby's Union Brigade (the Royals, Scots Greys, and Inniskillings – 900 sabres in all) wheeled into action with the Household Brigade (1st and 2nd Life Guards, the Royal Horse Guards, and the 1st King's Dragoon Guards – 1,220 sabres). The result was spectacular, devastating, and immediate. The Household Brigade squadrons bore down upon the cuirassiers as they were scrambling in and out of the sunken road; taken by surprise and faced by heavier horses, they were at a disadvantage, and were soon scattering in a headlong rush and riding over their own infantry. Other French troops on this same side of the road were caught in the act of deploying and thrown into utter confusion. The story was much the same to the east of the road, where the Union Brigade tore into the mass of Donzelot's and Marcognet's troops still fighting in a formation totally unsuited to resisting cavalry. The carnage was fearful.

Before long the two brigades joined together, and galloping – by now virtually out of control – across the smoke-filled valley they swept all before them and thundered into the French position, overturning guns and sabring gunners. But Nemesis, in the form of 30,000 fresh French troops, now took a hand. Both brigades were assailed by regiments of lancers and cuirassiers, and were only saved from complete disaster by the timely arrival from the left of Sir John Vandeleur's light dragoons.

As it was, almost half of these magnificent brigades, with their horses, were lost. Nevertheless, d'Erlon's corps had been driven off with heavy losses. Two Eagles had been captured in the cavalry charge and some twenty-five guns had been disabled.

It was now around 3 p.m. and the second phase of the battle had ended. Wellington's hard-tried infantry had been granted a respite. The Mont St Jean ridge was clear of Frenchmen (other than their dead), Hougoumont and La Haye Sainte stood firm, and the lightly held Papelotte, which General Durutte had captured from the Nassauers, had been retaken by Prince Bernhard. The Duke set about reorganizing and strengthening his line. La Haye Sainte was reinforced, the sandpit was reoccupied and General Lambert's 10th British Brigade was brought into the line from reserve. As the threat of an outflanking movement on the right had clearly receded, troops originally positioned west of the Nivelles road were brought across to form a close reserve, and two battalions (Brunswickers and du Plat's KGL) were sent to replace Byng's brigade, north of Hougoumont, which had gone to reinforce the garrison.

By about 3.30 p.m. d'Erlon had re-formed his shattered battalions and Napoleon, who was at Rossomme, ordered Ney to renew the attack on La Haye Sainte. The third phase of the battle was about to begin. Napoleon had realigned his artillery and now opened up with the heaviest barrage of the day. The terrible storm of iron that hurtled through the air made it, in the words of Captain Mercer 'seem dangerous to extend the arm lest it should be torn off'. It was the prelude to the appearance of 5,000 horsemen, in some 43 squadrons, advancing in perfect order in echelon from the right – slowly, majestically, and totally unaccompanied by infantry. Such a manoeuvre astounded Wellington and every experienced commander in the Allied army. The fact is Ney had mistaken the partial withdrawal of the Anglo–Dutch infantry to new positions for the beginning of a general retreat, and he thought he could achieve a speedy victory by the use of cavalry alone. Then in the excitement of successive charges, all of which he led personally, he seems to have forgotten the 6,000 men of Reille's corps – who had hardly fired a shot all day – until it was too late.

On came this mass of horsemen at a measured trot, for riding almost knee to knee their formation forbade a greater speed, and anyway it was their custom to ride into battle unhurried. Milhaud's cuirassiers, the sun glinting on their breastplates, led in the first line, then the cavalry of the Guard – Grenadiers à Cheval – with plain uniforms, but huge bearskin caps. The 'Red' Lancers with their tall white plumes, and Chasseurs à Cheval in green dolmans were followed by squadrons of hussars, dragoons, and carabiniers. It was a formidable and, to the inexperienced, a terrifying sight. But the troops knew their drill.

Wellington gave the command to prepare to meet cavalry, and the battalions formed square and the squares were staggered so as to be in some degree self-supporting and to allow room for manoeuvre. The gunners were ordered to fire their guns up to the last moment, and then to run for the shelter of the squares.

When the French horsemen were less than 100 yards away all hell was let loose; case and shot hurtled into the solid mass and whole ranks were shorn away. But still they came on, and when the gunners had taken refuge Ney's horsemen swirled around the squares trying every means, short of a suicidal charge, to gain entrance. Inevitably the squares took punishment. Captain Gronow, who was inside one, said they were nearly suffocated by the smoke and smell from burnt cartridges, and 'It was impossible to move a yard without treading upon a wounded comrade, or upon the bodies of the dead'.* But as men fell in the first two ranks their places were taken by men in rear. The bristling bayonets of the first two ranks and the terrific fire power of the third and fourth took terrible toll, and all the time the French cavalry were harried in close combat by the Allied horse. As soon as Ney's battered squadrons withdrew to re-form at a distance out ran the gunners. Nobody could count how many times Ney charged the squares; some say it was fifteen, and every time the pattern was the same; and every time the gunners found their weapons intact, for the French never thought to spike them.

Napoleon was angered at seeing his cavalry used in this wasteful way, but he felt he had to support Nay with more squadrons. By 5 p.m. he had no cavalry reserve left and some 9,000 men were riding against the squares. But by now most of the British cavalry had been expended, and all the infantry reserve had been committed. And then at last – it was shortly after 6 p.m. – Ney resorted to the proper tactics of using all three arms in a combined assault on La Haye Sainte with entirely successful results. Major Baring's KGL fought with utmost courage until their ammunition was expended, when the survivors withdrew as best they could.

Ney immediately brought up a battery to within 300 yards of the weakening British centre and let fly with a concentrated and destructive fire. But he had not sufficient troops to clinch the victory he felt sure was in his grasp. He sent urgently for reinforcements. The Emperor's reply is a part of history: *'Des troupes! Ou voulez-vous que j'en prenne? Voulez-vous que j'en fasse?'* Ney had made a similar request at Borodino and then, as now, it had been turned down. Almost certainly Napoleon was right at Borodino, but had he sent the Guard in now he could

*Gronow, p. 190.

perhaps have won the battle. However, there were many 'ifs' at Waterloo, and there were reasons for withholding this last reserve.

It was about 6.30 p.m. that La Haye Sainte fell, but for more than two hours before the Prussians had been in action at Wavre and on Napoleon's right flank. Their intervention at this time and later was one of the most important factors of the battle, and will be recounted later. Suffice it to say here that Grouchy, having failed to interpose his force between the Prussians and the French army, was now engaged at Wavre with Thielmann's III Corps. Meanwhile, Blücher, in compliance with his promise to Wellington, had ordered Bülow's IV Corps, followed a little later by Pirch's II Corps, to march via St Lambert to attack the French right. Napoleon had been aware of this movement since the early afternoon and, as already related, had sent two cavalry divisions and Lobau's VI Corps to hold back these Prussians while he made haste to finish off Wellington. From 4.30 p.m. onwards there was some very fierce fighting round Frischermont and Plancenoit.

The crisis of the battle was fast approaching. Napoleon felt, and he was right, that the Anglo–Dutch army had been dangerously weakened by his constant pounding and charging, and he also knew that the Prussians were almost upon him. He could now only withdraw under cover of the Guard, or throw those fine troops in against Wellington's thinning line in one last bid for victory. Predictably, he chose the latter course.

But Wellington had seized the opportunity afforded him by a brief lull in the fighting after the fall of La Haye Sainte to make certain adjustments to lend what strength he could to his battered line. In particular he brought Vivian's and Vandeleur's cavalry brigades from the left to the centre, where they were urgently needed. This was possible because Zieten's corps – after a misunderstanding that caused a slight loss of time – had now arrived and could guard the left flank. To face Napoleon's last great throw Wellington probably had no more than 35,000 men fit for battle, but because his flanks were secure – Hougoumont, although ablaze, still held – he was able to place most of these in that vital sector of his line from the *chaussée* to Hougoumont, where he would now have twice as many brigades as were there in the morning.

It was gone 7 p.m. when the lowering rays of a sun that had made only fitful appearances in the afternoon were glinting on 6,000 bayonets of the Imperial Guard as they formed up before their Emperor for what was to be their last parade. The French artillery had stepped up its firing rate, Reille was preparing one more assault on Hougoumont, d'Erlon's weary men were yet again re-forming in the centre, and Durutte was worrying the Nassauers and Prussians on the Allied left.

There are many differing accounts of this last act in the battle of

Waterloo. After eight hours of murderous mayhem it is not surprising that wits should have become dulled and impressions blurred. Subsequently memories were allowed free licence with a result that although there are extant French and Allied contemporary accounts, there is no really reliable description of the defeat of the Guard. But what seems quite certain is that these magnificent troops with their long blue coats and tall red-plumed bearskin caps, rifles at the shoulder with bayonets gleaming, marched into battle in column on a two-company front, so that each battalion had a frontage of between seventy and seventy-five men and was at least nine ranks deep. Wellington, observing this splendid spectacle through his telescope, may have seen Napoleon at the head of seven of these battalions, but some say there were as many as ten. Between each battalion came two guns, and a seemingly endless supply of tirailleurs stretched a protective screen across the entire front.

At the cutting in the road south of La Haye Sainte Napoleon handed over to Marshal Ney. Shortly afterwards Ney did what appeared to be a foolish thing. Instead of continuing up the axis of the Brussels road with its sheltering banks, he swung the column to its left across churned-up ground and over heaped-up corpses towards Wellington's strongest sector, and where his gunners were ready for this perfect target. After leaving the *chaussée* the column split, and advanced by battalions in echelon from the right; but they lost direction in the smoke and general confusion, and when they started to ascend the ridge they had come together in two columns. Although many of the Allied guns were either out of action or short of ammunition, there were enough batteries positioned to give a devastating frontal fire, or echeloned to pour canister, grape and shot into the exposed flank of the columns.

The effect of this fire on the densely packed ranks was appalling; men went down like swathes of corn before the reaper. Ney had his fifth horse shot under him but, nothing daunted, continued to lead his troops on foot. Wellington had ordered the infantry to lie down behind the crest in four ranks. The honour of being first to receive the attention of the Imperial Guard fell to Maitland's 1st Guards Brigade, and when the leading files of the enemy were less than fifty yards from the country road the silence behind the ridge was broken by the Commander-in-Chief's 'Now, Maitland, now's your time!' and then, carried away by the excitement of the moment, he gave direct orders to the men, 'Stand up Guards', and in an instant some 600 muskets were discharged at the astounded and thoroughly unprepared Grenadiers and Chasseurs of the Guard.

Immediately the 69th and 33rd Regiments (Halkett's brigade) on Maitland's left moved round to give him support, but the second column of the Guard now attacked the left battalions of this brigade, and, with the Brunswickers and Nassauers beginning to give ground, the situation for a while remained critical. But the Duke was everywhere urging and rallying any faltering battalion, and soon Maitland's men, helped by Detmer's Dutch–Belgian brigade, drove the enemy down the slope. However, the Guard quickly rallied and the 4th Chasseurs, now supported by cuirassiers, came up to extricate their comrades, and the Allied infantry, covered by the 23rd Dragoons who took care of the cuirassiers, were driven back to the crest. The fight all along this sector of the ridge now became the most bloody and desperate affair. Every attempt by fresh battalions of the Guard to drive Wellington's men from the ridge was stubbornly resisted, and gradually the intensive fire power and high degree of courage and leadership of the latter made their mark. The spirit and élan of these superb French troops began to wilt. The end came suddenly and dramatically.

Colonel Colborne's 52nd Regiment of Foot was the right battalion of General Adam's brigade, which was stationed immediately on Maitland's right. It had remained concealed on the reverse slope but now, showing splendid initiative and anticipating his Commander-in-Chief's orders, Colborne advanced his men in unhurried drill-book precision and wheeled them into line opposite the flank of the advancing Guard. The 52nd then halted and the two front ranks poured a withering volley into the flank of the Guard, with the two rear ranks passing through to fire in their turn. Then Adam, having appreciated Colborne's purpose, ordered his remaining two regiments (the 71st and 95th) to comply. The Guard had rallied, and indeed taken heavy toll of Colborne's men, but this sudden appearance through the smoke of fresh troops on its flank caused dismay, and when Colborne – closely supported by the other two regiments – led forward his men in a charge the grenadiers and Chasseurs turned and fled. The terrible and unheard of cry went up, '*La Garde recule*'.

It was a little after 8 p.m. when Wellington judged it the moment to give the signal for the general advance, which he did by raising his hat and waving it three times towards the French. Soon, in a moment of immortal glory, every man in the Allied line capable of moving was advancing down the slope in pursuit of a broken enemy. Wellington had won a great victory, but it had been a terrible battle; more than 40,000 men lay dead or wounded upon the field, of which nearly 15,000 were from his own army.

In this great battle there were a number of important events which had, or would have had, a bearing on the way the day went – Napoleon's line of attack and delay in opening it, Grouchy's dilatoriness, Ney's use of unsupported cavalry and Napoleon's refusal to reinforce him, to name just four. But often there were reasons for these and other actions, and

even excuses where there was lack of action, and although an accumu-
lation of these seeming errors undoubtedly contributed to the French
defeat it could not be said that any one of them caused it. There were,
however, two positive factors that undoubtedly saved the day for
Wellington. The holding of Hougoumont, and the coming – in the nick of
time – of the Prussians.

Wellington, seeing immediately the importance of Hougoumont,
ordered the light companies of the 1st Guards Brigade (Maitland) under
Lord Saltoun, together with those of the 2nd Battalion Coldstream
Guards and 2nd Battalion Third Guards (both of which belonged to
Byng's 2nd Guards Brigade) under Colonel Macdonell to go there on the
evening of the 17th. Saltoun's men were to hold the orchard and
Macdonell's the château and buildings, which they fortified as best they
could during the night. On the morning of the 18th, after a visit by
Wellington, the garrison was reinforced by the 1st Battalion of the
2nd Brigade of Prince Bernhard of Saxe-Weimar's Nassauers, a company of Hanoverian riflemen and 100 of Count Kielmansegge's 1st
Hanoverian Brigade; all these reinforcements were positioned in the
wood.

General Reille entrusted the attack on Hougoumont to Prince
Jerome's division, and his first objective was the wood. Supported by
heavy artillery fire and General Piré's Lancers the leading brigade
began the attack shortly after 11.30 a.m. In the first assault the brigade
commander (General Bauduin) was killed, and it took more than an
hour to dislodge the Nassauer and Hanoverian troops from the wood. A
great deal of fire power was now directed upon the French as they
debouched from the wood to assault the château, for Wellington had
ordered Sir Augustus Frazer to bring up Major Bull's howitzers to fire
over the heads of the Allied troops – a very delicate task. Jerome's men
were also hit by enfilade fire from the buildings and orchard. The
Prince's chief-of-staff, General Guilleminot, urged him to pull back, but
Jerome would not hear of it and immediately brought forward his second
brigade (Soye), and he also sent urgently for help from General Foy's
division. He then continued the attack through and down the side of the
wood from a westerly and south-westerly direction.

At this time Saltoun's light companies were in the orchard, and the
light company of the 2nd Coldstream held the southern wall of the
garden, with its right in the main building, while the light company of
the 3rd Guards held the lane to the west of the enclosure. A counterattack by the companies, together with the Germans, was only partially
successful. But the French, on reaching the thick hedge that bounded
the wood, were completely surprised by the murderous fire of the
Coldstreamers from the loopholed garden wall and buildings as they
attempted to cross the fifty yards of open ground that separated the wood

from the garden. They came on with great courage, and were driven back into the wood with very heavy losses.

It was now shortly after midday, and the situation – especially on the right flank of the defence – was becoming extremely critical. The 3rd Guards in the lane, with a blazing haystack at the south end and Soye's troops coming at them from the west, were being forced back towards the main gate. It was the only gate left open, and the outflanking French troops had seen it; if they could seize the gateway and hold it Hougoumont would be lost.

The 3rd Guards succeeded in falling back into the yard to join the Coldstreamers, and the gate was closed. But the French were hard by, and at their head was Sous-Lieutenant Legros of the 1st Light Regiment – a huge man aptly nicknamed L'Enfonceur (the Smasher). Seizing a sapper's axe he smashed open one part of the gate and forced his way into the yard closely followed by a number of men. The party was quickly engaged in some fierce close-quarter fighting in which all the intruders were killed – Legros, still with axe in hand, fell at the door of the chapel. Meanwhile, Colonel Macdonell – himself a large man – seeing what was afoot and collecting a small party, which included the burly Sergeant Graham of the Coldstream, rushed from the garden to the gate around which some heavy fighting was now in progress. Soon the French were forced back and Macdonell and Graham managed to fix the heavy crossbar that secured the doors.

Some time after the battle Wellington, when asked to award the £500 bequeathed to 'the bravest soldier in the British army at Waterloo', wrote 'The success of the battle of Waterloo turned upon the closing of the gates of Hougoumont. These gates were closed in the most courageous manner at the nick of time by Sir James Macdonell.'* He therefore gave the prize to Macdonell, who passed the money on to Sergeant Graham.

The immediate peril had been averted, but the French continued to hack and batter at the gate with an alarming intensity, despite suffering heavy casualties from the defenders' rifle fire. So close was the fighting that Bull's guns were no longer able to give support, but the arrival of Colonel Woodford with his Coldstream battalion – less two companies – drove the French away from the gate. His men then entered the enclosure by the small gate at its west side, and brought the garrison added strength at an important moment, for Foy was about to throw in his last brigade (Gautier's). These men made a frontal and flank attack on the orchard, and Saltoun with his left flank threatened had to withdraw to the Hollow Way. But this dangerous move by the French was taken care of by Lieutenant-Colonel Home of the 3rd Guards, who

*King, p. 124.

led two companies to outflank the outflankers and drove the enemy from
the orchard. Saltoun's men then re-established their position along the
south hedge.

The fight had now been raging for one and a half hours, and it was
time to relieve the sorely tried light companies of the 1st Guards
Brigade whose men had done a magnificent job. The remaining companies of the 3rd Guards were now brought into the Hollow Way
together with the Hanoverians, and the 2nd Coldstream occupied the
château buildings. By 1.30 p.m. the whole of the 2nd Guards Brigade
were in or around Hougoumont, and the pressure on this vital bastion
had eased. Somewhere around 2,000 Guardsmen and Hanoverians had
kept 10,000 of Napoleon's best troops from gaining the important prize
for which they had been striving during two hours of most bitter
fighting. But there was still much more to come, for fighting at
Hougoumont would continue for the rest of the day to occupy many
enemy formations. Moreover, the action in this part of the field denied
the French the space they needed if their massive assaults were to be
successful.

At about 7 p.m. on 17 June Grouchy and his two corps (Vandamme and
Gérard) had reached Gembloux after a leisurely march. Earlier in the
day he had heard from Exelmans, whose cavalry were in advance, that
he was keeping careful watch on a Prussian corps (Thielmann's) in the
area of Gembloux, but by the time Grouchy arrived they had given
Exelmans the slip unnoticed. Grouchy then sent out a cavalry patrol

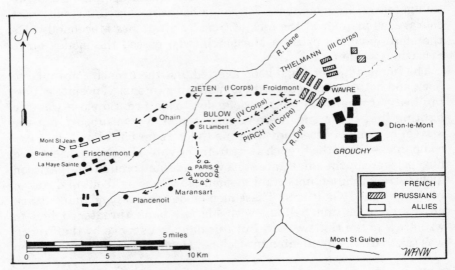

Waterloo: The Prussian Approach Marches

which brought back information that the Prussians seemed to be retreating on Wavre. At 10 p.m. he passed this information to Napoleon, indicating that the Prussians had divided in two columns, one apparently heading for Wavre, and the other most likely for Liège. This dispatch reached Le Caillou at 2 a.m. on the 18th, but Napoleon did not see it until 4 a.m., and then took no action until 10 a.m. by which time it was too late, for Grouchy, still undecided in his movements, had directed his corps on Sart à Walhain – away from Napoleon and the advancing Prussians.

Meanwhile, Blücher, having outmanoeuvred Grouchy, concentrated his army round Wavre on the evening of the 17th. The Ist and IInd Corps, which had borne the brunt of the fighting at Ligny, arrived at noon and that night were at Bierges and Aisemont respectively. III Corps, which had covered their retreat, crossed the Dyle and camped at La Bavette, while IV Corps, which had taken no part at Ligny, had arrived via Walhain and bivouacked some two miles south-east of Wavre at Dion-le-Mont.

The order of march for the Prussian army on 18 June has come in for much criticism. Gneisenau issued the orders, and because the hindmost corps was ordered to take the lead in difficult circumstances he is often accused of still being mistrustful of Wellington's determination to fight that day, and therefore anxious not to commit the Prussian army prematurely. Perhaps he was, but it seems unlikely that this was the cause of the delay, for although the chief-of-staff may have issued the orders Blücher would have masterminded the plan, and he was both committed and content to give maximum assistance to Wellington. No doubt he wished Bülow's completely fresh corps to spearhead the attack, and he seems to have underestimated the difficulties of terrain and certain other hazards.

Bülow's IV Corps was ordered to move off at 4 a.m. through Wavre to Chapelle St Lambert and, if the battle had started – but not otherwise – he was to engage the enemy's right flank; II Corps would follow close behind, while I Corps would be despatched later, marching via Froidmont and Ohain, to join Wellington's left; III Corps was to hold itself in readiness to march if no French force appeared before Wavre.

The Prussian commanders were well aware that the fate of the battle hinged upon their timely arrival, and it was unfortunate that the freshest corps had the farthest to march. Both IV and II Corps had to cross the Dyle and IV Corps had to pass through II Corps and then negotiate the bottleneck in Wavre. Bülow got the leading elements of his corps through Wavre without much difficulty and these troops were at St Lambert by about 10 a.m., but soon after they had got through Wavre a fire broke out there, which added very considerably to the existing chaos in and around the town. Nor was the pace of the march helped by the appalling condition of the ground. There were no roads and very few tracks, and after the extremely heavy rain these and the surrounding fields were a sea of mud. As a result Bülow's main body did not reach St Lambert before midday, and his last brigade considerably later. Moreover, II Corps could not march until IV Corps had cleared it, and it was midday before the corps started.

It was about 1.30 p.m. when Napoleon received confirmation (from a captured Prussian) that the troops he had seen on the heights above St Lambert were a part of Bülow's corps. It was an important turning point in the battle, for although Napoleon did not at this time consider the threat too serious (he still relied on assistance from Grouchy) he nevertheless had to detach Domon's and Subervie's cavalry divisions and Lobau's two infantry divisions to hold the Prussians. These troops proved to be insufficient and before long they had to be reinforced by battalions of the Guard. The contribution by the Prussians in the fighting that was soon to take place tends to be overshadowed by the opportune arrival of I Corps on Wellington's left flank later in the day, but it was every bit as important.

Blücher joined IV Corps at St Lambert about midday, and accompanied it on the desperately tiring march across the swampy Lasne basin to the Paris Wood, from the edge of which most of the battlefield could be seen. He had never been anxious to commit his troops piecemeal to the battle, but when – at about 4 p.m. – it became obvious that Napoleon's colossal pounding was in danger of breaking the Anglo–Dutch line he ordered Bülow to attack with his 15th and 16th Brigades and not to wait the arrival of the 13th and 14th, which were a little way back. It was fortunate for the Prussians that Lobau had failed to occupy the Paris Wood, for it would have greatly held up their advance. However, the French fought stubbornly, and Bülow was not able to press them back and through the village of Plancenoit until his missing brigades had come up.

Plancenoit was to become the centre of some extremely fierce fighting. It was close enough to the French line of retreat to cause Napoleon anxiety, and its capture by the Prussians could have a demoralizing effect on his troops. Somewhere around 6 p.m. the 16th Brigade of IV Corps fought its way into the village, but it was fairly soon evicted by the Young Guard whose eight battalions and twenty-four guns had been recently despatched by Napoleon. Prussian reinforcements from the 14th Brigade were hurried to the scene, and the Young Guard in their turn were thrown out. But the place changed hands for a third time when Napoleon ordered two battalions of the Old Guard to hasten from La Belle Alliance, and after a hard fight the Prussians were thrown back on to their original positions. It was now 7 p.m., and although Bülow's corps had failed to take Plancenoit it had pinned down about half the

French reserve. Soon II Corps would be arriving on this front, and less than two miles to the north I Corps was about to enter the battle.

Zieten received orders from Blücher at about 11.30 a.m. to join Wellington's left flank, but he was unable to move until 2 p.m. because II Corps blocked his line of approach to Froidmont. A few hours later, what might have been a disaster was narrowly avoided by General von Müffling's confidence in his own judgement and Zieten's willingness to disobey his chief's orders. Blücher, in his anxiety to take Plancenoit, had sent new orders to Zieten to march south in order to support IV Corps. These reached him at about 6.30 p.m. when his 1st Brigade was past Ohain, and the main body about level with it. Müffling had ridden to Wellington's left flank with orders for Vandeleur's and Vivian's troops to move to the centre, and for arrangements to be made for Zieten's corps to join the battle in that area.

When Müffling arrived Zieten was already turning his 2nd Brigade south (the 1st had gone beyond the Frischermont turning), and a difficult decision had to be taken. General von Müffling knew how shaky was the state of Wellington's defence on the left flank, where the French had just captured Papelotte and La Haye. He genuinely believed that without the assistance of Zieten's corps the battle would be lost. On the other hand Blücher's messenger painted a grim picture of the Prussian position at Plancenoit. Probably the forceful persuasions of Müffling, and the time it would take to close his corps up and point it southwards, decided Zieten that he would be justified in disobeying Blücher's order.

Undoubtedly it was the right decision, for had Zieten turned, his corps would very likely have been in the same position as d'Erlon's at Ligny – inactive between two battles. As it was the Prussians reached the battlefield at a critical time. The Imperial Guard was marching up the slope at Mont St Jean when Zieten's men were throwing the French out of Papelotte and La Haye, and then swinging across the Smohain valley they smashed into Durutte's and Lobau's troops round La Belle Alliance and Plancenoit, and together with IV Corps broke the French resistance in that part of the field.

The unnerving effect on the French at the appearance of the right wing of the Prussian army was given added poignancy through it being hoped by many that these were Grouchy's troops. But this was not to be, for all along that marshal's contribution had been too little and too late – although Napoleon must bear some blame for this. The battle Grouchy fought at Wavre until almost 11 p.m. on 18 June has received little attention, for apart from keeping a Prussian corps occupied it had no bearing on the principal event. It was mainly notable for Grouchy's indifferent tactics, but great personal courage, and for the very able way Thielmann's III Corps held at bay the repeated attacks of double their number of Frenchmen. Yet another example of the dogged determination of the Prussian troops, who in the three days' fighting had played such a vital part in the Allied victory.

Napoleon's physical deterioration has been mentioned earlier, and it undoubtedly played a prominent part in his defeat, for it resulted in his fighting an offensive battle which was no match for the skill of Wellington's defensive one. This was the deciding factor between victory and defeat, although there was another that raises a tempting speculation.

Grouchy's performance on 17 and 18 June comes very close to being an example of how a battle can be lost by the action of a subordinate commander. The mystery of Napoleon's message dispatched at 10 p.m. on 17 June has never been solved. Grouchy later said he never received it, Napoleon thought his disregard of it cost him the battle. If the Prussians had been held at Wavre, could Napoleon have won? It is conceivable, but unlikely. Nevertheless, such incompetence or disobedience can easily lose a battle.

At Waterloo there was no decisive factor outside the control of either commander, although on the evening of the 17th Napoleon might have caught Wellington's withdrawal from Quatre Bras but for an unexpected flash storm, and this could have had an important bearing on the fighting next day.

13   **Battle of the Alma**
20 September 1854

THE immediate dispute leading up to the Crimean War was a religious one, but what had become known as the Eastern Question – principally involving the conflict between Russia and Turkey – went back many years. The expansionist policies of successive Russian Tsars, and their desire to obtain access to the Mediterranean through the Black Sea, was a constant cause of friction between the two countries, and while Britain was anxious to maintain peace in the Balkans she found it necessary to safeguard the ailing Turkish empire which, until the opening of the Suez Canal, controlled the important overland route to the Indies.

Ever since 1812 Russia had exercised the right of protection over the Orthodox Christians in the Turkish provinces of Moldavia and Wallachia (now part of Rumania), which gave her an undesirable influence into Turkish affairs. In 1850 the French Emperor Louis Napoleon further complicated the religious question by demanding from the Turks a similar right of protection for the Roman Catholics in Palestine. Tsar Nicholas I not only protested to the Sultan at this, but a little later demanded the protectorship of Orthodox Christians throughout the Turkish empire, under threat of invading Moldavia and Wallachia. The Sultan, prompted by Lord Stratford de Redcliffe, the British ambassador at the Porte, refused, and the Russian troops marched.

On 23 October 1853 the Turks declared war. France and Britain had hoped that by showing a firm hand the Tsar could be persuaded to withdraw his troops, and to this end they sent a joint fleet into the Black Sea the day before the Turkish declaration. But far from having the desired effect, while the Allied fleet was off Constantinople the Russians put to sea and on 30 November completely destroyed a Turkish squadron off Sinope on the southern Black Sea shore with enormous loss of life and damage to the town. This 'massacre' as it was termed, although a legal act of war, so infuriated the British public that the Prime Minister, Lord Aberdeen, could no longer hold back. On 27 March 1854 Great Britain declared war on Russia. The French had done so the day before.

At the end of February and early March some 25,000 troops sailed from England. The first port of call was Valetta in Malta, where they were to spend two or three weeks before the political situation was resolved, and the journey to Turkey could be resumed. The French had already sailed from their Mediterranean ports, and they landed at Galipoli in early April. The British found that town both dirty and crowded so they moved on to Scutari, which was just as dirty but not so crowded.

The British force consisted of five infantry divisions – the Light Division, the 1st, 2nd, 3rd and 4th Divisions – and each had two brigades. The cavalry division (under Lord Lucan) comprised the Heavy and Light Brigades, and divisional artillery was made up from nine field batteries and three troops of Horse artillery (in all sixty guns). The total infantry and artillerymen was 24,400, and the cavalry had available 1,000 sabres. The French had only four divisions, but they were much larger than their British counterparts, and they put into the field almost 40,000 men and 8 batteries of field artillery. They had no cavalry. The Turkish contingent (under Suleiman Pasha) numbered 7,000 men. The French soldiers were armed almost entirely with the new Minié rifle, but this superior weapon was not in universal supply in the British army, many of whose soldiers still carried the faithful Brown Bess. The Russian muskets and their bayonets were inferior to those of the Allies.

The administrative and medical arrangements were disgraceful. In the long annals of the British army it would be difficult to find an occasion when a force was sent into battle lacking so many essentials for its welfare. This was largely due to forty years of peace during which time the emphasis was almost entirely on the naval arm, the army tending to be neglected. The disbanding of the Royal Wagon Train and Staff Corps after the Napoleonic wars was now seen to have been a particularly retrograde step. This belief in a purely garrison army inevitably had its effect on readiness for battle, and the quality of leadership. Discipline, however, had not suffered, for constant ceremonial and drill parades took precedence over field training. Only the handful of officers old enough to have fought in the Napoleonic wars, and those few who had served in India, had any experience of active service.

The army was commanded by Lord Raglan, who had lost an arm at Waterloo when on the Duke of Wellington's staff. He was now sixty-six, and although he had been on the fringes of high command he had never actually exercised it, having spent most of his service in an administrative capacity. He was always charming and courteous, and his courage was second to none. Throughout the battle he would lead his staff into the most uncomfortable places, always remaining steadfast and indomitable in peril.

Of the divisional commanders whose divisions bore the brunt of the fighting at the Alma two, Sir George Brown and Sir George de Lacy

Evans, had fought in the Peninsular campaign. Brown, who commanded the Light Division, was probably the most hated peacetime officer in the army, for his ideas of discipline went far beyond the norm – which in all conscience was harsh enough – and he was extremely fond of applying the lash. But his unparalleled bravery in battle won him many admirers, if not friends. The Duke of Cambridge, who commanded the 1st Division, was the grandson of George III; he had seen no active service, but he possessed many of the qualities that make for a good commander. The French were commanded by Marshal St Arnaud, who had gained his position through helping Louis Napoleon to the throne. He was in bad health,* and although he had battle experience he was quite unfitted for high command.

While the Allied armies were in Turkey the Russians had invaded the two principalities, and were heading for Constantinople. It was therefore decided to move both armies to Varna on the south-west coast of the Black Sea, which was some sixty miles from Silistria, then being besieged by the Russians. The move was made at the end of May and beginning of June, and with it came the most frightful epidemic of cholera, which claimed thousands of victims in both armies. The gallant defence of Silistria by the Turks, and the threat from Austria – who had assembled a large army on the frontier – persuaded the Russians to withdraw their troops across the border. There now seemed little reason for further hostilities, but the British public would not hear of peace until Sebastopol had been taken and the Russian fleet destroyed. Louis Napoleon was perfectly happy to go along with this jingoism in the pursuit of glory, and so early in September the Allied armies were despatched to the Crimea.

The place that Lord Raglan selected for disembarkation was an ideal beach in Kalamita Bay some twenty miles south of Eupatoria and thirty miles north of Sebastopol. The landing of the three armies, which was unopposed, began on the morning of 14 September and took almost five days to complete. On the beach all was chaos and confusion, men and horses† jumbled together, no organization, no tents on the first night, and the rain came down in torrents. Transport was virtually non-existent. However before the army marched on the morning of the 19th a number of very rickety local carts, sufficient to carry three days' hard rations and reserve ammunition, had been pressed into service, but tents and heavy equipment had to be left behind.

The Turks marched on the extreme right along the coast, and then came the French. The British troops marched in column on a two-

*St Arnaud died a few days after the battle, and was succeeded in command by his senior divisional commander, General Canrobert.

† All the horses had been sent from England by sail and had suffered terribly from the effects of the journey and lack of water.

division front. The 2nd Division was on the right, marching to the left of Prince Napoleon's division, and the Light Division was on the left. Behind the 2nd Division came the 3rd, and in rear of the Light Division was the Duke of Cambridge's 1st Division of Guards and Highlanders. One brigade of the 4th Division (the other had been left at Kalamita Bay) followed some distance in rear and echeloned to the left of the 1st Division. The infantry (less the 4th Division) were therefore advancing in two parallel columns sufficiently spaced to allow for deployment into line, and with Riflemen on the flanks and in front. Somewhat in advance of the infantry were regiments of Lord Cardigan's Light Brigade (the Heavy Brigade had been left at Varna). The 13th Light Dragoons in skirmishing order, and the 11th Hussars with a troop of Horse artillery, were in the van, and some way to the left of the army were the other two regiments (8th Hussars and 17th Lancers) of the brigade.

It was a brave display of scarlet tunics, bayonets sparkling in the sun, drums beating and Colours carried proudly aloft, but looks were a trifle deceptive. Cholera still stalked the army, and men were dropping out from sickness and lack of water (exacerbated by the salted pork ration) on this very hot day.

At about 2 p.m. the Bulganak river was reached, and Lord Raglan ordered the cavalry to investigate a party of Cossacks who were hovering on the far bank. It was soon realized that these Cossacks screened a reconnaissance in force of cavalry and infantry. Raglan hastily ordered the four squadrons to withdraw, for they were hopelessly outnumbered and to have attacked would have been disastrous. Some gunfire was exchanged but little damage done, and despite an unseemly, but not unusual, argument between Lord Lucan and his brother-in-law Lord Cardigan the cavalry carried out a well-executed disengagement. The army stood to arms that night on the south bank of the river, but an expected Russian attack never developed.

The advance to battle was continued on the morning of the 20th with the Turks and French somewhat ahead of the British divisions. On the previous night Marshal St Arnaud had produced a completely unrealistic battle plan, whereby General Bosquet's right division and the Turks were to roll up the Russian left, while the British performed a similar feat on the Russian right. At that stage all the commanders knew about the terrain, the Russian position and their numbers was what little they had been able to see from the ships as they sailed up the coast. Lord Raglan, who had no intention of carrying out his part of this plan, had been politely noncommittal.

At about 11 a.m. the Russian position came into view on the heights above the Alma river, and soon afterwards the army was halted. It was now possible for the generals to go forward and make a proper appreciation. The ground on the north side of the river sloped down quite gently

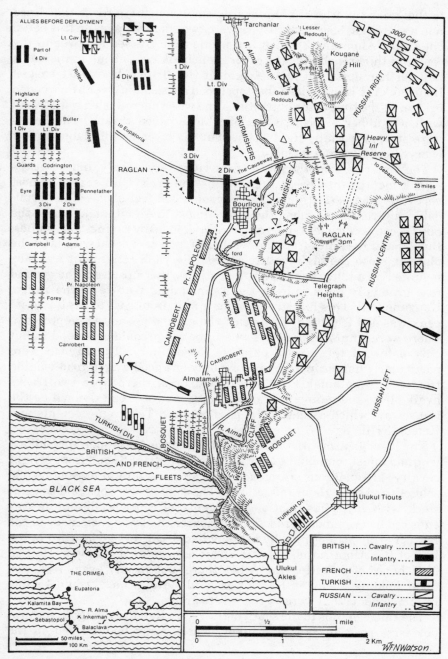

The Battle of the Alma: 20 September 1854

to the green luxuriance of vineyards and colourful gardens that lined much of the northern bank. There were two small villages on this bank, one called Almatamak which lay a mile from the sea and was in the centre of the French line; the other, Bourliouk, was about a mile and a half farther upstream at the right of the British line. Just east of Bourliouk the Eupatoria–Sebastopol road crossed the river by a wooden bridge. At the time of the battle the Alma was a narrow, sluggish stream with a number of pools, some of which proved trappy. The banks were steep, especially the left one, but the river was fordable almost everywhere except at its mouth.

The land rose from the south of the river very steeply. Indeed at the river's mouth what became known as the West Cliff soared almost vertically to a perfectly flat plateau some 350 feet above. This formidable cliff continued along the river almost to Almatamak, where the bluff became much less steep and was broken up by ravines and gullies. But some three miles from the West Cliff, and connected with it by the plateau, stood the high feature called Telegraph Heights (it was surmounted by a telegraph tower), and still farther upstream the ground rose gradually for a mile to the commanding feature of the range, Kouganè Hill. This hill stretched for a mile from east to west, and its peak was 450 feet high. To its east the ground presented no problem. There were a number of places where the range could be ascended, but only a few of these were passable for artillery. The French were particularly handicapped by having only one good wagon road leading from the Almatamak ford, but at Bourliouk there were two tracks available to the gunners, besides the Sebastopol road (known as the Causeway) which ascended the pass between Telegraph Heights and Kouganè Hill.

The Russian army was commanded by Prince Alexander Menshikov, who had under command 42 battalions of infantry, 16 squadrons of light cavalry, 11 squadrons of Cossacks and 48 guns, a total force of 38,000 soldiers and a few thousand sailors.* The soldiers were of stolid peasant stock with little imagination but plenty of courage; discipline was enforced by even more Draconian measures than was customary in the British army at the time. Menshikov had decided to go forward to the line of the Alma rather than to await a siege in Sebastopol. He had high hopes of defeating the Allies there, but in any event reckoned upon holding them at bay for several days, which would enable reinforcements that were on the way to arrive.

The range of hills to the south of the river offered a very good natural defensive position, but Menshikov, whose army had arrived on the

*Figures from Seaton, pp. 56, 61, 62.

heights on 14 September, had not personally reconnoitred the position. He was told that the West Cliff was impregnable, and so beyond placing a battalion and four guns in the small village of Ulukul Akles he had no troops west of Almatamak – a serious error. The Russians had done virtually no digging nor created any earthworks in the five days prior to the battle, the only exception being a breast-high earthwork on the north-west slope of Kouganè Hill to shelter a field battery of twelve guns, and a similar, but smaller, work to the right and rear near the crest of the hill. These two gun emplacements were grandiloquently called by the British the Great and Lesser Redoubts. The Russians fought the battle in close columns of companies, a ponderous, unwieldy formation that was at a disadvantage in manoeuvre and fire power.

Having made the initial error of leaving the west undefended, Menshikov covered the ground from opposite Almatamak to the east of Kouganè Hill quite skilfully. He had eight battalions bordering the river near Telegraph Heights, and on that feature he placed four battalions with two batteries that had a clear field of fire over the forward troops. On the Causeway, as it climbed to the plateau, he sited two light batteries of sixteen guns and a further four battalions. Higher up the road were seven more battalions and two batteries intended as a tactical reserve, but they were too close to the forward troops for this purpose. There were sixteen battalions dispersed around Kouganè Hill, including four from the Kazan regiment that flanked the Great Redoubt. Besides the guns in the two redoubts there was a Don Cossack battery on the southern slopes of the hill. The cavalry were massed on the right flank.

In spite of being able to see the position quite clearly the two Allied commanders appear to have been unable to arrive at a concerted plan, and at 1 p.m. the British army resumed its march to the river. At the same time a Russian gun opened up. The battle of the Alma had begun, and although this particular gun had fired short Lord Raglan judged it the time for the two leading divisions to deploy into line. Never an easy operation with a huge number of men, the manoeuvre on this occasion was made more difficult because during the march the columns of both armies had slightly lost direction. The 2nd Division was being pressed to its left by the French, and the Light Division was out of its ground. The result was that units of the 2nd Division overlapped those of the Light Division, and this led to some brigade deviations in the forthcoming battle.

The advance continued with the divisions in rear still marching in column, but soon round-shot, bouncing and skidding away across the hard ground like huge cricket balls, was beginning to reach them, and the 1st Division was given the order to deploy. The 3rd Division remained in column and fell back to come alongside the incomplete 4th

Division, while the 1st Division extended its line to overlap the rear of both leading divisions.

Lord Raglan was still ignorant of French intentions, but he imagined that Bosquet, who was nearing the river, would follow St Arnaud's original plan and endeavour to turn the Russian left. The remainder of the French were still in column, and marching roughly parallel to his own troops. He therefore decided to await the French attack on the Russian left before crossing the river and assaulting their right and centre. Meanwhile, as the Russian gunners were getting the range of his leading troops they were ordered to lie down.

The battle of the Alma, although it lasted for only a few hours, cannot be told briefly in detail. It was not fought to any overall plan, and indeed the Commander-in-Chief had virtually no control of it after the troops had crossed the river – although Lord Raglan's personal intervention at one point was of vital importance. It was not a soldiers' battle to the extent that Inkerman was, for divisional and brigade commanders influenced its course at certain stages, but much of the fighting was done on an independent battalion level. In outline it is best told in four phases, which were to a considerable extent interlocking – the French attack on the Russian left, the British capture of the Great Redoubt, their repulse, and the final assault by the Guards and Highlanders.

The part played by the French in the battle is fairly simply told, because Prince Menshikov in making his dispositions had completely neglected their front. General Bosquet, whose 2nd Division was to turn the enemy's left flank, sent General Bouat's brigade and the Turks to cross the river at its mouth by a difficult passage across the sandbar, while he accompanied the other brigade across the ford at Almatamak. Bouat's men took some time to cross the river, and then had to make a steep and tortuous ascent up the cliff along a very narrow track. Their guns had to be sent to the track opposite Almatamak, and the brigade did not reach the plateau until the battle was almost over.

General Autemarre's brigade on the other hand had a fairly easy and, like Bouat's, unopposed ascent, and with the Zouaves – always bursting for a fight – well in advance, his men gained the plateau before any enemy were about. The Russians, when they realized what was happening, ordered their detachment at Ulukel Akles to move forward, and their four guns caused a few casualties. Later General Kiriakov, commanding the Russian 17th Division, brought some artillery up, but by that time Autemarre had his own guns ready to neutralize them. Menshikov himself, in a moment of panic, galloped to the scene and ordered the reserve battalions to follow him, but when they arrived he decided the French threat was not so great as the British and turned them back. Autemarre's brigade remained in its position on the plateau.

St Arnaud had ordered that as soon as Bosquet's men appeared on the plateau the 1st and 3rd Divisions (commanded by Canrobert and Prince Napoleon respectively) were to cross the river. Canrobert was to ford it about a mile upstream of Almatamak and ascend the cliff by what seemed to be a reasonable track, and Napoleon was to cross with his division just below Bourliouk. Canrobert found he could not get his artillery up the track, and had to send it back to Almatamak where it was delayed through one of Autemarre's guns having blocked the path. As it was axiomatic in the French army that you did not attack without the support of artillery Canrobert halted his men along the sides of the ravine, where they were protected from the enemy guns on Telegraph Heights which had been causing some casualties during the river crossing. Prince Napoleon's division never even crossed the river at this stage, but coming under heavy cannon fire the battalions sought shelter in the gardens and vineyards of the north bank.

When around 3 p.m. the two leading British divisions were engaged in fierce combat with the Russian centre and right the French were almost in a state of suspended animation, and except for an artillery duel on the plateau had not been in action. St Arnaud, instead of ordering Canrobert to ascend the plateau with or without guns, thought he could best support Bosquet by bringing up a brigade from his 4th Division. This achieved nothing, and merely made the crossing places and tracks even more congested. Four battalions of Prince Napoleon's division were at last across the river, but Canrobert's men were still in the ravine awaiting their artillery to gain the heights.

The final scene on the plateau west of the Eupatoria road gave the French some cause for satisfaction, although their own account differs somewhat from most of the others. When the battle was at its height General Kiriakov led eight battalions to drive Canrobert's men back across the river. Canrobert declined battle and retired down the track towards the river, but at much the same time his guns, concealed from both friend and foe, arrived at the top of the escarpment, and the officer in command seeing the Russian columns in a solid mass sent ball and canister screaming into them. Lacking their own artillery support the eight battalions made haste to withdraw, and joined the beginning of what became a general Russian retreat.

The men of Canrobert's division learning of their gunners' success swarmed up the ravine, and the Zouaves – as always to the fore – soon had their Colours proudly displayed on the Telegraph tower. The French say they were not in fact driven from the ravine, but on the contrary closed with the eight battalions in a deadly hand-to-hand combat in which they lost a great many men before clearing the enemy from the field. But this is not borne out by the official casualty figures.

When Lord Raglan saw that the French were making little or no progress, he decided to abandon his original plan and take the risk of going forward on his own. At about 2.30 p.m. he gave orders for the 2nd and Light Divisions to advance. Men of the Rifle Brigade had been ranging ahead and engaged with Russian skirmishers who had occupied, and prepared for burning, Bourliouk village. This they achieved, although the Riflemen drove them across the river before they could destroy the bridge. Much attention was paid to the dressing of the line by the many drill sergeants, but the array was somewhat spoilt through the right brigade (General Adams) of the 2nd Division having to split to avoid the burning village. Two battalions went to the west of the village, but the third (the 47th) advanced on its eastern side, thereby closing on General Pennefather's brigade which now had four somewhat bunched battalions.

The first objective was the left bank of the river; beyond that little was known and no plan could be made. The steady advance of disciplined, well-drilled ranks stretching for almost two miles spurred the Russian gunners into rapid action, and the left brigade of the 2nd Division had a front that could be commanded by many of their guns. The rumbling thunder of iron shot echoed flatly from the hills and crashed about the garden walls. Soon wide gaps and shapeless heaps appeared in the lines. This heavy concentration of fire and the difficulty encountered in passing the burning village meant that the Light Division, which was not so heavily engaged, was the first across the river and into action. Five thousand men tried to sort themselves out on the broad ledge of the southern bank, where for a time they were safe from cannon, although spasmodic volleys of enfiladed musket fire caused casualties.

On the division's extreme left General Buller's brigade found more open country and a receding line of hills. No orders being received, he took it upon himself to safeguard the open flank against cavalry by forming square. Two of his battalions therefore did not go forward with the divisions; the third had become detached in the overall confusion and had joined General Codrington's brigade. Codrington was shortly to lose the 7th (Royal Fusiliers), who under their blood-and-thunder colonel, Lacy Yea (pronounced Yaw), were to drift away to fight a gallant action on their own, but in the original distortion of the lines this brigade had somehow gained the 95th from the 2nd Division.

Codrington, a good fighting soldier, would welcome any man or battalion that would follow him, and he had very soon ridden his white horse up the bank to lead his brigade through a hell of whistling metal and exploding shells towards the Great Redoubt. On both sides of this key point stood two battalion columns of the Kazan regiment, placed as it were in a funnel to challenge the attackers to enter their trap. For a time the Russian guns were silent, but when Codrington's men were closing the enemy gunners opened up a tremendous fire. Sponging out

reeking barrels and ramming down shot they kept up a steady cannonade for several minutes, while all the time the Kazan muskets were
doing what damage they could. But troops in line have greater fire
power than those in column, and beset by Major Norcott's Riflemen on
their flank and Codrington's men to their front the left column of the
Kazan regiment was being forced back, while Yea's Royal Fusiliers
were fiercely engaged with the right column.

The brigade was suffering grievous casualties, but it pressed forward
inexorably towards its objective, which by now was almost concealed by
a sulphur fog of powder smoke and dust. But as this cleared the British
could see that the Russian gunners, their sweat-streaked faces black-
ened with smoke, were limbering up and making off, for they knew their
Tsar did not tolerate a gun lost. General Codrington, miraculously
untouched, leapt his charger on to the parapet, and an ensign of the 23rd
rushed forward to place the Queen's Colour of his regiment upon it.
Sadly he was shot down, but the Great Redoubt had been captured.

The Russians had suffered a setback, but it was only a temporary one.
They would come again in strength on the British left. Meanwhile,
Colonel Yea's men were struggling to overcome the right-hand Kazan
column, and the Causeway guns were keeping the 2nd Division from
ascending the plateau. The 1st Division was not in close support, which
meant that the five battalions of the Light Division that had successfully stormed the Great Redoubt were now in grave peril, and in no
position to resist a strong counterattack.

The lack of immediate support for the Light Division stemmed from
inexperience and failure in command. When Lord Raglan ordered the
two leading divisions to advance to the river, and the Duke of
Cambridge to support the Light Division, they were his last executive
commands in the battle. The Duke had had no battle experience, and
once he had got his division across the river he felt the need for further
orders. But by then Lord Raglan was out of touch with the battle. He and
his staff had crossed the river between the British right and French left,
and ascended the ravine seemingly oblivious of the fact that they were
riding through and into the Russian lines. Here, on a curious-shaped
ledge, the Commander-in-Chief was to be seen by an amazed friend and
foe alike calmly surveying the battlefield,* and despatching aides to
bring up guns to his fortuitously found vantage point. But luckily his
quartermaster-general, General Airey, had seen how critical was the
situation and took it upon himself to instruct His Royal Highness, in
Lord Raglan's name, to advance immediately.

But it was too late to prevent Codrington's men, and a battalion from

---

*The telescope used by Lord Raglan, mounted on a skeleton-framed musket for his one
arm, can be seen in the National Army Museum, Chelsea.

Buller's brigade which had joined them, from being forced out of the Great Redoubt. Directly after its capture there had, inevitably, been considerable chaos with men milling about trying to find their units and crowding into the Redoubt for protection, which in fact was unwise, for Russian gunners in the Lesser Redoubt and on Kouganè Hill soon got the range. Moreover, there were sixteen fresh battalions poised to advance against them. When the first of these men, from the Vladimir regiments, appeared from the slopes of Kouganè Hill they were (although there was no similarity in dress) thought to be French, and the order went out not to fire. No sooner had the error been realized than confusion was worse confounded by some bugler being ordered to sound the 'retire' call, which was shortly taken up by others. What was at first an orderly retirement deteriorated into a disorganized tumble down the hill under pressure from heavy Russian musket fire. General Codrington, appreciating the seriousness of the situation, had sent a message to hasten troops from the 1st Division, and as the first of these appeared they were rolled back by the tide of retreating men.

At this juncture (it was about 3 p.m.) the battle was shaping none too well for the Allies. The French on the Russian left had yet to get to grips with the enemy; the British 2nd Division was still partly pinned down by the Causeway guns; the Light Division had been pushed back, temporarily disrupting the advance of the Scots Fusilier Guards; and there were at least 5,000 Russians preparing to advance. Only the Royal Fusiliers were still fighting, hanging on with commendable tenacity.

The crisis of the battle was now at hand, and the 1st Division was to play a decisive part in restoring the situation and preparing the way for final victory. The division advanced with the Guards Brigade under General Bentinck on the right, and the Highland Brigade under General Sir Colin Campbell on the left. The Scots Fusilier Guards, the centre battalion of the Guards Brigade, had gained the top of the bank slightly ahead of the other two battalions, but without their Left Flank company which – with the Coldstream – had had to cross the river three times owing to an S-bend. They had answered General Codrington's call, but when they were some fifty yards from the Great Redoubt they came under heavy fire, and were seriously buffeted by the men in retreat. They were thrown back, but soon resumed their former position in the line.

Meanwhile, the Grenadiers on the right and the Coldstream on the left came forward. High and proud was their bearing as they advanced in perfectly dressed lines towards the enemy. Only a little way behind the Coldstream and to their left came the three battalions of the Highland Brigade – the 42nd on the right then the 93rd and the 79th on the left – men as tough and hardy as any that fought that day. The gap between the two Guards battalions was quickly closed partly by those companies of the Scots Fusilier Guards that had rallied at once, and partly by some 300 men of the Light Division that Codrington had collected. The epic fight of the Royal Fusiliers, assisted by the 95th, against the two Kazan battalions had now been brought to a successful conclusion, and Yea was eager to pursue. But Sir George Brown, whose wounded horse had carried him most gallantly through some of the thickest fighting, ordered him to retire his sadly mauled battalion and let the Guards go through.

The defeat of the Russian masses in the fight that now ensued was very largely due to the superiority of line formation over column, for this was a fire fight not a hand-to-hand one. The Russians outnumbered the 1st Division by many thousands, but so great was the fire power of the two brigades, coming into battle almost simultaneously, that the enemy were first halted in their tracks, with men sinking to the ground in tangled heaps, and then thrown into disarray and precipitous retreat. On the left the Russians were also making a hasty withdrawal, for the two brigades of the 2nd Division had by now been in action for a little while, and Canrobert's Frenchmen had at last gained the heights.

But all was not quite over. At the eastern end of the Kouganè Hill there were still four fresh battalions of the Uglitz regiment, whose colonel had drawn them up across their retreating comrades, and 3,500 cavalry, which had taken no part in the battle, were waiting on the wings. The Light Brigade, like the Russian cavalry, had also done no fighting and now, acting without orders, Lord Lucan brought them up together with a battery of Horse artillery on the army's left, and the guns went into action at the soft target of some 10,000 Russians gathered together in a huge mass. Had there been time to get these men into proper formation so that they could be led into battle there would have been another hard fight before victory had been gained, for throughout the afternoon the Russian soldiers had resisted with the utmost constancy and courage. But when gunners on both sides of them emptied shot into their midst, shivering their vulnerable ranks like cornstalks, the last bonds of discipline snapped and they joined the stream across the plateau making for the safety of Sebastopol.

As the last Russian gun fired a single round in defiance, Colonel Gough Calthorpe looked at his watch and saw it was 3.40 p.m. The war correspondent W. H. Russell said the battle ended just before 5 p.m. This discrepancy in time is not of great moment. The fact is the battle was over in a few hours of very severe fighting. The Russians stated their losses as 5,709 killed and wounded, the French lost 60 men killed and 500 wounded, and the British casualties were 2,002 of which 362 men were killed. The state of the wounded was pitiable; there were far too few surgeons with quite inadequate equipment, and so most of the seriously wounded died. Some of the Russians lay on the field for more than twenty-four hours before attention could be given them.

There was to be no pursuit. The Light Brigade was in an excellent position to ride down the fast-fleeing Russians, and the British 3rd and 4th Divisions were fresh and eager for battle. But Lord Raglan, much to Lucan's bitterly expressed fury, was not prepared to risk his small number of sabres against a greatly superior Russian force, and Marshal St Arnaud refused to join in any full-scale pursuit. The French had taken off their packs before crossing the river, and the Marshal said they could not go forward without them. Lord Raglan, having urged the need for joint action, feared the political consequences of taking too much of the glory for the British.

The Alma was a decisive battle only in so far as, had it been lost, the Allies would have been driven off the peninsula and very likely there would have been no Crimean War. Therefore in considering the decisive factors of the battle the behaviour of the Russian commander should be examined. Prince Menshikov's decision to hold the line of the Alma rather than to await the Allies in Sebastopol was undoubtedly right, but could he have won the battle by offensive action on the Bulganak? His reconnaissance in force must have shown him that the British army was not in good shape to resist an attack by superior numbers of cavalry and infantry swinging in on its left flank. About the French he had less information, but roll up the left of the line and all three armies could have been driven into a corner from which neither the guns of the fleet nor the re-embarkation facilities could have saved them.

There were risks, of course, but a more enterprising and experienced commander might well have taken them, and with every chance of success. But perhaps an even better opportunity was missed at the crisis of the battle. When the Light Division had been forced back, and the 1st Division was with some difficulty fording the river, an attack on the Allied left with his large cavalry force combined with a frontal thrust by the many battalions on Kouganè Hill that had not yet been committed, might not have won Menshikov the battle but it could have gone very close to doing so.

That much is speculation, but in the fighting there were two factors, one of which was decisive while the other contributed considerably to the victory. They were the line formations adopted by the British divisions, and the guns that Lord Raglan ordered up to the jutting outcrop on which he watched the battle.

The Russians had never fought in line and Menshikov based his plan on defence by counterattack in column. There were to be no entrenchments, no dependence on rifle fire – although cannon were to play an important role – but principally avalanche attacks with the bayonet. The Russians still held to Suvorov's dictum, 'the bullet is a fool, but the bayonet a fine fellow'. The plan never got underway in time to oppose the river crossing, and later was defeated by the foolish bullet. Major Chodasevitch, writing of the battle, was to say about the British line: 'We had never before seen troops fight in line two deep, nor did we think it possible for men to be found with sufficient firmness of morale to be able to attack in this apparently weak formation our massive columns.'

The value of line over column can be shown by simple mathematics. In a formation of 1,000 strong the regiment drawn up in two lines can bring 500 rifles to bear on a column. Assuming a column of eight files facing to a flank it can then discharge 125 musket shots, if advancing head-on only eight. This preponderance of fire power enabled the Royal Fusiliers to take on and defeat the columns of the Kazan regiment which had twice the number of muskets; during the advance of the 1st Division two Guards battalions, separated a little distance from each other, out-gunned four Vladimir battalions and remnants of the Kazan regiment.

There are, of course, certain limitations to line formation. It can be used only in open country, and it depends very much on a perfect alignment to enable each man to have a wide angle of fire. It was therefore as much for its virtues as for its vanities that divisional commanders insisted on halting and dressing the lines at the crossing of the Alma. A further disadvantage was evident at the time of the Light Division's repulse from the Great Redoubt. Men advancing in line are more likely to be swamped than those advancing in columns which can be infiltrated. Nevertheless, the enormous value of line over column was clearly shown in this battle.

When Lord Raglan, with his entourage, decided to ride ahead of his army crossing the river – greatly amazing the French skirmishers as he rode through them – the party came under considerable enfilade fire which caused two casualties to his staff, and might well have wiped them out had the Russians not been firing high. However, they rode on along a track that became ever steeper until, quite by chance, they found a ledge jutting out from the hillside, which had been recently oc-cupied by the enemy, but was now isolated and seemingly out of range of their guns. It offered a splendid view of much of the battlefield, and was large enough to hold cannon which could, as Lord Raglan was quick to see, reach at least two of the Russian batteries from the elevated position.

Urgent messages were sent to Adams's brigade to detach guns for this purpose, and after some delay* – due to a gun overturning and blocking the track when a wheel-horse was killed – two 9-pounders of Captain Turner's battery arrived. For some unexplained reason they had come short of gunners, but were brought into action by Colonel Dickson, who was on the staff of the Commander Royal Artillery. The immediate target was the Causeway batteries, and the first two shots fell short. But then Dickson and his assistant gunner got the range and sent a ball into a tumbril, killing two horses, followed by another straight into the battery itself. This brief, but quite unexpected, enfilade fire was enough to make the Russian commander give orders to limber up, and the entire sixteen guns withdrew in good order to another position higher up the hill.

By then Captain Turner had arrived in person with two more guns and the complete gun team. After they had hastened the departure of the Causeway batteries the guns turned their attention to the seven battalions of heavy infantry that formed Menshikov's tactical reserve. These troops were well within range astride the Eupatoria road, and as they were massed in columns a great deal of damage was done before they withdrew. But the battery and troops in and around the Great Redoubt were just out of range of the 9-pounders. However, at the time when the Light Division was being pushed back, and the 1st Division was coming into action, the gunners loaded and reloaded with canister and ball which they pitched sufficiently close to cause General Kvetzenski, commanding the Russian right, to halt the advance of his columns at the critical moment of the battle.

Lord Raglan has been criticized for taking up this position of considerable danger from where he was quite unable to issue commands. But there is no doubt that, admittedly quite fortuitously, he was in fact able to influence the course of the battle to a much greater extent than had he remained in a more orthodox command post. The removal of the Causeway guns was all that de Lacy Evans needed to enable him to cross the river and go into action with the three regiments (30th, 47th and 55th) of his division which hitherto had been pinned down and out of the fight. Moreover, General England, commanding the 3rd Division in reserve, had offered him his artillery, and so Evans came in on the left of the Russian centre – where the Royal Fusiliers were so fiercely engaged – with something like thirty cannon. Turner's guns were also partly responsible for the ineffectiveness of Menshikov's reserves, and they had given the 1st Division the time it needed to get into its stride for the final advance.

---

*Colonel Gough Calthorpe, who was present on Raglan's staff, says the guns were ordered up before the party reached the ledge, for Raglan was so sure they could be used to bring enfilade fire on the forward troops. Other accounts say the order was not given until he reached the vantage point.

For this reason, if for no other, Lord Raglan's contribution to the victory should not be belittled. His generalship has come in for much armchair censure over the years, and among other things it is often suggested that instead of an uninspired frontal attack he should have rolled up the Russian right flank into the waiting French. But that would have involved a long detour over unreconnoitred ground with an army weakened by disease, short of water and on limited rations. Even Menshikov might have been tempted to swoop upon it with his great preponderance of cavalry.

The fact remains that Lord Raglan won the battle, and he would have been the first to give the credit for this to the incredible courage and tenacity of purpose displayed throughout by all ranks, and to the magnificent leadership of the regimental officers and non-commissioned officers.

Courage, resilience and patient endurance by the troops of both sides were the hallmarks of this battle. Lord Raglan was uninspiring, and Prince Menshikov was unintelligent. And so it could be said that the British gained the victory through the bravery of all ranks, and superior tactics; the Russians lost it through incompetent leadership.

---

14 The American Civil War 1861–1865
Background to the Seven Days' Battle

THE American Civil War, or the War Between the States, as it is more usually called by the American people, started in the early hours of 12 April 1861 when Confederate batteries opened fire on Fort Sumter – a fortress built on a shoal to guard the entrance to Charleston harbour. The next day the Federal commander surrendered, and on the 14th he and his small garrison marched out of the fort with the full honours of war. What was to be a long and bitter struggle, with all the tragic consequences of a civil war, became inevitable.

The Confederate States of America established their government first in Montgomery, Alabama, and a little later in Richmond, Virginia, and they elected a soldier turned politician called Jefferson Davis to be their President. In Washington President Lincoln had taken office at the head of a Republican administration just a month before Fort Sumter, and he went to war primarily to preserve the Union. Eleven slave-holding states of the South had recently seceded, ostensibly because they considered their sovereign rights under the constitution had been violated, but *au fond* it was fear of the abolition of slavery that drove them to this step.

As the two sides clattered into war neither realized how long the struggle would last nor how cruel the losses would be. The United States army numbered little more than 13,000 officers and men, and the state militias were outdated and regarded with derision. There was a situation not entirely dissimilar to that which existed in the Indian army at the time of partition in 1947 when Hindu and Moslem officers found themselves with divided loyalties. So it was for some 300 United States army officers, who although in many cases set great store by the Union decided that their allegiance to their state came first.

Both sides entered the war entirely unprepared, and both armies had to resort to a *levée en masse*, obtained first from volunteers and later by conscription. The difficulty was not in procuring recruits, but in arming and equipping them. This was especially so for the South whose industrial capacity could not match that of the North. Training for the Southerners was also a problem, for many of the senior non-commissioned officers were of German or Irish extraction, and having no state ties remained loyal to the government, while the officers who had 'defected' to the South were mostly needed to fill technical and staff positions.

When war broke out the overall commander of the United States forces was General Winfield Scott, who was an old and virtually immobile seventy-five. But he had been a good general, and he was sufficiently perspicacious to see that although the war could be lost (as it nearly was) in the east it would be won eventually (as indeed it was) in the west. However, Lincoln was right to remove him soon after the Federal defeat in the first major engagement of the war. Until almost the end of the war the North suffered from dissension among its senior generals, and constant obfuscation of command led to frequent changes in the higher echelons.

The most outstanding general of the South, and arguably the most outstanding of either army, was Robert E. Lee, who was one of those regular soldiers who had resigned his commission to fight for his native state of Virginia. Appointed Commander-in-Chief of the State Militia, he was unsuccessful in his campaign in West Virginia, but Davis knew his worth and he rendered his President good service as his military adviser before being appointed to command what became known as the Army of Northern Virginia when General Joseph Johnston was wounded. Lee was a general who never lost the offensive spirit, and time and again he proved a master of manoeuvre. Moreover, he possessed those two important attributes of a successful commander – the will to win and the ability to inspire confidence. His principal fault was, perhaps, to trust far too much in the ability and willingness of his subordinates, which led him at times to issue discretionary orders. The Confederate field armies had independent commanders until February 1865, when Lee was appointed to supreme command.

The first important battle was fought on 21 July 1861, when General Scott sent five divisions under General Irwin McDowell to seize the important Manassas Junction just south of Washington. The Confederates were commanded by General Beauregard, and Scott had hoped that McDowell would defeat him before General Johnston's troops could come up from the Shenandoah Valley. But in the event Johnston was able to join forces with Beauregard, and the Confederates took up a strong defensive position. Both sides were fighting with untrained recruits, and in such circumstances the defenders had the advantage. After some initial success the Federal troops were severely defeated.

In November Scott was replaced in command by the young (he was thirty-five years old) and popular George B. McClellan. McClellan had been a government observer in the Crimean War (which cannot have helped him very much!), he had distinguished himself in the Mexico fighting, and he was fresh from a triumph in West Virginia. His was a most promising choice, but he never succeeded in fulfilling expectations, and very soon he had lost the confidence of his President and Secretary of War. He is chiefly remembered for the excellent work he did in training, organizing, and inspiring that fine fighting force the Army of the Potomac rather than for his prowess in the field. He was a man of considerable intellect, but little perception and no dynamic force. His plans were bold, but in execution his constant caution lost him battles that a more resolute general would have won.

McClellan remained inactive throughout the winter, for he was under the impression – quite erroneously, for his intelligence system was very bad – that Johnston, who remained strongly entrenched at Manassas, more than matched his own army in numbers and equipment. Lincoln soon became impatient at McClellan's inaction, and towards the end of February 1862 ordered him to make a move. And so McClellan planned an attack on Richmond by way of Urbano, a town at the mouth of the Rappahannock. The Confederate capital was only sixty miles away, and McClellan felt sure that Johnston would have to move from the Centerville area to meet the threat, and his line of withdrawal would be blocked. But Johnston pre-empted this plan by withdrawing to a position on the Rapidan. However, only with difficulty had McClellan persuaded Lincoln to permit an amphibious operation, and he was not prepared to forgo the chance. The Federal ironclad *Monitor* had recently neutralized the famous Confederate vessel *Merrimac*, and the navy reported Hampton Roads as safe. It was therefore decided to land at Fortress Monroe, and to advance on Richmond between the York and James rivers.

On disembarkation at the beginning of April McClellan had some 58,000 men from three corps, the IInd, IIIrd and IVth under generals Sumner, Heintzelman and Keyes respectively, a small cavalry force and about 100 guns. He knew that the Confederates held Yorktown, but he had no knowledge of the country nor reliable maps, and his head of Intelligence constantly misinformed him. He supposed, although he had no reason for doing so, that by a rapid march he could turn the Confederate position and defeat his enemy before Johnston could arrive with reinforcements. And so he did not wait for the rest of his army to join, but set off for Yorktown on 4 April.

In fact General Magruder had 30,000 Confederates behind fieldworks that stretched for some 13 miles across the breadth of the peninsula, and his position certainly could not be turned. Finding these defences too strong, McClellan decided upon a siege. The navy had made it clear to him that they were still too busy with the *Merrimac* to give the army any assistance, but McClellan intended bringing up his Ist Corps (General McDowell) to take Gloucester on the north bank of the York. However, he had scarcely left Fortress Monroe before he was informed from Washington that this corps was to be detained to safeguard the city. There was to be constant, and at times fractious, communication concerning this corps between McClellan and Secretary Stanton, and McClellan was certain that the withholding of it lost him Richmond. He may well have been right.

McClellan's immediate complaint was that Stanton held out hopes that McDowell could soon be spared, and therefore he (McClellan) was not to adopt his proposed line of advance up the James but to extend to his right so as to be on hand for McDowell. This was to mean splitting his army across the Chickahominy, a forty-foot-wide river bordered by swampy forest land. However, before that occurred there was to be a fight at Williamsburg. On 17th April Johnston arrived at Yorktown and took over command. He never intended the troops to withstand a lengthy siege, for once the *Merrimac* had been scuttled (rather than surrender) Federal gunboats could blast the Yorktown defences, and so on the night of 3 May the Confederate troops slipped quietly out of their lines, leaving the Federals in possession of some seventy-seven guns and ammunition for them.

McClellan, whose persistent importunities had eventually induced Lincoln to relent so far as to send him Franklin's division of McDowell's corps, caught up with the Confederates in their previously prepared position at Williamsburg – at least his troops did, for McClellan seemed to make a habit of missing battles, although no one could impugn his courage. In his absence, supervising the landing of more troops, General Sumner took command at what was an untidy battle fought by the Federals (mainly Hooker's division) without plan or concerted action. For a comparatively small affair the casualties on both sides were heavy, the Federals losing 2,228 men and the Confederates 1,500. Longstreet, who commanded the Confederates, disengaged on the night of 5 May and continued the withdrawal towards Richmond, with the Federals following at a leisurely pace.

McClellan set up his headquarters at the White House on the Pamunkey on 17 May, and here with the reinforcements he had received he organized two new corps – the Vth commanded by General Fitz-John Porter and the VIth by General Franklin. The Confederate garrisons of Norfolk and Gloucester had been withdrawn, and with the *Merrimac* out of the way the James was open to within six miles of Richmond. McClellan was still hopeful that McDowell would join him, and he felt confident that the Confederate capital would soon be his.

He did not, however, proceed towards his objective at any pace, and meanwhile Johnston had four strong divisions entrenched around Richmond on the south bank of the Chickahominy. On 20 May and again on the 25th McClellan sent a corps across the river, keeping the

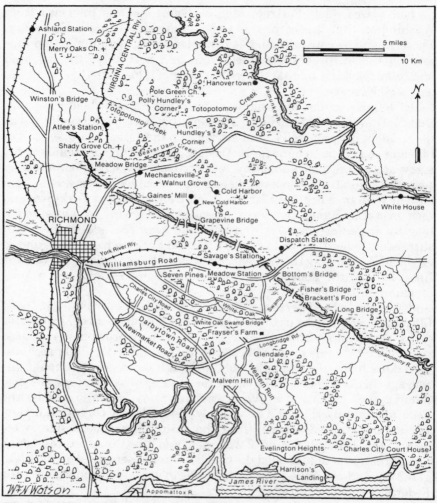

The Seven Days' Battle: 26 June–2 July 1862

remainder of his army on the north bank. On his right flank, in the area of Hanover Court House, there were two Confederate brigades (Anderson's and Branch's) which lay between him and McDowell. Even after McClellan learnt that he would not be receiving the remainder of McDowell's corps these troops had to be cleared, and this task was successfully undertaken by Porter's corps. This removed any immediate danger, but the right wing was still vulnerable, and the army precariously poised on two sides of the Chickahominy.

Johnston was not slow to take advantage of this favourable situation, and decided to attack. Originally he planned an offensive against the whole Federal line in the hope of encompassing its defeat before McDowell could arrive, but when he learnt (from a cavalry vedette) that McDowell was moving in an opposite direction he decided to attack the two corps on the south bank of the river at once. The battle of Seven Pines, or Fair Oaks, fought on 31 May–1 June was the first large-scale engagement of the campaign.

The country in which this battle, and indeed much of the campaign, was fought was pretty unpleasant. The Chickahominy was subject to fluctuations, and rainstorms – which were frequent – would cause a rapid rise that often washed away the bridges and made the river impassable. There were large tracts of scrub and thicket, and there was a certain amount of swamp. The valleys were crisscrossed with sluggish streams and dying vegetation, making camping sites unattractive and malarial. The tracks, especially in times of rain, were deep in mud. Fieldworks were built up – for which there was plenty of material – not dug down, and the two Federal corps about to be attacked were well prepared.

Seven Pines should have been a certain victory for the Confederates, but the ground was unstudied, the plan unformed and the commanders– headed by Longstreet – made a mess of it. In the end the result was indecisive, although the Federals claimed the victory. On the evening before the battle the rain poured down, making the Chickahominy almost – but not quite – impassable. On their right the Confederates eventually drove the Federal line back, and their attack here might have been decisive had Longstreet understood his orders and the staff work been better. As it was, Huger's division and six brigades of Longstreet's command never got into the fight. On the left the Confederates were also successful at first, but after a desperate struggle with the elements Sumner got his corps across the river, and entering the battle at about 5 p.m. drove the Confederates back and ended the day on their line. Thus both sides had some success on opposite wings. The next day Longstreet failed to carry out his orders correctly for an attack, and the Union troops made no move. The Confederate losses were around 6,000 and the Federals about 1,000 less.

The Confederate commander, General Johnston, had been severely wounded in the late evening of 31 May, and the command had devolved upon General G. W. Smith. As Johnston was being borne from the field President Davis, who had an instinctive affinity for the front line, was riding with General Lee to view the fighting. Having spoken to Smith and seen for himself what a fearful muddle the Confederate commanders were making of the battle, he decided to give Lee command of what now became the Army of Northern Virginia, whose exploits under their renowned chief were to vie with those of the Army of the Potomac.

Lee planned to take the offensive. After Seven Pines McClellan had transferred the rest of his army, less Porter's corps, to the south of the Chickahominy, and Lee was particularly aware of McClellan's weakened right wing. But first he needed to know the exact situation beyond Porter's right flank, and how and from where the Federals were being supplied. He was also interested in the Totopotomoy creek (a tributary of the Pamunkey river) across which he planned to bring reinforcements, and required general information as a guidance for future operations. Lee's cavalry commander was the young, picturesque, flamboyant but exceedingly capable Brigadier-General 'Jeb' Stuart to whom was entrusted, with many cautionary admonishments – for his excessive zeal was well known – this delicate mission.

A delighted Stuart rode away on 12 June at the head of three regiments numbering in all 1,200 sabres, and a section of horse artillery. In the course of four days he marched right round the Federal army, crossed the Chickahominy well below Bottom's Bridge and was back at Richmond by 15 June having covered 150 miles, destroyed a wagon train, brought back a number of prisoners and a wealth of information, all for the loss of one man. There had, however, been some unnecessary recklessness, and had the Federal cavalry not been so dispersed he might well have been cut off and severely mauled. As it was he had had to ask Lee for a diversion to prevent this. Moreover, he had alerted McClellan to the vulnerability of his lines of communication from the White House, and this was probably responsible for that general's decision to shift his base to the James river.

But Lee was happy to overlook his cavalry commander's minor peccadillos – indeed he commended this daring ride in general orders – for he had brought back an obviously accurate report of the enemy's positions, strengths, and limitations. From Stuart's observations it was clear to Lee that he could bring General Jackson from the Shenandoah valley, and launch his offensive against the Federal right with every prospect of success. The Seven Days' Battle was about to begin.

15   The Seven Days' Battle
26 June–2 July 1862

BETWEEN 26 June and 2 July there were fought four battles and one or two minor engagements which collectively became known as the Seven Days' Battle. Lee's opening move was a plan to wipe out Porter's corps (of somewhere around 30,000 men)* north of the Chickahominy by an enveloping movement against his right flank, before McClellan had time to reinforce him from south of the river. It was a plan of the boldest conception, for although it related strategy to what was tactically possible with the troops at his disposal, it left Richmond at McClellan's mercy. All but Magruder's command of 27,000 men were to be transferred to the north bank, and Magruder was left to defend Richmond against McClellan's force of almost three times his number. But it was not quite so rash as at first it seems, for Lee knew McClellan well (possibly the only advantage of fighting a civil war), and he was fairly certain that with his right being assailed he would fear to advance his left and centre.

An integral part of Lee's plan was the bringing of General Thomas ('Stonewall') Jackson's corps from the Shenandoah valley, where its successes had already gained its commander legendary fame. Jackson, who was later killed at Chancellorsville, was to become one of the folk-heroes of the war. He was indeed a strange man. Six feet tall, well built, with a luxuriant beard which partly concealed a face that reflected the pride and strength of the warrior, he was a strict disciplinarian, and an intensely religious man, who for his chief-of-staff selected a Presbyterian minister. It is not difficult to imagine Jackson animating his troops with one of the comminatory passages of the Old Testament. His modern counterpart was, perhaps, General Orde Wingate, and like him he was frugal in habit, sparing in conversation, and untidy in dress. Jackson was to play an important and enigmatic part in the forthcoming battles.

*In many of the Civil War battles contemporary and near-contemporary accounts of figures vary considerably. Porter's strength at Mechanicsville and later at Gaines's Mill is given by Henderson as 25,000 (p. 10), by Alexander as 'not over 30,000' (p. 112), and by Webb as only 19,864 (p. 129).

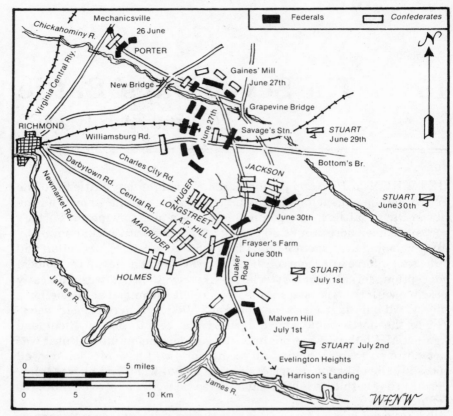

The Seven Days' Battle: 26 June–2 July 1862

Lee had written to him on 8 June suggesting that he should leave the valley to unite with Lee's troops before Richmond, having first taken steps to deceive the enemy as to his intention. Further letters on the 11th and 16th strengthened the suggestion into a command, urged speed and ingeminated the need for secrecy. To reinforce the deception plan Lee sent Whiting's division and Lawton's brigade ostensibly to strengthen the Valley Army, neither commander being told that they would have to turn round and march back again. On 23 June Jackson, after a long ride delayed through his strict principle of Sunday observance, met Lee at Fredericks Hall. His troops were following in twenty freight cars down the Virginia Central Railroad. Also present at this meeting were A. P. and D. H. Hill and Longstreet.

Lee explained to these generals that Richmond could not withstand a siege, and so in order to avoid this he must attack. The main Federal line was too strong and their artillery too powerful, and so it was necessary to launch the attack against Porter's corps. To destroy these troops would seriously threaten McClellan's lines of communication, and cause him either to leave his entrenchments and cross to the north bank of the river, where his army could be more easily dealt with, or to withdraw. If the latter, Lee thought and hoped that McClellan would head down the peninsula the way he had come, and he planned accordingly. But in this he was to be proved wrong.

Jackson was to be the linchpin of the attack, his troops were to turn Porter's right and to threaten his rear. He was to march from Ashland to Merry Oaks Church, cross the Totopotomoy creek and head towards Hundley's Corner and Cold Harbor. His role in the forthcoming battle was to hit the right of Porter's defences at Beaver Dam Creek; Stuart's cavalry would guard his left. A. P. Hill was to send a brigade (Branch's) up the Chickahominy to cross at Winston's Bridge and make for Mechanicsville. Branch was to make contact with Jackson, and as he advanced he would push in the enemy's outposts, and uncover Meadow Bridge. As soon as this had been accomplished A. P. Hill would cross the rest of his division at that bridge, clear the town and open up the Mechanicsville bridges for D. H. Hill and Longstreet. The former would then pass behind A. P. Hill's division and give support to Jackson. Longstreet's division would be the last to cross the river, and be in support of A. P. Hill.

The verbal orders (they were confirmed, rather ambiguously, in writing on 24 June) were quite clear to all except Jackson, upon whose movements the whole operation hinged. He, unlike the others, knew nothing of the country which although not so wet as the Chickahominy valley was well wooded, with numerous roads running in all directions on which a body of troops could easily mistake the way. Jackson said at first that he would be ready to attack on 25 June, but at Longstreet's instigation, and having been told something of the country, he wisely changed this to the 26th. In the written orders, therefore, he was instructed to cross the Virginia Central Railroad early that morning, and to make contact with General Branch who would then cross the Chickahominy as planned.

Lee had recently received reinforcements, and at the time of Mechanicsville – the first of the Seven Days' Battles – his total was in the region of 85,000 all arms. This included Jackson's troops which, together with Whiting's division and Lawton's brigade now with him, amounted to 18,500, and also those of Generals Holmes and Wise (8,000 men and 10 batteries)* which comprised the River James defence force. Lee now planned to bring against Porter's 30,000 some 56,000 men including Stuart's cavalry. He began his offensive only just in time, for

*Figures from Freeman, R. E. Lee, pp. 116, 117.

on 25 June McClellan had pushed his line forward preparatory to thrusting towards Richmond with two-thirds of his army.

Meanwhile, McClellan had been warned of Jackson's movements by a deserter, and Porter had been alerted to the possible danger on his right. His main position behind the left bank of Beaver Dam Creek was a very strong one with his left resting on the Chickahominy, and his right protected by dense woods beyond Mechanicsville. An advancing enemy would find his front and flanks exposed to batteries firing from well-constructed fieldworks. As the battle developed the Confederates were to discover this, and Jackson's turning movement failed to develop.

His men found marching conditions appalling. The streams were in spate after recent heavy rain, the bridges broken and no pioneers to mend them, and the roads were deep in mud. He eventually reached the Virginia Central Railroad at 9 a.m. on the 26th, six hours behind Lee's timetable. He met resistance at Totopotomoy creek, where the enemy destroyed the bridge before withdrawing, and it was not until 5 p.m. – several hours late – that he reached Hundley's Corner close to his appointed place in the line. Here he could hear the fighting to his south, but there was no sign of the troops that should have been on his right, and no orders reached him. Jackson therefore decided to bivouac for the night. Thus the troops which formed the key to unlock the defence played no part in the battle.

Jackson's failure to turn Porter's flank at Beaver Dam Creek ruined Lee's chances of victory, but the ensuing débâcle and the heavy casualties suffered by the Confederates was due to lamentable liaison between commanders, bad staff work and, above all, disregard of the orders by A. P. Hill. Branch had heard from Jackson at 9 a.m., but thereafter he received no reports. Imagining him to be well on his way to Hundley's Corner he took his brigade across the Chickahominy at about 10.30. He immediately turned south towards Atlee's Station and soon disposed of Federal skirmishers on his line of advance. At Atlee's Station his brigade was again in action, thereafter he lost touch with his divisional commander, although at one time they were on the same road only a mile apart. He had, however, contacted Ewell in the late afternoon, but Ewell (who had left Jackson after crossing the creek) was also groping in Cimmerian gloom, and A. P. Hill knew nothing of Jackson's, Ewell's, or Branch's movements. Such confusion among colleagues can only cause chaos.

At about 3 p.m. A. P. Hill, at Meadow's Bridge, became impatient and decided it was time to take action if Lee's plan was to succeed, even though he would appear to be totally unsupported. He forced a crossing at Meadow's Bridge and advanced towards Mechanicsville, where his leading troops came under artillery fire. When the rest of his division had come up he dispersed the enemy troops facing him, and by soon after

4 p.m. he had taken the village and uncovered the Mechanicsville bridges for D. H. Hill and Longstreet to make use of. But there was some delay in getting their troops across, for the bridges needed repairing and there were no pioneers to hand.

The Mechanicsville plain was now clear of enemy, and A. P. Hill pressed forward on a front of over a mile and in the face of a withering fire from Porter's strongly positioned men. Lee, riding up to the bridge at 5 p.m. together with his redoubtable President, was horrified at what he heard and saw, and sent a message urging Hill to press no further against the impregnable front until Jackson had come in on the flank. But heavy losses had already been suffered by the division, whose troops had been fighting virtually without any cover.

Darkness was fast approaching, and with the Confederate left bogged down Lee attempted to retrieve something from the fiasco by an attack on the extreme right, where the ground was slightly more favourable as it sloped towards the river. D. H. Hill's division had taken some time in crossing the river (Longstreet's leading brigade was not across until 10 p.m.), and in the failing light his two forward brigades (Ripley's and Pender's) lost time through not knowing the ground, and were easily held by well-sited infantry which poured volley after volley into them at very short range. The battle ended at 9 p.m. with Lee's plan to sweep the Federals down the Chickahominy in tatters. Of the 56,000 men he had attempted to get across the river only 14,000 had been in action, and about 1,350 (including 14 field officers) were lost, while the Federal casualties amounted to less than 400.*

Lee had been right in forecasting that while Porter was being attacked McClellan would make no move towards Richmond with the bulk of his army south of the Chickahominy. Now the Federal commander was in a dilemma, for with Jackson poised to pounce upon his lines of communication and Magruder's energetic deception plans misleading him as to the Confederate strength in front of Richmond, he had been forced on to the defensive. About 18 June he had begun to consider the desirability of changing his base from the White House to Harrison's Landing on the James river, and the heavy pressure building up on his right decided him to act at once.

Porter was ordered to fall back to a very strong position behind Boatswains' Creek, south of Gaines's Mill. Here he was to accept battle while the wagon trains got underway. His line was a semicircle of some two miles with his left again resting on the Chickahominy, and his right on some fairly dense thickets. These thickets were scattered throughout the front, and the approach was made more difficult by the swampy creek, and the high ground behind on which Porter's batteries were

*Alexander, p. 121.

positioned. He had 3 divisions of infantry, 6 regiments of cavalry and 80 guns, and his total strength of 30,000 had been scarcely diminished by the Mechanicsville fight. Only on his extreme right was the line weak, and this he knew was where Jackson might attempt to break through.

The pattern of attack was to be much the same as on the previous day. Jackson, who now had D. H. Hill with him,* was to assail the Federal right and rear, and Lee calculated that this threat to his line of retreat would cause Porter to weaken his centre and left, and thus enable A. P. Hill's men, who were again to bear the brunt of the battle, to make a break in the centre. Longstreet was to attack the Federal left, but was to be held in reserve until Jackson's attack had had the expected result of drawing troops away.

Once again the attack suffered from lack of co-ordination and bad staff work with the result that troops were thrown in unsupported, and not until the end of the day was a co-ordinated frontal attack along the whole line achieved. Jackson was again late in coming on the scene: his line of march from Walnut Grove Church to Cold Harbor was obstructed by fallen trees and skirmishers, and it was 2 p.m. before he reached the latter place. 'A captain in the time of war, hath not the ordering of his hours.' D. H. Hill's division had forged ahead of Jackson's column, and brought a battery into action that had been quickly silenced. When Jackson arrived he ordered Hill to withdraw his division into some woods in rear. All his divisions then remained inactive. The presence of Jackson's troops, although perfectly known to Porter, did not cause that general to weaken his left or centre to meet the threat.

A. P. Hill sent his men in to the attack about 2.30 p.m. In well-ordered lines these troops, who had been so hardly battered on the previous day, went forward with great courage through the scattered thickets, down the valley, into the swamps and across the hastily erected abatis on the banks of the creek. But again they suffered appalling punishment; men were mown down in ugly swaths, their blood on the damp earth steaming as the sun warmed it. But where was Jackson? Later he said he was waiting for Hill and Longstreet to drive the enemy towards him, and had selected a suitable killing ground when this should occur.

At last, at about 4 p.m., realizing the battle was clearly not going according to plan, he sent his troops in to the attack. But D. H. Hill's division could make little progress, and Ewell's division on Hill's right was even less successful, while two brigades of Whiting's division, through a staff officer's mistake, were late in coming into line. At this time Longstreet was also ordered to attack on the right in support of A. P. Hill. Thus when Whiting's brigades, personally directed by Lee,

---

*Jackson's command now comprised Whiting's, his own, Ewell's, and D. H. Hill's divisions.

had been brought up the Confederate force was, at about 7 p.m. and for the first time, attacking in unison along the whole front. But McClellan, who had proved loath to weaken his troops on the south bank, had eventually sent Slocum's division of Franklin's corps to bolster Porter's line, and the battle hung in equipoise, going first one way and then the other.

However, Porter's men had not only given but taken terrible punishment, and when the Confederates, striving desperately for one further effort, pierced the Federal centre the line was broken in two. Porter, as darkness fell and with his gunners still pounding away, withdrew his troops in a fairly orderly manner across the Chickahominy and destroyed the bridges as he went. The battle of Gaines's Mill had been a victory for Lee, although it might well not have been had McClellan had the sense to send more than one division to Porter's assistance. It had been a Pyrrhic victory with little to show for it. The Confederate losses were 8,358 men, and the Federals lost 6,837 and 22 guns.*

Through the action at Gaines's Mill the huge wagon train (5,000 carts), reserve artillery and 2,500 head of cattle had escaped the danger of being cut off by Jackson's troops. But had McClellan got them underway twenty-four hours earlier he might well have reached his new base on the James without having to fight two skirmishes and a battle. Large quantities of rations, ammunition for siege guns, and hardware of various sorts that could not be loaded had to be abandoned. Neverthless, the withdrawal of the whole army across very difficult country, which started early on 28 June, was extremely well organized, for McClellan was nothing if not a good organizer.

On the night after Gaines's Mill he told his corps commanders of his decision to withdraw to the James, and General Keyes's IVth Corps was to march with artillery and baggage across the White Oak Swamp, and from positions on the far side to cover the passage of other troops and transports. Keyes had carried out this order by midday on the 28th. Porter's corps also crossed the swamp that day, and took up a position covering the roads leading from Richmond.

Lee still clung to the possibility that McClellan would withdraw down the peninsula, and Ewell's division was sent some seven miles down the north bank of the Chickahominy to Despatch Station, and Stuart's cavalry was ordered to support it and ride down the river to Bottom's Bridge. Stuart in fact pressed on to the White House where he and his troopers greatly enjoyed themselves ransacking what was left of McClellan's stores, and in consequence of this Lee was without his cavalry until after the battle of Malvern Hill. The 28th was a wasted day for the Confederates and gave McClellan a welcome start. It was not

---

*Alexander, p. 131.

until that evening Lee became finally convinced that the Union troops were making for the James. It was essential that they should be caught and destroyed before they reached a base from which it might be hard to dislodge them.

Orders were immediately issued for a vigorous pursuit, which unfortunately got off to a bad start. Jackson, who was to cross the Chickahominy at Grapevine Bridge was, for one reason or another, incredibly slow in crossing. He was, therefore, not available to aid Magruder when the latter bumped into the Federal rearguard on the Williamsburg road near Savage's Station. Magruder felt it necessary to summon assistance from Huger, who was marching parallel to him on the Charles City road. Huger halted his troops and sent four brigades across to take part in two inconclusive engagements. This loss of time, particularly Jackson's, was serious, for he had the shortest march and could quite possibly have caught a part of the Union troops before they crossed the White Oak Swamp.

As it was McClellan had his whole army across by 10 a.m. on 30 June. He now had only about six miles to march to the comparative safety of the Malvern hills, and in another day his column would have closed up, leaving no exposed flank, and with his wagon train quite secure. June 30 was, therefore, to be a vital day offering Lee perhaps his last chance to gain the victory, which through misadventures, misunderstandings, and a degree of incompetence had so far eluded him.

Lee's plan to concentrate his troops parallel to McClellan's line of withdrawal would bring the bulk of his army in to the attack on an eastward axis, with the exception of Jackson's 25,000 (he still had D. H. Hill with him) who were to hit the rear of the Federal army, and his line of attack would be from north to south. It was a good plan allowing for convergence of the divisions along separate roads, but it called for a high degree of liaison and co-operation.

General Holmes was to bring his division across the James and march down the New Market road. He would thus be on the extreme right of the Confederate line. Longstreet with A. P. Hill's division was to move down the Darbytown road (where they had bivouacked the previous night) to the Long Bridge road. Magruder's six brigades were withdrawn from Savage's Station and were to march down the Darbytown road in support of Longstreet. Huger was to form the left of the east-facing attack, and his troops were to march on the Charles City road to its junction with the Long Bridge road. In rear of the enemy Jackson's force was to cross the swamp by White Oak Bridge. He had about seven miles to march, and was likely to have an opposed crossing.

Lee now had some 70,000 men with which to retrieve the Confederate fortunes that were manifestly running his enemy's way. And once again his carefully laid plans were to go awry. Out of this sizeable number of

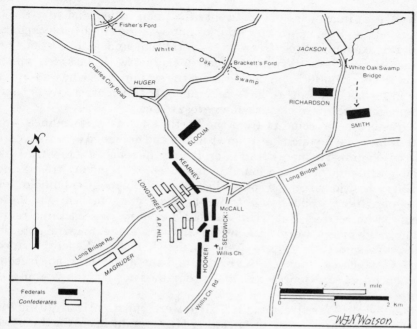

The Seven Days' Battle: The Battle of Frayser's Farm 30 June 1862

troops no more than 20,000 (two divisions) were to engage the enemy, and even they did not go in together, but one division after the other.

Holmes's, Magruder's, Huger's, and Jackson's troops played virtually no part in the battle of Frayser's Farm (sometimes called Glendale), which was fought on 30 June. Holmes, having crossed the river, came down the New Market road to within sight of Malvern Hill. To his front and at no very great distance was a large part of the Federal wagon train. The target was too tempting to be ignored and Holmes brought up six guns to blast these wagons, but this drew a fierce fire from the heavy guns of the gunboats in the James and the Field Artillery Reserve, as well as from men of Porter's corps which had just arrived on the heights. Holmes's division was soon scattered and making for cover. Lee, who had been in touch with Holmes and approved his cannonade, ordered Magruder to bring his six brigades to his assistance, and then realizing there was little they could do countermanded the order. Hence there were some 18,000 men milling about ineffectually on the right of Lee's line.

On the 29th Huger's division, as already related, had been delayed in its march down the Charles City road through having to halt and send troops to assist in the affair at Savage's Station. For the rest of that day and on the 30th his progress was appallingly slow. There were skirmishes (in which he lost twenty-five men killed and fifty-three wounded), and his approach to the swamp was continually blocked by Federal axemen felling trees as they retired, and at one stage he detached a brigade (Wright's) to make contact with Jackson, which spent much of the 30th wandering about the swamp. Lee, who was only a few miles away, seems to have taken no steps to contact Huger, and Huger never reported his lack of progress to Lee.

Jackson was to come in from the north, and his performance – or rather lack of it – which has been attacked and defended over the years will be examined in more detail later. Briefly, he reached the White Oak Bridge at about noon and found it destroyed, with enemy troops and artillery positioned on the south side. By 1.45 Colonel Crutchfield, his chief-of-artillery, had brought twenty-eight guns to bear on these troops, who retired. But when Jackson's cavalry crossed the stream other field pieces were brought up and drove the horsemen back. Jackson's smooth-bore guns were no match for the Federals' rifled barrels which commanded the bridge and the approach road. In consequence Jackson's fourteen brigades remained north of the swamp and out of the battle all day.

Meanwhile, Longstreet and A. P. Hill were impatiently awaiting the signal (the opening salvoes from either Huger or Jackson) for their two divisions to be launched. Lee was with them as the hours went by and no action. Longstreet was becoming impatient, and just before 4 p.m. he ordered a limited attack to silence an aggressive Federal battery, and this brought on the main battle of the day. Two Confederate divisions, of which one (Hill's) was at first held back to be fresh for the expected pursuit, threw themselves against Heintzelman's IIIrd Corps and McCall's division of Porter's corps, supported by two further divisions in a second line, in what has been described as the most desperate encounter of the whole war. The outstandingly courageous and sustained attack of these two divisions, in the face of a murderous fire from well-sited positions, broke McCall's division in the centre. But on the flanks the Federals stood firm, and when night came the line had been re-established. Longstreet's losses of about 2,600 and Hill's of about 1,700 speak for themselves.

McClellan had won a victory in a battle at which he himself was not present, for incredibly he had decided, on this day of crisis, to carry out a reconnaissance in the Malvern Hill area. Lee, partly through his fault of refusing to interfere with his subordinates when things were not going as planned, had lost what was almost certainly his last chance of striking a decisive blow at McClellan. That night (30 June – 1 July) the Federal troops who had been fighting at Frayser's Farm withdrew to join Keyes's and Porter's corps in a strong position on Malvern Hill.

The hill – or more accurately hills – rose about 100 feet from the valley of the James river. There was an open plateau at the top which to the north and north-east fell gradually through corn-covered slopes to forest and marshy land. Both flanks of the Federal position were partly protected by forest, and on the right by a watercourse known as the Western Run. It was a desperate position to take by storm, for its marshy and wooded approach severely hampered any effective artillery support, while the commanding position of McClellan's 300 guns could blast any infantry as they approached over the open ground.

Nevertheless, Lee was determined to attempt it. He well knew that it would be a stern struggle and the losses would be cruel, but the victory, if it could be gained, would make amends for all the disappointments that had gone before. Longstreet had carried out a careful reconnaissance, and persuaded Lee that it would be possible to position 100 guns in the open ground beyond the swamp. These could bring a cross-fire from the left and centre to neutralize the Federal batteries and permit the infantry to make a successful assault.

The battle of Malvern Hill was fought throughout most of 1 July, and quickly became a hard-hitting, bloodthirsty affair in which the Confederates suffered appalling casualties without achieving a breakthrough. It will not be described in great detail, because it is not a battle from which can be developed any decisive collective or individual actions which, had they been ordered differently, might have affected the outcome. It is true that after the battle Jeb Stuart certainly eliminated a possible chance of Lee gaining an eleventh-hour victory, but that intrepid cavalry commander's constant impetuosity was too often the cause of Confederate consternation to be singled out as an unusual factor.

Longstreet's promised barrage was a ghastly failure. It was found impossible to get the batteries through the tangle of scrub, thicket, and morass in time for a co-ordinated shoot. Many guns never got into action at all, and those divisional batteries that managed to overcome every impediment that nature could put in their way came up at varying intervals (with never more than twenty guns firing at one time), and were blasted to smithereens by the powerful Union cannon firing almost hub-to-hub. No passage was cleared for the assault, and the brigade detailed to lead could do no more than disperse the Federal picket and sharpshooter line. Thus the first phase of the battle, which ended about 2.30 p.m. with hardly a Union infantryman engaged.

As a frontal assault in the face of massive artillery had clearly proved too hazardous, Lee decided upon a flank attack. But before this could be mounted information reached him (erroneous as it transpired) that the leading brigades of the original assault had at last made some progress, and so he countermanded the flank attack and decided to reinforce success. General Magruder was therefore ordered to press forward with his whole command.

Magruder had been delayed in reaching Malvern Hill, because his guide had led him down the wrong road, and his artillery had not yet arrived. But sensing the urgency he decided to attack without adequate artillery support. His nine brigades charged through a hail of shot with desperate courage but no co-ordination, and as each one emerged from cover it was dealt with unmercifully. Then D. H. Hill on Magruder's right, responding to the drumming thunder of the cannonade, launched his brigades up the slope. This attack, like so many others, was un-supported and unco-ordinated and the Union artillery, which was the queen of this battle, wiped out huge numbers.

Soon it was all these two divisions could do to cling to the slippery, bloodstained hill and A. P. Hill's and Longstreet's troops came to their assistance. Later Jackson sent four brigades to prop up D. H. Hill's attack in the centre of the line, which had run out of impetus. But bravely as the Confederate troops struggled, the position was too strongly held, and as the swirling mists of evening added to the con-fusion the Union men, scenting victory, pressed inexorably forward and drove the Confederate left into the thickets from which they could not easily be rallied. When Magruder's weary reserve brigades had been thrown off the battle-scarred heights for the last time and darkness descended over this field of fearful slaughter, the last orange tongues of flame spurted from the Union batteries, and the battle was over. The Confederate losses had been over 5,000 (mostly from gun fire), while their opponents probably lost no more than 1,500 or 1,600.

All that night it rained in torrents, and when the moiled and bed-raggled Confederates gazed upon the battlefield in the early hours of 2 July they saw only the dead, the dying and a handful of stragglers. McClellan, despite the urgings of his generals, had refused to renew the attack and during the night his troops slipped away to Harrison's Landing. His men, although recently victorious, were in low spirits from constantly marching backwards and fighting and dying in appalling conditions. His withdrawal to Harrison's Landing had every appear-ance of a shambling retreat with men falling out, and equipment and material abandoned everywhere.

Jackson was anxious to go in pursuit at once, but Lee – who had again been joined by President Davis – was unsure of the exact route McClellan would take, and thought that his army needed a day to recover before attempting another march along roads knee-deep in mud. Stuart had, at last, rejoined the army and Lee sent him off to keep in touch with the Federals. He planned to resume the march the next day with Longstreet's and Jackson's comparatively fresh troops in the van.

As it turned out, the delay of a day may well have lost Lee his very last chance of destroying the Federal army. On arrival at Harrison's Landing McClellan's troops were so exhausted and disorganized that they left unguarded a commanding feature known as Evelington Heights. Stuart, when he caught up with the Union army, sent back word to Lee of their whereabouts. But instead of keeping them carefully and quietly in sight, impetuous as ever he needs must occupy the dominating feature, and with his only howitzer empty its few remaining shells into their camp. Irritated by this harmless pricking, and made suddenly aware of their tactical error, Federal troops quickly pushed Stuart's men off Evelington Heights and occupied it themselves in strength. Lee examined the position, and saw at once that it was impregnable, being even stronger than Malvern Hill. After three days he withdrew the Army of Northern Virginia to Richmond, leaving Stuart to observe the Federals.

Towards the end of August McClellan embarked the Army of the Potomac from Yorktown and Fortress Monroe. His campaign had ended in failure and had cost his army 16,000 casualties, and 6,000 men taken prisoner. Lee had taken colossal risks, and although he had failed to destroy his enemy he had at least preserved Richmond from tramontane occupation – but at a staggering cost of 20,000 casualties. Perhaps the saddest outcome of these battles was that there could now be little chance of a quick end to this disastrous war.

In the course of this campaign there were a number of mishaps and missed opportunities. McClellan could almost certainly have taken Richmond had he been better supported by Washington and less cautious. His original design showed an offensive spirit, but as he progressed up the peninsula this was replaced by an unwelcome catalepsy, from which he eventually emerged to conduct a masterly retreat. Lee's daring plan was worthy of greater fortune, and better support from his subordinate commanders. His strategy was excellent, but his tactics faulty.

Both sides were affected by an absence of reliable maps and by bad staff work. Little had been done to map the country before the war, and there was an acute shortage of topographical engineers. A map had been prepared for Lee, but he soon discovered that it was full of errors. Proper maps, or a better knowledge of the roads, would have saved long delays in bringing troops from one position to another, and might have avoided battles.

McClellan's staff officers were marginally more experienced than Lee's, but they left much to be desired, and he was handicapped through receiving faulty tactical information, or sometimes none at all. His Intelligence service misled him, and was largely responsible for his failure to take Richmond. Some of Lee's personal staff were inexperienced and not properly trained, and Lee himself was not good at handling them. He also suffered from having his cavalry off the battlefields for much of the campaign.

To these general observations can be added three factors, two of which – McDowell's absence, and McClellan's failure to attack Magruder on 27 June – most probably saved Richmond; the third, the most intriguing of all, the strange behaviour of Stonewall Jackson throughout the campaign, which most probably saved the Army of the Potomac.

Major-General Irvin McDowell commanded the Ist Corps of the army, and should therefore have embarked with McClellan for Fortress Monroe at the end of March. However, Jackson's brilliant campaign in the Shenandoah valley so alarmed President Lincoln that he temporarily withheld McDowell for the defence of Washington, even though there were 18,000 troops in and around the city, and a further 55,000 in the neighbourhood. Lincoln could never understand that Washington could be better safeguarded, and troops better employed, through a successful attack on Richmond than by keeping them idle in the vicinity of the capital.

Soon after landing McClellan was making plans to take Yorktown, and these included the use of McDowell's corps of 30,000 troops – which he understood was then embarking from Alexandria – for the capture of Gloucester. However, on 6 April he received word from Secretary of War Stanton that the President was still not willing to release the corps. This meant that the York river remained closed to Federal shipping. However, by the beginning of May when Johnston had been withdrawn from the Rapidan, McClellan had cleared him from the Yorktown line, and the Confederates had abandoned Gloucester, Lincoln felt that the threat to Washington was less immediate. Thus in response to further urgent appeals Stanton informed McClellan, in a letter dated 18 May, that McDowell whose strength had been increased to between 35,000 and 40,000 men would be marching to join him, and that McClellan was to extend his right wing to the north of Richmond in order to make contact with McDowell's left.

If these troops had been sent by sea, as McClellan had wanted, he could have carried out his cherished plan of advancing on Richmond by the line of the James river. As it was he was forced to split his army, for in order to take Richmond a part of it had to cross the Chickahominy to the south bank while another part must remain on the north side in order to join up with McDowell. This was to expose the Federal right, and to give Lee an excellent opportunity to wipe out at least one corps. McClellan was to say later, 'Herein lay the failure of the campaign.'*

* McClellan, p. 346.

McClellan established his headquarters at the White House on the Pamunkey, and in order to facilitate the passage of McDowell's corps he ordered Porter to clear the Hanover Court House area of a Confederate force under Brigadier-General Branch. This was accomplished successfully by 12,000 men of Porter's corps on 27 May, and at that time McDowell's van was only about twenty miles from McClellan's right. But Lee, realizing the serious threat to Richmond posed by McDowell's imminent approach, had earlier arranged for Jackson in the Shenandoah valley to be reinforced, and to create such a diversion there as to frighten Lincoln into again withholding McDowell.

This ploy was entirely successful. Jackson defeated General Banks at Strasburg on 23 May, and the next day an order was sent to McDowell to abandon any idea of Richmond and to put 20,000 men in motion at once for the Shenandoah. And so when he was so close McDowell had to turn away his 40,000 men. General FitzJohn Porter was to write, 'If McDowell had joined McClellan then, it would have resulted in the capture of Richmond.'* And there can be little doubt that he was right. No government should remove a corps from an army engaged in carrying out a well and carefully planned operation.

On 25 June, two days before the battles of Gaines's Mill, the Federal left and centre had engaged the forward Confederate pickets just north of Seven Pines, and after a skirmish at Oak Grove McClellan had advanced his line to within about four miles of Richmond. Here two-thirds of his army faced Magruder's division of 13,000 and Huger's of 9,000 men. In addition the Confederates had 5 regiments of cavalry (2,000 sabres) and 3,000 reserve artillerymen on this south bank of the river. Holmes's division of 6,500 was some distance away on the far side of the James river. Opposing this Confederate force of 27,000 men McClellan had, from right to left, Franklin's, Sumner's, and Heintzelman's corps with Keyes's in reserve. Each corps had two divisions (although Slocum's of Franklin's corps was later sent across the river to assist Porter), and the force was around 62,000 effectives. Apart from this disparity in numbers the Confederate artillery and small arms were considerably inferior to Federal weapons both in range and accuracy.

It would seem, therefore, that if McClellan was to mount a vigorous offensive with his centre and left, leaving Porter to hold the large-scale Confederate attack on his right, he must capture Richmond. Magruder in his official report has this to say concerning the threat to his command: 'Had McClellan massed his whole force in column and advanced against any point in our line . . . its momentum would have

*Johnson and Buel, p. 325.

insured his success.'* The question is was he wrong in failing to take this seemingly golden chance to attain his objective?

In defence of his failure to attack (*McClellan's Own Story*, pp. 422, 423) McClellan puts forward three points. There was a large force of the enemy (presumably Jackson's troops) in rear of his army which would sever communications with his supply depot at the White House, and he had insufficient rations to complete the operation. Had he taken Richmond the Confederates could have come between his overland and up-river supply line, thereby turning success into disaster. Moreover, he thought there was always the possibility that the enemy might concentrate his entire force, give battle, defeat his army, and cut him off from his supply trains before he could regain the flotilla on the James.

These might be considered specious excuses, but the question of supplies does stand up to some examination. Richmond was a great prize, and its capture might well have shortened the war. The Union government would have done all in its power to sustain the Army of the Potomac, which anyway had an overall superiority of more than 20,000 men with which to beat off any counterattack. Lee would have found it very difficult to bring troops across the river to retake the capital, for most certainly McDowell with his 40,000 men would be close behind him. But having defeated Porter at Gaines's Mill he might well have caught up with and destroyed the Federal wagon trains. This could have been very awkward – but probably not disastrous – for unless the conquered capital was able to supply the army until such time as the way was cleared by force of arms for fresh supplies to be brought in overland or by river, the troops would be on unpleasantly hard rations.

This introduced an element of risk, and McClellan was a cautious general. But in fairness to him it is most probable, although he refrained from giving it as an explanation, that he remained inactive in the centre and left of his line because he believed that Magruder had a great many more than 27,000 men. The head of Army Intelligence, Allan Pinkerton (known at headquarters as Major E. J. Allen), had told McClellan, when the army first landed, that he was opposed by 200,000 Confederate troops. Situation reports from Gaines's Mill informed him that Porter was facing 70,000 of these (a much-exaggerated figure), which left Lee, after allowing for casualties, something like 120,000 with which to defend Richmond (an estimate borne out, to a certain degree, by Magruder's deception plan of marching the same men in and out of thickets). McClellan had been let down by the too-vivid imagination of a great detective but an indifferent intelligence officer, and in the course of three months he had made no effort to check the information supplied.

A more daring commander would have gone for Richmond, certainly

* Alexander, p. 135.

have taken it and probably retained it, and thereby shortened the war. But McClellan had made up his mind before Gaines's Mill to 'change his base', as he euphemistically described his withdrawal. In doing this he lost the initiative, put his army in peril and virtually gave up any hope of achieving his objective.

The behaviour of General Jackson almost from the moment he was summoned by Lee to march from the Shenandoah valley, where he had so distinguished himself, is one of the great puzzles of the war. He failed to arrive at the appointed place on 26 June, the day that he himself had chosen. He halted in sound of the guns that evening, and took no part in the attack on Beaver Dam Creek, where his was the vital role. Moreover, he was late at Gaines's Mill, and when he did arrive he withdrew D. H. Hill's division at a critical time of the battle, and did not commit his troops until it was almost too late. He took no part in the engagement at Savage's Station, while at Frayser's Farm his attempts to get across the White Oak Swamp were half-hearted and ineffective; and at Malvern Hill, in Alexander's words, 'he took no initiative'.

Of these many uncharacteristic aberrations it would be true to say that at the battles of Mechanicsville and Frayser's Farm Jackson's failure to implement his commander's plans almost certainly saved the Army of the Potomac from destruction. How then did this come about?

Lee's orders to Jackson gave him a march of almost twenty miles on 24 June for him to be at Ashland that night. On the 25th he was to move six miles east of Ashland to camp at Merry Oaks Church just west of the Virginia Central Railroad, and to leave camp at 3 a.m. on the 26th, marching on the road leading to Pole Green Church. That morning he was to liaise with General Branch whose brigade would then cross the Chickahominy and make for Mechanicsville. General A. P. Hill's division was to cross the river as soon as Jackson's and Branch's troops were 'discovered' (a vague and unsatisfactory word). Longstreet and D. H. Hill would cross when the enemy had been cleared from Mechanicsville. Jackson, marching well to the left but *en échelon* with the other divisions, was to turn Beaver Dam Creek and then proceed towards Cold Harbor, so as to be in Porter's rear.

Jackson had rejoined his troops at Beaver Dam Station the morning after his conference with Lee on 23 June. The march to Ashland was made over appalling tracks and across country of which he knew nothing. This was the beginning of his troubles from which he never fully recovered. By the evening of the 25th his exhausted troops had scarcely made Ashland, six miles short of Merry Oaks Church, their objective for that night. Jackson, much distressed by this loss of time, ordered the march on the 26th to begin at 2.30 a.m., but from an administrative angle – ration carts not up, water not readily available, etc. – this proved impossible. It was 9 a.m. before the column was at the Virginia Central Railroad – six hours behind the time set in Lee's operation order. The troops were not across the railroad until 10 a.m., for an hour was spent in dispersing a party of Federal cavalry. At this stage Ewell left the column, and marched his division south for the Shady Grove Church area, where he made contact with Branch's brigade, but their paths soon diverged.

At 3 p.m. the Totopotomoy creek was reached, where another enemy picket had to be driven off, but not before it had destroyed the bridge. However, the engineers soon had it repaired, and the column crossed at 4 p.m. when gun and musketry fire to the south first became audible. The march continued towards Hundley's Corner which the van reached about 5 p.m. Here Ewell rejoined the column, but he could give Jackson no information about either of the Hills (A. P. should have been on his right and D. H. in support). Gunfire could now be plainly heard but Jackson, without any information and unsupported on his right for the advance to Beaver Dam Creek, decided to bivouac for the night.

Such were the facts concerning Jackson's orders and how he carried them out. Over the years he has had his detractors and defenders. There can be no doubt that the difficulties his troops experienced in the long marches of 23 to 26 June were extremely formidable. At the conference on 23 June, Jackson, at Longstreet's urgent instigation, changed the date on which he would be ready to give battle from 25 to 26 June. He has been criticized for being overoptimistic, which he certainly was, for he had no knowledge of the ground and no reliable maps. In the circumstances he overestimated the abilities – which were considerable – of his troops and the condition of the ground, but he was very much aware of the need for haste. It was important that Porter be attacked before McClellan reinforced him, and as it happened information was on its way to the Federals of Jackson's approach. Lee knew only a little more about the country than Jackson did, and unwittingly he may have set him too tight a marching schedule to Ashland. Both before and after Ashland, Jackson did what he could to adhere to the timetable, but the task proved beyond him. His fault here was in not communicating his lack of progress to Lee.

His behaviour at Hundley's Corner is less easily excused. Part of the trouble may have been that he did not properly understand Lee's orders, which in the written memorandum differed slightly from the verbal ones, in that Jackson's march was to be farther to the east than originally planned. This was to assist his turning movement and would still enable him to advance *en échelon* with the other divisions to Beaver Dam Creek. It may not have been clear to Jackson (although there seems little reason why it should not have been) that in sending him farther east Lee still expected him to attack Porter's right flank, and not merely to make for Cold Harbor and take him in rear. If there were doubts it would not have been easy to clear them up, for since the 25th the telegraph line was down, and he was some distance from Lee.

As already related, at 3 p.m. (at which time Jackson's column had only just reached Totopotomoy creek) A. P. Hill became impatient and opened the battle on his own account and unsupported. D. H. Hill and Longstreet were not across the river until much later, and so when Jackson eventually reached Hundley's Corner there was no sign of any support on his right. This, of course, was due to the slowness of his march and the fact that there was virtually no communication between A. P. Hill, Branch, and Jackson. At 5 p.m. Lee attempted to halt an attack that should never have started until Jackson had come in to line. A. P. Hill had disobeyed orders, which presumably must have been quite clear to him, with disastrous results.

Some of Jackson's subordinate commanders tried to press him to march to the sound of the guns when these were clearly heard from Hundley's Corner. Jackson said later that he thought the firing might indicate something other than a full-scale battle, and his orders were to advance in co-operation with the other divisions, of which there were no signs. He decided to obey them to the letter, and remained inactive.

One can dismiss the accusations sometimes levelled that Jackson resented being under command and taking second place: these are palpably false; nor was the need to spend time in religious observance responsible, on this occasion, for the slowness of his march. But it is difficult to acquit him of failing to march to the assistance of his colleagues when some sort of battle was obviously in progress. This was not the action of a good commander, nor characteristic of Jackson. His 18,500 men might not have retrieved the blunder caused by A. P. Hill, but had they arrived at the fight by, say, 7 p.m. there was a good chance they could have done so.

The gravamen against Jackson at the battle of Frayser's Farm on 30 June (which was the crisis day of the Seven Days') was that he made no real effort to get his troops across the White Oak Swamp and attack the rear of McClellan's army in accordance with Lee's plan. And a careful examination of the evidence, even though some of it is conflicting and not absolutely clear, tends to uphold the charge.

In the pursuit after the Gaines's Mill battle, which Lee hoped to get under way early on the 29th, Jackson, less Ewell's division, was to cross the Chickahominy at Grapevine Bridge and head south past Savage's Station and on to the road leading to White Oak Bridge. The rest of the army would attack the retreating Federals in flank. Jackson did not cross the river until after midnight of the 29th–30th, and his seven-mile march to White Oak Bridge was so slow, owing to the taking of many prisoners and the clearing of tracks, that he did not reach the bridge until noon. Had he been three hours earlier he would have caught part of the Federal army crossing the swamp.

Because 29 June was a Sunday, and Jackson was well known to keep that day for rest and divine worship, he has been accused of deliberately delaying his march. His own account states that repairs to the bridge took a very long time, but this is contrary to what his engineer officer told Magruder. In any event there were two bridges in working order only three and four miles respectively up stream, which he never even reconnoitred. It is possible, therefore, that strict observance of the Lord's Day did account for this unfortunate delay.

While Jackson was marching in the early hours of the 30th an exceptionally violent thunderstorm broke, and as the dawn filtered through the dark, heavily laden clouds much of the surrounding land was deep in mud and slush. The White Oak Swamp was approached by fields of rough, tufted grass that merged into a tangle of thickets reaching down to the White Oak stream, which was subject to flash floods after such rain as had just fallen. It was a wild primeval place of bog, brambles, and stunted trees, with a few rickety bridges across the stream, and some fords. Nothing lived within this hostile morass: it was a landscape charged with silent menace.

When Jackson arrived the bridge was down and Federal artillery, supported by infantry, guarded the crossing and commanded the approach. General Franklin was in command and he had with him two complete divisions, three brigades from other divisions and three batteries, a total of 22,000 men with which to oppose Jackson's force that amounted to rather over 25,000 when Ewell, who had been north of the Chickahominy, rejoined him at about 4 p.m.

At 1.45 p.m. Colonel Crutchfield opened up with twenty-eight guns. The concentrated fire from these silenced the Federal artillery, and Jackson brought a gun forward to dislodge the sharpshooters from the area of the bridge. He then ordered Colonel Munford and his 2nd Virginia Cavalry to splash their way across the stream and storm the Federal position. Jackson and some of his staff followed, but no infantry were ordered across. The party ran into artillery fire from batteries moved to the east side of the road, and they were forced to make a hasty withdrawal. For the whole afternoon a furious artillery duel ensued in which both sides expended a large quantity of ammunition, firing blind with no appreciable results, other than the Federal skirmish line being re-established under cover of their artillery. Jackson, believing that the Federals held the crossing too strongly and that he could never get his artillery over the swamp to support any attack, remained inactive. To his south the noise of Longstreet's attack could be clearly heard.

There is little doubt that in doing nothing Jackson lost Lee the battle, and there is also little doubt that he could have done something. He could certainly have got his infantry across – if not to his immediate front (where in fact D. H. Hill did get some over) then farther up and down the stream. Wright of Huger's division had crossed the swamp and reported to Jackson, who sent him back to cross again which he did, not at Brackett's Ford which he found too well guarded, but at Fisher's Ford only some three miles from Jackson's position. However, Wright had no instructions to report, and Jackson made no attempt to learn of his progress. He might have had trouble in getting his guns across, but a large infantry force could on its own have posed a serious threat to Franklin's rear.

It has been argued that Jackson was correct in not marching up the stream to cross his troops, for his orders were quite definitely to endeavour to force White Oak Bridge, to protect Lee's left flank and to stay on the White Oak Bridge until he received further orders. And Jackson was a man who believed implicitly in obedience to orders. However, there is good reason to think that Jackson did receive fresh orders at the bridge urging him to give immediate support to Longstreet. But even if this was not the case an opportunity was to occur for him to take a decisive part in the battle so close to the White Oak Bridge that no one could justly assert that he had deviated from his orders.

One of his brigade commanders, Wade Hampton, while reconnoitring during the artillery battle discovered at the edge of the swamp an easy crossing place where the stream had a firm bottom and was only some fifteen feet wide. At this place there was a clearing from which could be seen the Federal position, well sited against a frontal attack, but extremely vulnerable to a flanking movement. Hampton reported this place as admirably suited for an attack, and when asked by Jackson said that he could very quickly construct a bridge for infantry, but surprise would be lost through making a larger one for artillery. Jackson appeared very interested, and ordered Hampton to build the infantry bridge. But when the latter reported the work completed, and begged to be allowed to take his brigade over in the van, Jackson said nothing and walked away. And so 25,000 men were held back when their presence at the battle would almost certainly have proved decisive.

Over the years many excuses have been made for Jackson's totally uncharacteristic performance at White Oak Swamp, but none is satisfactory. The kindest explanation, for Jackson was a great soldier, was made by Major Dabney, his chief-of-staff, who was convinced that his lapse here was due to complete physical exhaustion caused by practically no sleep over the last two or three days, and exacerbated by constant worry and responsibility.

In the course of this campaign there were a number of factors that could be said to have influenced victory or defeat. But perhaps three stand out above the others – political poltroonery, bad intelligence and the third, a factor beyond the control of the Confederate commander.

The political interference from Washington was not of the same kind that Burgoyne had to endure from Whitehall, and although it did not result in defeat it bent the chances of victory. Battles are not likely to be won when politicians are fearful of taking risks, and deprive a commander of a large part of his force to guard against an imaginary danger.

McClellan's information during his advance up the peninsula was hopelessly at fault, and was one of the principal causes of his failure to take Richmond and win the campaign. Good or bad intelligence can have a decisive effect on the outcome of a battle; in more recent times this was brought very much to the fore by the Allied possession of the Enigma machine in the 1939–45 war.

General Jackson was one of Lee's most talented and trusted lieutenants, but his performance at Beaver Dam Creek, Gaines's Mill and Frayser's Farm was so far below his usual high standard that it deprived Lee of the chance to defeat decisively the Federal army. Lee did what he could to urge Jackson to greater efforts, but this was an occasion when almost certain victory eluded a commander through a factor beyond his control.

16   The Battle of Gettysburg
1–3 July 1863

IN the course of the twelve months that separated the battles of Malvern Hill and Gettysburg there was to be some severe fighting, and on the Union side constant changes in the army command. General Lee remained in command of the Army of Northern Virginia, and for him a most gratifying event of these months must surely have been the return of Stonewall Jackson's undoubted ability to the height it had achieved before the Seven Days' Battle. His first success was on 9 August 1862 at Cedar Mountain, north of Gordonsville, where he defeated a Federal force under his old opponent General Banks.

While McClellan was still in the peninsula Lincoln put Major-General John Pope in command of McDowell's, Freemont's, and Banks's corps with the task of safeguarding Washington. Towards the end of August Lee formed one of those daring plans in which he split his army. He was to hold Pope on the line of the Rappahannock while Jackson marched round his rear to destroy his base. But Pope, learning of Jackson's movement, fell back to Manassas Junction and was followed by Lee who, joining forces with Jackson, defeated him at the Second Battle of Manassas on 29 and 30 August. It was a victory that did not achieve very much and cost him nearly 20 per cent of his army. Nor was any immediate progress possible, for McClellan had arrived from the peninsula, and he now marched towards Lee with superior numbers.

At the beginning of September Lee, short of provisions and clothes, headed for the well-stocked depots of Maryland and Pennsylvania. In another risky manoeuvre he again split his army, sending Jackson to clear the enemy from Harper's Ferry and Martinsburg, while Long-street marched for Hagerstown. A copy of his plan fell into McClellan's hands, and had he taken advantage of the information he must have defeated the Army of Northern Virginia in detail. But he dallied, and Lee had time to reunite his army, and on 17 September he accepted battle north of Sharpsburg (the Battle of Antietam). The result was inconclusive, and costly for Lee who lost over 13,000 men; but McClellan had – for the time being – halted the Confederate invasion.

A few days later the Army of Northern Virginia recrossed the

Potomac and fell back to Opequan Creek, and later to Culpeper Court House. McClellan moved leisurely to Warrenton, where on 7 November he was informed that General Burnside had superseded him in command. Burnside planned to make his base at Aquia Creek and move by Fredericksburg on Richmond. But, like McClellan, he moved in no hurry, and Lee was able to concentrate his army and take up a strong defensive position above the small town of Fredericksburg. Burnside crossed the Rappahannock on 11 and 12 December, and his army of some 120,000 men assaulted the Confederates during the whole of the 12th. But the position was far too strong, and the Federals were continually repulsed, with very heavy losses. Lee's victory was convincing, but the commanding position of the Federal batteries on the Stafford Heights made it too dangerous to turn a successful defensive action into an attack.

The winter of 1862–63 was comparatively quiet. Burnside recrossed the river on 15 December, and in January was succeeded in command by Major-General Hooker. The Army of Northern Virginia, holding a line between Fort Royal and United States Ford, faced the Army of the Potomac across the Rappahannock. At the end of April Hooker made an attempt to turn Lee's left which resulted in the battle of Chancellorsville, fought on 1–4 May. The Confederates won this fiercely contested battle, but it decided nothing and Lee suffered the very grievous loss of Jackson. The victory also had the damaging effect of increasing Lee's misplaced confidence in his ability to ride roughshod through the Union army, whose soldiers he was inclined to regard with contempt. In fact the morale of the Army of the Potomac was not long in recovering from Chancellorsville, and Lee had failed to differentiate between bad soldiers, and good soldiers badly led.

In this euphoria of invincibility the decision was taken to send the Army of Northern Virginia into Pennsylvania, rather than to detach a part of it to the Mississippi, where Grant and Rosecrans were posing a serious threat to the Confederate forces. There were many good reasons for such a move. The Army of the Potomac's position opposite Fredericksburg was one that could not be easily attacked, and in drawing it away north of the Potomac a more favourable opportunity to engage it might be found, and at the same time the lower part of the Shenandoah valley could be freed from troops that had occupied it during the winter. Supplies of every kind were urgently needed, and these could be obtained from the well-stocked Northern States. There were other less obvious reasons for this decision, such as to strengthen the hand of the Northern peace party, and perhaps encourage foreign intervention on the Confederate side. But an invasion of the North was more likely to unite than divide, and the epoch-making Proclamation of Emancipation (1 January 1863), declaring that from henceforth all slaves would be free, would divert to the North what sympathy there might previously have been among European states for the South.

Accordingly Lee began his move north from the Rappahannock on 3 June. He had organized the infantry of his army into three corps each of three divisions. I Corps was commanded by General Longstreet; II Corps by General Ewell; and III Corps by General A. P. Hill. The field artillery had fifteen battalions of four batteries each, and General J. E. B. (Jeb) Stuart commanded six brigades of cavalry and a battalion of horse artillery. The contempt with which Lee regarded Hooker was clearly shown by the risky flank march he now undertook, and the way in which he was to extend his army over many miles in enemy country. Hill's corps was left for a brief period to watch Hooker on the Rappahannock, while Longstreet's and Ewell's made for Culpeper and then to the Blue Mountains. Hooker had every chance to seize the Blue Mountain gaps, divide the Confederates and defeat them in detail, but this he failed to do.

He did order General Sedgwick, commanding his VI Corps, to send troops across the river to reconnoitre, and this provoked a cavalry engagement at Brandy Station, which although not much more than a skirmish was important, for it was the first occasion in which the Federal horsemen showed themselves to be the equal of the Confederates. This battle was fought on 9 June, and it enabled General Pleasonton, commanding the Federal cavalry, to confirm the forward movement of Lee's army – Ewell's corps by now was advancing down the Shenandoah valley on Winchester – and so on 13 June Hooker left Fredericksburg, and marched his army north on a parallel line to Lee's.

On 14 June Ewell's II Corps engaged and defeated General Milroy at Winchester, and with Hooker now coming up on his right flank Lee made for the Potomac. Longstreet was advancing along the eastern edge of the Blue Ridge, while Ewell's and Hill's (who had now rejoined) corps moved down the Shenandoah valley. The Potomac was crossed at Shepherdstown between 15 and 22 June by Ewell's corps, and at the same place by Hill's corps between the 24th and 26th. Longstreet crossed at Williamsport also during the 24th to 26th.

About a week previously there had occurred the first of the five factors which were in each case to have a decisive effect on the course of the battle, and very possibly on its result. Lee decided to divide Stuart's cavalry; he retained two brigades to give close protection to his main body. Jenkins's brigade accompanied Ewell's corps in the van of the army, and he sent Stuart with the remaining three brigades to ride round the right flank of the Federal army. They were to protect the flank of the leading corps (Ewell's), and to send back information. He never heard of Stuart again until the battle of Gettysburg had begun.

Hooker crossed the Potomac at Edward's Ferry on 25 and 26 June, and the next day he submitted a plan to General Halleck (Commander-in-Chief of the Union forces) which that general overruled. Annoyed at this – for it was not the first time it had happened – Hooker submitted his resignation, and on 28 June General Meade took command of the Army of the Potomac. Meanwhile, Ewell's leading division had reached Cashtown and Longstreet and Hill were at Chambersburg and Fayetteville respectively. Lee, without Stuart's cavalry, had little idea of Meade's whereabouts, but thanks to a report from a man called Harrison who acted as Longstreet's private intelligence, he knew he was across the Potomac and he realized that a battle was imminent. He therefore hastily ordered his far-flung divisions to concentrate at Cashtown, eight miles west of Gettysburg. By now units of both armies ringed Gettysburg at various distances, but no thought had been given to fighting a battle there.

It was the events on the afternoon of 30 June when General Heth, commanding a division of Hill's corps, ordered a brigade into Gettysburg to procure boots for his men, that decided the place of battle. These men met a column of Federal cavalry sent to cut across Lee's expected line of advance, and retired to report. The next day Hill (Lee had not yet reached Cashtown) ordered Heth's and Pender's divisions to advance on Gettysburg, and a mile west of the town, on McPherson Ridge, the first engagement of the battle took place. These troops, Heth's division in particular, had a very hard fight. But once the 24th Michigan and two regiments from New York and Pennsylvania broke, the remainder did not stop until they were well beyond the town of Gettysburg.

In this preliminary action the Confederates were driven from the ridge, and the Federals suffered a severe blow when losing one of their best generals, John F. Reynolds. Meanwhile divisions of both armies were being hastened to the field. Early on the scene were the Union troops of I and XI Corps, which took up a position west and north of the town. Lee had ordered Ewell to redirect his divisions from Cashtown to Gettysburg, and by midday on 1 July Rodes's division had occupied Oak Ridge, where he was soon heavily opposed by the Federal XI Corps. Heth's division – later reinforced by another division from Hill's corps – engaged the Union's left, where General Doubleday's I Corps were mostly deployed.

It was now a matter of time as to which army would receive reinforcements first, and strenuous efforts were made by both sides. But it was the appearance of General Early of Ewell's corps along the Harrisburg road that made the Union position untenable. Lee arrived on the battlefield in time to witness the discomfiture of the Union troops: XI Corps were streaming through Gettysburg to the area of Cemetery Hill, and I Corps (which had been terribly mauled) hardly paused on Seminary Ridge before crossing the intervening fields to Cemetery Ridge.

Lee's rapid concentration of force had been masterly, and he now felt (understandably) that if he could push home his advantage and drive the enemy troops back upon those corps that had not yet reached the field, the battle would be his. But it was not to be, for at this juncture there occurred the second of those five factors. Culp's Hill was a key feature of the northern part of the battlefield, and it was unoccupied. It could have been taken that evening, and the whole Federal line swept away, but General Ewell felt the task beyond him, and by the next morning it was too late. As it was, the day's fighting had cost the Federals not less than 10,000 men in killed, wounded and missing, besides 5,000 prisoners.

During the night of 1–2 July the Federal army was busy consolidating its position. General Meade and his headquarters arrived from Taneytown at 1 a.m., and when dawn broke he could see the strength of the position by riding round it: XI Corps occupied Cemetery Hill in a half-circle reaching back to Culp's Hill (the feature that should have been in Confederate hands), where Wadsworth's division of I Corps faced a division of Ewell's which had not been in time to fight on the first day. Later in the morning XII Corps took up a position on Wadsworth's right; I Corps was placed behind Cemetery Hill; Hays's Division of II Corps was in Ziegler's Grove; and the remainder of II Corps, and III Corps were allotted the line of Cemetery Ridge from Ziegler's Grove to Little Round Top. On arrival V Corps went into reserve until VI Corps reached the battlefield. It was a very strong position, although there were those who thought it had been jeopardized by the action of General Sickles, commanding III Corps, who on his own authority advanced his corps to occupy a salient on higher ground.

At a somewhat confused informal Confederate council, at which many contradictory opinions were voiced, it was eventually decided to attack the position before Meade's army could be fully concentrated. Undoubtedly Lee's confidence had been further strengthened by the fighting on the first day, and certainly an invading army living on the land had need to be aggressive, but he was taking a great risk with this decision, especially as with Stuart away he was short of proper information.

The obvious start line for any Confederate offensive was Seminary Ridge, which is a longer feature than Cemetery Ridge, and lies about a mile to the west across a shallow valley. Ewell's and Hill's corps, which had borne the brunt of the fighting on the previous day, were holding a position on the north end of the ridge and in the Gettysburg area. Ewell covered the Federal right, and Hill's men were opposite the centre. Longstreet's troops were fresh, although short of Pickett's division, and they held the right of the Confederate line.

Lee decided to make his main thrust against the left of the Union line with Longstreet's corps, and ordered Hill to strike the centre on Cemetery Ridge, and Ewell to co-operate on the enemy's right flank as soon as they heard Longstreet's guns. There then occurred the third crucial event of this battle; for one reason or another Longstreet (who never liked the plan, and had strongly advocated outflanking the enemy) delayed his attack by several hours, and then on finding himself observed by the enemy he carried out an unnecessarily long countermarch. This gave Meade the vital time he needed to bring up his reserves, and it also meant that VI Corps, which had arrived in the battlefield area at about 2 p.m., was in time to fight.

Sickles's advanced position stretched from the Peach Orchard to a rocky outcrop, aptly named the Devil's Den, which firmly anchored the left of his line. Against this fairly strong, but exposed salient Longstreet eventually (about 4 p.m.) hurled his 12,000 men. His two divisions had marched in column from Herr Ridge with McLaws's in the van, but on coming opposite the Peach Orchard McLaws deployed to his left, allowing Hood to pass to his rear and come into line on his right. The battle, especially in the area of the Devil's Den, became a desperate affair, lasting upwards of two hours. Gradually the Federals were forced out of their position and fell back fighting furiously.

Shortly before Longstreet's attack Meade had ridden over to see Sickles, and to register his disapproval of that general's decision to advance his corps. He had seen at once that Sickles could not hold the salient without help and now, with the Confederates pressing hard, he rode off to order forward Sykes's V Corps to shore up the position, and sent Brigadier-General Warren – his Chief Engineer – to examine and report upon the perilous situation that seemed to be developing on his left flank. This resulted in the fourth of those unpredictable events upon which the fate of a battle often hinges. Warren was instrumental in securing the Little Round Top, which had it fallen would have resulted in Meade's left flank being turned and enfiladed.

Meade's left flank was saved, but the crisis was not over, for in the centre of the Federal line gaps were occurring, and these were filled partly by troops brought from the right. This opened the way for Ewell, who it will be remembered had been ordered to co-ordinate his attack with Longstreet's, to sweep down upon the weakened Federal right. The action of his corps forms the last of the five factors that so greatly influenced the course of the battle. His first attack was unco-ordinated and went in far too late, and his second was called off. A good chance of rolling up the Federal right had been lost for ever, for during the night Meade returned the regiments he had withdrawn to the Culp's Hill area.

Thus ended the second day of the battle – a day that had seen some very gallant fighting and a good deal of muddled generalship. The Confederates had gained some ground on their right, both sides had suffered heavy casualties and nothing decisive had been accomplished. At a council of war on the night of 2–3 July Meade decided to stay on the defensive, but Lee's courage and optimism remained buoyant, and his thoughts centred entirely on the offensive. He now had three extra brigades (those of Pickett's division newly arrived), Stuart's cavalry was at last on hand, and he had gained a foothold – albeit a very slender one – on each of Meade's flanks.

Lee eschewed Longstreet's advice to attempt a flank attack, and decided to launch a frontal one against the centre of the enemy line (which was now weaker than either flank), with his cavalry operating to the east and rear of the Federal line to harass the expected retreat. The battle on this day was a much more straightforward affair than the manoeuvres of the first two days, and the centrepiece was the magnificent, but unavailing, charge of Pickett's division.

Early on the morning of 3 July Ewell's forward troops on Culp's Hill were engaged by men of the Federal XII Corps, and in a battle that lasted from 4 a.m. until 11 a.m. they were worsted, and thereafter could be of little use in supporting the main attack. This was opened at 1 p.m. with the thunderous roar of 138 cannon. When, at 2.40 p.m., the bombardment was over Longstreet gave Pickett the order to advance, and 11,000 men (Pickett's division and elements from all three divisions of A. P. Hill's corps) strode across the valley towards the enemy on Cemetery Ridge, and into the very jaws of death. The battle was most savagely contested, men were mown down in hundreds by shot and shell, but to no avail. In the late afternoon Pickett was forced to give the signal to retire, and by then 67 per cent of the total force that had charged with him were casualties. It was the end of the battle of Gettysburg. Meade failed to counterattack, and on the late afternoon of the next day (4 July) Lee began a perfectly orderly retreat to the south.

At much the same time as Pickett's men were suffering so severely one other action was taking place about three miles to the east of the battlefield. Some 8,000 Union cavalrymen forced Stuart to fight on ground not of his choosing. It was a grand battle fought in the old style, and lasting about three hours, before Stuart was forced from the field and quite unable to give aid to the infantrymen.

In a concluding passage of his account of this battle Winston Churchill wrote of Lee's withdrawal from the field, 'he carried with him his wounded and his prisoners. He had lost two guns, *and the war*' (my italics). There are those who argue that the Vicksburg campaign was the most decisive of this long and bitter war between the states, but had Lee smashed Meade's army at Gettysburg it is quite possible that the South could have gained, if only for a short time, independence. Conversely, the crippling casualties Lee suffered in the battle ensured that there could be no other invasion of the North, nor indeed could Lee mount another major offensive with the Army of Northern Virginia.

In this battle there were five important events any one of which, had the situation been handled differently, could have given Lee the victory. But before taking a closer look at them it is necessary to examine the conduct of Lee himself, for the overall responsibility for victory or defeat must lie with him.

He was undoubtedly a great general, but like everyone else he had his faults, although these were outweighed by his overall genius for war. He was not a good quartermaster, and he must take at least part of the blame for his troops being often ill-clad, poorly equipped and fed; he was sometimes irresolute in opposing the wishes of his subordinates, and he placed far too much trust in them. This latter fault resulted in the giving of discretionary orders, and in leaving his lieutenants strictly alone once these orders had been given. These defects were apparent before and during the battle of Gettysburg. That he was let down by some of his senior officers is an indisputable fact which the following accounts will show, but a proportion of the blame for this was of his own making.

The secret of Stuart's blunder lies in the character of the man. In the words of a Union general he was 'the best cavalry leader ever foaled in North America', and that is almost certainly true. He was all that a *beau sabreur* should be; easily distinguished through being the most magnificently dressed man in either army, he rode into battle literally with a song, and sometimes accompanied by a man playing the banjo. But besides his elegance and panache there was an abundance of courage and intelligence. Jeb Stuart was highly skilled in reconnaissance, and possessed all the qualities required for a successful leader of cavalry. The one flaw was an overriding desire for glory, which unfortunately usually sprang from impulse rather than from reason.

Ever since he had commanded the Confederate cavalry his men had seemed invincible, but on 9 June 1863, at the time when Lee was beginning his invasion of the North, this image of invincibility was sadly dented at the Brandy Station action. And in the succeeding days General Pleasonton, the new commander of the Federal cavalry, continually harassed Stuart's brigades as they formed the protective screen for Lee's advance.

There was criticism of Stuart's performance at Brandy Station in which engagement there were 523 Confederate casualties, and the *Richmond Examiner* wrote, 'If the war was a tournament, invented and supported for the pleasure of a few vain and weak-headed officers, these disasters might be dismissed with compassion.' This may have been a little unfair, but it badly bruised Stuart's pride, and no doubt prompted him to seek permission for a ride round the rear of the Federal army as it

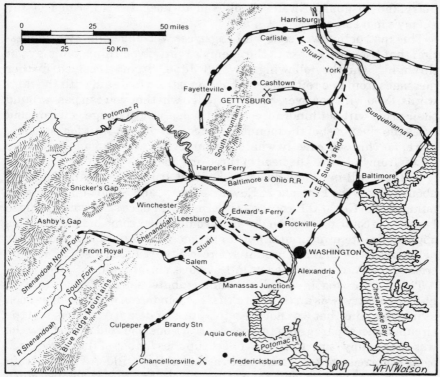

The Gettysburg Campaign: Stuart's Ride 25–29 June 1863

marched for the Potomac crossing above Washington. He had done such
a ride with success a year previous in the Seven Days' Battle, causing
General McClellan considerable discomfiture, and it offered opportunities for a glorified foray and the chance to restore his slightly
creased reputation.

Lee needed information and saw some merit in Stuart's suggestion,
but he knew that the first priority was to protect the flank of Ewell's II
Corps, which was marching down the Shenandoah valley in advance of
the army, and by 22 June had crossed the Potomac and was approaching
Chambersburg. With his army well strung out Lee decided to divide
Stuart's five brigades (Jenkins's was already detached) in order to get
more information and provide wider protection. To this end he sent
Stuart, both direct and through Longstreet, a number of vague and
somewhat confused instructions – they could not be called orders. Stuart
was to leave two brigades to guard Snicker's and Ashby's gaps in the
Blue Ridge and to watch Hooker's Army of the Potomac (whose exact
whereabouts were as yet unknown), and move with the other three into

Maryland to guard Ewell's flank and to keep Lee informed of the enemy's movements.

This instruction was sent via Longstreet who added his own suggestion that 'you are to pass to the enemy's rear, if you think you may get through'.* On the following day, 23 June, Stuart received further messages from Lee reiterating what Longstreet had said with the fatal words, 'You will, however, be able to judge whether you can pass around their army without hindrance, doing them all the damage you can, and cross the river east of the mountains.'† Stuart did not wait for anything more, for this was exactly what he wanted. Before dawn on 25 June he set off from Salem at the head of three brigades.

Hooker, still in command of the Federal army, was at this time just about to cross the Potomac at Edward's Ferry, and Stuart unexpectedly bumped into General Hancock's II Corps. He at once sent word of this to Lee, which could have given the army commander some indication of his opponent's intentions, but this, the only message Stuart sent, was never delivered. This chance encounter forced Stuart to turn south, and he crossed the Potomac only a few miles above Washington.

The detour this involved was unfortunate, for Lee, operating in hostile country, was anxious for Stuart to join forces with Ewell as soon as possible. But that was not the only cause for delay. An unwise (in the circumstances) paragraph in Lee's instructions had told Stuart that he was to take any opportunity to collect supplies for use of the army. Such a one occurred while his men were resting at Rockville. A Federal train of 150 wagons was espied by one of his patrols, and those vehicles which were not captured were chased almost to the environs of Washington. Colonel Blackford of Stuart's command described it 'as exciting as a fox chase for several miles'. Further time was lost cutting telegraph lines, ripping up the Baltimore and Ohio railroad, and carrying out other swift and unexpected strikes.

This no doubt was good fun, but it was not what Stuart was originally meant to do; his cavalry were the eyes of the army, without them Lee was virtually blind. Moreover, Stuart was to safeguard the right flank of the leading corps, but through these marplot peregrinations he was too late to rendezvous with General Ewell's leading division at York on 27 June. He not only failed to send Lee any information, but he was unable to obtain sufficient for his own purposes. He was groping in the dark on the fringes of the armies, and he never found Lee, who eventually located him at Carlisle on the second day of the battle.

To what extend did Stuart's absence affect the result of the battle? In respect of the actual fighting probably not very much. He did not appear

*An Aide-de-Camp of Lee, Papers of Colonel Marshall, p. 204.
†The War of the Rebellion, Vol. XIV, p. 923.

on the scene until early on the third day, when Lee ordered him to take position on the left of the line. Later on that day, as has been related, his men were engaged in a major fight with the Federal cavalry. It is possible that had it not been for their long ride of inroad and foray, which had taken the stuffing out of men and horses, he might have broken through General Gregg's squadrons and caused a great deal of trouble in the Army of the Potomac's rear. But even so this could hardly have been decisive.

Undoubtedly the greatest embarrassment Lee suffered was his total ignorance of Meade's whereabouts until Longstreet's spy got through the enemy lines and reported that the entire Federal army was across the Potomac and heading for the South Mountain, but Lee still had no idea of their route nor order of march. What he did know was that his lines of communication could now be cut, and that he would have to abandon his original plan of marching to Harrisburg and Baltimore, and instead call in his forward troops and concentrate for battle.

But what was very much worse, having accepted battle he had to fight the first two days not knowing properly the whereabouts of a substantial part of Meade's forces. This caused him to make what was almost certainly the wrong plan of attack when on the second day he ordered a frontal assault with inferior numbers against a strongly positioned enemy. To have moved round their left flank and attacked in rear would have been a bold manoeuvre and open to a Federal cut-off attack, but it offered the best chance of success. However, without precise knowledge of Meade's 'missing' corps a flank operation might court disaster.

There seems little doubt that Stuart took undue advantage of the loose wording of his instruction. He was an experienced and skilled cavalry commander, who on this occasion allowed personal consider-ations to outweigh what he must have known were his general's paramount wishes. Lee never censured Stuart for this dereliction of duty, perhaps because he realized, unlike his chief-of-staff who wanted Stuart court martialled, that his orders were not sufficiently forceful. Nevertheless, his dalliance quite possibly affected the outcome of the battle. Indeed General Fuller goes so far as to say this was 'the blunder which as much as any other wrecked Lee at Gettysburg'.*

If lack of information from Stuart caused Lee to make a wrong plan of attack, lack of initiative by Ewell on the afternoon of the first day allowed Meade to remain in the field and eventually win the battle. When a general commits a serious, perhaps even battle-losing, error (and at Gettysburg Ewell committed two) there is often a personal reason outside of the battlefield. In the case of Stuart it was, at least

*Fuller, p. 158.

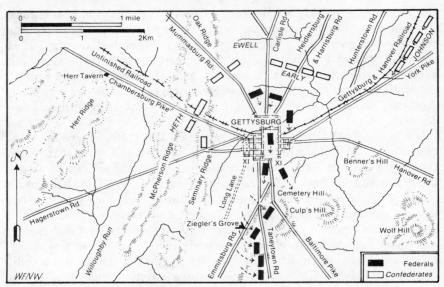

The Battle of Gettysburg: II Corps 1 July, p.m.

partly, vanity; in the case of Ewell unfitness (for even in the less taxing campaigns of the last century a general needed to be fit if he was to function properly); and in the case of Longstreet, whose performance will be examined later, it was probably pique.

General Ewell had taken command of Lee's II Corps in place of General Jackson killed at Chancellorsville. Apart from his strange lapse in the peninsular campaign Jackson had shown himself to be a commander of the very highest order, and in consequence a most difficult man to follow. Lee had come to rely upon him very greatly, for not only was he a brilliant general but he supplied Lee with that resolution he sometimes lacked. Not long before his own death Lee was talking to the Reverend William Jones of certain incidents in the battle, and banging his fist upon the table Lee exclaimed, 'If I had had Stonewall Jackson at Gettysburg I would have won that fight, and a complete victory there would have given us Washington and Baltimore, if not Philadelphia, and would have established the independence of the Confederacy.'* And what is more Lee, when he said that, was thinking of Ewell's failure to launch his troops against the enemy on the evening of the first day of the battle.

It came about like this. On the afternoon of 1 July the Federal I and XI Corps were being hard pressed by Ewell's leading divisions – Rodes's from the direction of Oak Hill, and Early's from the Harrisburg Road –

* Gordon, p. 154.

with two divisions of Hill's in support, and it was clear that the Federals were about to break. Indeed, the men in front of Ewell's leading brigade had been taken in flank, and those not in full retreat were laying down their arms. Lee, who had arrived in time to witness Heth's earlier attack, now saw his enemy streaming through Gettysburg in total disarray. He quickly appreciated the value of Cemetery Hill, and as neither Ewell nor Early was around he sent an urgent message to Ewell to seize this key point, but characteristically he added the two words 'if practicable' at the end of the message.

Ewell's position at this time is uncertain; he may have been at Rodes's divisional headquarters, but he does not appear to have been in touch with the situation. This was uncharacteristic, for although he was renowned for his eccentricities these did not include fighting battles from the rear. On the contrary, in the past he had proved himself an excellent fighting commander of considerable ability. He was almost certainly not himself throughout the three days of Gettysburg. He was known to be afflicted with chronic dyspepsia, which may have been troubling him at the time, he had lost a leg in an earlier battle and was only beginning to master a wooden one (which parried a musket ball as he was riding through Gettysburg on the evening of 1 July!), and this was his first command of a corps. All of which probably contributed to the catalepsy with which he was now smitten.

Ewell did not go forward to see for himself, but sent for Early (who also appears to have been somewhat out of touch with front-line events) to find out the state of his troops, whom he felt must be extremely tired after their long, hard fighting day with some heavy casualties. He was also without his third division (General Johnson's), which was two miles away when he received Lee's message, and so he decided that any further attack was impracticable until Johnson's comparatively fresh troops were to hand. While he waited Culp's Hill was occupied and Cemetery Hill strengthened.

An extra punch late that afternoon, even with tired troops, had every chance of defeating the scattered and battered Federals before any organized defence was ready. Jackson would have done it, and although it is impossible to say that it would have won the battle for Lee, with hindsight it seems to have offered him the best chance. But even if it had not proved decisive, Early's division could have occupied the vitally important Culp's Hill unopposed, where the following evening Ewell's corps was to suffer grievous casualties trying to take it.

The Times correspondent (Lawley) in an excellent from-the-field dispatch, published on 18 August 1863, has this to say on the subject: 'It is the belief of many that if General Ewell, after driving his enemy for four miles and through the town of Gettysburg, had not, by superior orders, stayed the pursuit within the town itself, his victorious troops would have camped on the night of 1st July upon the top of that ridge [Cemetery] which upon the two subsequent days all the desperate efforts of the Confederates were inadequate to storm.'

This is absolutely true, except for the words 'by superior orders'. Whose orders? Certainly not Lee's, for he was some distance away at the time. No, the decision to call a halt was taken by Ewell.

After their narrow escape, those units of the Federal army already on the battlefield spent most of the night 1–2 July consolidating and strengthening their positions. Their Vth and VIth Corps (especially the VIth) were still some miles distant, although Lee was unaware of this, and it was that fact which decided him, on the evening of 1 July, to put in a frontal attack the next morning with Longstreet's corps against Meade's left. At the evening council, and again at 3 o'clock the following morning, Longstreet argued hotly to be allowed to put in a flanking attack to seize the prominent position Little Round Top. He did not like

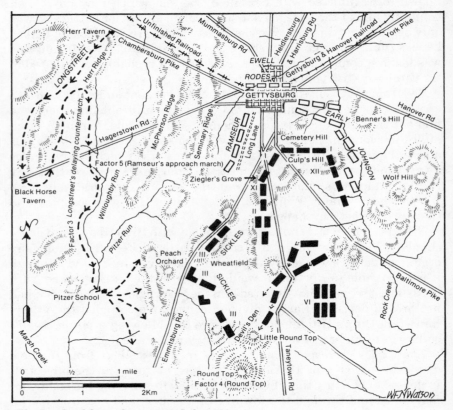

The Battle of Gettysburg: 2–3 July 1863

the idea of a frontal assault against a strongly defended position, especially as he was still without Pickett's division; but Lee was adamant, for he was not prepared to risk a flanking movement without precise information. And so after he had ridden over to confer with Ewell on his part in the forthcoming battle he sent positive orders to Longstreet to mount his attack, and to mount it that morning.

Lee could not have found Longstreet (Old Pete) an easy subordinate. He was contumacious, argumentative, and conveniently deaf – but for all that he was a great soldier. At Gettysburg he was particularly difficult. On the morning of 2 July his corps was encamped on the Chambersburg road, and the orders he received were to take position on the Emmitsburg road and to attack the Peach Orchard, which Lee (erroneously) thought was the left of the Union line. He intended the attack to go in before midday, but Longstreet said later that he did not receive the orders until 11 a.m., a fact that is not borne out by General Hood, commanding his 1st Division.

When Longstreet eventually began his march, at about midday, Hood's and McLaws's divisions marched west of Herr Ridge to Black Horse Tavern on the Hagerstown road. Crossing the road the troops ascended the high ground and then Longstreet realized that his column could be seen by Federal signallers on Little Round Top. He then made an extraordinary decision. He was already hours later than he should have been in launching his attack, but instead of going forward along the track to the Pitzer School, where he would have been (for part of the time) in view of the Little Round Top observation post, he doubled back to the Herr Ridge and renewed his march to dead ground along the west bank of Willoughby Run. He does not appear to have gained surprise by this move, and he certainly lost valuable time during which the Federal V Corps reached the battlefield and took up position, and their VI Corps also arrived in time to form a reserve.

No satisfactory reason has ever been put forward for Longstreet's performance on 2 July; it has every sign of being due to pique because his plan (which as it turned out would have been the better one) was not adopted. It cannot be said positively that his disobedience of orders (and he was to repeat the offence the next day) lost the battle, although Lee died believing it did; but his stubbornness and dilatoriness in launching his attack four hours late taken in conjunction with another key event – this time concerning the Federal army – must have diminished Lee's chances of victory.

The fight in the Peach Orchard, where Sickles had positioned his corps, was some of the fiercest of this very fierce three-day battle. And during this epic struggle, through a strange concatenation of events, an army was probably saved from defeat. A general, without orders, places his corps in advance of the line; his chief, realizing the error and its damaging consequences, orders up the reserve; he then details a staff officer to reconnoitre an exposed flank; and because the reserve has been ordered up and is to hand the staff officer is able to make safe, in the nick of time, a vital key point.

When the battle was raging in the Peach Orchard and towards the Devil's Den, Meade was with Sickles (who later lost a leg in the fight) and saw that III Corps was about to break and that the left flank of Hancock's II Corps had been exposed by Sickles's forward movement, and was in danger of being turned. Fortunately, through Longstreet's tardiness, it was possible to move up General Sykes's V Corps from reserve and replace it with the newly arrived VI Corps. While Meade went off to attend to this he ordered General Warren to reconnoitre the extreme left, which was causing him anxiety.

Warren ascended the Little Round Top, manned by a signal section. It was very obvious to him that this feature could hold the key to the battle. From its rocky eminence he could see Confederate troops forming up in the woods on the west side of the Emmitsburg road preparatory to attacking the extreme left flank of the Union line. 'The discovery was intensely thrilling and appalling,' wrote Warren in his report. He at once sent an urgent message to Meade for a division to be sent to this point, but before the messenger could arrive the threat to the hill became imminent, and Warren took immediate action. 'I rode down the hill, meeting my old brigade,' he writes. 'The commander had already passed, so I took the responsibility to detach Colonel O'Rorke's regiment, which moved at once to the hilltop.'* Soon a battery of rifled cannon arrived, and although the fighting round the huge boulders raged for a long time, through Warren's prompt action the Little Round Top was denied the enemy, and the left of the line was secured.

General Warren concluded his report by saying, 'I was wounded slightly by a musketball while talking with Lieutenant Hazlett [the gunner officer who was later killed]; seeing the position saved, though the whole line to the right and front of us was melting away under the enemy's attack, I left the hill to rejoin General Meade near the center of the field, where a new crisis was at hand.' It was this new crisis that brought about the fifth and last of the decisive factors in this battle, for it entailed Meade weakening his right in order to shore up his centre, and thereby giving Ewell the chance – the very last chance – to roll up Meade's right, and perhaps win the battle.

At the time Longstreet opened his attack Ewell had two divisions (Rodes and Early) in the west and east parts of Gettysburg town respectively,

*Civil War Times Illustrated, p. 46.

and his third division, commanded by Johnson, was farther east. He had received orders early on 2 July to demonstrate in force against the right of the enemy line, and it was intended that his attack should coincide with Longstreet's. But once again Lee had given Ewell a fatal degree of latitude in allowing him to judge when conditions seemed suitable for him to commit his troops.

It seems that in the ample time available the divisional commanders had done little in the way of reconnaissance. It is true, the Federal right was to a certain extent screened by woods and skirmishers, but much could have been learnt concerning lines of approach and timings for the attack. There was also some bad staff work and an appalling lack of liaison within the corps and with Hill's left brigades. It was not until 5.30 p.m., after the Confederate batteries on Benner's Hill had been silenced, that Ewell decided it was time for his corps to attack. Since he had ordered the three divisions to go in simultaneously, and Johnson's was still a mile from its objective (Culp's Hill), there was bound to be further delay, even if the approach to the start line was carefully co-ordinated – which it was not.

Meade, with his reserves fully committed and Longstreet's men aided by Hill's about to break through, had been forced to denude the right of his line. Two of Geary's brigades were taken off Culp's Hill (leaving only Greene's brigade) and brought, via the Baltimore Pike, to Rock Creek, and Williams's division from the centre was brought to the left, as were Caldwell's division of II Corps and parts of two other divisions also from that corps. But the whole of XI Corps was still on Cemetery Hill. The key to a Confederate success lay with Ewell, whose corps should have been poised for a knockout blow on the hook which bent round from Cemetery Hill to Culp's Hill, but throughout the operation neither Ewell nor Rodes, commanding his right division, appeared to have a proper grasp of the situation, and the latter in particular remained remote from the battle.

Rodes planned that his attack should be mounted from a start line along a track that paralleled the Emmitsburg road, but having done that he left the actual operation in charge of a young brigadier-general called Stephen Ramseur, who was faced with the longest approach march and consequently was not ready to engage at 7.30 p.m. when the other two divisions were at last committed to battle. Early's and Johnson's divisions fought furiously for over an hour in rapidly failing light and across unreconnoitred ground, striving to gain a foothold on Cemetery and Culp's Hills. Meanwhile Rodes's men had still not emerged from Gettysburg, and although liaison with III Corps' left brigade was eventually achieved, this information never reached Ewell, who fought the battle believing his right to be in the air.

By the time Ramseur had the division ready to attack Cemetery Hill it was almost dark, and he could dimly discern Union batteries and two lines of infantry behind formidable breastworks. Ramseur decided, after consultation with a neighbouring brigade commander, that the position was too strongly held and the hour too late for him to launch an attack. He consequently recommended to Rodes that the attack should be cancelled. Rodes gave the order and Ewell concurred. This decision was undoubtedly correct in circumstances that should never have arisen.

In the opinion of some historians the costly and calamitous struggle that took place on the evening of 2 July around Cemetery and Culp's Hills was arguably the most crucial action of the whole battle, and one which should have given Lee the victory. It is dangerous to be dogmatic on such occasions, and this phase of the battle has been re-fought over the years possibly more times than any of the other episodes. In spite of – or perhaps because of – all the attention every aspect of the Gettysburg battle has received there is a surprising disagreement as to the Federal strength on Culp's and Cemetery Hills directly after Longstreet's attack, and on the time that reinforcements arrived there. It is generally assumed that by about 6 p.m. there were at least 6,000 men and 38 guns in position, and that by then the crisis was over and the Confederates were too late.

If this was so Ewell's opportunity was fleeting, and that after 6 p.m. however hard he had pressed his attack he would not have dislodged the Federals and taken Cemetery Hill. But in the absence of absolutely reliable evidence as to numbers and timing of Federal reinforcements it is impossible to be certain, and in any event there are some questions to be answered germane to Ewell's failure to attack the feature a great deal earlier than he did, and before the Confederate batteries had been knocked out. It would seem that this was principally because Johnson's division was so far back, but why was it so far back, for it was known to be within two miles of Culp's Hill the previous evening? Why was the importance of reconnaissance neglected? And why did Rodes virtually opt out of the attack and leave much to a comparatively junior officer?

Short of satisfactory answers to these questions it is difficult to avoid the conclusion that Ewell's corps missed a very fine chance of unhinging the Union line, and gaining a victory which might have rendered unnecessary the gallant but forlorn charge which extinguished the Confederate hopes on the following day.

If one were to select a single factor that lost the Confederates this battle the choice would probably be Stuart's absence at a critical time. To pinpoint the factor that gave the Federals the victory is more difficult; no isolated event, other than perhaps the action on Little Round Top, stands out and the award must go to Meade's handling of a defensive battle.

If it is agreed that Stuart's escapade lost Lee the battle through causing him to fight it partially blind, it illustrates once again how disastrous can be lack of accurate information, and it shows how a personal characteristic – vanity – can influence the course of a battle.

It is sometimes argued that Meade was a puppet in the hands of two of his corps commanders – Generals Howard and Hancock – but this is a little unfair. It must be remembered that he took command only a week before an important battle was forced upon him on ground not of his choosing, and he lost his best general in the very earliest stage of the battle. Moreover, the decision to stand firm after the second day's fighting rather than withdraw – as so often in the past – was almost certainly his, and the handling of his corps (and at times divisions) to meet threatened points of attack cannot be faulted.

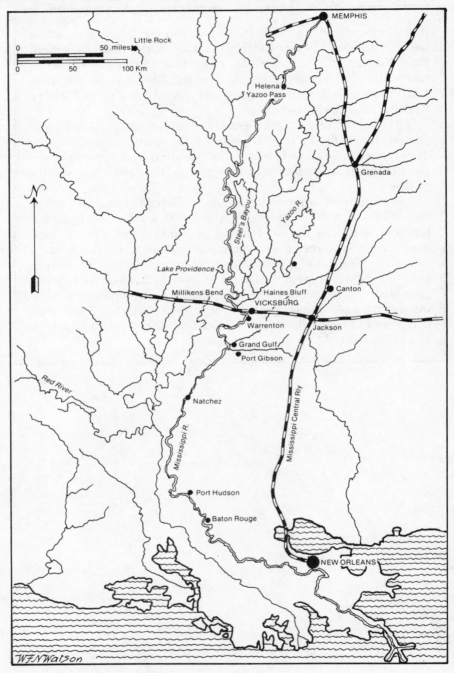

The Vicksburg Campaign: January–July 1863

17 The Vicksburg Campaign
January–July 1863

VICKSBURG is situated on the east, or left, bank of the Mississippi some 400 miles from its mouth at New Orleans. This great waterway was of enormous importance to both the Union and the Confederacy. For the Union it formed the main artery, in a part of the country that was short of roads, for the transportation of industrial products from the north to much-needed markets, and for transportation of troops and supplies which, using the various navigable tributaries, could campaign into the very heart of the Confederate south. For the Confederates, the loss of the river meant the isolation of a large chunk of their territory in the west, from which they obtained (by way of the Red River, which joins the Mississippi north of Port Hudson) big quantities of food, military supplies, and personnel from Louisiana, Texas, and Arkansas.

In this matter the Union, with its greater industrial potential, had the advantage where ironclads and other vessels were concerned, and so the Confederates had attempted to close the river to their opponents by a series of strongly fortified points from Columbus in the north to New Orleans in the south. During the first half of 1862 the Federals had systematically taken all these strongpoints save for Vicksburg. Here the powerful batteries on the bluff above the river defied the Federal Admiral, David Farragut, who having destroyed the Confederate fleet attempted to land troops and take the city. This proved impossible, and in July the Federal fleet had to withdraw, leaving Vicksburg quite intact, and the Confederates were once again in control of the river from there to Port Hudson, with supplies readily available down the Red River.

Vicksburg, the key to the river, had to be taken, for, as President Lincoln said, the war could not be won 'until that key is in our pocket'. The man selected to do it was Major-General Ulysses Grant, who in the autumn of 1862 was given command of the Army of the Tennessee. Earlier in the year he had carried out a successful advance, capturing Forts Henry and Donelson, and driving back the Confederate forces covering Nashville, the capital of Tennessee. He was not a very prepossessing officer to look at, but he was a first-class fighting general, who in the forthcoming battles was to show energy and enterprise that quite outmatched anything his opponents could bring against him. He was about to conduct and win one of the great campaigns of history.

In November 1862 General Joseph E. Johnston was given overall command of the Confederate armies in the West. The Army of the Mississippi, which was the one chiefly concerned with the defence of Vicksburg, was commanded by Lieutenant-General Pemberton. He was a sound administrator, diligent and hard-working, but he was not a good general. Apart from his initial problem of having to defend, virtually without the aid of cavalry, a very wide front, his task throughout was made more difficult through receiving contradictory orders from Johnston, his immediate military superior, and Davis, his President and Commander-in-Chief. By April 1863, when Grant began his campaign to take Vicksburg from the rear, Pemberton had around 50,000 troops under command, but they were dispersed from near Memphis in the north to Port Hudson in the south.

Grant's first attempt to take Vicksburg was a two-pronged attack launched in December. Pemberton's main body, commanded by General Van Dorn, held the line of the Yallabusha river, near Grenada, and Grant planned that he would keep these men fully occupied while Major-General Sherman, with a force of 32,000 aboard six transports, would sail down river to the mouth of the Yazoo, land them and attack Vicksburg. The venture ended in disaster, largely because the Confederates managed to get behind Grant's line of advance and destroy large quantities of military material and supplies at his base. Cut off from his supplies Grant had to fall back, which allowed Pemberton to switch some 12,000 men against Sherman. That general succeeded in landing his troops, but on unsuitable ground and at the battle of Chickasaw Bluffs, fought on 29 December, he was defeated with the loss of about 2,000 men.

The failure of this overland attempt to take Vicksburg prompted the Federal Commander-in-Chief, General Halleck, to urge that the next move should be by water in conjunction with the navy. Grant's army was now organized into four corps, one of which – the 16th under General Hurlbut – was left at Memphis to protect communications; the other three were camped wherever there was sufficient dry ground amid the swamps, creeks, canals, and bayous* of the Mississippi delta. Two corps – the 13th and 15th under Generals McClernand and Sherman respectively – were at Millikins Bend, and the 17th Corps, commanded by General McPherson, was at Lake Providence. Grant's problem was to use these troops, in conjunction with Admiral Porter's fleet, to turn the right or left flanks of the Vicksburg defences. To attempt this the men

---

*Intersecting streams or channels amid the large alluvial deposits.

were put to labour unremittingly in dredging and digging – as well as some fighting – for a part of January and all of February and March 1863.

The operations, of which there were four, were somewhat complicated and need not be gone into in any detail. The first was to dig a mile-long canal across the peninsula opposite Vicksburg to enable the unarmed transports to bypass the garrison's guns and land an army on the left bank below Vicksburg. All went well to start with, but at the beginning of March a sudden flood drove the troops out, and by then enemy guns near Warrenton were beginning to take toll, and so the project was abandoned.

While the canal was being dug men of McPherson's corps were put to work on opening a route from Lake Providence through some bayous to the Red River, so that the Mississippi could be entered by that river and Vicksburg could be assaulted on the left flank. It was a most formidable undertaking involving the clearance of trees and stumps above and below water. The scheme when completed would have opened up a safe route of some 400 miles, and indeed by the end of March, when the dry weather gave Grant other ideas, much progress had been made.

The other two operations aimed to turn the right flank of the defences. The first was another most ambitious project involving a route of 700 miles, and known as the Yazoo Pass expedition. The Yazoo Pass was a bayou that had been blocked by an earthwork which was to be demolished by a mine, giving access for transports from the Mississippi through other waters to the Yazoo river, and so to turn the right flank at Haines' Bluff. As soon as Pemberton got knowledge of this move he had little difficulty in blocking it with troops stationed at Grenada whom he ordered to hold the line of the Yallabusha river, ninety miles north of Vicksburg. Here General Loring, at the head of a 1,500-strong Confederate force, based on a hastily improvised cotton-bale fort, defied all attempts of the Union gunboats to get through.

The fourth and final attempt was made by General Sherman and Admiral Porter, with eleven vessels, by way of Steele's bayou into the Sunflower and Yazoo rivers to Haines' Bluff, a sailing distance of about 200 miles. Pemberton again got early information of this design and was able to make the passage of the troops impossible, and indeed this expedition might have ended in disaster when the Confederates blocked the river behind the fleet, and there was a sudden fall in the waters. Sherman's men managed to drive the Confederates off, and in the course of three days the fleet backed its way to safety.

Grant was to say later that he never had much hope that these canal-bayou expeditions would succeed, but during the wet months they served to keep the troops fully occupied, alert and in good condition while at the same time he was able to examine all possibilities however remote. None of this thinking was known to the mounting number of his critics in the North, who out of envy or mistrust took pains, and in some cases pleasure, to underline these costly failures and urge Grant's replacement. But President Lincoln never lost faith in him. 'I think we'll try him a little longer,' he said, and so the way was clear for a masterstroke of genius and triumph in the West.

In the winter months the roads, or tracks, on the west bank of the Mississippi in this area were usually feet under water, but in April they began to emerge and Grant was able to begin operations on a plan he had envisaged for some time. This was for the navy and transports to run the gauntlet past the Vicksburg batteries at night, and to be at hand to ferry his troops across the river at Grand Gulf or some point below. Once across the river the original plan was to send the leading corps – McClernand's – to aid General Banks to reduce Port Hudson, and then for Banks to combine with Grant in taking Vicksburg from the rear. Sherman's corps was to remain in the Vicksburg area, and a division would create a diversion about 150 miles up river. And in order to confuse Pemberton still further, and at the same time to inflict maximum damage, Colonel Grierson with three cavalry regiments was to raid the country in Pemberton's rear. This epic cavalry raid – worthy of the best that Jeb Stuart could accomplish – eventually ended up at Baton Rouge.

On the night of 16–17 April Porter's fleet successfully carried out the

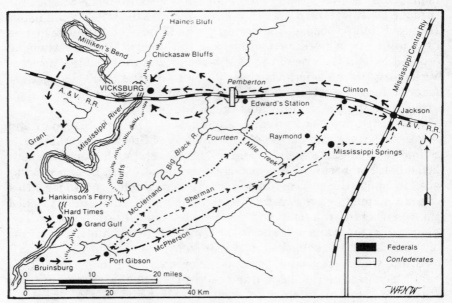

The Vicksburg Campaign: Grant's March

hazardous operation of running past the Vicksburg batteries with the loss of only one vessel. A few nights later the operation was repeated with six transports and twelve barges carrying supplies; on this occasion one transport and six barges were lost. Meanwhile, a scheme to open up a number of bayous in order to float troops down on flats proved impracticable, and they had to march over very difficult country the whole way to a place aptly named Hard Times, just opposite Grand Gulf. But the naval bombardment of Grand Gulf failed to neutralize the defences, and so the troops made a further march of six miles and then crossed the river unopposed opposite Bruinsberg.

Pemberton's troops were very scattered, and Grant's diversions had been entirely successful. General Bowen's force of 8,000 at Grand Gulf was clearly insufficient to hold McClernand's corps and two divisions of McPherson's,* but the Federal advance along the two roads leading to Port Gibson was stubbornly contested by four brigades fighting on ground ideal for defence. However, numbers prevailed and McClernand's men were in Port Gibson on the morning of 2 May. Grand Gulf was not tenable after Port Gibson fell, and Bowen evacuated it, retreating across the Big Black River to Hankinson's Ferry on 3 May, while McClernand's troops spent that night at Willow Springs. Grant, from his headquarters at Grand Gulf, ordered Sherman to join with two divisions and some supply wagons, and the army did not resume the advance until 7 May.

Grant now faced the crisis of the campaign. He had information that General Johnston was heading for Jackson with an army that was being reinforced from various Confederate strongholds, and he also heard that General Banks was in no position to co-operate with him.† Bold action was now imperative and speed vital. Grant decided to cut himself off from his base, to supplement what few rations he had from the country (which in this region was quite possible), and to march for Jackson in order to beat Johnston's force before it could unite with Pemberton's.

Pemberton, meanwhile, was in a most unenviable position. Through his lack of cavalry he was uncertain of what Grant was doing. He felt it essential to protect Vicksburg, but he also feared for his important railway communication between that town and Jackson. As a result his brigades were scattered, thereby making it much easier for Grant to defeat him in detail, as well as to cope with any threat from Johnston.

---

*Grant's strength for this campaign was about 50,000 men, but troops had to be detached for various duties, and his numbers actually engaged in rear of Vicksburg prior to the siege varied between 40,000 and 45,000.

†It appears (see Grant Papers p. 91) that as early as 19 April Grant had abandoned any idea of fulfilling the original plan to send troops to Banks, although in his memoirs (p. 410) he says the decision was not taken until 3 May when he received a letter from Banks saying he could not be at Port Hudson before 10 May.

On 7 May Grant moved forward in a north-easterly direction with a view to holding a line parallel to the Vicksburg–Jackson railroad. McPherson's corps was aimed for Jackson slightly ahead and on the right; Sherman's was to come up into the centre and McClernand had the left with a division guarding the line of the Big Black. On 12 May Fourteen Mile Creek was crossed, and in the vicinity of Raymond, General Logan's division of McPherson's corps met Brigadier-General Grigg's Confederate brigade that Pemberton had ordered out from Jackson. There was a stiff engagement lasting between two and three hours, until the Confederates abandoned the field and headed back for Jackson, suffering 505 casualties of which 73 were killed. Logan had 65 men killed and 367 wounded or missing.

At about the same time as Grigg's men were straggling into Jackson, General Johnston arrived to take command in the field. He had with him about 12,000 men, and he knew that Grant's army was between him and Pemberton, whose main force was now in the area of Edwards' Station. He sent a dispatch to Pemberton urging him to attack Sherman's (he meant McPherson's) rear at Clinton, and then telegraphed his President, ending with the words 'I am too late', which might appear to be an attempt to divert responsibility for what was likely to be the loss of the state capital. Thereafter he took few steps to defend Jackson, but he did make arrangements to evacuate valuable material by the Canton railway.

On the 14th Grant's leading corps closed in on Jackson. Sherman now held the right, moving from Raymond through Mississippi Springs, while McPherson had moved from Raymond to Clinton and thence towards Jackson. McClernand, who had successfully withdrawn his troops from in front of Pemberton's army at Edwards' Station, now had divisions well placed to support both the leading corps. It rained in torrents on the night of the 13th and on the early morning of the 14th, and so the assault on Jackson was postponed until 11 a.m. in order to safeguard the powder. The brunt of the attack fell to McPherson's corps, and in particular to the three brigades of General Crocker's leading division, but Tuttle's division of Sherman's corps played an important part with a right hook that captured ten guns. Opposition from troops in the forward entrenchments facing Sherman's men (mainly those men who had been defeated at Raymond) was negligible, but on the left McPherson met with slightly stiffer resistance. However, by 4 p.m. both corps were in Jackson, having suffered between them 300 casualties. The Confederates lost 845 men and 17 guns.

After his defeat at Jackson, Johnston moved a few miles north towards Canton, and the Confederates were about to get themselves into a terrible tangle. Pemberton had disregarded Johnston's order to attack McPherson; instead he struck south-east against Grant's supply line, which had never existed.* Meanwhile, the defeated Johnston was marching north, and so there was the ludicrous situation of some 45,000 Confederate soldiers well separated in three different areas (Vicksburg, south of Edwards' Station, and north of Jackson) faced with about an equal number of Union troops all within close support of each other.

Johnston's dispatch of 13 May had been sent out by three messengers, one of whom was in Federal pay, and so on the 14th Grant was aware of its content, although he was not to know that Pemberton had disobeyed the order. He at once ordered McPherson and McClernand to about turn their corps and head west, while Sherman was left in Jackson with orders to destroy all military and manufacturing installations and to rip up the rail track.

On 14 May Johnston, from six miles north of Jackson, sent another dispatch to Pemberton, informing him of the loss of the state capital and urging him to make all speed to unite with his force. This time Pemberton obeyed, and countermarched back to Edwards' Station intending to take the road north to Brownsville. Grant had no indication of this last order, but he knew the approximate whereabouts of the two Confederate forces, and he possessed that essential gift of a good commander of being able to put himself into the mind of his opponent. He felt sure that a united Confederate army would cross the Big Black and attempt to bar the way to Vicksburg. He therefore took steps to hasten an engagement against Pemberton before he could join Johnston.

Unlike his enemy he was working on interior lines, and the concentration of his army, given the nature of the country, was a comparatively simple matter. Three roads led to Edwards' Station. The northern one from Jackson through Clinton ran parallel and just south of the railroad, and there were two emanating from a fork about a mile from Raymond, and then running roughly parallel to each other but about two and a half miles apart. McPherson had been ordered to make for Bolton on the 14th when Grant obtained a copy of Johnston's dispatch, and his corps would therefore use the top road. But McClernand's divisions were well spread, Hovey's also being on the top road but some four miles ahead of McPherson's leading troops. Of McClernand's remaining three divisions those of Osterhaus and Carr took the middle road, and A. J. Smith's men, backed up by Blair's division of Sherman's corps, marched up the direct (or lower) Raymond road.

Pemberton's men had experienced some confusion in negotiating Baker's Creek on their way south-east, for the rains had swollen the

---

* As it happened General Blair's division of Sherman's corps had now joined, bringing 200 wagons of rations – the only supplies received until the time of the siege – and these were at Auburn, but strongly protected.

waters, and by the 15th they were under orders to countermarch back to the Jackson road. Very early the next morning Grant got information via railway workmen that Pemberton was heading east with about 25,000 men. He at once ordered Sherman to leave Jackson and come up on the army's extreme right; McClernand was ordered to press on to gain contact, and he was given Blair's division. McPherson was also told to press forward in close support of Hovey's division.

The position taken up by Pemberton to fight what became known as the battle of Champion's Hill (sometimes Baker's Creek) was an extremely strong one, but it was probably chosen fortuitously. The Federal troops had made contact while Pemberton's men were still countermarching, forcing him to take up the best available defensive position. Confederate pickets on all three roads were quickly driven in, and the first serious fighting was on the top road. This road on meeting Champion's Hill turns south and runs over a ridge for about a mile to join the middle road. The hill itself is a commanding feature although only about eighty feet high, and on its east side a thickly wooded ravine runs north and west to Baker's Creek. Pemberton took up a position covering all three roads, with Stevenson's division on the left holding the northern section of the ridge, Bowen in the centre and Loring on the right. The heaviest fighting took place on his left and in the centre, for

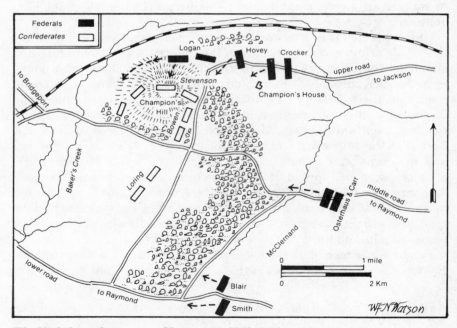

The Vicksburg Campaign: Champion's Hill 16 May 1863

Loring's division was little troubled by McClernand who was extremely dilatory.

The battle proper began a little before 11 a.m., and there was a lot of very hard fighting for about four hours before the Confederates on the left broke. Hovey's division on the top road spearheaded the attack, and in order to protect its right flank Logan's division of McPherson's corps was put in to engage Stevenson's men on the north side of the hill. Logan's brigades were so successful that they worked round parallel to and then behind the Confederate left, and were in a position to cut off their line of retreat. But Grant lacked knowledge of the country, and did not fully appreciate this tactical advantage. And so when Hovey's hard-pressed and courageous fighters called for assistance from their precarious hold on the ridge, Logan was ordered to disengage and fall back to help.

Before this occurred Hovey had gained the crest of the ridge and captured eleven guns, but Pemberton ordered Bowen to support Stevenson, and after some desperate fighting Hovey's men were thrown back across open country to Champion's House, losing all but two of their captured guns. But when his call for help, mentioned above, was answered by Crocker's division of McPherson's corps the ridge was again successfully assaulted, and Stevenson's division was routed, which left Bowen little choice but to withdraw.

Loring, who had not been much engaged on the Confederate right, was ordered to send two brigades to assist the left and centre, but they were not in time to do more than take up a position covering the withdrawal. Stevenson's and Bowen's men failed to hold the ford at the creek for Loring, and his division, unable to discover another lower down, were cut off and had no alternative but to break away south, and then by a circuitous route to join Johnston. This was the biggest engagement of the campaign. Pemberton lost 3,839 men (380 killed), 24 guns and, of course, the future use of Loring's division, while Grant's army suffered 2,408 casualties which included 397 men killed. Hovey's division lost exactly half of Grant's total casualties.

From the moment Grant was known to be heading for Grand Gulf with the obvious intention of attacking him in rear, Pemberton had decided to hold the Big Black River, and to this end he had constructed a number of bridgehead defences. It was to the one opposite the Black River Bridge (where the railway crossed) that he now fell back, and prepared to resist Grant's further advance. Unfortunately he was handicapped in this through not knowing what had become of Loring's division, which he had intended should hold the advantageous ground on the west bank. He had called up two brigades from the Vicksburg garrison, and one of these he posted at Bovina, and the other joined Bowen's division holding the prepared defences east of the Big Black.

Sherman, most of whose corps had not fought at Champion's Hill, was ordered to make all speed for Bridgeport, a place a few miles up river, where his 5th Division (Blair's) would join him complete with pontoon-train for the crossing, and from where he would be in a position to outflank the enemy – for Grant was fairly certain that Pemberton would try to hold the Big Black. In the event this was not necessary, for a frontal attack routed the Confederates.

McClernand's corps, which was quite fresh, was now in the van, and when Carr's division met the enemy line at about 8 a.m. on the 17th he at once deployed his troops to the right of the road. Osterhaus came into position on the left of the road, and Smith's division was on Osterhaus's left. McPherson's corps marched in column behind the centre ready to give support where needed. The ground was open except to the right of the road where Carr's men were able to make use of woodland for an assault against Vaughn's brigade, which was entirely successful. Bowen's division fought on for a short while, but with Vaughn's men gone, and no back-up troops on the high ground west of the river, they considered the position hopeless and made for the bridge. Some 5,000 men had one bridge and a deep river to cross; a number got away – often without arms – some were drowned, and 1,751 were captured along with 18 guns. Grant's troops suffered 276 casualties of which 39 were killed.

The whole affair was over soon after 9 a.m., and for the rest of the day the Federals were building bridges. Bowen's men, much to their credit, for they had been given a suicidal task in front of the river, managed to destroy the bridge; but working by the light of torches the Federals had three bridges completed by midnight, and there was Sherman's pontoon bridge up river. The delay in bridge building gave the Confederates time to call in the brigade at Haines' Bluff, which place Sherman had rendered untenable, and to withdraw their troops in moderately good order to the prepared defences at Vicksburg. Grant was now faced with a siege, although he hoped his enemy was sufficiently demoralized to allow him to take the town's defences by storm.

The campaign was not over, Vicksburg had yet to be taken, but Grant could look back with very considerable satisfaction to the achievements of the past eighteen days. With virtually no supply train the Union troops had marched an average of 180 miles, fought and won 5 battles, and had accounted for some 12,000 Confederate soldiers captured, wounded, or killed, for a total loss to themselves of 4,379. This is a measure of Grant's tactical and strategical superiority over Johnston and Pemberton, who allowed themselves to be manoeuvred into a situation where their numerically superior troops could be defeated in detail.

The ground around Vicksburg was ideally suited for defence. The town itself stood on a plateau commanding an approach of broken, hilly country intersected by a crisscross of ravines and gullies that were very formidable obstacles for any attacking force. Pemberton had constructed a strong defensive line on commanding heights of redoubts and artillery positions protected by massive earthworks (there were 128 pieces of artillery in all, of which 36 were siege guns), and connected by rifle pits so laid out that an enemy making use of the obvious approaches would be smitten by heavy enfiladed fire. This powerful line began near the river two miles north of the town, and ran east and south to Glass's Bayou (a ravine with precipitous sides), on to the Jackson road and then south-west along the Arrenton ridge reaching the river again three miles south of the town. In all a wide arc some nine miles in length.

To defend the perimeter Pemberton had at least 20,000 troops fit for duty. He placed General M. L. Smith's division at the northern end, General Formey was on his right, and then came General Stevenson's division. Bowen's troops, which had performed so well in the earlier fighting, were in reserve. By mid-morning on the 19th Grant had his three corps in position, with Sherman's close up to the Confederate emplacements. This corps was on the right covering the high ground from where it overlooked the Yazoo, on his left was McPherson astride the Jackson road, and then came McClernand stretching as far towards Warrenton as a two-division front would allow.

Sherman's corps was so close to the troops of the Confederate left that skirmishing had been taking place for most of the morning, but both McPherson's and McClernand's were some way back from the defences when at 2 p.m. Grant ordered an all-out assault. He had hoped to rout the enemy by a *coup de main*, but far from the broken morale he had expected, he found that once behind their solidly constructed defences they had taken fresh heart and were full of fight. Sherman's corps did its best, but was repulsed all along the line, and got no support from the other two which were too far back. All this assault achieved was to bring McPherson's and McClernand's men into closer contact with the defenders.

Grant, however, remained unconvinced as to the impregnability of the Confederate line, and ordered another assault to begin at 10 a.m. on the 22nd. He had many reasons for making this fresh attempt. His men were eager to fight, rather than to dig, Johnston had a strong force in his rear, and a siege was bound to be protracted and would require more troops, for at present he was thin on the ground with a large gap to the river on McClernand's left. But once again the defences proved far too strong, and the defenders – despite the courage and determination of the attackers – too resolute. And this time the Federal casualties were very heavy. Time and again Grant's men reached the ditches and stormed the heights. The Colours, borne forward in commendable devotion, were planted on the parapets, but nowhere could the troops achieve a breakthrough. This assault was made on a three-mile front and 35,000 troops were driven back, with over 3,000 losses, by not more than 13,000 defenders actually attacked.* These casualties need not have been so heavy had McClernand not continually asked for diversionary attacks to support what was in fact a completely forlorn situation on his front.†

There was now nothing for it but to get out the spades and dig entrenchments, rifle pits, saps, and artillery emplacements, for a siege had become inevitable. These were achieved at a most satisfactory speed, and a plentiful supply of ammunition enabled Federal gunners and sharpshooters to keep Confederate heads down while the work was in progress. On 25 May Grant was able to report to Halleck, 'Vicksburg is now completely invested.'

In due course the besieged were to suffer all the usual horrors – shortage of food, water, ammunition, and medical supplies, and long hours of waiting under a blazing sun. For the besiegers life was more tolerable, although never pleasant. There was a plentiful supply of food and ammunition (although water was a problem), and in the end there were sufficient troops – over 70,000 and nearly 250 guns. But to begin with there was every reason to fear an attack from the rear by Johnston, who was assembling a large force. To meet this threat Grant had to construct lines of contravallation as well as circumvallation, and to man them he had stripped Hurlbut's corps at Memphis almost completely, and Halleck had sent him troops from Ohio and Missouri.

Grant was right, Vicksburg was indeed completely invested, for the navy had the river exit securely blocked. Nor could Pemberton hope for much from Johnston, who never really believed that Vicksburg could be relieved, and was most half-hearted in his efforts. All the time the Federals sapped steadily forward, and on 25 June and again on 1 July mines were exploded in the defences causing considerable damage. Grant judged the defenders' position to be so desperate that he ordered a large-scale attack for 6 July. But before this could be launched Pemberton had confirmed his judgement, and on 3 July he asked for terms. At first Grant demanded unconditional surrender, but this was soon modified and on 4 July 1863, 31,000 men marched out of their defences, placed their colours on the top of their stacked arms and then returned to the town where they were fed from Union stores.

The campaign had been a great personal triumph for Grant, whose fortunes since the capture of Fort Donelson over a year previous had

---

*Greene, p. 184.
†McClernand was relieved of his command soon afterwards, although not for this blunder but for breaking army regulations. However, his removal was overdue, for his performance throughout the campaign had been distinctly disappointing.

been on the wane. At Vicksburg he showed what a good general he was. He had made a clean sweep of Confederate forces in the area, and for the loss of only 8,873 of his own men – killed, wounded, and missing – his troops had accounted for at least 45,000 of Pemberton's Mississippi army. In addition he had taken the capital of that state, and a great deal of booty.

On the day that Pemberton sought terms from Grant at Vicksburg, General Lee had been decisively beaten at Gettysburg. These two Confederate defeats, and the loss in less than six months of Chattanooga, were the turning point in this bitter civil strife. There was to be much more fighting, and the Federals were to suffer cruelly for Grant, who on 9 March 1864 had been given command of all their armies, was lamentably prodigal with his troops. But there were now few, if any, in the South who thought in terms of victory.

On 9 July the commander of Port Hudson, who had been under siege since 23 May, hearing of the loss of Vicksburg, surrendered. The last of the Confederates had been cleared from the banks of the Mississippi and now, in Lincoln's memorable words, 'The father of waters rolls unvexed to the sea.'

In the course of the last two months of the Vicksburg campaign, when Grant had launched his offensive designed to take the town in rear, there were – if one discounts a possible opportunity missed by the Confederates to defeat McClernand's corps on 13 May – five principal factors that had, or might have had, a definite bearing on the outcome of the campaign. But in general the Confederate defeat was caused by a lack of authority emanating from Richmond, which produced damaging disorder in the field command.

This occurred even before the campaign started when General Holmes, in command of the Trans-Mississippi Department and some 25,000 troops, defied urgent appeals from Davis, the Secretary of State for War, and Johnston to send troops to aid Pemberton. And once the campaign was under way the undefined relationship between Johnston and Pemberton led to confusion and disobedience. Pemberton undoubtedly believed that he was responsible direct to Davis (who seemingly did nothing to disabuse him), and not to Johnston, for the defence of Vicksburg, while Johnston seemed more concerned to divest responsibility for failure than to assert authority for success.

The first of three occasions when Pemberton was in disagreement with his immediate superior occurred at the time of Grant's crossing of the Mississippi. From 28 April the transmission wires had been busy relaying messages and dispatches between Pemberton at Jackson, Bowen in command at Grand Gulf, Johnston at Tullahoma, and

President Davis in Richmond.* Pemberton communicated with equal frequency to Davis and Johnston, without apparently sending copies, so that Johnston was not always in immediate touch with the situation. Nevertheless, he had been informed on 29 April of the naval bombardment of Grand Gulf, but it was to Davis that Pemberton reported on 1 May the furious battle taking place for Port Gibson. Johnson, therefore, was unaware of the landing when he telegraphed that same day, 'If Grant crosses unite all your troops to beat him. Success will give back what was abandoned to win it.'

Pemberton has been criticized for not obeying this order, but all along he considered Johnston's communications to be only of an advisory nature† and that he, the man on the spot, should use his own judgement, which in this case was that Vicksburg should be held at all costs. In fact by 1 May it was too late to concentrate sufficient troops to drive Grant back across the river; this should have been done days ago. But should Pemberton, once he knew for certain (on 17 April) that Grant intended to cross and take Vicksburg in rear, have anticipated Johnston's order and assembled sufficient troops to defeat the Federal army before there was a chance to establish a corps on dry land?

At the beginning of April Pemberton had slightly under 50,000 troops fit for duty, of which 16,000 were at Port Hudson. Some 22,000 held the line from Haines' Bluff through Vicksburg to Grand Gulf, where Bowen had 2,500 of these men. There were 7,000 at Fort Pemberton, and 4–5,000 were away to the north keeping a watching brief on Hurlbut's corps and the Memphis–Corinth railway.‡ As late as 10 April Pemberton was convinced that his left flank was not threatened, and that Grant had gone up river to Tennessee. He telegraphed this to Johnston who ordered him to send reinforcements to General Bragg. Four thousand men recently arrived from Port Hudson, a brigade from Vicksburg and another from Fort Pemberton were ordered to leave for Chattanooga. But these had to be recalled from the various stages of their journey when Pemberton realized his mistake, and steps were hurriedly taken to reinforce Bowen at Grand Gulf with Green's brigade from Edwards' Station.

Pemberton was very short of cavalry, and this prevented him from knowing the intention or precise whereabouts of his enemy. He had reason to believe that a Federal force from the north was about to descend on his Vicksburg–Jackson line of communication, and Colonel Grierson's spectacular and damaging cavalry raid all along his rear

---

* For these various communications see *War of the Rebellion*.

† Understandably perhaps, for Johnston's orders, or instructions, were often couched in vague terms, such as 'would it not be better. . .'

‡ Figures, Greene, p. 117.

caused him to send out detachments from bases that stretched from Vicksburg to Port Hudson in an attempt to intercept these horsemen.

On 20 April these detachments were called in and centred on Jackson against a possible attack from the north, and Stevenson, commanding in Vicksburg, was ordered to hold 5,000 men in readiness to march either to Grand Gulf or Warrenton. Tracey's brigade from this division did march, and reached Grand Gulf on 30 April, but Bowen was told not to call upon the remainder unless absolutely necessary. Pemberton was clearly alive to the danger of Grant's landing, but he still feared for his right flank, which he felt certain Sherman's corps was about to attack. That general had been left by Grant as part of his deception plan and had sailed up the Yazoo with ten regiments. Pemberton, who had had specific orders to hold Vicksburg, dared not strip the garrison too drastically or Sherman would have the town.

Grant got McClernand's corps (18,000 men) across the river quite quickly, and these were closely supported by two divisions of McPherson's corps. Even with topographical and tactical advantages Pemberton would have needed 30,000 troops to be certain of throwing this force back before it got established. He had the men and he had the time, and if he was uncertain as to whether Grand Gulf or Warrenton was to be the landing point he could have concentrated his army between the two, ready to pounce on either place. With hindsight this may seem obvious, but in fact much of what Pemberton did was very understandable.

He was not a general of genius and he was being tried beyond his limits with contrary orders, and many points to guard with insufficient information. It is true that he disssipated his forces to too great an extent, and it was quite wrong to have concentrated only 8,000 of some 40,000 troops available to oppose Grant's landing. However, Vicksburg was still secure and he felt confident that as Grant advanced his line of withdrawal could be blocked, and he would be forced to fight at a disadvantage. This would require his whole army; it could not be easily, or even safely, assembled once Grant was underway, but with Vicksburg no longer threatened now was his best chance of victory. Unfortunately, he lacked the audacity to take it. Surely that was his mistake, more than his initial failure to prevent the river crossing.

From the very start Grant had placed more confidence in taking Vicksburg from the rear than in the various bayou expeditions, but after he had crossed the Mississippi, fought the first of his five battles and reached Grand Gulf he had to make a momentous, and as it turned out, campaign-winning decision. General Halleck had been urging on him the importance of co-operating with Banks at Port Hudson, and McClernand's corps had been earmarked to go south for this purpose. But owing to the delay in communications Banks was up the Red River before hearing of the plan, and in a letter which reached Grant at Grand Gulf informed him that it would be 10 May before he was back.

Time was the essence of the daring plan Grant had in mind, and he was certainly not in the mood to play safe and wait, nor could he afford to send troops to Port Hudson to await Banks's return. He had to take advantage of what had been achieved in the fight at Port Gibson and strike quickly. The obvious course would be to march north by the comparatively short route to Vicksburg, which after all was the primary target. But Grant at the time was uncertain of the enemy numbers, although he did know that the Confederates were being reinforced from the east and that Jackson, on account of the railway system, would be the collecting point. He therefore deemed it essential not to be confronted with superior numbers through these two forces combining, but to move north-east to drive a wedge between them, take Jackson, and thereby isolate the troops in Vicksburg, and defeat the two Confederate forces separately.

It was a plan of great boldness, and one which his able lieutenant, Sherman (who incidentally was to indulge in similar risks later on), urged Grant to abandon on logistic grounds. But Grant told him, 'I do not calculate on supplying the army with full rations from Grand Gulf . . . what I do expect is to get up what rations of hard bread, coffee and salt we can, and make the country furnish the balance.'* And that is what happened. When the army set off from Grand Gulf on 7 May they marched with no more than three days' rations. The rich farmland of Mississippi would supply all that was needed provided – and only provided – the army kept moving.

But feeding the army in this fertile country was the least of risks. Once away from his river base Grant was exposing his line of withdrawal to what he believed at the time was a force on his left flank of greatly superior numbers. He could not afford to leave troops to guard this line, and if Pemberton got behind him he had either to beat all the Confederate troops in the Jackson–Vicksburg area or perish. It was a plan that risked all to gain all, and one that required a commander who was gifted, vital, and adventurous, proof against the incalculable hazards of the battlefield, and possessed of a little luck.

Grant knew very well that his cautious and completely orthodox commander-in-chief would not, even in the best of circumstances, agree to such a daring manoeuvre, and certainly not at this time of crisis in the Union's military affairs. On 3 May General Hooker had been well beaten by Lee at Chancellorsville, and Grant's proposal to launch his army into the very heartland of the enemy without a supply line

---

* *War of the Rebellion*, Part 3, pp. 284, 285.

would convulse army headquarters, and considerably ruffle the normal urbanity of the President's office.

Fortunately the telegraph system from Washington did not go south of Cairo (Illinois), or else the Vicksburg campaign might never have got under way. On 3 May Grant reported to Halleck in a long dispatch* his plan in all its detail, and thereafter he kept his chief constantly informed of the army's progress. But none of these dispatches had reached Halleck by the time he sent a letter, via Memphis, on 11 May saying, 'If possible, the forces of yourself and General Banks should be united between Vicksburg and Port Hudson, so as to attack these places separately with the combined forces. This has been urged upon General Banks.' It was delivered to Grant as he was watching the preparations being made for the assault of the Black River Bridge. Grant felt that it called for neither action nor answer, and rode off to supervise the attack that would bring him to the battlements of Vicksburg.

The second time that Pemberton failed to carry out Johnston's instructions was shortly before and just after the loss of Jackson. Pemberton had three divisions (about 23,000 men) at Edwards' Station, and Johnston (in Jackson) was aware that Sherman (in fact it was McPherson) stood between him and Pemberton with four divisions. On the evening of 13 May he sent a dispatch to Pemberton, who was at Bovina (a copy of which fell into Grant's hands on the 14th), saying, 'If practicable come up on his rear at once; to beat such a detachment would be of immense value. The troops here could co-operate.' To which Pemberton replied, 'I move at once with all my force . . .' ending his dispatch, 'In directing this I do not think you fully comprehend the position that Vicksburg will be left in, but I comply with your order.'

However, not long afterwards he had second thoughts and summoned a council of his senior officers, and put Johnston's order before them. The majority were for complying, but his two senior generals headed a minority that were in favour of attacking Grant's mythical lines of communication in the area of Raymond. Pemberton himself favoured waiting to be attacked, and certainly considered he had too few troops to move against McPherson, but to satisfy the eagerness of his officers he agreed to march south. A splendid example of leadership by minority vote!

Therefore that same day (14 May) he telegraphed Johnston, 'I shall move as early tomorrow morning as practicable with a column of 17,000 men to Dillon's. The object is to cut the enemy's communications and force him to attack me.' It is particularly interesting that Johnston, having ordered Pemberton on 13 May to attack Sherman (McPherson),

* *WR*, Part 1, p. 32.

is now thinking along much the same lines as Pemberton's minority group, for on the 14th he wired, 'Can he [Grant] supply himself from Mississippi? Can you not cut him off from it, and above all, should he be compelled to fall back for want of supplies, beat him?'

However, on the 15th he tells Pemberton, 'Our being compelled to leave Jackson makes your plan [the march to Dillon's] impracticable. The only mode by which we can unite is by your moving directly to Clinton . . .' Pemberton actually obeys this order, but any attempt to unite was now too late, and he gets caught at Champion's Hill and defeated. Seldom can one find a more damaging obfuscation of command, and seldom such sophistry as Pemberton's dispatch to Davis of 19 May: 'Against my own judgement, but by instructions from superior authority, sustained by the unanimous voice of my general officers, I felt myself compelled to advance my position beyond Edwards' Depot, and offer or accept battle according to circumstances.'*

On 4 July, after a long and costly siege, Grant's army was victorious. But had General McClernand displayed any kind of initiative, or shown haste to obey his commander's instructions, Pemberton's army would almost certainly have been destroyed at Champion's Hill on 16 May, and Vicksburg taken without a siege.

The Federals' approach to the battlefield was along the three roads, already described, leading from Raymond and Jackson to Edwards' Station. McClernand had four divisions of his corps present but one, Hovey's, was detached and marching ahead of McPherson's corps on the top road from Jackson. However, Blair's division of Sherman's corps, which had only recently joined, was placed under command of McClernand, giving him 15,000 men with which to fight the battle. Blair's and A. J. Smith's divisions were ordered to advance by the lower road (which ran parallel, but about two miles south of the middle road), and Carr's and Osterhaus's were to use the middle road.

On the evening of the 15th, and again early on the 16th, Grant sent orders to McClernand, whose headquarters was on the middle road some two to three miles from Grant, to move his divisions forward cautiously, but not to bring on a general engagement unless sure of success. McClernand seems to have taken this too literally, for caution was the keynote to his entire performance on the 16th. Admittedly he had some very difficult country in which to deploy his troops, heavily wooded with a number of rugged ridges and ravines, and he was opposed by about 7,000 men (mostly Loring's division), but he commanded more than twice that number.

Early on the 16th Pemberton's army was countermarching in order to

---

* For these various communications see *WR*, Part 3, pp. 870–82.

comply with Johnston's order to join him north of the Jackson road, and
it was Smith's and Osterhaus's divisions that made first contact, driving
rebel skirmishers through the woods back on to their main army, which
was hastily taking up a defensive position on Champion's Hill. But it
was Hovey's division, soon reinforced by the divisions of McPherson's
corps, that opened the battle proper on the top road. Pemberton had
dispersed his troops to cover all three roads with Stevenson's division on
his left, Bowen's in the centre, and Loring's on the right. The battle was
fought almost entirely round Champion's Hill, and for the Federals by
Hovey's, Logan's, and Crocker's division, and for the Confederates by
Stevenson's and Bowen's divisions.

Grant wanted to withhold a general engagement until he was
satisfied that McClernand's men, who initially had a shorter distance to
march than McPherson's corps, were closed up and ready for action. But
although the leading troops of two of his divisions had been skirmishing
with Pemberton's pickets, it seems that at 9 a.m. his main body was still
some two miles from the Confederate line. Grant sent successive
messages by staff officers urging him to press forward and attack in
force. The last of these was despatched at 12.35, but did not reach
McClernand until after 2 p.m., on receipt of which he ordered Smith and
Osterhaus to 'attack the enemy vigorously, and press for victory'. For
some reason, not easily understood, those two commanders took very
little action on receipt of these orders, although Osterhaus did engage
Loring's division at the end of the battle when the latter was covering
the Confederate retreat.

Meanwhile, on the Federal right intense skirmishing for more than
two hours developed into a full-scale battle around 11 a.m., and not long
afterwards Logan's division had manoeuvred itself into a position to be
able to cut off the Confederate line of retreat to the only bridge across
Baker's Creek. But Pemberton, free from any pressure on his right or
centre, was able to reinforce his hard-pressed left and Grant, who had
not appreciated the importance of Logan's position, withdrew him to
assist Hovey and Crocker. Shortly afterwards Stevenson's division was
in full flight, and Bowen's was forced to make a hasty withdrawal. There
was nothing to impede their escape across the creek both by the bridge
and by the ford lower down.

There is very little doubt (and Grant himself was convinced of it)
that had McClernand shown the same initiative and enterprise as
McPherson had, and personally pushed his commanders into swift and
resolute action, Logan would have been able to maintain his position
and cut off the bridge, while McClernand's leading troops could have
reached the ford in time to prevent a large part of Pemberton's force from
getting across. It is entirely possible that Pemberton would have been
faced with total surrender. The casualty figures for McClernand's corps

in this battle speak for themselves. The four divisions directly under his command lost 15 men killed, 100 wounded and 26 missing.*

The last occasion on which the fate of Vicksburg was open to question occurred at the time of the siege. After the fight at the Big Black Bridge Grant had sent Sherman's corps to cross the river at Bridgeport thus rendering the Confederate position at Haines' Bluff untenable, and Pemberton ordered the troops there to fall back into Vicksburg, at the same time – by letter written from Bovina on the 17th – informing Johnston of the situation.

Johnston received this note the same evening at his headquarters on the Brownsville road. He immediately replied, 'If Haines' Bluff is untenable, Vicksburg is of no value and cannot be held. If, therefore, you are invested in Vicksburg you must ultimately surrender. Under such circumstances, instead of losing both troops and place, we must, if possible, save the troops. If it is not too late, evacuate Vicksburg . . . and march to the north-east.' Pemberton received this dispatch on the afternoon of the 18th, and was visibly shaken by the thought of abandoning what he considered to be the linchpin of all Confederacy operations in the West.

However, he resorted to his usual ploy of calling a council, and this time his officers were unanimous in their opinion that 'it was impossible to withdraw the army from this position with such morale and material to be of further service to the Confederacy'. Pemberton in reporting this decision of his council informed Johnston that 'I have decided to hold Vicksburg as long as possible, with the firm hope that the government may yet be able to assist me in keeping this obstruction to the enemy's free navigation of the Mississippi. I still conceive it to be the most important point in the Confederacy.'†

However wrong and uncertain Pemberton may have been at Grand Gulf and Edwards' Station, he now rightly and obdurately resisted this proposal to abandon Vicksburg. Grant had swiftly blocked all the exits by land and the Union navy controlled the river. Pemberton's officers were right, the morale of the troops, which had risen rapidly when they got behind their well-prepared defences, would never have withstood the consequences of another murderous mêlée so soon, even had it been partly successful which was most unlikely. The Confederates had a strong position, and a defending force of at least 20,000 troops fit for battle (31,000 were surrendered) of which 8,000 had not been recently engaged, and sufficient food and ammunition to last a full month, before which time Pemberton could confidently hope to be relieved.

*Greene, p. 160.
† WR, Part 3, pp. 889, 890.

In general it was Confederate policy to fight a defensive war of attrition, so as to blunt the Union weapon and wear down the will of the Northerners to prosecute a long war, but instead to make them seek a compromise. Vicksburg, besides being of vital importance, was a pulsing symbol of this policy and Pemberton was right to see it that way. On this occasion it was for Johnston to attempt a decisive action. By the beginning of June he had an army of 30,000 men near Canton and was under considerable pressure from Richmond to use it in relief of Vicksburg. In co-operation with Pemberton he had a chance to raise the siege before Grant's massive reinforcements were assembled. But he was a defensive general who did not thrive on the adrenalin of risks, and he had not the mind to put it to the test.

Vicksburg is the perfect example of a campaign being lost through obfuscation of command. It is probable the Federals would have won anyway, for apart from the advantage obtained through their navy in General Grant they had a commander much superior to General Pemberton. However, the latter was very gravely handicapped by receiving contradictory orders from his president, who was also his commander-in-chief, and from his immediate military superior. The result was complete confusion in the giving and receiving of orders, which was cleverly exploited by Grant. This is a quite unnecessary way to lose a battle or campaign, but one which occasionally occurs when the head of state is also commander-in-chief of the army – more especially when that dignitary was formerly a prominent soldier.

18   The Chickamauga–Chattanooga Campaign
June–November 1863

SHORTLY after Vicksburg Grant's army was split up. Some detachments were sent to occupy territory, while other troops were required to deal with isolated Confederate forces in such places as Texas, Arkansas, and Missouri. The principal scene in the West now shifts to Tennessee, where Major-General Rosecrans commanded the Federal Army of the Cumberland, and Lieutenant-General Bragg the Confederate Army of the Tennessee. At the turn of the year (31 December 1862–2 January 1863) Rosecrans had defeated Bragg at the battle of Murfreesboro (or Stones River) and the latter had withdrawn to the line Shelbyville–Wartrace, with another prepared position farther in rear at Tullahoma. Some twenty-five miles separated the two armies, and for the first six months of 1863 fighting was confined mainly to cavalry raids, in which arm Bragg was considerably superior.

Rosecrans, despite many calls for action from his commander-in-chief, General Halleck, did not make a move forward until 23 June. The prize he sought was Chattanooga, which although only a small town was of the greatest strategical importance, for the loss of its railway junction and the surrounding rich, fertile farming land by the Confederates must considerably hasten the end of the war. At the time of his advance, excluding the emergency reserve corps of 12,575 men, Rosecrans had three corps comprising a total of 40,746 infantry, 6,806 cavalry and 3,065 artillerymen with which to oppose Bragg's 30,449 infantry, 13,962 cavalry and 2,254 artillerymen.* While Rosecrans was to take Chattanooga, General Burnside's Army of the Ohio had been directed to move on Knoxville, a town 100 miles north-east on the Tennessee and Virginia railway.

When Rosecrans did eventually advance he carried out a series of well-conceived flanking manoeuvres which, together with a clever deception plan, quite outwitted Bragg, who was forced to retire from his first position by 27 June, and to fall back on the Tullahoma line. The terrain was rough and the rain came down in torrents, which together

---

*Figures from *Johnson and Buel*, p. 636.

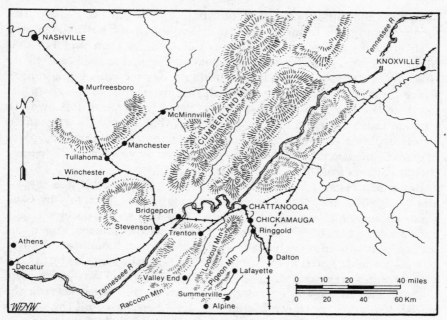

The Chickamauga Campaign: June–November 1863

with some stubborn Confederate resistance made progress painfully
slow. But a mounted infantry raid that tore up the rail track and
destroyed a depot south of Tullahoma, together with a wide flanking
movement by two infantry brigades, decided Bragg to fall back yet again
and consolidate in Chattanooga.

In the course of eight days the Confederates had been brilliantly
manoeuvred out of two strong positions with a loss of 1,600 prisoners
and 11 guns, while Rosecrans's casualties were only 560. But for the
appalling weather (so often the arbiter of battles and campaigns) and
ground conditions, Bragg's army might have been severely mauled on
the west bank of the Tennessee. Having driven his enemy across the
river, Rosecrans was not prepared to continue his advance (although
pressed to do so by Halleck) until he had repaired the rail track in his
front and rear, and harvested a quantity of corn. It was not until 16
August that he advanced from his Winchester–McMinnville line and
prepared to cross the Tennessee.

The country which he was about to enter, and in which the battles of
Chickamauga and Chattanooga were to be fought, was laced with
mountain ranges, which on the eastern side of the river sloped south-
west from Chattanooga across the north-west corner of Georgia and far
into Alabama. The westernmost one (running parallel to the river) is
called Raccoon Mountain, Sand Mountain is slightly to its south and

east, and then comes Lookout Mountain (2,200 feet) which is 100 miles long, reaching the Tennessee a mile or two south of Chattanooga, and with crossing places widely spaced. Between Raccoon and Lookout Mountains lay a valley drained by Lookout Creek, and rising steeply to this valley's east was another formidable barrier called Missionary Ridge (approximately 400 feet) which ran forty miles to the river just north of the town. To the east of this ridge the ground fell away to Chickamauga Creek, a fairly wide stream that wound its way across lonely fields tangled with brambles and dense patches of thicket: a place of grim associations from Indian days reflected by its name, said to have meant River of Death.

Rosecrans began his river crossing on 29 August with three corps – the 14th, 20th, and 21st. They were commanded respectively by Generals Thomas, McCook, and Crittenden. His plan was to deceive Bragg into thinking that he intended to cross north of Chattanooga, and to this end he sent two infantry brigades, some cavalry and mounted infantry to make a feint north along the river from Chattanooga as far as the Confederates were guarding the crossings. The ruse was a complete success, and Bragg concentrated his troops in that area, leaving the crossing places lower down unguarded. By 4 September all three corps were across on a wide front; Crittenden had crossed at Shellmound, Thomas near Bridgeport, and McCook at Caperton's Ferry. No sooner had Bragg realized that the Federal army was across below Chattanooga than he ordered an immediate withdrawal from the town in order to protect his vital supply line to Atlanta.

This hasty withdrawal convinced Rosecrans that he had Bragg on the run, and on 9 September he ordered McCook to cross Lookout Mountain at Winston's Gap (some forty-six miles south of Chattanooga) and make for Alpine with the intention of cutting off Bragg's retreat; Thomas was near Trenton and ordered to cross the mountain at Cooper's Gap and make for McLemore's Cove (a valley between Lookout and Pigeon Mountains); and Crittenden was to garrison Chattanooga with a brigade, and pursue the Confederates down the Ringgold road with the rest of his corps. Rosecrans had, therefore, well and truly split his army with his left and right forty miles apart. In difficult mountainous country his three widely separated corps were at the mercy of the Confederates, should they not be in full retreat, for individual support was an impossibility.

In fact Bragg had ordered a withdrawal only so far as Lafayette, a town twenty-two miles south of Chattanooga. Here he concentrated his army (which was three times the strength of any one of Rosecrans's divided corps), and he was well aware that the Confederates had walked into a trap. However, the steps he took to close it had nugatory results, and although he was inclined (with some justification) to blame his corps

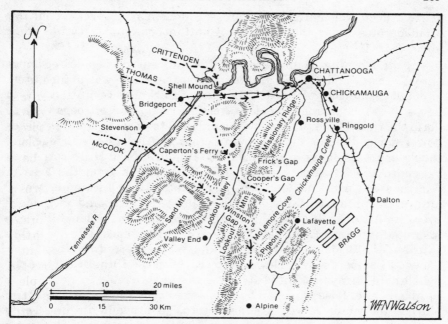

The Chickamauga Campaign: Rosecrans's three-pronged advance
9 September

commanders for failure to carry out his orders he himself was by no means blameless.

He had at this time three corps commanded by Generals Polk, D. H. Hill, and Buckner – the latter had very recently arrived from Knoxville – and he had received two divisions from General Joseph Johnston's army. General Longstreet's corps from the Army of Northern Virginia was to join him shortly, but with Burnside occupying the important railway centre of Knoxville this was seriously delayed through having to make a circuitous journey of some 900 miles. On 10/11 September an opportunity was lost to defeat two Federal divisions in McLemore's Cove, and on the 13th orders to attack Crittenden's divided corps were never carried out. Bragg's failure to defeat the Union troops in detail at this time was one of the deciding factors of the Chickamauga campaign, and will be discussed later.

It was not until 18 September that Rosecrans had managed to regroup his army in the Chickamauga valley; the delay was caused by McCook taking an unnecessarily long route from Alpine. He now had Crittenden's corps on his left in front of Lee and Gordon's Mill, Thomas at Pond Spring, and McCook on the right at Stevens Gap. His reserve corps (Granger) was at Rossville. Bragg, having allowed Rosecrans to escape the trap, now planned to attack the left of his line in strength so as to roll it back upon the centre in the area of McLemore's Cove, cut off the Confederates from the roads to Chattanooga, and reoccupy that town.

On the morning of the 18th the three advanced brigades of Longstreet's corps, under General Hood, arrived, and one was immediately ordered to join B. R. Johnson's division of Buckner's corps that was to cross the Chickamauga Creek at Reed's Bridge. These troops were to form the right of the turning movement, and to uncover crossing places lower down. Walker's corps was to cross at Alexander's Bridge and Buckner's (less Johnson's division) at Telford's Ford. Hill's corps was to guard the left against a possible flank attack from the area of McLemore's Cove. The Confederates' advance to the Chickamauga over difficult mountain tracks was slow, and Reed's and Alexander's Bridges were stoutly defended by Colonel Minty's cavalry and Colonel Wilder's mounted infantry. Eventually these were driven back, but not before Alexander's Bridge was destroyed and Walker forced to cross lower down at Lambert's Ford. However, by early on the 19th, Bragg had the whole of his army (less three divisions) across the creek.

Meanwhile, Rosecrans had become aware of Bragg's intentions, and during the night moved Thomas's corps to prevent his line being outflanked, and to guard the approaches to Chattanooga. This corps extended beyond and behind that of Crittenden which was slightly in advance at Lee and Gordon's Mill; McCook's corps had not moved from the extreme right at McLemore's Cove. Thus on the morning of 19 September the two armies faced each other west of Chickamauga Creek in lines that stretched for about six miles, but which were in places only a few hundred yards apart. The country was densely wooded and the commanders on both sides scarcely knew the whereabouts of their own men, and were certainly in the dark regarding the position of their enemy.

The action began on the Confederate right where that fine cavalry officer, General Forrest, and his men were fighting dismounted. Two brigades of Brannan's division (Thomas's corps) reconnoitring the river drove Forrest back after a very sharp engagement, but the Confederates were soon reinforced by Walker's corps and Brannan's men in their turn were thrown back, as was Baird's division which had come to their assistance. The situation was becoming critical on Rosecrans's left, and McCook's corps was hastened to give assistance to Thomas. The Confederates kept feeling for the Federal left, not realizing that it had been considerably extended. The fighting on this flank became confused and very bitter. Bragg ordered his left-flank divisions (from Hill's and Polk's corps) to cross the Chickamauga and join the battle, which now favoured one side and then the other. The Confederates fought with great courage, but they lacked concerted action, and opportunities (such as a gap of nearly two miles, between Thomas's and Crittenden's corps, which they could have exploited) were missed.

By midday all the Federal troops, less Granger's reserve corps, and all but three of the Confederate divisions had become engaged in this savagely contested battle in which the slaughter was very heavy. Shortly after 2.30 p.m. Hood's men, fighting in the centre, had pushed back the Federal divisions of Reynolds and Van Cleve to gain a footing on the Lafayette-Chattanooga road. But in fighting that lasted almost to darkness they were forced to abandon their hard-won prize, and this gory day ended with little satisfaction for the Federals, and none (save in the valour of their soldiers) for the Confederates. Rosecrans's army had at least staved off all attempts to turn its left, and he was still in possession of the Chattanooga road.

That night Longstreet joined Bragg with some more brigades, but not all of his corps arrived in time to take part in the forthcoming battle. The Confederate commander now reorganized his army and divided it into a right and left wing, with Polk (the bishop who had turned from the crosier to the cannon) commanding the right and Longstreet the left. Polk had Hill's and Walker's corps, and Cheatham's division from his own corps, giving him a total of 18,794 infantry and Forrest's 3,500 cavalry; Longstreet had Hood's and Buckner's corps and Hindman's division from Polk's corps. He had the larger wing with 22,849 infantry, and 4,000 cavalry under General Wheeler.*

Bragg determined to persist with his plan of the previous day to make his main attack against the Federal left, to force it away from the Chattanooga road and to break it up in difficult country. Polk was ordered to begin the attack at daybreak with Breckinridge's division, which had not fought on the 19th. But once again Bragg's plans went awry. What happened to his orders, and the whereabouts of two of the corps commanders who were to receive them on the night of 19–20 September, has never been satisfactorily resolved and has been the subject of recriminatory accounts by or on behalf of the three principals concerned. Suffice it to say that it was not until 9.30 a.m. that Breckinridge eventually opened the battle.

During the night Rosecrans had made changes in his dispositions, strengthening his left both by additional manpower and with hasty but effective improvisation of breastworks of logs and rocks. In his new order of battle divisions were intermingled irrespective of corps, and as their positions in the subsequent fighting were important they need to be detailed. The Federals began the battle with Baird's division holding the left of the line, and then came R. W. Johnson's, Palmer's. Reynolds's, Brannan's, Negley's, Davis's, and Sheridan's. Wood's and Van Cleve's

---

*Johnson and Buel, p. 652.

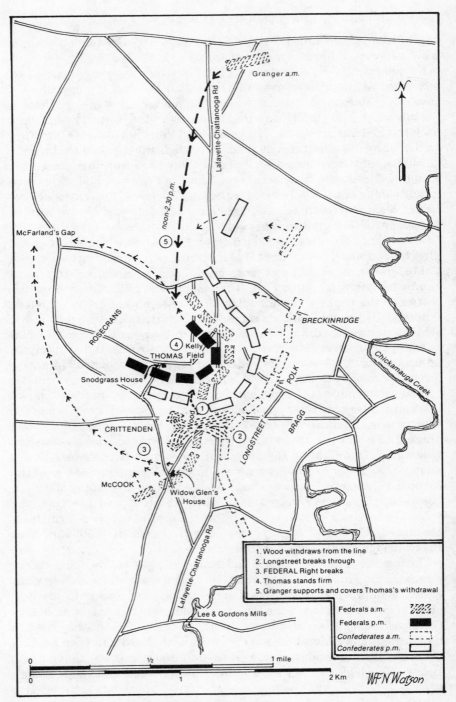

The Battle of Chickamauga: 20 September 1863

Map labels:

Granger a.m.

Lafayette-Chattanooga Rd

N

noon-2.30 p.m.

⑤

McFarland's Gap

BRECKINRIDGE

Chickamauga Creek

ROSECRANS

④ Kelly
THOMAS Field

Snodgrass House

POLK

①

CRITTENDEN

Wood

②

LONGSTREET

BRAGG

③

McCOOK

Widow Glen's
House

Lafayette-Chattanooga Rd

Lee & Gordons Mills

1. Wood withdraws from the line
2. Longstreet breaks through
3. FEDERAL Right breaks
4. Thomas stands firm
5. Granger supports and covers Thomas's withdrawal

Federals a.m.
Federals p.m.
Confederates a.m.
Confederates p.m.

0   ½   1 mile
0   1   2 Km

WFN Watson

were in reserve, and Granger's corps was still near Rossville. Thomas, on the left, commanded six divisions, McCook on the right two and Crittenden had two in reserve ready to reinforce either right or left. At the start of the day the extreme left of the Federal line faced north along the north-east corner of Kelly Field close to the Lafayette road, it then swung east in a slight semicircle crossing the Lafayette road and extending south-west to Widow Glen's House.

The fighting had not long started when Thomas's troops were in trouble, for Breckinridge had enveloped the left of his line. He sent an urgent call for another division, and Rosecrans ordered Wood from reserve to relieve Negley in the line, and Negley to march to Thomas's aid. But Negley's division became temporarily lost in the thick country. Therefore Thomas clamoured for still more support, and Rosecrans continued to weaken his right to strengthen his left. At about 11 a.m. Reynolds and Brannan in the centre were engaged by Stewart's division, which forced these troops across the Lafayette road, but the Confederates were driven back and the line re-established. Walker's corps then entered the battle against the hard-pressed Thomas, and shortly afterwards the Federals suffered a major misfortune.

Bragg's plan had been for Longstreet's wing to come in when the Federal left had been forced back, the whole of the Confederate line would then pivot on the left division and complete the rout. Longstreet's troops had been in position ready for this manoeuvre when an unexpected chance opened up. When thousands of men are engaged in close and mortal combat, and a yellow fog of powder smoke and dust blots out the sun and obscures the action, commanders are at a great disadvantage, and in this battle their problems were compounded by the dense nature of the country. Through an unfortunate misunderstanding, and perhaps the failure of the commanding general to make himself properly aware of the situation, Wood was told to take his division to assist Reynolds whose right was said to be in trouble. To accomplish this Wood had to bring his division out of the line and march it behind Brannan's. McCook was to send Davis's division to replace Wood.

Longstreet seized his chance and poured eight brigades into the gap created by Wood's withdrawal. The result was a Federal disaster. Sheridan's entire division, two brigades of Davis's and one of Van Cleve's were swept from the field (although two brigades rejoined about 7 p.m. to cover the final retreat). The army was virtually split with the right flank gone, and gone with it were Rosecrans and two of his corps commanders – McCook and Crittenden. Now only Thomas remained to take charge of the battered Union army. But he was a general imperturbable and dependable; Longstreet, his friend and comrade from the Mexican War (such is the tragedy of civil war), prepared to swing his troops right-handed and complete the rout, but Thomas took swift and positive action to resist the coming blow.

A wide gap had appeared between Brannan's and Reynold's divisions, which had not Wood, with commendable speed, moved his division into Longstreet must have pierced, and got behind those divisions fighting to fend off Polk's attack on the left of the Federal line. Wood's determined resistance gave Thomas time to form a new line, almost at right angles to his bulging front, and facing south along the commanding Horseshoe Ridge below farmer Snodgrass's house. Here he held off a series of determined attacks by Longstreet until ordered by Rosecrans to withdraw. The action fought by the Federal left under Thomas was a major factor in saving Rosecrans's army, and the disposition of the troops will be dealt with in more detail later.

At about this time, or a little later, Longstreet reported to Bragg and urged him to hold hard on the right and reinforce the left so as to cut Thomas off, but according to Longstreet he found Bragg quite out of touch and even believing his army was facing defeat. No reinforcements from the right could be spared, he said. And so Longstreet assaulted the ridge again, this time with three divisions, and once more in a short period of swift destruction men were mown down in tangled heaps, and the Union line held. As the long hours of heavy fighting wore on Federal ammunition became scarce, and anyway muskets were becoming too hot to load. Thomas was everywhere giving encouragement and shouting, 'Use your bayonets . . . the position must be held.' And held it was for more than five hours by 30,000 embattled men heavily outnumbered and almost surrounded. At the end of the day, and only just in time, Thomas withdrew his troops. It was a tired and ragged force that he led back, but their heroic stand had saved the Union army from total destruction.

Rosecrans maintained the position round Rossville Gap throughout the 21st, and on the 22nd withdrew to Chattanooga. Bragg was urged to pursue the Federals on the 21st, and hit them hard while they were off balance. The battle of Chickamauga had been won, but the prize was Chattanooga and that had not been attained. However, Bragg would not hear of it. He seems to have been overcome by his losses, which were indeed heavy,* and he spent the 21st burying his dead and collecting arms and stores. General Hill, writing at a later date, gave it as his opinion that the élan of the Southern soldier was never seen after Chickamauga. 'He fought stoutly to the last, but after Chickamauga,

---

*The numbers that fought and died at Chickamauga have been variously given by a number of authorities, and are not known for certain. But the Federal losses, killed and wounded, were probably between 14,000 and 16,000, and the Confederates' between 18,000 and 20,000.

with the sullenness of despair and without the enthusiasm of hope. That "barren victory" sealed the fate of the Southern Confederacy.'*

Rosecrans, when he withdrew to the lines around Chattanooga, had decided against holding Lookout Mountain and Lookout Valley, which divided the mountain from Raccoon Mountain. He felt it would be impossible to maintain communications with outpost troops, but it was a most unwise decision, for Bragg at once occupied positions from Missionary Ridge to Lookout Mountain connected by a line of earthworks, and he sent a strong force into Lookout Valley. He therefore controlled the Federal supply line from Bridgeport to Chattanooga, and he imposed a virtual stranglehold upon Rosecrans. He strengthened his position, harassed the Union troops with cavalry raids, and confidently expected that starvation would soon cause Rosecrans to beat the chamade.

But Washington reacted strongly to the situation. Troops from the Mississippi under Sherman, and from the Rappahannock under Hooker were hastily despatched to the beleaguered garrison; on 3 October General Grant was given overall command of the Military Division of the Mississippi (which covered the Departments of Ohio, Cumberland, and Tennessee), and General Thomas replaced Rosecrans in command at Chattanooga. McCook and Crittenden were relieved of their corps, and Granger took command of a combined corps.

The first, and most urgent, priority for the besieged was to open a viable supply route from Bridgeport, for the Army of the Cumberland was by the middle of October on half rations, many of the horses were dead, and ammunition and medical supplies were dangerously low. With the arrival of Hooker's troops at Bridgeport at the end of October a combined operation between his men and Thomas's was successfully executed against the Confederates at Brown's Ferry, and their troops in Lookout Valley. Once these had been removed the men on Lookout Mountain did not matter, for the road across Raccoon Mountain was now open. Henceforth the Federals could obtain supplies along what was known as 'the Cracker Line', which ran by river from Bridgeport to Kelly's Ferry, from thence across Raccoon Mountain to Brown's Ferry, where a pontoon bridge had been constructed, and from there across Moccasin Point to Chattanooga. The siege was virtually over.

In the Confederate army Bragg, disappointed by Polk's performance at Chickamauga, had replaced him by General Hardee from the Army of the Mississippi, and D. H. Hill had also been relieved of his command. There had been murmurings against Bragg himself. He had often been at loggerheads with his subordinate commanders, and shown little emanation of authority, but he survived. Now, at the beginning of

* *Johnson and Buel*, p. 662.

November, apparently unaware that the fate of Chattanooga for which he had striven for so long and at such cost, was soon to be decided, he despatched Longstreet's corps more than 100 miles to wrest Knoxville from Burnside.

This certainly caused Grant some uneasiness, for he was still short of Sherman's corps, Burnside had to look after himself, which he did admirably despite Bragg reinforcing Longstreet with Buckner's corps just a day before Grant was ready to attack. The battle of Chattanooga was fought on 23–25 November, and Grant's offensive was to be three-pronged. Sherman was to attack the north end of Missionary Ridge, Thomas was to carry out a holding operation in the centre, and Hooker was to bring his troops from Lookout Valley to Chattanooga Creek and assault the Confederate left.

There was little fighting on the 23rd, but on the 24th Hooker became involved in a battle on Lookout Mountain which, fought in mist and rain, later became known as the Battle Above The Clouds. He considerably outnumbered his opponents under General Stevenson, who withdrew during the night on to the main position. The decisive action took place on 25 November against what Bragg had, understandably, considered his impregnable position on Missionary Ridge. It was the only occasion in the whole war in which troops successfully assaulted successive lines of strongly held positions on a steep boulder-strewn hillside.

Sheridan was to continue his tough battle against the northern end of Missionary Ridge, while Hooker drove in the Confederate left flank; meanwhile Thomas's Army of the Cumberland was to launch a diversionary attack on the lower row of trenches in the centre of Missionary Ridge to keep Bragg from reinforcing his flanks. But Sherman and Hooker were destined to play the lesser roles. It was the Cumberland men, no doubt animated by their desire to wipe out their recent defeat at Chickamauga, who were to deliver the hammer blow that sent the Confederates flying from the field. As the sound of cannonade rolled down to them from batteries higher up the ridge these tough men crashed through first one line of trenches and then another. On and up they stormed, the very embodiment of the offensive spirit, watched by their surprised generals until their demoralized foe broke and ran. Casualties in this battle were much lighter than at Chickamauga. The Confederates suffered 6,667 and the Federals 5,824 killed and wounded.

The Confederacy had lost the strategically important Chattanooga, and almost all of Tennessee; moreover the road into Georgia was rapidly opening. Grant had achieved this very praiseworthy success, but Chickamauga was the key battle, where Bragg let victory elude him and Thomas made Chattanooga possible.

*

The battle of Chattanooga was a straightforward, hard-hitting fight. It is difficult to single out any particular factor that had a direct bearing on the result – other than courage and élan. But in the case of Chickamauga, not the most decisive of the two battles but the greater, there were three factors that had a definite bearing on the outcome: Bragg's failure to defeat Rosecrans's army in detail; the withdrawal of Wood's division from the line on 20 September; and Thomas's heroic stand later that day.

When Rosecrans succeeded in moving his three corps across the Tennessee and around Bragg's flank the latter judged Chattanooga to be untenable, and ordered a withdrawal to safeguard his communications in north Georgia. But this was not, as Rosecrans unwisely thought, a headlong flight but a planned withdrawal to Lafayette, where Bragg presided over a masterly concentration not only of his own army but of troops from East Tennessee, Mississippi, and Virginia. The Federal commander walked into this trap which Bragg had further baited by sending 'deserters' into Chattanooga with depressing stories of Confederate loss of morale and genuine despondency.

When Rosecrans learnt, on 9 September, that Bragg had abandoned Chattanooga and was retreating southward he ordered his three corps commanders to make a rapid pursuit. On the right McCook with all the cavalry (less one brigade), and Wilder's mounted infantry, was to make for Alpine and Somerville. Thomas, who was in the centre, had his two leading divisions (Negley's and Baird's) over Lookout Mountain and heading for McLemore's Cove, and they were now to continue their march by the Trenton–Lafayette road. Crittenden on the left had occupied Chattanooga, where he was ordered to leave a brigade and with the remainder of his corps to pursue the enemy down the Rossville–Ringgold–Dalton road. Rosecrans thus had his two flanks forty miles apart, and each of his columns well separated. McCook, whose three divisions reached Alpine on 10 September, found himself entirely isolated with the enemy in between him and Thomas's corps.

Bragg, spider like, had been watching these columns walk into his web, and by 9 September had his own force well concentrated centrally from near Lee and Gordon's Mill to Lafayette, with Cleburne's division of Hill's corps occupying the gaps of Pigeon Mountain. He decided to deal with Rosecrans's centre (Thomas's corps) first, and then turn upon the two flanks. On the evening of the 9th he issued orders for a two-pronged attack the following day on Thomas's leading divisions in McLemore's Cove. Hindman's division of Polk's corps was to advance from the north-east while Hill was to send, or take in person, Cleburne's division marching west through the Pigeon Mountain gaps. But Hill on receipt of these orders immediately replied that they were impracticable, because his divisional commander was ill and the two gaps in the mountain were blocked by fallen timber and could not be cleared in under twenty-four hours.

Meanwhile, Hindman had marched some ten miles during the night of the 9th and by morning was in striking distance of Negley's and Baird's divisions. Bragg therefore decided to proceed with the plan and ordered Buckner to march his corps to assist Hindman. This he did during the afternoon of the 10th. But when these two commanders met they agreed that Bragg's plan was not the best, and submitted one of their own. A good deal of time was lost in awaiting an answer, and when it came it was to say that they were to attack as ordered. Bragg then ordered Polk to send his remaining division to cover the rear of the attack, and Walker's corps to move at once in support of Cleburne's division at Dug Gap. This division was to join the battle as soon as Hindman opened the attack. Early on the morning of the 11th Bragg himself came forward to Cleburne's headquarters – Cleburne having apparently recovered from his illness – and together they waited until well after noon before Hindman's first gun opened up. The obstructions in Dug's and Catlett's Gaps having been previously removed, Cleburne then went forward, only to find that Thomas's advanced divisions had withdrawn from their precarious position.

Hindman's and Buckner's failure to move until after midday has never been properly explained, but it seems they were piqued at not being allowed to fight the battle their way, and anyway they did not like Bragg. But their behaviour, and that of Hill too, was unpardonable. Bragg, having concentrated some 30,000 troops into a position whereby they could crush two-thirds of Thomas's corps, was confounded by the contumely of his subordinate commanders.

Having failed against the centre Bragg now tried to defeat Crittenden's corps in detail, and to this purpose he issued orders to Polk at 6 p.m. on the night of the 12th. Up to this time Crittenden's corps had been divided; he had two divisions east of Chickamauga Creek and one in the vicinity of Lee and Gordon's Mill. These troops had been vainly marching and countermarching, quite oblivious of the danger they were in, trying to locate Confederate positions. But by the afternoon of the 12th the corps was concentrated at Lee and Gordon's Mill.

Bragg's orders to Polk, issued at a distance of some ten miles, were most insistent but not very clear. This was scarcely surprising, for the army commander had no conception as to the whereabouts of Crittenden's troops. He thought there was only one division east of Chickamauga, and he ordered Polk to engage it south-west of Ringgold on the Pea Vine Creek, whereas there had been two divisions, but by the time Polk received the dispatch they had united and were behind the creek. Polk therefore informed Bragg that far from attacking he had assumed a defensive position in the face of a superior force and needed reinforcements. He was told that he outnumbered the enemy and was to proceed at daybreak on the 13th with his attack. But later that morning Bragg went to the front in advance of Buckner's corps, which was to assist Polk, and saw for himself the true situation, and that Crittenden had escaped the trap.

By now Rosecrans had fully realized the appalling danger he was in, with thirty miles separating his left flank at Lee and Gordon's Mill and his right at Alpine. McCook was ordered to march immediately and close up on Thomas's corps, while the latter and Crittenden's corps remained in position to await McCook. Bragg did not avail himself of the opportunity to strike before McCook had reached Thomas. Having seen the fruits of his intelligent stratagems wither, he now determined to await the Virginian reinforcements before confronting the Federal army in a set-piece attack.

General D. H. Hill, in a later account of the battle, has not much that is good to say about Bragg. Some of the mud he slings sticks, but he had an axe to grind. There is no doubt that Bragg was quite often out of touch with the prevailing situation; he relied too much on his excellent cavalry, but they had many problems, and he took few steps to improve his intelligence system or to supervise his orders. This was the principal reason for his failure against Crittenden. But it is not true to say that he was confused and bewildered by the opportunities that presented themselves as a result of what was a clever piece of strategy. Bragg had a very clear idea of the overall picture when he made his first plan to spring the trap; a plan that should have succeeded had he been properly served. But there was no empathy between him and his subordinates, and he was an unlucky general – two factors that seldom make for success.

When Bragg eventually opened his attack on the morning of 20 September he packed a powerful punch at the Federal left, and General Thomas was soon calling for assistance. Rosecrans ordered Negley's division, which held a position on the right centre, to pull out of the line and march to Thomas. The gap was filled by Wood's division which, together with Van Cleve's, was in reserve. Shortly afterwards Rosecrans further weakened his right in response to urgent appeals from Thomas, and he does not seem to have been aware (although a quick reconnaissance could have told him) that Longstreet with eight brigades posed an ominous threat to his depleted right wing.

Shortly after 11 a.m. a member of Thomas's staff (Lieutenant-Colonel Von Schrader), while reconnoitring the defences, failed to appreciate that Brannan's division was somewhat withdrawn (although still in the line between Reynolds and Wood) and concealed by woodland. Thinking there was a dangerous gap he reported this information to Rosecrans, who without seeking corroboration sent an order to Wood to close up to his left in support of Reynolds, while McCook was told to send Davis's division into the gap that would be caused by Wood's move. Units from Van Cleve's division in reserve, and Sheridan's holding the extreme right of the Federal line were in the process of moving to strengthen the left, and so this latest complicated manoeuvre presented Longstreet with a situation he could scarcely credit.

It was a case of the right man in the right place at the right time, and into the gap caused by the disappearance of Wood, Longstreet poured his brigades. McCook had only two brigades of Davis's division and one of Sheridan's left with which to try to stem this onslaught, although others farther up were hastily ordered to change front and form a line. Wood had moved just far enough to uncover Brannan, and both these divisions were struck in flank by Longstreet's avalanche, while Davis's division was overwhelmed and scattered before it could get up to fill the gap vacated by Wood. Sheridan's division and Wilder's brigade were cut off and forced to quit the field, and indeed the whole Federal line from Brannan's centre to beyond Widow Glen's House was in confusion. According to the Confederate general, Daniel Hill, the Union right lost in this attack 1,100 prisoners, 27 guns and numerous wagon trains.

Such were the facts that caused the Federal disaster at Chickamauga. A disaster which might have been far worse – and indeed led to the annihilation of Rosecrans's whole army – had Bragg spared Longstreet's troops to cut off Thomas's line of retreat, and to pursue the flying Federals down the Dry Valley road. Although he was understandably anxious to break through on the right he still had Cheatham's division uncommitted, and through failing to reinforce success he quite probably let slip the chance of total victory.

Nevertheless, the disintegration of the Federal right ensured that Bragg would eventually win the battle, for however valiantly the remaining Federals fought – and they did fight most valiantly – they could never repel Bragg's whole army. It is interesting, therefore, to consider just why Wood carried out a manoeuvre which brought disaster to half the army. There are two reasons usually put forward: that the order he received was not clear, and that his withdrawal from the line was an act of spite against Rosecrans. The order read: 'The General Commanding directs that you close upon Reynolds as fast as possible and support him.' There does not seem to be anything ambiguous about that, and so one is left with vindictiveness.

Earlier in the morning Rosecrans, no doubt under pressure from Thomas's predicament, had censured Wood for tardiness in relieving Negley in the line, and it is thought by some that Wood now deliberately carried out an order knowing it to be impracticable, but hoping it would cause Rosecrans embarrassment. Wood is said to have asked for the order to move to be put in writing, and it is suggested that this supports his maleficent behaviour. It is true that there had been occasions in this campaign when general officers, acting out of antipathy, had ruined their commander's plans, and this might have been yet another instance of such lamentable business. But it is difficult to believe that any man would deliberately endanger perhaps thousands of his comrades merely to avenge a minor rebuke. More particularly is it difficult when one remembers how magnificently Wood fought an hour or so later on Horseshoe Ridge to prevent Longstreet from sweeping to the rear of what remained of the Federal army.

Surely it is possible that although he knew the situation to his immediate left and right, and therefore this order may have seemed somewhat strange, he had no idea of the overall picture, which was exceedingly confused with troops hastening to the left, and that he felt it his duty to comply with the army commander's order right or wrong. Rosecrans, not Wood, should take the blame for this incident that was to cause the Federal defeat.

The battle was lost, but the army could still be saved – a factor of the utmost importance. In the wake of Longstreet's first devastating thrust there appeared a wide gap between Brannan's division, which had been hastily brought to the right to face the attack, and that of Reynolds. It has already been related how Wood filled this gap just in time, and held it with stern resolution. The subsequent short lull in the fighting enabled Thomas, now the senior officer left on the field, to realign his troops to meet the new threat.

The left of his defence, facing Polk's continuing attacks, was held by Baird's, Johnson's, and Palmer's divisions in that order. Then came Reynolds, and after him a new line was formed almost at right angles to the original one, and just south of Snodgrass House on a commanding eminence known as Horseshoe Ridge. This was held by 1,200 men of Harker's brigade (Wood's division), two regiments (19th Illinois and 11th Michigan) of Stanley's brigade of Negley's division, Brannan's division (less a brigade) and on the extreme right Colonel Sirwell's brigade of Negley's division. These assorted troops faced south in the direction of Longstreet's advance.

This new alignment was intended to prevent Longstreet from turning Thomas's right and cutting him off from his line of withdrawal to Rossville Gap. Longstreet for the rest of the day made repeated attacks in an attempt to break through, and very nearly succeeded. At about 2 p.m. Anderson's brigade of Hindman's division and Kershaw's of McLaw's division fought desperately to gain the crest, and for a brief moment succeeded, before being hurled back. The 21st Ohio Regiment did tremendous execution with their Colt's revolving rifles. The situation was becoming critical, for Longstreet had many brigades not yet committed, but help was at hand.

Granger's reserve corps had been positioned on the Ringgold road. Hearing heavy firing coming from between the Lafayette and Dry Valley roads he judged the time appropriate for intervention, and disregarding his orders he despatched two brigades (Whitaker's and Mitchell's) of Steedman's division to report to Thomas, and instructed his third brigade (Dan McCook's) to cover the Ringgold–Lafayette road. Steedman had marched the three and a half miles to Horseshoe Ridge by 3 p.m., and here he found Thomas supervising the struggle to keep Longstreet's men, now reinforced by troops from Hindman's and B. R. Johnson's divisions, from their attempts to turn both his flanks. Mitchell and Whitaker brought their brigades into the right of the line.

At the same time as Steedman's brigades arrived Van Derveer's from Brannan's division also reported to Thomas, and took its place alongside the other brigades of that division whose men were almost totally exhausted and very short of ammunition. But besides troops Steedman had brought 95,000 rounds of spare ammunition, and through these most fortunate acquisitions Thomas was able to withstand Longstreet's constant batterings. However, it was not only the attacks on Horseshoe Ridge that the embattled Thomas had to hold off: the left of his line was assaulted at about midday by a strong attack commanded by Bragg in person. Breckinridge's division of Hill's corps managed to outflank Thomas's left on the Chattanooga road and attempted to take Baird's division in rear. But he was met and thrown back by the reserve brigades (which included Van Derveer's not yet sent to Horseshoe Ridge). Baird's, Palmer's, and Johnson's divisions were all engaged frontally at this time by Polk's corps, which kept up a steady pressure on the Federal left.

At about 3.30 the crisis of this great battle was reached. Longstreet, hoping to make a complete breakthrough and trap all the Federal troops, asked Bragg for reinforcements from the right, but Bragg refused. Longstreet then brought up his reserve division (Preston's), and extended his line beyond the Federal right. A wide gap had occurred between the two wings of Thomas's force, and Longstreet has been criticized for not exploiting it in preference to another frontal attack. In the general confusion of this closely contested battle the gap may not have been apparent to Longstreet, but it is strange – in view of his appeal to Bragg – that he did not, at this critical moment, commit the whole of Preston's division to the attack, but held back a brigade to deal with a mythical cavalry threat.

The battle for the annihilation of Thomas's force lasted until dark, and was fought with the utmost savagery. Longstreet threw in Hindman's and B. R. Johnson's divisions on the left against Steedman's, beating it back to a ridge in rear and gaining ground on Brannan's right, but these troops could get no farther. On the right of his line he passed Kelly's and Gracie's brigades of Preston's division through Anderson's and Kershaw's, both of which had been hard engaged for some time. But these two brigades were firmly held on the vital crest by Harker's, Hazen's, and Van Derveer's men, and forced to withdraw after suffering heavy casualties. Meanwhile, from 4 to 6 p.m. Hill's corps supported by Walker's, and Cheatham's and Liddell's divisions, pummelled the Union left and for a time cut off the Rossville road. But Reynolds's division, which was beginning to withdraw, pushed them back to the east of the road.

As the sun went down Thomas's weary troops, now again short of ammunition and relying on the bayonet, were still intact on the ground they had defended with such courage and resolution for more than five hours of bitter fighting, but the time had come to be gone. During the afternoon Rosecrans had sent an order to Thomas to withdraw by way of McFarland's Gap, and to take up a defensive position at Rossville Gap with McCook and Crittenden. The order was received shortly after 4.30, and seems to have been acted upon fairly promptly with Reynolds's division instructed to leave first. As already mentioned this division had to fight its way out, and so did Baird's and Johnson's divisions, for the left flank was almost enveloped by the Confederate right, but the men on Horseshoe Ridge slipped away in orderly fashion, and unmolested, as darkness covered the bloodstained field.

During the night of 20–21 September Thomas's troops passed through McFarland's Gap, and on the 21st the whole army took up a position in Rossville Gap and along the crest of Missionary Ridge to Lookout Mountain. That night it was withdrawn to Chattanooga, from where in two months' time it was to emerge to gain a famous victory. Thomas, 'the Rock of Chickamauga', has been rightly acclaimed the hero who saved the army; but General Granger needs to be remembered for, marching to the sound of cannon contrary to orders, he and his men arrived just in time to save Brannan's division from being enveloped, and had this occurred the whole position would almost certainly have been lost.

General Bragg won the battle of Chickamauga, but he failed in his principal task of saving Chattanooga. The reason for this can be traced to the débâcle that occurred in and around McLemore's Cove between 10 and 13 September. There have been instances described where battles were probably lost through the incompetence, and on one occasion even the vanity, of a subordinate commander. But here there was contumely, amounting almost to insubordination, by generals who refused to operate the plan of their commander, who was himself at the time too far back to influence the battle. In the circumstances it was amazing that the Confederates eventually achieved what they did. But the opportunity for total victory was lost at this time by an unpopular commander, often out of touch and badly served by at least two of his generals. Great events are unlikely to be recorded by such an unhappy combination.

However, this was a battle where – in pleasing contrast to some already related – final victory was gained by the action of a subordinate commander. The Union army would have been swept from Chattanooga had Thomas's corps not held firm at Chickamauga.

19 Background to Isandhlwana

IN January 1879 a British force was outnumbered, outmanoeuvred, beaten and broken by Zulu valour. It was a disaster which shook the nation, and one that had certain similarities with what had occurred in the valley of the Little Big Horn three years earlier, when five troops of the US Seventh Cavalry were wiped out by Sioux Indians. In both instances the fight was against a proud and warlike race striving to preserve their homeland; in both instances the white men were heavily outnumbered; in both instances they unwisely split their force; in both instances a degree of incompetence and misjudgement was partly compensated for by extreme courage; and in both instances the disaster should never have occurred.

Isandhlwana (pronounced I-san-shwana) was not a great battle, nor had it the slightest political or military significance, but it was a great epic upon which posterity has bestowed a large measure of honour and glory. In the shadow of a majestic hill on a rock-strewn plain hundreds of young Englishmen and thousands of young Zulus, who might have lived together in peace, died heroically.

The Zulus were a comparatively insignificant Bantu clan until, in the early years of the nineteenth century, a particularly bloodthirsty chief called Shaka welded them into a nation based largely on superstition and militarism, and became their first king. They were a very fine people, physically superb, athletic, intelligent, and amenable to discipline. This, together with their great courage, made them excellent soldiers. Military service was universal and compulsory, young men being conscripted at an early age and sent to live in military kraals where they were forbidden to marry without the king's consent, which was often withheld until the man was forty. Men were drafted to regiments according to age groups, and there was frequently a small percentage (usually less than 10 per cent) of very old warriors – in Shaka's Usixepi Regiment, for example, there were 2,000 men between the ages of thirty and eighty.

While the number of men and regiments which fought at Isandhlwana is fairly accurately known, the total force under arms in the kingdom at that time is less authentically documented; but it is usually accepted that there were 26 regiments containing some 40,000 warriors under the age of 60, and a further 7 of older men – although in a few regiments age groups were still mixed. The principal weapon was the assegai. The short-handled variety was used for close-quarter stabbing, and the larger one (sometimes two) was carried in the left hand inside a strong oxhide shield that gave the man almost full protection. This throwing assegai was often launched from the incredible distance of seventy yards. There were a number of muskets and rifles in the army, perhaps as many as 15,000, but of these not more than 2,000 would have any degree of accuracy, and marksmanship was bad.

Each regiment had its distinguishing marks – worn on the shield or headdress – and was commanded by the chief induna who had a second-in-command called the second induna. The regiment was divided into two wings and subdivided into companies. There were no recognized drill movements, but a few useful formations were practised, and obedience to superiors was absolute. Tactics were simple, but extremely effective. In the attack an impi (as an army was called) would have two wings or horns and a chest. It was the duty of the horns to circle the flanks of the enemy in a huge pincer movement, and when this manoeuvre was completed the chest, of many ranks deep, would advance to the kill. In much of the rugged country these athletic Zulus could outpace a horse, and their capacity for concealment among the hills and kranzes of their native land was very impressive. They travelled light and needed virtually no commissariat.

Shaka's tyranny was widespread and effective. By 1823 he was master of vast tracts of land including what is now Natal, but in 1828 he was murdered by his brother Dingaan who then became king. Dingaan was scarcely less cruel than Shaka, and even more treacherous. In 1837, in return for carrying out a service, he promised the Boers a tract of land, but when in February 1838, their task accomplished, a delegation came to the royal kraal to ratify the treaty of settlement Dingaan massacred the whole party.* This base act did not go unpunished, and although they were to suffer a further disaster at the hands of the Zulus, in January 1840 the Boers won a decisive victory. They then supported Dingaan's half-brother, Mpande, who chased Dingaan across the Pongola river into Swaziland, where shortly afterwards he was killed, probably by the Swazis. Mpande reigned from 1840 to 1873, first as a vassal of the Boers and then from 1843, when the British annexed Natal, of the British. He was a good-natured, easy-going valetudinarian whose effective rule ended in 1857 when his son, Cetshwayo, took over the administration of the kingdom.

*H. Rider Haggard, in his novel *Marie* (Macdonald 1912), gives a good account of this unpleasant, but characteristic, piece of treachery by Dingaan.

Cetshwayo had fought and killed his brother in 1856, and was soon recognized as Mpande's heir. He was the fourth King of the Zulus and an undoubted improvement on his predecessors. He was intelligent, and popular with his people whom he ruled firmly and on the whole justly. But in him the forces of light and darkness constantly strove, for on occasions he could be devious and extremely cruel. At his coronation Sir Theophilus Shepstone, representing the British government, extracted certain promises from him to rule humanely, but these he found difficult to keep. His primary task was to strengthen and expand the already formidable army that his uncles had created, and inevitably he found difficulty in resisting the pressures put upon him for action by this powerful military machine. There was, however, little evidence to show that he ever intended to invade Natal.

But there were those among the British who thought otherwise, and there is little doubt that the white colonists mistrusted this powerful black neighbour on their boundary. Moreover, Zululand would be a rich and fertile acquisition. The British had taken Capetown in 1806, and were soon at loggerheads with the Dutch Boers who had been there for more than 150 years. Such acts as the abolition of slavery, which seriously affected their economy, and other meddlesome measures, resulted in the Great Trek, which started in 1835. Before long the Boers were stubbornly resisted by the Basutos and the Matabeles. The latter, a people akin to the Zulus and ruled by Mosilikatzi, one of Shaka's generals, proved to be exceptionally tiresome foes. But the Boer commandos were expert at this type of fighting, and after some hard battles they drove the natives north and established themselves in what became known as the Orange Free State and the Transvaal Republic.

However, they were not yet fully satisfied, and looked for more space across the Drakensberg Mountains into Natal. Here, after the trouble with Dingaan mentioned above, they formed another independent republic. This was not to the liking of the British government which sent troops to Durban, and the Boers gave way. By a treaty of 1852 the British acknowledged Boer independence of the Orange Free State and the Transvaal, and the boundaries of the Zulu kingdom were also defined. For more than twenty years there was no trouble, but in 1877 – for a number of good economic and military reasons – the British annexed the Transvaal. The Zulus now, if they wished to expand, must do so at the expense of the British. And Sir Bartle Frere, appointed Governor-General of Cape Colony in 1877, quickly convinced himself that that was exactly what they did want to do.

Frere was a highly intelligent, dedicated, and able proconsul. He had behind him long and excellent service in India, where among other posts he had been Governor of Bombay and a member of the Governor-General's Council. The Colonial Secretary, Lord Carnarvon, was anxious for him to promote some form of federation, but the ill-feeling caused by the annexation of the Transvaal made this impossible for the present, and so Frere directed his gaze on native affairs. His arrival at the Cape coincided with a certain amount of native trouble; the ninth of the so-called Kaffir Wars was being fought, there was a serious drought, and more than one native uprising in Boer territory. Frere was a firm advocate of British paramountcy and the need to bring the native population out of savagery and corruption, and to combat famine and disease. These were admirable sentiments, but they were seldom shared by the natives, who were conservative in their ways and greatly valued their independence. But for the moment Frere was more concerned to forestall, by a pre-emptive strike, an imaginary threat of invasion by what he called Cetshwayo's 'celibate man-slaying machine'.

During 1878 he had constantly assured the Colonial Secretary that in order to safeguard the Natal colonists, as well as to put an end to internecine warfare and ritual massacre, the Zulu nation must be brought to heel. However, the government was anxious to avoid war, and instructed Frere to do all that he could to reach a peaceful and amicable settlement with Cetshwayo. But South Africa was a long way from London, and Frere felt that as the man on the spot he knew best, and that the situation called for quick and resolute action.

When the British annexed the Transvaal they inherited a serious dispute between the Zulus and the Boers over a large tract of territory in the north-west of Zululand. Frere proposed, and Cetshawyo agreed, to refer the dispute to a Boundary Commission whose members Frere appointed. Much to his chagrin, at the end of 1878, the Commission found in favour of the Zulus. Frere had to return them their land, but in a declaration sent to Cetshwayo on 11 December the award was hedged with impossible restrictions, and accompanied by an ultimatum that had to be complied with in twenty days. The ultimatum was in two parts; the first dealt with the surrender of certain border raiders (principally the sons of an aged chief called Sirayo, who had violated British territory to seize their father's adulterous wife), and the second part contained a clause demanding the disbandment of the Zulu army. Frere knew that Cetshwayo was unlikely to comply with the first of these demands, and most certainly not with the second.

The ultimatum expired on 31 December, and on 2 January 1879 Sir Bartle Frere issued a final notification explaining in eleven points why it had become necessary to invade Zulu territory. This somewhat sanctimonious document included towards the end that familiar but distinctly cynical, even deceitful, sentence, 'The British Government has no quarrel with the Zulu nation . . .' On 11 January (the deadline set) a British army crossed the Buffalo and Tugela rivers in the opening moves of a war that was to blot out that nation with which its government had no quarrel.

The man who was to command the troops in this – to many people's thinking, unnecessary – war was Lieutenant-General Lord Chelmsford. At the time he was fifty-two years old, and the archetypal mid-nineteenth-century British general. Courteous, courageous, honourable in his dealings, loyal, and generous to his subordinates – indeed an exemplar of the virtues of a civilized nation – but sadly, for the great part, he was ineffectual. He had served with distinction in the Crimean War in a junior capacity, and on Napier's staff at Magdala, but as yet he was untried in high command in war. Although painstaking and conscientious he was to display few of the talents that make for a great commander. At times indecisive he did, however, share Frere's decisiveness over the need to invade Zululand and, also like Frere, he underestimated the skill and resolution of the enemy.

The Battle of Isandhlwana
22 January 1879

CHELMSFORD's plan was to invade on a wide front (some 200 miles) with three main columns, which were to drive the Zulus before them and to converge on Cetshwayo's capital, Ulundi. He thought that to strike straight for Ulundi with one large column would run the considerable risk of allowing the Zulu army, or part of it, to get behind him and raid into Natal. The right column (No. 1), commanded by Colonel Pearson, was to cross the Lower Tugela near its mouth and its first objective was Eschowe; the centre column (No. 3), under Colonel Glyn, would cross at Rorke's Drift and march eastwards, clearing the border and keeping in touch with the neighbouring columns. Lord Chelmsford and his staff were to accompany this column. The left column (No. 4), under Colonel Wood, was to march south-east from the direction of Utrecht and cross the Blood River. A fourth column (No. 2), commanded by Colonel Durnford, was initially left on the Middle Tugela at Kranz Kop to form a protection for the border, while a fifth column remained on the Pongola river at Luneberg.

The strengths of the four columns were 4,750, 3,871, 4,709 and 2,278 respectively; in all 15,608 officers and men, 756 drivers, 110 horses and 285 wagons.* The composition of the columns were broadly speaking much the same with the exception of Colonel Durnford's which had a rocket battery, and was comprised almost entirely of native troops. Colonel Glyn's column, which was the one principally involved at Isandhlwana, was made up of six staff officers, N Battery 5th Brigade RA (Lieutenant-Colonel Harness), 1st Battalion 24th Foot (Lieutenant-Colonel Pulleine), 2nd Battalion 24th Foot (Lieutenant-Colonel Degacher), No. 1 Squadron Mounted Infantry (Lieutenant-Colonel Russell), Natal Mounted Police (Major Dartnell, later transferred to HQ), Natal Carabiniers (Captain T. Shepstone), Newcastle Mounted Rifles (Captain Bradstreet), Buffalo Border Guard (Captain Smith), 1st and 2nd Battalions of the 3rd Regiment Natal Native Contingent (Commandants Hamilton-Browne and Lonsdale respectively), and No.

---

* Figures from French, pp. 391–7. Other accounts vary slightly but not significantly.

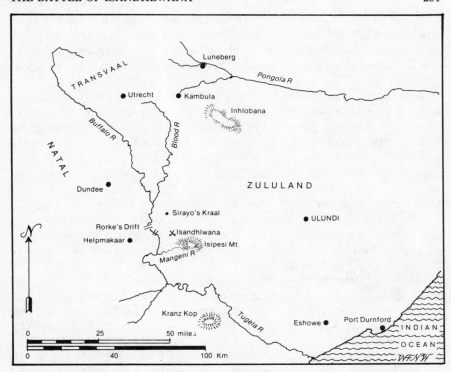

Zululand 1879

1 Company Natal Native Pioneer Corps. There were 1,747 Imperial and
Colonial troops and 2,866 native troops in this column as well as
conductors and drivers employed to drive 220 wagons and 82 carts.

On paper Chelmsford commanded a formidable force, and the greater
part of it was to fight with extreme courage, but some of the native troops
left much to be desired. Durnford's Basutos were excellent, but the
Natal Zulus (perhaps understandably) were in some cases unreliable,
and did not take kindly to the rigid formations and training unwisely
imposed upon them. Chelmsford took enormous trouble in the organization and administration of the force, issuing regulations to cover
almost every contingency, but unfortunately in none of the columns
were these always carried out. And Chelmsford, himself, having sought
what information he could on the Zulus from Boer commanders, did not
take heed of what they had told him.

Cetshwayo, unlike his uncle, Shaka, was not a great warrior. He did
not lead his troops in person, but his authority was absolute and he
strictly forbade the first strike. He mobilized his entire army, and the
regiments rallied at the royal kraal. He had no plan for them, the

indunas were to wait upon events with the paramount duty not to cross the border, but to drive the invaders from their land, and to rely as much as possible on surprise and ambush. When Chelmsford's troops crossed the Zulu frontier on 11 January Cetshwayo's warriors were ready to give battle.

What befell Nos 1 and 4 Columns will be recounted briefly later. The story of Isandhlwana concerns only No. 3 and a part of No. 2 columns. The first brush with the enemy occurred some six miles east of the river in the early hours of 12 January, when the 1st/24th with a contingent of native troops engaged a party of Zulus defending Sirayo's (he whose sons had caused such trouble) kraal from the nearby krantzes. The action lasted only a short time before the Zulus were driven off with the loss of thirty men, and the troops then burnt the kraal and rounded up 500 head of cattle. The column remained on this site for seven days, carrying out work to the track to make it passable for wagons. The road at best was very rough, and the incessant heavy thunderstorms made drainage necessary and repairs a problem.

While this repair work was in progress Chelmsford and his staff went forward to select the next camp site, and the one they chose was in the immediate vicinity of the strangely shaped Isandhlwana Mount. This flat-topped, elongated hill with steep sides rising 500 feet above the surrounding plain, runs north and south and is about 300 yards long at the top. It is connected by a col, or neck, to a lesser hill to the south known as Stony Hill, and across the col was the only possible route for the wagons, because elsewhere the ground was very broken and rough. East of the hill the ground sloped gently down to a dry donga which ran parallel to the hill, and beyond it was a plain some four miles wide and extending for eight miles east to west. To the south the land was open for some distance to the Malagata Range, but in the north the plain ended abruptly at the Ngutu Hills, a range as high as Isandhlwana Mount itself, and only 2,000 yards distant at its nearest point.

The camp was to be pitched on the plateau immediately east of the mount which would therefore protect its rear. In the shadow of this majestic feature – in whose shape men of the 24th recognized the Sphinx, their regimental badge – and on the rock-strewn plateau around it, one of the major dramas of war was shortly to be enacted. Chelmsford has been criticized for its choice, and certainly the range to the north was too close for comfort, and gave ample opportunity for concealment. But it had its merits, and had it been properly defended would probably have been as good as any other site in the neighbourhood.

Most of the troops were at the camp site by midday on the 20th, although some of the wagons had to be outspanned a mile away owing to the exhaustion of the oxen. The camp was formed from left to right by the two battalions of the Natal Native Contingent, the 2nd/24th, gunners, mounted troops, and the 1st/24th. No orders were given to entrench or laager the camp, although only a few days earlier while at Sirayo's kraal Chelmsford had been earnestly advised by a Boer commander to do this. While the camp was being set up Chelmsford, with an escort, made a reconnaissance to the south-east where a Zulu stronghold had been reported, but he returned at 6.30 p.m. having seen nothing.

However, that evening on receipt of further reports on the presence of an impi to the south-east, he decided to despatch the next day a reconnaissance in force. Three parties went out: two battalions of the Natal Native Contingent under Commandant Lonsdale left camp at 4.30 a.m. with orders to work round the southern side of the Malagata Range; they were followed an hour later by 150 mounted police – under Major Dartnell – who were to reconnoitre along the track that Chelmsford had followed the day previous; and a third, smaller party of mounted infantry was to carry out a short independent reconnaissance towards Isipesi Hill.

Early in the afternoon Chelmsford, who was still in the camp, received a message that Dartnell had linked up with Lonsdale, and although a few hundred Zulus had been seen they had soon cleared off. But at 4 p.m., while Chelmsford was riding with Glyn to inspect some advanced vedettes, another message from Dartnell reported a large force of Zulus in the hills to his front. As it was too late for him to take action that day Dartnell intended bivouacking and resuming operations next day. Meanwhile, could food and blankets be despatched for his and Lonsdale's troops? This request Chelmsford complied with, but not unnaturally he was considerably annoyed, for Dartnell's orders were to reconnoitre and return, not to stay and fight.

He was probably still more annoyed when at 1.30 a.m. on the 22nd he was roused with another message from Dartnell to say that the Zulus were too large a force for him to tackle, and he urgently required reinforcements. This information, although it proved to be incorrect, for those Zulus were a comparatively small body on their way to join the main impi, did tend to confirm an earlier report that the Umcijo regiment was assembled near Isipesi Hill, and so Chelmsford ordered reinforcements to be ready to leave under Colonel Glyn at first light. These consisted of six companies of the 2nd/24th, the Mounted Infantry, four of Colonel Harness's guns, and the Natal Native Pioneer Corps. Chelmsford would accompany them, for in any event it was his intention to reconnoitre the next camp site.

This left in camp, under the command of Lieutenant-Colonel Pulleine, a mixed force of European and native troops which included 2 guns and 70 gunners – in all about 1,200 men of which some 800 were

Europeans. However, before he left camp Chelmsford had sent an order to Colonel Durnford (who with part of his No 2 Column had been left at Rorke's Drift) to bring up his five troops of mounted Basutos, the rocket battery, two companies of the 1st Regiment Natal Native Contingent,* and ten wagons. These troops arrived at Isandhlwana at about 9.45 a.m. when all was still quiet in the camp.

Glyn's reinforcements, accompanied by Chelmsford and his staff, reached Dartnell's position at 6.30 a.m. There followed a strange concatenation of events, mistakes and misunderstandings that had a definite, although indirect, bearing on the disaster that was shortly to engulf the camp at Isandhlwana. Dartnell and Colonel Russell (in command of the Mounted Infantry) with four guns were ordered to go forward to discover the dispositions and strength of the Zulu force seen the previous night. They became engaged in a running fight, for it seemed this small force of Zulus was anxious to draw them on, and although they killed about eighty they achieved very little.

While they were away a message from Pulleine, timed 8.05 a.m., reached Chelmsford at 9 a.m. Pulleine had been informed by one of his vedettes that a strong force of Zulus was advancing towards the camp from the direction of the Ngutu Hills. Chelmsford, still thinking he had the main impi in front of him, found this difficult to believe, but he sent his ADC, Lieutenant Milne of the Naval Brigade, to the high ground where, through his powerful telescope, he could see the camp. Milne reported that all seemed normal and the tents were still standing. This was a significant factor, for in the face of danger they should have been struck.

Pulleine's report carried no hint of urgency, and was anyway second-hand. Chelmsford had just sent Hamilton-Browne with his NNC battalion back to help Pulleine strike camp, and anyway Durnford's men should have reached Isandhlwana by now. It would have required at least three hours to get the troops back to camp, and Chelmsford was not unmindful that his principal objective was Ulundi and his immediate one was to get the column to the next camp site. He decided to continue his march. Had he returned he might have been in time to save the camp. There would have been no Rorke's Drift, and many brave deeds would have perished unborn. But it cannot be considered a wrong decision, for in the circumstances any commander would have done as he did.

As Dartnell's and Russell's troops were unable to bring the enemy to bay Chelmsford ordered them back, and the entire party, less the guns, moved forward to the proposed new camp site at the head of the Mangeni

---

*Some accounts say Durnford brought only one company of 1st NNC. They were infantry, and were not in fact listed in Chelmsford's order.

Valley. The time was now about 12.30 and gunfire from the direction of the camp could be clearly heard. This time Chelmsford himself rode up a nearby ridge from where through his glass he could see the camp with the tents still standing, and as the gunfire had died down he imagined Pulleine must have beaten off a small impi and there was no cause for alarm. But troops nearer to the camp were soon thinking otherwise.

To reach the new camp site Colonel Harness and his guns had to backtrack for two miles on account of the ground, and while engaged in this they heard firing from the direction of Isandhlwana, and saw a large body of natives between them and the camp. These turned out to be Hamilton-Browne's men on their way back to the camp, who sent urgently for Harness to join them, for they believed the camp to be surrounded and about to be taken. Major Gossett, Chelmsford's senior ADC, was marching with Harness and he strongly advised him to carry out his orders to rejoin Chelmsford, for he felt Hamilton-Browne's report was exaggerated, but Harness ignored this advice. Whereupon Gossett rode back to Chelmsford. Whether he communicated the urgency of Hamilton-Browne's plea for troops to either Chelmsford or Colonel Crealock, his staff officer, is in doubt. But in any event he returned with orders for Harness to turn about and march to the new camp site.

Hamilton-Browne had, before his troops were seen by Harness, sent back two urgent messages to Chelmsford, and these reached the general at about the same time as Gossett's probably watered-down report. Chelmsford was still unconvinced that there was serious trouble at the camp, but he decided to ride back and investigate for himself. He set off at about 2 p.m. with Russell's Mounted Infantry as an escort. An hour and a half later he came up with Hamilton-Browne's battalion, whose native soldiers had refused to go farther without support, and ordered them to fall in behind the Mounted Infantry. A few minutes later a badly frightened Commandant Lonsdale rode up. He had become detached from his troops while reconnoitring the Malagata Hills and becoming unwell had allowed his horse to head back for camp and its fodder bucket. He came out of a lethargic doze to find himself in the camp amid the carnage of black and white bodies, all of the latter having been disembowelled. He had speedily turned about and only by urging his weary animal did he avoid death.

Chelmsford, who appeared quite unmoved by the narrowness of his personal escape, for his party was almost in sight of the camp, was dumbfounded that such a disaster could have occurred. He immediately ordered Glyn's force to return, and with Hamilton-Browne's Natal Native Contingent advanced in battle order to within three miles of the camp, there to await the arrival of Glyn. By the time he reached the stricken field night had cast a veil over the grisly scene.

Meanwhile, what had occurred at Isandhlwana? When Durnford

arrived he took over command (by virtue of seniority, if not by direct order – for there is some doubt about the latter) from Pulleine. Durnford had been commissioned into the Royal Engineers in 1848, and in the course of his thirty years' service had had much experience with native troops for whom he had a great respect, which was mutual. He was an excellent fighting soldier, competent and exceptionally brave, but he liked to go his own way, and hated being left out of a fight. The usually placid Chelmsford had been stirred to administer a severe reprimand for his independent action with No. 2 column while at Kranz Kop, and there were those who later asserted that his actions at Isandhlwana were at least partly responsible for the disaster.

Pulleine would, of course, have told Durnford about the Zulus seen to the north-east a couple of hours before his arrival, and that may have prompted him to send out troops some way in advance of the camp. He had sent back one troop of his Basutos to protect his wagons that had not yet come up, and two troops were despatched to reconnoitre on the left flank towards the Nguto Hills, while he himself advanced into the plain with the remaining two troops of Basutos, the rocket battery, and one company of the 1st NNC. He had asked Pulleine to lend him two British companies to strengthen his force, but Pulleine demurred, reminding Durnford that the orders were to defend the camp and the troops were already dangerously extended. Durnford did not press his request. But before leaving he ordered a company of the 1st/24th under Lieutenant Cavaye to the heights some 1,500 yards north of the camp, and the remainder of the troops, who had stood-to after the 8 a.m. alarm, he stood-down.

Durnford and his men rode east and passed to the south of a prominent feature called Conical Hill. He had sent some of his Basutos to climb the plateau and reconnoitre along it. These troops at first saw only a herd of cattle, which they intended to round up, but on coming to the edge of the ridge they saw to their utter amazement a vast horde of Zulus in the valley below. These were at ease although in full battle array, and yet another large body was moving off to the north. This was the main impi whose regiments were quietly and cunningly taking up position for their attack the next day. Surprise having been lost the Uve regiment – almost certainly without orders – rushed to the attack, and other regiments necessarily followed.

Durnford, some four miles from the camp, was a little ahead and to the flank of the patrolling Basutos, but he had no need of the warning they sent him, for by now the great wave of the impi's left horn could be seen breasting the ridge. The rocket battery, which had perforce become somewhat detached in rear, were the first to feel the tide of Zulu storm; bravely they attempted to discharge their missiles, but only one could be launched before a party of Zulus swept upon them. In hand-to-hand fighting the battery commander, Major Russell, and all but four of his men were killed, and the rocket-guns had to be abandoned. Meanwhile, Durnford and his men fought their way back to the dry donga some 800 yards in front of the camp. They reached it at about the time (around 12.30 p.m.) the Zulu regiments were closing in upon the camp.

The gravamen against Durnford was that on taking over command from Pulleine he disobeyed orders that officer had received from Chelmsford, by which he should automatically have been bound. In so doing he had dissipated what strength Pulleine had (the latter had to send two other companies to defend the forward troops when attacked), his departure from the camp and subsequent withdrawal created a wide gap on the right of the line between his troops and Lieutenant Pope's, and his premature engagement with the Zulus resulted in their attack being put forward more than twelve hours.

Durnford was undoubtedly guilty of disobeying orders, and that was to form Chelmsford's principal apologia. It certainly made Pulleine's task more difficult, but in itself it could hardly have affected the issue. And if it was true that on account of inauspicious omens the Zulu assault was not scheduled until the early hours of the 23rd, their attack would

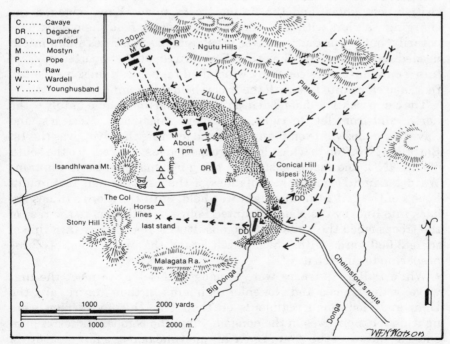

The Battle of Isandhlwana. 22 January 1879.

have been just as devastating and probably completed more quickly, for the troops would have been caught while striking camp.

Pulleine got his first intimation of serious trouble from the political agent, Captain George Shepstone, who had accompanied Lieutenant Raw's Basutos. These men, while reconnoitring the high ground some three or four miles from the camp, gave chase to a party of Zulus herding cattle, only to find – like their colleagues with Durnford – that they were suddenly almost on top of a huge mass of men making straight for the camp, while others (the right horn) were circling round to the rear. Lietenants Raw and Cavaye fell back, the latter's company engaging the horn at long range. Shepstone arrived with this alarming news at the same time as an order from Chelmsford to strike camp. Clearly this latter could not be done, but after some hesitation – for his troops were dangerously extended – Pulleine agreed to send two companies of his own battalion (1st/24th) under Captains Mostyn and Younghusband in support of Raw and Cavaye. Once more, and very hastily, the camp was stood-to, with those troops not on outpost duty ordered to form line some 500 yards from the tents, facing north-east and east.

The Zulus adopted their usual tactics of pressing forward with the chest while the right horn swept round in an attempt to encircle the camp from the west and south of Isandhlwana Mount. The two forward British companies, and the native troops under Raw, engaged the charging warriors with well-aimed volleys which held them back temporarily, but the pressure was too great, and in some cases ammunition needed replenishment. They therefore retired, ably supported by Captain Younghusband's company which had taken position somewhat to rear, and came into line with the troops before the camp.

The camp was now defended in a right-angled line. Immediately to the north, and from left to right, were Younghusband's, Mostyn's, and Cavaye's troops while on their right, and forming the pivot, was the 1st Battalion NNC (on to which Raw's troops had just retired). To the south of the NNC, and facing east, were the guns and then came Captains Wardell's and Degacher's companies of the 1st/24th and Lieutenant Pope's of the 2nd/24th. The right was held, until Durnford's troops fell back into line, by the Natal Mounted Police. A little way to the rear of the troops stood the tents and wagons. It was a perilously thin line of some 3,000 yards with which to withstand the black cloud of Zulus preparing to envelop it.

While Pulleine's troops were bracing themselves to meet the first wave of the Umcijo and Nokenke regiments in their centre, and the Undi and Nodwengu regiments on their left, Durnford's men were fighting for their lives in the donga against the Ngobamakhosi regiment. The nature of the ground gave his men and horses a fair measure of protection, and soon dead Zulus littered the earth in front of the donga, but his ammunition was running out (repeated requests for more had not been answered), and the enemy's left horn threatened to cut his force off. Realizing the danger, he withdrew his troops to the high ground between the mount and Stony Hill. By this time some of his native levies had had enough and began to melt away, but the Basutos stood firm and fought most courageously, dying to a man on the right of the line.

Durnford's men had reached Stony Hill at almost the same time as the Zulu avalanche began to pierce the defensive line. Rank upon rank* these magnificent warriors, the pride of their race and all utterly contemptuous of death, advanced steadily and silently into the fray, accepting terrible punishment from the well-trained British soldiers firing in two ranks. When the Zulu mass was some 200 yards from the British line the leading files faltered momentarily, for so great was the havoc wrought. But just then two vital incidents occurred. Ammunition began to run short, and there was no organized supply from the wagons only a few hundred yards in rear. At this slackening off of the fire the Zulus took fresh heart, and now uttering their terrible war-cry they advanced to within assegai distance. This was too much for the Natal Native Contingent, who had had no battle experience and were themselves Zulus of a sort. They broke and ran, thus creating the second of those two crucial misfortunes.

The line had become unhinged at a critical point. The defenders continued to fire while ammunition lasted, the two guns getting off a few fairly harmless rounds, and then the long assegais gave place to the short and the bullet to the bayonet. Through the two gaps (the one at the hinge and another between Pope's and Durnford's men) the black men poured, and black and white quickly became entangled in bloody mortal combat. There were many acts of great gallantry, but only a handful of the British lived to tell the tale. The highest encomiums came later from the Zulus themselves, who bore honourable witness to the tremendous punishment they had received, and to the skill and daring of those who had administered it. By 1.30 p.m., just an hour and a half since the impi had descended the hill, the two horns had virtually joined, and the camp was in Zulu hands.

When further resistance was hopeless there were some who managed to break away and make for the nearest point on the Buffalo River. But the ground was rough and the Zulus were swift. Here again there were great acts of heroism both on the way to the river and in the actual crossing. Lieutenant Teignmouth Melville (Adjutant of 1st/24th) made a determined effort to save the Queen's Colour. He galloped to the river

*The number of Zulus in this impi is said in some accounts to have been 20,000, but the official War Office account (p. 36) gives it as about 14,000 of whom 10,000 attacked the camp, while 4,000 later peeled off to attack Rorke's Drift. The defenders, therefore, were outnumbered by almost ten to one.

with it and plunged in. His horse sank and he was swept away, but helped by Lieutenant Higginson, and still clutching the colour, he was anchored by some rocks, and was by now totally exhausted. Lieutenant Coghill had gained the safety of the Natal bank, but seeing Melville's plight he at once jumped his horse into the swirling water, and although almost collapsing himself from a previous injury, he managed to get Melville ashore. However, the colour had by then slipped from his grasp and the two men, now scarcely able to move, were killed by the Zulus. Twenty-eight years later their gallantry was rewarded with post-humous Victoria Crosses.* The colours of the 2nd Battalion 24th Regiment were in the guard tent at the time of the attack and were lost. Among those who had a miraculous and hairsbreadth escape was Lieutenant (later General Sir Horace) Smith-Dorrien, but he was among the few lucky ones. In all 1,329 men perished in the battle or attempting to escape. Certainly 2,000, and probably more, Zulus died on that bloodsoaked plain, and countless numbers crept back to their kraals greatly stricken.

That night Lord Chelmsford and the troops that had gone forward bivouacked on the battlefield. All around them the bodies of the fallen lay in mangled heaps. It must have been a grim and grisly night, full of apprehension, for these men who had so narrowly escaped the fate of their comrades. Before first light Chelmsford had them on their way to Rorke's Drift, for no one knew where the Zulus had gone and when they would next attack. The plain was a shambles, and the sickly smell of death pervaded the air, but at least by marching when they did the troops were spared the full horror of a tragic spectacle.

In fact they were heading in the right direction, but before they could reach Rorke's Drift one of the many glorious episodes in the history of the British army had already been enacted. A tiny force of 104 officers and men (there were 35 others in the hospital) withstood the furious attack of 4,000 Zulus of the Undi Corps, and after a long night in which great acts of heroism inside the hospital and mission house had been performed, fought the Zulus to a standstill and drove them back.

The Undi Corps were the right-hand regiment of the Zulu right horn at Isandhlwana, and the direction of their attack took them to the west of the mount, where they might have expected to cut off the fugitives. But most of these had taken a shorter – although rougher – road to the river, and so the Undi Corps' commander, Dabulamanzi, decided to break off and attack the Oscarberg mission station at Rorke's Drift.†

---

*Captain Harford (and two other men), rescued the Queen's Colour a day or two later from among debris that had drifted from the river. It was carried with pride by the Regiment (which later became The South Wales Borderers), until after the First World War, when it was laid up.

†This was contrary to Cetshwayo's orders, and Dabulamanzi would probably have paid for such disobedience with his life had he not been the king's brother.

Lieutenant Chard, who found himself in command when his senior officer left for Helpmakaar, had little time to improvise the defence of the buildings, for the Zulus came into sight at 4.30 p.m. The battle raged for twelve hours, and on more than one occasion the Zulus penetrated the defences and were thrown back. When Chelmsford's troops arrived at 7 a.m., some 350 Zulus lay dead in front of the compound, while 15 men of the garrison had been killed and 12 others (2 of whom died later) were wounded. Lieutenant Chard and his handful of assorted soldiers and civilians may have aborted a serious raid on Natal. For their valour in this epic defence no fewer than eleven Victoria Crosses were awarded.

After the débâcle at Isandhlwana the British invasion of Zululand was temporarily halted. Native morale had been badly shaken, and four battalions had disbanded themselves; reinforcements were urgently needed, a fact that the British government at last recognized. No. 3 column was withdrawn to Helpmakaar, where it remained in a defensive role. Colonel Pearson's No. 1 column had fought a battle against à large Zulu force at Inyezane on the same day as the Isandhlwana fight. In this his troops had come off best, inflicting considerable casualties on the Zulus. The next day he reached Eshowe (which was his first objective), and here his column was invested by a large force of Zulus until being relieved by Lord Chelmsford on 3 April.

Colonel Wood's left column (No. 4) was to suffer two serious reverses and gain a significant victory during March. On the 12th a company of the 80th Regiment escorting a number of supply wagons was caught quite unprepared on both banks of the Intombi river by a regiment of Zulus, and only saved from annihilation by the fortuitous arrival of the Luneberg garrison (No. 5 column). As it was, sixty-two British soldiers and seventeen wagoners were killed. And then on the 28th, when Wood had been ordered to create a diversion while Chelmsford was relieving Eshowe, his column stirred up a hornets' nest of some 20,000 Zulus, which included regiments that had triumphed at Isandhlwana.

He had split his force into two parties to make a steep and difficult ascent of Inhlobana Mountain. One party under Colonel Redvers Buller (who was subsequently awarded the Victoria Cross) was almost cut off on the summit, and twelve officers and eighty soldiers were killed. But for Buller's superb leadership in getting the men off the mountain the whole 400 might have been lost. The impi subsequently attacked Wood's camp at Kambula, but a Zulu deserter had brought information in time for Wood to strengthen the defence with a close-knit wagon-laager. Even so the attack was pressed home remorselessly and the fight was the hardest of the campaign, and Wood's victory the most complete.

In April massive reinforcements arrived, and with them the French Prince Imperial, so sadly to be killed on patrol on the first day of June. Lord Chelmsford, whose conduct of the campaign had been, at best, undistinguished had nevertheless borne his misfortunes with dignity, and after Isandhlwana had offered to resign. The offer had not been accepted at the time, but now General Sir Garnet Wolseley was on his way to take over. However, before he could arrive Chelmsford was able to complete the business, and in the final victory make some amends for what had gone before.

He now had under command a force of 17,528 men which included over 9,000 British infantry and 1,190 British cavalry. The advance into Zululand, which began in June, was cautious and comprised two main columns. The 1st Division, commanded by Major-General H. H. Crealock, marched up the coast unopposed to Port Durnford, while Major-General Newdigate's 2nd Division struck east from Dundee to Cetshwayo's kraal at Ulundi.

In the early hours of 4 July the last battle began. Newdigate's men advanced in a hollow square containing 4,000 British and 1,000 native infantry and 12 guns, and the square was protected by cavalry. The most suitable ground on which to offer battle had been chosen in advance by Buller, and on it the square halted and awaited the assault. Some 20,000 Zulus attacked with their customary courage, but the weight of fire power was too great for them. It was all over in less than an hour. The impi was shattered and scattered with heavy losses. The British force suffered just twelve men killed and eighty-eight wounded.

The war was over: it had cost the British almost a thousand lives and five million pounds. It settled nothing and was to lead to much trouble both in Zululand itself and, until 1901, with the Boers. After the final battle Cetshwayo's kraal was found deserted; he was captured six weeks later, reinstated in a divided kingdom and thrown out in a civil war. In 1894 he died. His splendid warriors, who had fought so bravely with so little, ceased to be part of a military machine, but for a while many were to keep their spears blooded in fierce internecine strife.

Shortly after the disaster at Isandhlwana Lord Chelmsford ordered a Court of Inquiry. Much of the evidence had been lost on the battlefield where key personnel, orders, and notebooks had perished in the fighting or in the subsequent looting. One notebook was found considerably later, which had a bearing on Chelmsford's order for Durnford to take command of the camp, but this scarcely affected the outcome. The evidence given by Chelmsford himself, some of his staff, and a few survivors, supplemented later by accounts from C. L. Norris Newman (war correspondent of the *Standard*), and Zulus who took part in the battle provide our only window on this vanished scene.

From these sources it is very clear that there were two serious acts of omission – lack of protection for the camp and ammunition failure –

which made it virtually certain the force would be wiped out, and it is entirely possible that had these been properly seen to the impi's attack would have been held and broken up.

The first of these important factors was the failure to provide proper protection for the camp. No European army has had so much experience as the British in operating in hostile native country, and it has always been axiomatic that every camp, no matter its size nor its duration, must be properly protected against surprise attack. Lord Chelmsford had laid down very comprehensive instructions for the protection of a camp site before the operation began, but for some reason he made no attempt to see them enforced at Isandhlwana. Furthermore, he had been specifically warned by Paul Kruger, and another experienced Boer fighter, of the need always to laager the wagons, to attempt some sort of entrenchment, and to send scouting patrols well ahead, for the Zulus were very swift of foot and experts at concealment. The first two of these three prerequisites were ignored, and the third only partly executed.

A properly constructed laager was a very formidable means of defence. The wagons would be drawn up in a square or circle, their wheels chained together and the gaps filled with brushwood or with what materials were available. The oxen and horses were then carefully tethered within the laager. Such an elaborate laager could not have been constructed at Isandhlwana, for by day the wagons had to journey to Rorke's Drift for supplies, and on the first night very few had arrived. But on the second night there were plenty in camp, and on the morning of the battle orders to despatch them were cancelled. But they were never put towards even a partial defence, and were mostly drawn up inspanned and haphazardly behind the troops. In mitigation of this negligence it must be said that to form an efficient laager is a time-consuming and burdensome task, and Chelmsford was well aware that with his slow oxen, logistics allowed him less than three months to reach Ulundi. But there were other means of defence that were neglected, or imperfectly carried out.

Any form of entrenchment was difficult, and could only be shallow, nor were there sufficient materials available for a complete defence – even had there been time to build one. However, that part of the line along the col, where the rear was not protected by the mount, could have been strengthened. Pickets were certainly posted, and vedettes sent out, but not far enough; at night all but one outpost was withdrawn to within a short distance of the camp. It was the usual custom to strike the tents at the first alarm, for standing they could greatly impede the defence. This was not done by Pulleine when the first report of a large enemy force in the Ngutu Hills was received, and this, incidentally, had a bearing on Chelmsford's decision not to return to camp.

When Durnford arrived at 10 a.m. he not only rode off with most of his force, but despite reports that Zulus were massing in strength he gave orders for one company of the 1st/24th, two native companies, and a troop of Basuto horse to move out on reconnaissance and picket duties, thus further dissipating the garrison's strength. On the other hand he gave no specific orders for the defence of the camp, but he did at least send a native sentinel to the top of Isandhlwana Mount, which had hitherto been neglected and was clearly the best observation post.

At the Court of Inquiry, and later, various excuses were made. The troops were too tired on the first day to carry out protection work; the camp was only intended as a short staging post and, most damning of all, no impi was thought to be in the neighbourhood. None of these is a plausible excuse for what was a dereliction of duty. Chelmsford, Pulleine, and Durnford were in varying degrees to blame. Durnford in particular one would have thought was well aware of the Zulu's propensity for speed and surprise, necessitating extreme vigilance and an all-round compact defence.

The failure to bring up the reserve ammunition is clearly connected with the failure to form a compact defence. After the campaign Zulu chiefs were to tell of the tremendous impact the steady and telling volleys of the British soldiers had on their resolve. There was a time when the whole line wavered, and some of the leaders were beginning to think the cost too high. But when the firing slackened, through shortage of ammunition, they took fresh heart. The fact that Pulleine's troops fought the battle several hundred yards ahead of the wagons would not have affected the supply of ammunition, had this been properly organized, for there were plenty of runners to bring up the boxes – although obviously a line extending some 3,000 yards would have made it more difficult – but even with plentiful ammunition the result was likely to have been the same. The Zulu chest might have been held under the sustained deadly fire, but the encircling horns would have swamped the defenders.

However, had Pulleine, as soon as danger threatened, struck the tents and formed a much shorter line with its rear largely protected by the mount, and amply supplied with ammunition from wagons close at hand, the Zulu attack would almost certainly have failed. This is what Chelmsford said afterwards he expected Pulleine to do, and it is perhaps what Pulleine would have done had he received clear orders and not been beset by difficulties, some of which were not of his own making.

But however compact the defence it could never have held without an efficient resupply of ammunition. For the failure of this Pulleine, who was left in charge of the camp, must take the full blame. There were plenty of boxes available with the wagons, but they were all secured with copper bands and six screws. It appears that only the two quartermasters had screwdrivers; a further supply had been indented for but the order had gone astray in Natal. Men sent back from the fighting line were soon pounding and tearing at the copper bands, but to no avail.

At the height of the battle there was a splendid example of quartermaster loyalty. When Smith-Dorrien eventually prised a box open, and attempted to rush the ammunition to hard-pressed troops of the 1st/24th the quartermaster of the 2nd/24th remonstrated strongly against his breaking open a box belonging to his battalion – a highly irregular procedure without a requisition order! In the end the Zulus got all the ammunition – without having to sign for it! – and a good many rifles with which to use it.

Of all the mistakes, miscalculations, and misunderstandings of the senior officers who marched to war with No. 3 column, the failure to provide the fighting troops with ammunition was the most unnecessary and the most unforgivable.

Isandhlwana was not truly a battle, it was a massacre, and it came about through human error. In those days of high Empire there were officers in the British army who firmly believed that no native force, however large, could ever defeat their well trained and disciplined troops. And even the Indian Mutiny had failed to lift this illusory veil from their eyes. The whole performance at Isandhlwana was casual in that orders were correctly given, but no trouble taken to ensure they were properly enforced. The disaster occurred not through any action outside the control of the commanders, but through disobedience, carelessness and above all complacency. It is an example of where the leadership was at fault.

21 The Battle of Tannenberg
26–30 August 1914

ON 28 August 1914, when General Erich Ludendorff was issuing orders for the pursuit of the beaten Russian Second Army, he began his dictation with the name of the small East Prussian town, Frogenau, where his headquarters was at that time. But his senior general staff officer, Colonel Max Hoffmann, apostrophized with the suggestion that the nearby town of Tannenberg might be a more appropriate heading. Ludendorff, who was later to claim the credit for this happy thought, agreed, and so what proved to be 'the greatest defeat suffered by any of the contestants during the war'* is known to history as the battle of Tannenberg. Here in 1410 the Teutonic Knights (among whose number could be counted a Hindenburg) were almost totally destroyed by a savage horde of Lithuanians and Slavs: 500 years later, in a brilliant victory which had devastating consequences, honour was restored.

For many years before the outbreak of the 1914 war, plans had been made, revised and scrapped by the major European powers to cover all likely contingencies. Of these the most perspicacious were made by General Count von Schlieffen, when he was Chief of the German General Staff. Fortunately for the Allies his plans were ruinously modified by his successor, Colonel-General Helmuth von Moltke, who had little more than a great name to commend him. Schlieffen had planned for a war on two fronts with the initial main offensive in the west and a holding operation in the east, and not until the sweep through Belgium and northern France had achieved an overall victory was it intended to launch a major offensive against the Russians.

The Franco–Russian alliance dated from 1892 and between then and 1913, when the final conference took place, the general staffs of both countries had drawn up, changed and revised a series of plans. The French were at pains to impress upon the Russians, whose attention was firmly fixed upon the Austro–Hungarian border, that the principal enemy would be Germany; defeat her and the Austrians would be no trouble. Moreover, it was important that the Germans should first be

*Ironside, p. 195.

defeated in the west, and therefore the Russians should pose sufficient threat to draw German troops to their eastern border. This in fact the Russians achieved, but with disastrous consequences to themselves.

The build-up after mobilization was an initial problem for the Russians, who found it physically impossible – due to bad communications, terrain, and the current reorganization of their army – to achieve concentration until the fifteenth day after mobilization, and that had been speeded up by twelve days from the original target. The French would be able to advance on the eleventh day, and the Germans earlier. There was, therefore, a dangerous gap for the French in the west. The Russians, in order to assist their allies – a fact that at the time and later they made very clear – agreed, in a plan formed after mobilization, to act offensively against the German forces in East Prussia with two armies, and to form a new army which in due course (it would not be ready before the end of August) was to move up on the left of the second Army to advance towards Berlin.

These two armies were to form the North-Western Group under the command of General Jilinski, whose headquarters was at Byelostok. The First Army was commanded by General Rennenkampf and was to advance north of the Masurian Lakes and turn the enemy's left flank; the Second Army was commanded by General Samsonov and would advance south of the lakes to cut off and destroy the German troops between the lakes and the Vistula.

At the outset of the campaign the Russian First Army comprised three corps (III, IV, and XX), supported by five cavalry divisions and the 5th Rifle Brigade. The Second Army had six corps (I, II – later transferred to First Army – VI, XIII, XV, and XXIII) supported by three cavalry divisions and the 1st Rifle Brigade. Their respective strengths of 200,000 and 250,000 men were numerically vastly superior to the German VIIIth Army that opposed them, but one of the decisive factors in this campaign – which will be discussed later – was the total unpreparedness of the Russians.

The German army, which was superior to the Russians in every way save numbers, was commanded by General von Prittwitz, and comprised four corps (I, XVII, XX, and 1 Reserve Corps), various garrison troops and the 1st Cavalry Division. General Ironside calculated their ratio inferiority to the Russians as 1 to 1.7 in infantry and 1 to 2.7 in cavalry.*

This numerical inferiority was amply compensated for by the superior German organization, administration, and leadership. There were four

---

*Hindenburg says (*Out of My Life*, p. 87) that 'During the months of August and September Russia brought up no fewer than 800,000 men and 1,700 guns against East Prussia, for the defence of which we had only 210,000 German soldiers and 600 guns at our disposal.'

outstanding senior officers in the German VIIIth Army who, under the stolid figure of their second commanding general, Hindenburg, were the architects of victory. Ludendorff, a stiff, proud man with an excellent brain and a totally tireless industry, was chief-of-staff; General von Grünert was the very competent quartermaster-general; François, a gifted and adventurous general, was the corps commander who achieved the most decisive tactical result, and Colonel Max Hoffmann, the general staff officer, who successfully combined an extremely active and penetrating mind with an indolent pleasure-loving nature, was perhaps the most brilliant of them all.

The Russian commanders fell sadly below the high standard of the German generals. Jilinski had commanded a cavalry division, but most of his service had been on the staff and he did not possess the confidence of his subordinates. Both Rennenkampf and Samsonov had commanded with distinction in the Japanese war and gained a high reputation. In the course of that war they had come to blows (literally, on a railway station) which is sometimes said to have been the cause of Rennenkampf's lack of co-operation with his fellow army commander during the battle. Both are said to have deteriorated in the peace years between the wars. Samsonov had been Governor of Turkestan since 1909; he was therefore out of touch militarily, and also not fully fit. Rennenkampf's fractious behaviour towards his staff made him an uneasy commander, and his dilatoriness was one of the principal causes of the Russian disaster.

The country over which the campaign was to be fought can be divided into four regions. In the north the fortified Königsberg zone would pose a difficult and costly operation for any attacking force. South of the fortifications, which stretched from Brandenburg in the west to Tapiau, and thence north to Laiau, there was the Insterburg Gap of forty-three miles through which ran the Insterburg–Allenstein railway across mostly open flat country, although the Romintern Forest was an obstacle. From Angerburg to the frontier at Johannisburg there stretched the line of the Masurian Lakes, with the narrow gaps well strengthened by the Germans. This impregnable barrier conveniently split any force attempting a simultaneous north and south attack. Finally, the Russians had added to their difficulties by having deliberately laid waste, against a German invasion, the country immediately south of the border. The land was mainly untended forest, marsh and swamp, with a few sandy tracks that passed for roads.

The First Army was ordered by Jilinski to cross the frontier on 17 August, and its objective was to be the line Insterburg–Angersburg. Rennenkampf was to employ a large proportion of his cavalry to cut off the German left flank from Königsberg. The Higher Command's overall plan was for the First Army to push forward in advance of the Second in

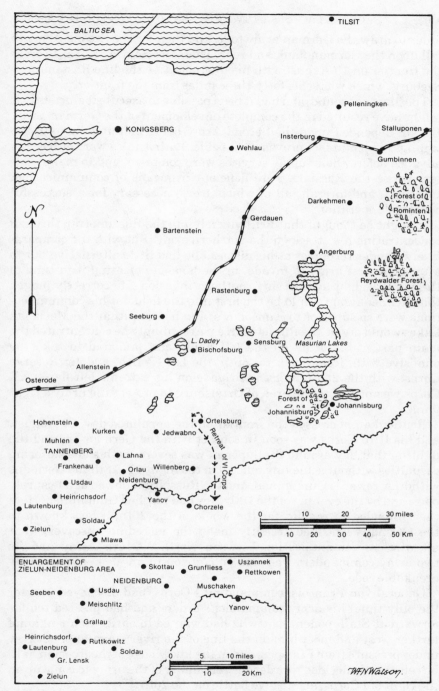

The Battle of Tannenberg: 26–30 August 1914

order to draw the German army to it, and then for the Second Army to fall upon the German flank and rear. Therefore Samsonov was to cross the frontier on 19 August with his first objective the line Rastenburg–Seeburg, which was some forty-three miles from the frontier.

The plan was sound, and had it been possible to execute it efficiently it might have resulted in the complete envelopment of the German army. But all depended upon the Second Army being able to adhere to the timings, which in fact proved impossible. Both armies were ordered to advance before their supply services were complete, and to make matters worse the Russians were deficient in means of communication, transport, and aircraft, all of which are so necessary for a successful concentric operation.

It might be thought that Prittwitz fell into the Russian trap through concentrating his attack on the northern army. But with the comparatively slender resources at his disposal he had little alternative but to attack the first army to invade, in the hope of defeating it in time to throw his weight against any southern invasion. He correctly judged that Rennenkampf would be the first into the field, for his communications were so superior to Samsonov's, and he knew that the Masurian Lakes would divide the Russian forces. Accordingly he concentrated the main part of his army on the left flank, and prepared to take the offensive with, from north to south, the Ist, XVIIth, and 1st Reserve Corps, with the 2nd *Landwehr* Brigade on his extreme left flank; XX Corps was moved to the area of Ortelsburg to protect the army's right flank.

Rennenkampf crossed the frontier on the appointed day, 17 August, and his IIIrd Corps was soon in contact with the German Ist, and the fighting that day around Stallupönen was severe, both sides suffering casualties without achieving much. On the night 17–18th the Germans withdrew towards Gumbinnen, and the Russians followed at a leisurely pace, and by the evening of the 19th they had reached Gumbinnen. Here they intended to remain for the whole of the 20th, a fact known to the Germans who had recently made the incredible discovery that all wireless communication between North-Western Army and its two army commanders was sent *en clair* on in an elementary, easily breakable code.

General von François, commanding I Corps, had disobeyed (not for the only time) his army commander's orders and had pressed too far forward at Stallupönen. Prittwitz had wanted to entice Rennenkampf farther west and meet him on the line of the river Angerapp, but now under pressure from François, and in the knowledge of the Russian halt, he reluctantly decided to order the remainder of the army to come up on the right of I Corps, and to give battle on the 20th.

The Russians were to claim Gumbinnen as a victory, but in this they exaggerated, for although the Germans withdrew at the end of the day it was a case of *reculer pour mieux sauter*. It might have been a victory had Rennenkampf's Cavalry Corps taken any part in the fighting, instead of remaining supine on the Russian right flank. The Russian cavalry in both armies was mainly Cossacks, and was of very little use through being badly handled. On their left and right the Germans had met with almost complete success, but in the centre Mackensen's XVII Corps had launched an attack which had been heavily defeated, and by the afternoon the corps had been rolled back some distance. However, provided these troops could rally – and there seemed no reason why they could not – the Germans had every chance of defeating Rennenkampf on the following day.

But some time during the evening of the 20th Prittwitz (and his chief-of-staff, General von Waldersee) panicked. He appears to have been more impressed with the defeat of XVII Corps than with the successes gained by the other two, and information had reached him that Samsonov, who had extended his line of march farther west, would be crossing the frontier the next day and would pose a serious threat to the German right flank. He therefore ordered the army to break off the engagement and to retire behind the Vistula. He overruled the objections of Grünert and Hoffmann, and telephoned his decision to Moltke. The latter (whose original orders, incidentally, had included the possibility of a withdrawal behind the Vistula) was so appalled by Prittwitz's telephone conversation that he took steps – without informing Prittwitz – to replace both him and his chief-of-staff.

Meanwhile, under the steadying influence of their subordinates who pointed the way to victory, Pritwitz and Waldersee regained their nerves, and although insistent that the battle in front of Rennenkampf should be discontinued agreed to a plan put forward by Hoffmann for an attack against the Russian Second Army. Unfortunately for Prittwitz – although it is doubtful if it would have made much difference, for Moltke never wanted him in command – he failed to inform Supreme Headquarters that he had cancelled the withdrawal to the Vistula.

Hoffmann's plan for the defeat of Samsonov was fraught with risk, and depended very largely on Rennenkampf's inertia. He felt that the latter, having been severely mauled, was unlikely to resume the offensive immediately, and that Samsonov posed the most pressing threat. Therefore the bulk of the army was to be switched to the south and west: XX Corps was to move to the Hohenstein area, I Corps was to be switched to the right flank south of XX Corps, and 3 Reserve Division, Unger's garrison troops, and 70 *Landwehr* Brigade were also to move to the area south of XX Corps. Thus there was a concentration of almost three corps for the coming battle. Both XVII and 1 Reserve Corps were to march west, and their employment was to be dependent on what action Rennenkampf took.

In the event Rennenkampf took virtually no action. He even allowed the Germans to disengage from his front and carry out a complicated entrainment, in some cases within twenty-five miles of the front line, without his knowledge let alone interference. He appears to have been convinced that a defeated German army was in retreat, and his cavalry made no attempt to disillusion him. It was to be two and a half days before he moved, and then still completely ignorant of where the enemy had gone he marched in a most leisurely fashion. His performance after Gumbinnen was decisive to the outcome of the battle.

To succeed Prittwitz and Waldersee, Moltke selected General von Hindenburg and General Erich Ludendorff as Commander-in-Chief and Chief-of-Staff respectively. Hindenburg was sixty-seven and had been retired for some three years, but he was the right man in the right place. His large proportions and steely composure inspired confidence, and he was the perfect foil to the mental superiority and lightning perception of his chief-of-staff.

Ludendorff received permission to issue orders before he had even met Hindenburg, and he bypassed army headquarters, going straight to corps. Apart from some minor detraining alterations, and the selection of Marienburg rather than Muhlhausen for army headquarters, his orders were almost identical to those framed by Hoffmann. But his decision to let corps commanders handle their corps independently until the arrival of the new chief had, as well as upsetting the army head-quarters staff, resulted in the commanders of XVII and 1 Reserve Corps giving their troops a day's rest. Time was of the greatest importance, and although the future movements of these two corps depended upon Rennenkampf, it was necessary to get them as far from the Russian First Army as possible in order to facilitate any march to the south, and this lost day had to be made good by strenuous forced marches.

Hindenburg and Ludendorff arrived at Marienburg on the afternoon of 23 August. Hindenburg tells us* that a paper had been found in the pocket-book of a dead Russian officer which gave a complete outline of the plan for the Russian concentric attack. He does not indicate when this information was to hand, but presumably about the time of his arrival, and it obviously accounts for the continual uncertainty at headquarters concerning Rennenkampf. It was not until the 25th that an intercepted wireless message made the slowness of Rennenkampf's movements clear, and enabled Ludendorff to leave just the cavalry division (and that less a brigade) on his front.

Samsonov's Second Army eventually shambled across the frontier on

---

*Hindenburg, p. 87.

21 and 22 August, well behind the original schedule. He had advanced before his mobilization was complete under extreme pressure from Jilinski. His men were in a desperately poor condition, short of food and tired from being hustled along over the deep sandy tracks with incomplete transport and a supply system that was in tatters. The army commander appears to have had no information as to the whereabouts of the enemy, or if he had he failed to pass it forward, and his leading troops were without the help of regular cavalry. There was little co-ordination between units of the army, and none between the armies. Samsonov should, of course, have made the position clear to Jilinski, who seldom came forward, and refused to advance until his army was in a far greater state of readiness.

The troops inched forward on a wide front of some sixty miles, for Samsonov had altered his orders from Jilinski – who took no action to countermand the infringement – and extended his line so far to the left that only VI Corps was heading for his allotted line of Seeburg–Rastenburg. He thought the Mlawa–Soldau railway might ease his supply problem, and he had developed exaggerated ideas of the turning movement. As a consequence of this extension to the left he had created large gaps within his own army, and drawn farther away from Rennenkampf's.

By 23 August VI Corps was at Ortelsburg, XIII at Jadwabno, XV nearing Frankenau, 2 Division of XXIII Corps north-east of Soldau and the remainder of XXIII Corps back at Mlawa. The First Army, meanwhile, had advanced cautiously to a line Pelleningken–Darkehmen. Second Army's first serious engagement took place on the evening of 23 August and was continued for the next two days. Leading troops of XV Corps made contact with the German XX Corps along the line Orlau–Michalken. There had been no reconnaissance and the Russians blundered into the enemy across an open field and whole regiments were shorn away under the flail of German machine-guns. The next day the battle was fiercely contested, with the Russians making small impact. On the 25th help was at hand from XIII Corps; and the German *Landwehr* units, who had fought an admirable delaying action, seeing a threat to their left flank, withdrew. General Ironside says XV Corps lost 50 officers and 2,000 men in this battle with only 2 guns and a few prisoners to show for it.* If this is really so their performance at Tannenberg was that much more creditable.

The incompetence of the Russian higher command, engendered largely through complete lack of information, now becomes once more apparent. Samsonov, as a result of the recent battle, considered the Germans to be drawing back their left flank, and in order to facilitate

*Ironside, p. 139.

the pursuit he asked Jilinski for permission to change again his axis of advance to the line Allenstein–Osterode. Jilinski, after some hesitation – for he was not certain (rightly) that Samsonov was fully in the picture – agreed to this on the understanding a corps and a cavalry division should cover the extreme right flank between the lakes and Allenstein. There appeared to be absolutely no reason for this proviso, and it merely meant that Jilinski was ordering Samsonov to put those troops out on a limb some thirty miles from the main body, which would allow them to be defeated in detail. And so by 26 August the Second Army stretched from Sensburg (VI Corps) to Zielun (6 Cavalry Division) with XIII Corps around Kurken, XXIII Skottau, XV Frankenau, and I Usdau. One division of XXIII Corps, two cavalry divisions, and a Rifle Brigade were placed under command I Corps to safeguard the army's left. There was thereafter a spread of some seventy-five miles with inter-unit communication weak to the point of nonexistence.

Meanwhile, the German concentration, which had gone smoothly and according to plan, was almost complete. Ludendorff had taken a calculated risk on the 24th in ordering XVII and 1 Reserve Corps to march south in order to attack the right of the Second Army. Rennenkampf still posed a serious threat, and it was not until the next day that intercepts confirmed that the decision had been a correct one. The German plan to annihilate Samsonov's army was simple in conception, but somewhat complicated in execution, for on account of the many natural obstacles it involved corps fighting independent battles. In brief Ludendorff planned to lure Samsonov to attack a somewhat weakened centre (half of XX Corps), while he struck hard on the right with I Corps and the other half of XX Corps, and on the left or north with XVII and 1 Reserve Corps. As soon as the flanks had been cleared the centre was to be enveloped in a large pincer movement.

There was a minor setback in these carefully laid plans when the contumacious François protested strongly against Ludendorff's orders for a frontal attack on Usdau, for his full artillery complement was not yet to hand, and he anyway preferred an indirect approach. However, Ludendorff overruled him. On the first day of this crucial five-day battle the fighting in the north and centre was extremely fierce. Samsonov, still without knowledge of his enemy's movements or intentions, continued his advance to the Osterode–Allenstein line, happily quite oblivious to the fact that on the evening of the 25th an intercept had given the Germans complete confirmation of all his objectives. At Thurau, 2 Division of XXIII Corps made initial progress driving out the Germans, but on being counterattacked and suffering heavy casualties they broke and fled almost to Neidenburg; XV Corps fought well and by evening it held the line Grieslienen–Mühlen; XIII Corps had little fighting, and spent the day marching and counter-marching without

positive orders because the telegraph lines had been cut and wireless
stations were jammed.

But disaster for Samsonov came in the north, where his VIth Corps
was utterly defeated and virtually out of the battle by the end of the first
day. It will be remembered that this corps was very isolated on the
Russian right and once Ludendorff, encouraged by informative intercepts, had been able to concentrate XVII and 1 Reserve Corps against it,
superiority of numbers – even though the Germans were desperately
tired through long forced marches – made the result inevitable. But
defeat was made more certain through lack of information, and mis-
interpretation by a divisional commander of what information there
was. In consequence the corps commander issued orders and counter-
orders which had the effect of getting two divisions into a terrible tangle
with the German flanking movement round Lake Dadey, and their
ordered retirement to Bischofsburg becoming a rout which, in some
cases, extended for twenty miles to Ortelsburg.

The crisis of the battle came on 27 and 28 August with action around
Usdau between the German and Russian Ist Corps. The battle was
opened in the early hours by the artillery of both corps in which the
Germans outgunned the Russians. Later in the evening, when the
German infantry stormed Usdau they met with little resistance, for

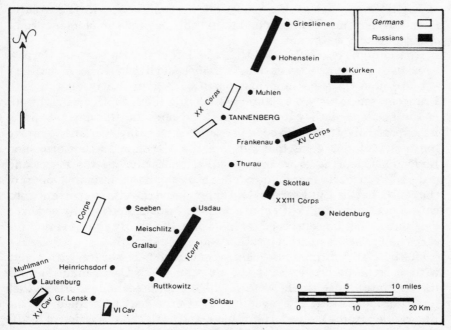

Tannenberg: The German attack on the Russian Left: 26–28 August 1914

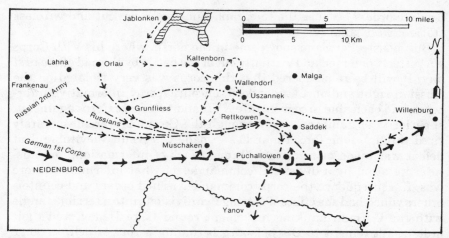

Tannenberg: Von François cuts off Russian lines of Retreat: 29–30 August 1914

those half-starved Russian soldiers who had survived the cannonade were in no mood to wait for German steel. By 11 a.m. I Corps had been torn asunder and the road to Neidenburg was wide open. However, an unexpected counterattack from the south of Soldau by 1 Rifle Brigade of XXIII Corps met with considerable initial success in the area of Heinrichsdort, and François had to halt his advance on Neidenberg in order to restore the situation.

By the night of the 27th all that was left of the Russian Ist Corps – some five regiments from various divisions and five batteries of artillery – had taken up a position just north of Soldau. Early on the 28th François issued his orders aimed at driving them south and right out of the battle, but they did not wait, and now the Russian left flank lay exposed and the centre open to encirclement. However, in the centre matters had not gone too well for the German XXth Corps and Ludendorff, fearing a breakthrough, temporarily lost his nerve and ordered François to march his whole corps north to Lahna in support of the centre battle. But François had appreciated the vital importance of a cut-off operation, and with characteristic insouciance for any order he disapproved of, he continued on his original line. By the next day his corps had closed the Russian escape route to the south.

On the 27th fighting in the centre continued to be severe, with heavy casualties on both sides, and the Russian XVth Corps made serious inroads into the German XXth – which prompted Ludendorff's order to François. But by the evening XV Corps had been held on the line Heidenmuhl–Wahlsdorf–Mühlen, and as the 2nd Division of XXIII Corps, operating on their left, had been thrown back almost to

Neidenburg the left flank of XV Corps had been dangerously exposed.

The next day Ludendorff ordered XVII and 1 Reserve Corps to break off their pursuit of the beaten VIth Corps and swing south-west to attack XIII Corps on the right flank of the Russian centre. General Kluev, the corps commander, having had no orders from Samsonov, was marching from Allenstein to Hohenstein to assist XV Corps. Throughout the day his corps was attacked from the north and north-east, and by nightfall it had not managed to take Hohenstein and could not make contact with XV Corps.

The Russian Second Army was on the point of disintegration. For the most part the soldiers had fought bravely under appalling conditions of near starvation, but by now they had had more than they could take. Communications, always bad, had virtually broken down, and corps commanders were out of touch with each other and without knowledge as to what was happening to their front or their flanks.

Samsonov had gone forward to consult with General Martos, the commander of XV Corps and his only really sound senior commander. Martos urged him to withdraw while there was still time, but Samsonov would not agree, for he felt that if they could hold Neidenburg the position could yet be stabilized. It was a totally unrealistic appreciation, which he soon had to change. On 29 and 30 August three German corps threw a band of steel around the Russian centre, driving them inexorably towards François's waiting corps that blocked their retreat along the Neidenburg–Willenberg road.

Samsonov had at last grasped the appalling entanglement his army was in, and in his last order he directed XIII, XV, and XXIII Corps to fight their way back to Chorzele and Yanov. Martos had been sent to reconnoitre a position round Neidenburg – where after a series of nerve-racking adventures he was eventually captured – and General Kluev had been put in overall command of the three corps. The XVth and XXIIIth, having fought a series of stiff rearguard actions, made an attempt to break through the cordon between Muschaken and Willenberg, but the Germans had all the exits from the forest in their machine-gun sights, and on 31 August near Rettkowen the majority of these totally exhausted, near-starved soldiers surrendered.

The XIIIth Corps had the longest march, and the hardest fighting of all. Weary beyond words, with no rations of any kind for men or horses, they covered at one stage 42 miles in 40 hours over atrocious tracks of heavy sand until, completely exhausted, two of their three columns came to Uszannek. Here they dug in and throughout the night 30–31 August they put up a magnificent fight against hopeless odds. On the 31st they surrendered.

The right-hand column of this corps was more fortunate, for on the 30th remnants of the Ist Russian Corps, which the Germans thought they had destroyed, rose out of the ashes for a final throw against Neidenburg. This town they briefly captured before being driven off by that part of François's corps that he was able to spare from guarding the forest exits. But the confusion caused by this counterattack enabled several thousand Russians from XIII Corps' right column to cross the frontier into safety. They and two well-led, determined bodies from XV and XXIII Corps, who broke out near Willenberg, were almost the only men from the Russian centre to escape.

And so in less than ten days from the time it crossed the East Prussian frontier the Russian Second Army had been virtually annihilated, and its luckless commander, knowing himself to be beaten and discredited, had slipped quietly away into the depths of the forest and shot himself. The full extent of the Russian losses is not known for certain, but was indeed grievous. The Germans claim they took 92,000 prisoners, killed 70,000 men, and captured or destroyed all the artillery and transport for the modest loss to themselves of 15,000 casualties.

Rennenkampf, who had made no effort to assist the stricken Samsonov, still maundered sullenly on the line Wehlau–Gerdauen–Angerburg. His hour was at hand, and in the battle of the Masurian Lakes he was to be driven out of East Prussia with a loss of some 60,000 men and 150 guns.

The consequences of the battle of Tannenberg were considerable. Great reliance had been placed by the Allies on the Russian 'steam roller', and the hasty collapse of their Second Army came a⸲ ⸱ very severe shock, and made it almost certain that the war would now be a long and costly one. But perhaps the most important effect of the Russian invasion of East Prussia was the influence it had on the fighting in the west, where it probably turned the whole course of the war.

At the time of Prittwitz's panic Moltke made the decision to reinforce substantially the Eastern Front, despite the fact that Ludendorff was insistent no reinforcements were necessary. Eventually two corps and a cavalry division were taken from the right of the German armies in France, and arrived in Russia for the Masurian Lakes battle. Both the Russians and the French said that this lost the Germans the battle of the Marne and saved France, and even Moltke admitted that taking these troops from the vital right wing was a serious error. It is difficult to be sure if crippling the Russian war effort saved the Allies in the west, but certainly success in the east encouraged the Germans to press harder for a conclusion on that front, and thereby lessened the pressure on the Allies in the west.

The principal factors that brought about the defeat of the Russian Second Army at Tannenberg were their complete unpreparedness for

war, together with the incompetence of their command; the failure of
Rennenkampf to join the battle; and in the realm of tactics the masterly
manoeuvre of François's corps at and after Usdau.

From the very first day of mobilization (31 July) Russia's timings were
at fault. There was almost no chance of her being able to honour the
commitment to advance fifteen days later. Everything militated against
this. The backward condition of the country generally was reflected in
her poor industrial capacity, which was not geared to expand rapidly; in
every branch of transportation – roads, railways, waterways, vehicles –
and in telegraphic and wireless communications she fell far short of the
requirements demanded of a modern military power.

Her army also was well below the required standard. A disastrous war
fought ten years earlier had brought to light many defects, and these
had been only partly remedied. The private soldiers were peasants
recruited from diverse races, who could fight extremely bravely if well
led, but who were mostly completely uneducated and lacking in initiative. There were insufficient long-serving non-commissioned officers to
train properly the three-year conscripts, and the officer class – despite
recent efforts to improve their lot – left much to be desired. The training
of regimental officers was sketchy, for the best were sent early to the
staff college, and in most cases returned to regimental duty only after
years on the staff, where they had little experience in man management
and none in leadership. Of the 800,000 men the Russians agreed to have
ready on the fifteenth day after mobilization, 300,000 would have to be
reservists who had received very little training.

If the condition of the Russian army generally was bad, that of the
Second Army was deplorable. The transport and supply services were
deficient throughout the army, worse in some corps than in others. In
the XXIIIrd for instance, transport was virtually nonexistent at the
time they crossed the frontier, and the troops had to manhandle
ammunition and stores in requisitioned carts, and/or borrow from
neighbouring units whose position was little better. The army had been
sent forward without field bakeries, and with railway and road communications appalling, unrealistic orders had to be given about living
off the country.

Samsonov's staff had been hurriedly assembled from officers who had
never met before let alone worked together, many of the original
headquarters, including the chief-of-staff, having been taken for North-
Western Army Group. Large numbers of recruits had only recently
arrived, and there had been no time for training, or even proper
administration. The communications department of the army was
almost totally lacking. On the higher level Samsonov had no direct
communication with Rennenkampf, and throughout the campaign
Jilinski failed to keep him properly informed. For what little signal

equipment was available the operators were mostly untrained. Because cipher keys had not been issued to corps, operation orders and information had to be sent in clear and were often intercepted.

Junior officers appealed to their corps commanders, and the latter appealed to the army commander for a six, or at least a four-day delay. But Samsonov would not support their representations, and committed the unpardonable sin of marching his army into battle before his troops were ready, and with his supply services in chaos. It is true that time was the essence of the plan, and that the Second Army was to deliver the decisive blow, but this had little chance of being achieved by an army marching to battle with its rear services lacking.

Jilinski had miscalculated the conditions of the countryside and the state of the Second Army, and Samsonov made no efforts to correct him, nor any attempt to get the schedule modified. The consequence was that the army crossed the frontier late and suffered throughout from being unreasonably hastened by Jilinski, who never himself appears to have visited the front. It must be said that it is doubtful if a delay of a week would have made much difference to the extent of the disaster. The defects went too deep to be eradicated in so short a time, but the soldiers would have had more chance.

If it be accepted that against all odds, other than numbers, the Russians could have defeated the German VIIIth Army then, according to Ludendorff, Rennenkampf held the key.

The First Army started the campaign on a much sounder footing than the Second. Rennenkampf's staff and troops were drawn mostly from the Vilna Military District which had been his peacetime command, and so they had worked and planned together; the supply services, although incomplete, were functioning reasonably well along road and rail communications of a kind that were denied Samsonov. But from the very start Rennenkampf's personal performance was sluggish, and he took nine days to reach the line of his first objective (Insterburg–Angerburg), a distance of only thirty-eight miles from the frontier.

Rennenkampf considered he had won the battle of Gumbinnen, and in so far as he had prevented the Germans from gaining the decisive victory they had expected, and caused them to withdraw, this was true; but they were most certainly not defeated, and at the very time he should have been following up his advantage he made no move for two and a half days. Moreover, he took no steps to ascertain in what direction the enemy had gone, being entirely satisfied that they were in full retreat – and by his reports he convinced Jilinski likewise. It was learnt later from a member of his staff that, believing the advance of the Second Army to have been delayed, he feared to push the enemy too far and upset the cut-off operation. As he was never in touch with the

Second Army this seems somewhat improbable, and anyway it does not excuse him from losing contact with the Germans on his immediate front, and remaining ignorant of the situation for the rest of the campaign.

When, on 26 August, the First Army eventually reached the line of their first objective matters were not made easier for Rennenkampf by Jilinski (who at no time had a realistic grip on the battle) issuing a series of instructions based on a completely false assumption of German movements. He was convinced that those Germans 'defeated' at Gumbinnen who did not shut themselves up in the Königsberg fortress would withdraw to the Vistula. He therefore instructed Rennenkampf to blockade Königsberg with two corps, and with the remainder of his army pursue those troops heading for the Vistula.

As late as 27 August, two days after Ludendorff had taken the colossal gamble of leaving only two cavalry brigades in front of First Army, Jilinski and Samsonov still believed Rennenkampf was in contact with a part of the VIIIth Army retreating from Gumbinnen, and they were blissfully ignorant of the impending danger from the north.

That same evening Jilinski ordered Rennenkampf to co-operate with the Second Army by moving his left flank to Bartenstein and his cavalry to Bischofsburg. He does not appear to have realized the extent of Samsonov's deviation to the west, and still thought him to be advancing northwards, nor was he yet informed of the defeats inflicted upon the army's Ist and VIth Corps. But he had at least by now appreciated that Second Army would need the assistance of the First, although he showed no uneasiness nor signs of urgency – a fact that communicated itself to Rennenkampf, who moved south leisurely and by the evening of the 29th had still no contact with the enemy.

Hoffmann is of the opinion that by this time Rennenkampf was too late to prevent Samsonov's doom, but he still could have interfered with the course of the battle. To meet this possibility the Germans considered moving a few divisions behind the river Alle, but in the event this proved unnecessary. Ludendorff's encircling manoeuvre was not planned well in advance, as is sometimes thought, but was considered to be an acceptable risk when it became clear that Rennenkampf seemed content to remain on the sidelines. The success of the whole operation depended upon that general remaining inactive. Ludendorff was to write, 'When the battle began in real earnest ... Rennenkampf's formidable host hung like a threatening thundercloud to the north-east. He need only have closed with us and we should have been beaten.'* A statement that does not entirely tie up with Hoffmann's thinking, but clearly shows the important part Rennenkampf could have played.

* Ludendorff, pp. 48, 49.

It only remains to consider why Rennenkampf allowed an integral part of the Russian war machine to be trampled out of existence without making any effort to come to its assistance. Colonel Hoffmann, writing a few years later, was firmly convinced that while Rennenkampf could not have expected his inactivity to have resulted in the disaster it did, it was motivated solely through his enmity towards Samsonov, which dated from their bitter quarrel in Manchuria that terminated in fisticuffs on a station platform. Shortly before he died Hoffmann said to Sir John Wheeler-Bennett, 'If the Battle of Waterloo was won on the playing fields of Eton, the Battle of Tannenberg was lost on the railway platform of Mukden.'*

For a senior general (even a Russian one) to carry on a vendetta for ten years, and still at the end of that time be prepared to exact vengeance at the risk of causing a national disaster, seems a little far fetched. Much more likely Rennenkampf was no longer up to his job, was naturally indolent, inclined to be complacent, and probably confused by Jilinski's constant interference with his command. But what is certain is that Hoffmann was instrumental in persuading Ludendorff that he could carry out the encircling manoeuvre in safety based upon his conviction that Rennenkampf would never come to Samsonov's assistance.

'On the morning of the 27th the battle was decided on its western wing by General von François's breakthrough at Usdau, and its exploitation.'† Thus wrote Hoffmann of a crucial action successfully brought about through disobedience. On the Russian left flank General Artamonov's 1st Corps had held the line Usdau–Meischlitz–Ruttkowitz since 24 August. The 6th Cavalry Division was at Gr. Lensk, and the 15th Cavalry Division was watching Lautenburg. Artamonov had detachments forward at Seeban and Grallau. He was totally unaware of any impending German attack, and had weakened his right (which was particularly vulnerable, for there was a gap of nearly seven miles to the nearest troops of XXIII Corps) in order to launch an attack on the only Germans he knew about, who were in Lautenburg.

On the 25th François's Ist Corps detrained within a day's march of Artamonov's main position without one cavalry squadron of the fifty he had available being aware of this fact. François's orders were to attack early on the morning of the 26th and take Usdau, but he was still short of some of his artillery, and did not consider himself ready. Nevertheless, Ludendorff insisted, but François was a general who would not hazard his troops if he felt the orders to do so were wrong, and although he attacked on the 26th it was a deliberately half-hearted affair. Seeben

*Frankland and Dowling, p. 18
† Hoffmann, p. 285.

was taken by midday, and Artamonov's attack on Mühlmann's 5th
Landwehr Brigade at Lautenburg was a typically muddled affair, which
François's men soon repulsed.

After these two successes the German line had advanced to
Heinrichsdorff–Grallau, and François and General von Conta, his
leading divisional commander, decided that in view of the tiredness of
the troops and lack of artillery the attack on Usdau should be postponed
until the following day. Hoffmann is quite certain that François's
refusal to attack on the 26th was the greatest contribution to the
destruction of the Second Russian Army. Had he attacked without his
full artillery complement he might well have been unsuccessful, and
Samsonov would have had time to withdraw his army before the trap
closed.*

François ordered his artillery to commence firing on Usdau at 4 a.m.
on the 27th, and an hour later his 1st and 2nd Divisions were to develop
a converging attack. But, as already recounted, the demoralized Russian infantry, despite the excellent defensive position they held, did not
stay to fight, and the 1st German Corps had a virtual walkover. But it
was after the capture of Usdau, with François once again showing his
independence, that the fate of the Russian centre was sealed.

Here XX Corps had met with stiff opposition and Ludendorff, showing
incipient signs of panic, had ordered I Corps to change their direction
and march north. But François, disregarding the possible peril facing
XX Corps, had his eyes firmly fixed on the Neidenburg–Willenberg
road, and the tracks that led from the forest. He knew that to cut this
conduit along which the Russian escape-line lay was to bring their
battle to a cataclysmic conclusion. He therefore ordered his troops to
march east and complete the iron ring that encompassed the grey ghosts
of what was left of Samsonov's ravaged army.

It is difficult to condone disobedience of orders, but if senior officers
never took risks and feared to hazard their reputations great opportunities would often be missed. François was an excellent fighting
general who was not afraid to take his own line and, what must have
been so infuriating for his superiors, his line was usually the right one.
His double disobedience at Tannenberg did not win Ludendorff the
battle, but it was responsible for the magnitude of his victory.

---

*Hoffmann, p. 331.

Tannenberg was one of those battles decided by the character and personal performance of the senior commanders. Moltke was almost certainly right to replace von Prittwitz. He had lost the initiative, the confidence of his staff and the will to win. In such circumstances it is not long before lack of morale seeps through the ranks. The combination of the elderly Hindenburg and the much younger Ludendorff was a happy inspiration: the former lent prestige, the latter professionalism. Moreover, Ludendorff, his general staff officer, Hoffmann, and the commander of his 1st Corps, von François, were all men prepared to back their judgement and take calculated risks.

In contrast the performance of the Russian generals was lamentable. The army group commander, Jilinski, inspired no confidence and was scarcely seen at the front, and the two army commanders were not prepared to co-operate and were anyway too old and out of date for the job. It is true, they were badly supported in rear by an antiquated organization, but that did not alter the fact that they were hopelessly outgeneralled.

22 The Battle of Warsaw
August 1920

THE Battle of Warsaw was not a great battle in so far as the actual fighting went, but it was probably more important to the civilization of Europe than any other described in these pages. After four years of a terrible war the working classes of many Central European countries, stimulated by the insidious and persistent propaganda that poured from Moscow, were ripe for revolution. Once before, in 1683, the Poles had helped to save Europe and now, in August 1920, had they not stood firm before Warsaw, Germany certainly, and no doubt other countries as well, would have suffered the malice and oppression of the Bolshevik barbaric hordes.

In great measure the salvation of Poland at this time was due to Marshal Joseph Pilsudski. Indeed, his story is, in epitome, the story of Poland's renaissance after more than a hundred years of Romanov, Habsburg, and Hohenzollern domination. Pilsudski was born in Vilna in December 1867, the son of Lithuanian parents whose family had been prominent in Lithuanian and Polish affairs for many generations. He was more a nationalist than a socialist, although in order to fulfil his ardent aspirations for an independent Poland he became prominent in the Polish Socialist Party and, to achieve his aims, a conspirator and revolutionary for which he suffered many years in a Tsarist prison. He may have dabbled in Marxism, but he was never a Bolshevik; rather was he a dedicated patriot.

Pilsudski's great opportunity came on the outbreak of the 1914–18 war, when he immediately led a small guerrilla force across the Russian frontier; thereafter he organized a Polish nationalist army, first covertly through Riflemen's Clubs, and later openly when he was given the rank of Brigadier-General and fought with his legions under Austrian command. But he spent the last eighteen months of the war incarcerated in Magdeburg Castle for refusing to co-operate with the Germans, whom he believed had permanent designs on Poland. On his return to Warsaw in November 1918 it quickly became apparent that he alone commanded the respect of both civilians and soldiers, and the moribund Council of Regency offered him command of the army. In the place of the

Regency, which he soon disbanded, he headed a nationalist government, and announced to the world an independent Poland.

Pilsudski could not have been an easy man to serve with. The mainspring of his life at this time was the liberation of Poland, and to this end he could be ruthless, rude, secretive, perfectly prepared to accept fearful risks, and to stake all on the hazards of war. He was a fighter, a man of great courage, but an unorthodox commander. His aim was to restore the Polish frontier to its 1772 demarcation, which reached

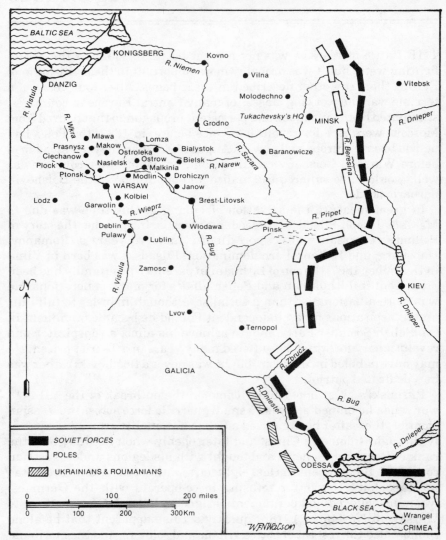

The Battle of Warsaw: April 1919

as far east as Kiev and the river Dnieper, and he knew very well that once their civil war was over the Bolshevik Red Army would have to be defeated if this objective was to be achieved.

Therefore in April 1919 he launched his troops on a large-scale and very successful offensive. Before the end of that month he had taken Vilna, in May 50,000 of his men were fighting their way across Galicia, reaching the river Zbrucz on 17 July, and on 10 August Minsk was occupied. All this was most creditable, with an army only very recently formed from disparate elements. There had been some hard fighting, but on the whole the Bolsheviks had not put up a strong resistance. This gave Pilsudski a misplaced confidence, which his enemy was soon to dispel.

At the end of 1919 and into the opening months of 1920 negotiations for peace went forward with small chance of success, for the Poles had set their sights on the 1772 frontier, and the Bolsheviks had completely different ideas. The diplomatic overtures were abruptly ended in April when Pilsudski opened a fresh offensive in the south-west which took his troops as far as Kiev. But his armies were now hopelessly over-stretched, extending in a line of about 1,000 miles, with lateral communications made virtually impossible by the large expanse of the Pripet marshes. They were far from their base and short of supplies of every kind, including horses. The Russians were ready to counterattack along the whole front, for by now they had defeated Denikin's and Kolchak's armies (leaving only Wrangel in the Crimea as a possible White Russian threat), which had enabled them to concentrate more men on their western and south-western fronts.

The Commander-in-Chief of all the Russian armies was General S. S. Kamenev, and he was about to attack on two fronts divided by the river Pripet. North of the river the Western Front was commanded by General M. N. Tukhachevsky who had under command the Third, Fourth, Fifteenth and Sixteenth Armies, and Gay Khan's Third Cavalry Corps. South of the Pripet the South-Western Front was commanded by General A. Yegorov with the Twelfth and Fourteenth Armies, and a substantial force of cavalry under General S. M. Budienny. The Poles faced Tukhachevsky with their First and Fourth Armies, and another was at Vilna in the process of forming. In the south they had three armies – the Second, Third and Sixth. The total forces engaged were probably in the region of 180,000 Russians and 120,000 Poles. Pilsudski's troops were therefore outnumbered (particularly was this so north of the Pripet), short of cavalry and inferior in arms and munitions.

In May 1920 Tukhachevsky launched an attack in the direction of Molodechno which failed, but in the south – where around Kiev the locals thoroughly disliked the Poles – Budienny with a large force of tough Cossacks, supported by the Twelfth Army, almost trapped the Polish Third Army. They managed to fight their way out, but the whole Polish front in this area was swept behind the river Zbrucz and back towards Lvov. This made it necessary for Pilsudski to withdraw his left, a process in which Tukhachevsky was very willing to assist.

The Russian advance in July was by any standards a very fine performance. Even in those early days they were masters of propaganda, deception, and sedition. Polish morale in and around Warsaw was cunningly undermined, whole hordes of unprivileged and uncultured serfs sunk in savagery* rolled forward in unstoppable masses, turning flanks, fording rivers, taking towns. In 30 days Tukhachevsky's men had marched and fought 300 miles, almost to the gates of Warsaw. Following the triumphant soldiers, and unsuccessfully trying to keep in touch with them, came the commissariat composed of some 33,000 farm carts, mainly manned by the local population.

In the first week of August the Poles faced a desperate situation. From north of Warsaw to Deblin their armies had been driven back to the Vistula, and from Deblin the line ran along the river Wieprz to Zamosc and Lvov. The Warsaw bridgehead was held, from left to right, by the Fifth, First, and Second Armies, in all about 84,000 tired and somewhat dispirited soldiers. The Vistula curves west just north of Warsaw, and the Polish left flank guarding Modlin and Plock, with troops along the river Wkra, was dangerously exposed. The Fourth Army was around Deblin, the Third farther to the south and east, the Sixth below Lvov and the Seventh still farther south in Galicia. In those early August days there were very few prepared to believe with Pilsudski that Warsaw could be saved, and with the dyke broken the bitter waters would flow onward in a deluge.

However, there were certain shafts of light that pierced this sombre scene. Strenuous efforts were now being made by the Poles to collect stragglers and sharpen discipline. Moreover, the very gravity of the threat hanging over the population had done much to close ranks and to strengthen morale. Internal differences and problems were, for the time being, forgotten. The Warsaw bridgehead was well laid out and covered by forty-three batteries, and the strongholds of Plock, Modlin, and Deblin could offer stout resistance to Tukhachevsky, who had his own worries.

His advance had been so rapid that he had hopelessly outrun his supplies. This meant that he had to go forward or starve, he could not wait for reserves which were badly needed. Morale played a big part in this campaign, and while that of the Poles was becoming stronger, in

---

*No doubt there was great brutality shown by both sides but Trotsky, in an Army Order of 17 July, had to admit '. . . maybe there have been isolated cases when more backward Red Army men . . . have torn the hearts out of captured Polish soldiers.'

Tukhachevsky's armies it was beginning to weaken. Not all his troops were dedicated Communists, many were humble peasants impressed to fight Bolshevik battles and kept in line by brutal commissars attached to the armies for that purpose. The Western Front was also weakened at this time through having to send assistance to the South-Western, where Budienny was taking his own unco-operative line, and Wrangel had emerged from the Crimea.

There was another factor which undoubtedly sustained the Poles, although they were not always disposed to think so, and that was the presence in Warsaw of the Anglo–French mission. At the end of June 1920 the Polish government applied to London and Paris for active support in their time of crisis. Mr Lloyd George and Monsieur Millerand at once agreed that an Anglo–French diplomatic and military mission should be sent to Warsaw. The duties of this mission were to advise their respective governments on matters connected with peace negotiations, to assist the Poles with military advice and to make arrangements for the supply of munitions. The British ambassador in Berlin and the French ambassador in Washington were accompanied by Generals Radcliffe and Weygand.

At the beginning of August various attempts to arrange satisfactory peace terms were made. The Poles met the Russians at a place called Baranowicze, and again on 11 and 12 August delegates assembled at Minsk. But the Russians were in a strong position to make impossible demands. Both Lenin and Trotsky were determined upon a universal, proselytizing ideology. Lenin thought this could best be achieved in conditions of peace, but Trotsky (who was War Minister) felt it could be more quickly gained by Bolshevik bayonets. Trotsky's views seem to have prevailed, for the Poles were offered terms they were quite unable to accept.

General Weygand, who was the dominant member of the mission on the military side, had a very frustrating time. Pilsudski was far more interested in supplies than he was in advice. These were not easily obtained, for the workers in Germany, Austria, and Czechoslovakia were refusing to allow trains to be loaded with war material to assist the Poles. Danzig offered a better chance, where the British officer commanding the troops dealt firmly with the work-force and some supplies were unloaded and despatched.

Anyone who has served on a military mission will know how necessary are the virtues of tolerance, patience, and persistence. Usually the members are groping in the dark, for their hosts are reluctant to give them full information – and sometimes they receive misinformation. Often Weygand's advice was not accepted, and when it was no action was taken. Eventually he was granted the post of chief-of-staff which gave him responsibility with power, and although Pilsudski was unimpressed by his suggestion to defend Warsaw on the Vistula and counter-attack from that base, his outward display of confidence, clear judgement and clarity of vision were of considerable moral support to the Polish commanders.

To return now to the battlefront, where the Poles were anxiously awaiting the Bolshevik onslaught that Tukhachevsky felt confident would give him Warsaw. When Weygand had produced his plan Pilsudski had said very little. That evening (5 August) he retired to the quiet of his room in the Belvedere Palace, and after intensive lucubration he emerged in the small hours with a plan of great daring.

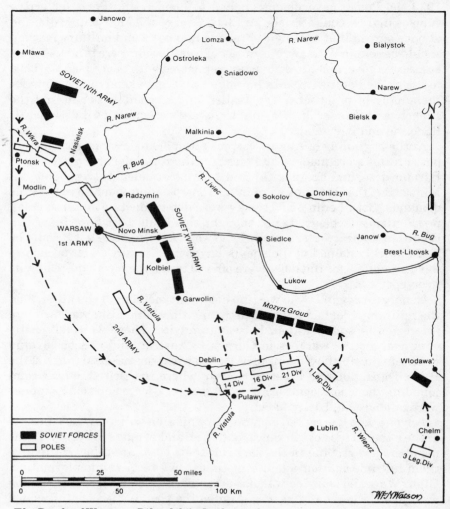

The Battle of Warsaw: Pilsudski's flank attack

He considered that the troops immediately before Warsaw, with their very strong artillery support, could hold Tukhachevsky's attack for three or four days while he led five and a half divisions in a counter-offensive north from the river Weiprz against the flank and rear of the Bolshevik Sixteenth Army. This was to be in the nature of a trigger attack, for he reckoned it should so disorganize and demoralize the Soviet troops that the way would be open for a massive advance of the Fifth, First, and Second Armies from Warsaw.

Pilsudski left Warsaw on 12 August, and motoring down the left bank of the Vistula he set up his headquarters at Pulawy. As the flank attack was to succeed beyond all expectations it must be emphasized that it was entirely his brainchild. It entailed too many risks to commend it to most of his generals, and these were very soon clamouring for him to return, or at least advance the timing of his attack, for on 13 August Tukhachevsky had set his armies in motion towards Warsaw in accordance with orders he had issued on the 8th.

The Russian attack was to be divided. The Third and Sixteenth Armies were to strike at the northern and southern parts of the bridgehead respectively. The Fifteenth Army was to pivot on Nasielsk, and crossing the Wkra was to assault Modlin, while the Fourth Army in the north was to swing west and south to threaten Plock, and with the Fifteenth take the Poles in flank and rear. Radzymin fell on either the late 13th or early 14th, and the Bolsheviks were within fifteen miles of Warsaw. At the same time the Polish Fifth Army was being hard pressed on the Wkra. It was now that the calm and confidence – at least shown if not felt – of Weygand and Radcliffe had a steadying effect on the Polish General Staff, for important personages were fleeing the capital and morale was suffering. Nevertheless, urgent messages were sent to Pilsudski, and he agreed to advance his attack to the 16th.

At this juncture Warsaw owed much to General Sikorski, who fought his Fifth Army with the greatest skill along the line of the Wkra, repulsing many Russian assaults. Even so the situation remained extremely critical, for although the First Army was still standing firm before Warsaw Sikorski's left was turned, and on the 16th the Russian Fourth Army came against his rear in the area of Ptonsk. But on that morning Pilsudski launched his counter-offensive from the line of the Wieprz, and the Polish situation was very soon to take a turn for the better.

The two Russian fronts, which should really have been under a single commander, were tenuously linked by the mysterious Mozyrz Group of indeterminate size, but which was apparently a part of the Russian 57th Infantry Division. These men, and those of the Sixteenth Army farther north, were taken completely by surprise when Pilsudski attacked. This need not have been the case had the General Staff not scorned their luck by disbelieving the Polish operation order which had come into the hands of the Twelfth Army a few days earlier. In consequence Pilsudski's first objective, the Brest–Litovsk–Warsaw road, was reached within the set time of two days.

Indeed, he was seriously worried by the lack of opposition and until the 18th, when contact was firmly established, he expected a trap. On that day his divisions were striking towards Novo Minsk on the left and along the line of the Bug on the right, with the Russian Sixteenth Army in panic and disarray retreating before them. The flank attack had been so successful that on that day Pilsudski, disdaining the danger of Cossack patrols, decided to return to Warsaw in order to take advantage of the favourable situation. Here he found his subordinate commanders still in the depths of despair, and totally mesmerized by the encircling threat of the Russian Fourth Army. Pilsudski had to overrule their reluctance to go over to the offensive in accordance with plans he had conceived.

His orders were for a forward thrust by the First and Second Armies, while the Fifth was to fight its way north towards the Prussian border in the hope of cutting off Tukhachevsky's Fourth Army. The Polish Fourth Army was to make all speed in the direction of Malkinia, on the Bialystok railway, to mop up the retreating Sixteenth Army. With the exception of that of the First, whose units had been too split up to enable it to perform as ordered, these offensive operations were entirely and rapidly successful. The Polish soldiers, who had at first been filled with doubts and hesitations, now put these aside and went forward with a stern and confident purpose.

On the other hand Tukhachevsky, in his distant lair, was becoming much less confident. He had not been informed of Pilsudski's flank attack until the 18th, by which time it was whipping the entrails out of his Sixteenth Army, and yet that army's commander – who himself had been ignorant of the action for almost twenty-four hours – reported that he did not consider it serious. But Tukhachevsky had a clearer picture of the battlefield. The commander of his Fourth Army had failed to encircle Sikorski's troops on the Wkra, and these were now pressing the Fifteenth Army, while on his left the situation was just as serious. Budienny had been repeatedly urged to strike north with his Cossacks, but he had refused to do so until he had taken Lvov, which he never did. Tukhachevsky rightly judged the situation to be critical, and he ordered an immediate withdrawal.

The orders he issued for the disengagement were clear and concise, but they were too late, and in some instances could not be acted upon because the Polish thrust was gaining momentum at a terrifying speed.

The Fourth Army was to concentrate by 20 August on the line Przasnysz–Makow, and while doing this it was – unless it seriously hindered its progress – to give what assistance it could to the Fifteenth

Army which, together with the Third, had been ordered to hold the enemy long enough for the concentration of the Fourth Army's reserves. The Sixteenth Army was to withdraw behind the river Liviec with the Mozyrz Group covering its left, and the Twelfth Army was to attack the Poles who had crossed the Wieprz. Finally – and what would seem to have been a very forlorn hope – the Third and Sixteenth Armies were to detach a division each to force-march to the Drohiczyn–Janow area to act as general reserve.

This was the plan, which in every quarter the Poles frustrated. On Tukhachevsky's right, the Fourth Army commander – an inexperienced general whom Tukhachevsky was later to blame for not defeating Sikorski and thereby taking Warsaw – had temporarily lost touch with command headquarters and with neighbouring units. He was therefore unaware of the orders to withdraw, and believing the general situation to be favourable he continued to attack along the line of the Vistula. When, on the 19th, he eventually regained contact with Minsk he was still optimistic, but received peremptory orders to withdraw at once. The Fifteenth Army, ably assisted by Gay Khan's cavalry corps, had put up a very stiff resistance in the region of Ciechanow in an attempt to keep open the narrow corridor between the river Narew and the Prussian frontier by which the Fourth Army might escape. But by now that army's chances had become slender.

On the 20th the Sixteenth Army had been broken, and were in headlong retreat. This allowed the triumphant Polish Second and Fourth Armies (always well beyond the Soviet Twelfth Army's reach) to hit the Russian Third and Fifteenth in flank, pushing them back behind a line Przasnysz–Makow–Ostrow–Bielsk. Two days later the Poles had advanced to a line Ostrolenka–Lomza–Bialystok, and the whole Russian front was crumbling with their Fifteenth and Third Armies swelling the broad stream of fugitives. Meanwhile the Fourth Army had managed to reach Mlawa, but the valiant efforts of Gay Khan, whose troopers had given the Poles in that area a rough time, could not prevent his own corps nor most of the Fourth Army from being swept across the German frontier.

On 25 August Pilsudski called a halt to the pursuit. His troops had reached a line from Grodno through Brest–Litovsk to Wlodawa on the river Bug. The Russians, with the help of their reserves, were hoping to regroup behind the Niemen. In the last two months, including prisoners and those men disarmed in Prussia, they had lost at least 150,000 men together with some 230 guns, more than 1,000 machine-guns and great quantities of ammunition. The Polish losses had been in the region of 50,000 men.

The Battle of Warsaw was over, but there was more fighting to be done. On 12 September the Poles resumed the offensive while the

Russians were still off balance. By the 18th Sikorski had occupied a line from Pinsk south to Ternopol, while Pilsudski won decisive victories on the Niemen in the area of Grodno, and then on the line of the river Szczara driving the beaten Bolsheviks back to Minsk. Their only offensive move was made by Budienny in the south against Zamosc, and that was repulsed. By 26 September four Bolshevik armies had been virtually destroyed, 50,000 prisoners and 160 guns had been taken. In October an armistice was agreed, which was followed in March 1921 by the Treaty of Riga. From this the Poles obtained a much more extended eastern frontier than the boundary line demanded by the Russians before the Battle of Warsaw.

Could Tukhachevsky have taken Warsaw, and if he had could he have fulfilled his dreams of watering his horses on the Rhine? The answer to the first question is almost certainly 'yes', and to the second 'quite probably'. What then saved Warsaw, and Central Europe as well? In this battle there were two decisive factors. Perhaps the most important was Tukhachevsky's remoteness from the battlefield, from which stemmed most of his trouble. But that is not to belittle the daring genius of Pilsudski's flank attack: that won the battle and was therefore a decisive manoeuvre. But had Tukhachevsky taken Warsaw before Pilsudski struck, which he almost certainly could have done, then the flank attack, if it could have been mounted at all, would have come too late.

Mikhail Tukhachevsky was a most remarkable man. At the time of the Battle of Warsaw he was twenty-seven years of age; he came from a good family, and he fought in the Great War – until he was taken prisoner – as a lieutenant in the Semenovski Guards, who were Household troops. However, a few months after his release from prison in the autumn of 1917 he joined the Communist Party, and largely through the influence of his friends Lenin and Trotsky he received rapid promotion. At various times, and on various fronts, between 1918 and 1920 he commanded with great distinction and élan the First, Fifth, Eighth, and Ninth Armies in the fighting against Admiral Kolchak's and General Denikin's White Russians. He was also successively Commander-in-Chief of the Southern, Caucasus, and Western Fronts.

Tukhachevsky was way ahead of his colleagues in military thinking; highly intelligent with considerable intellectual ability, he was convinced that war must be total, and became through his many learned lectures and writings an acknowledged expert on air, armour, and chemical warfare. His personal courage was never in doubt, and he possessed many of the qualities of leadership, And yet, completely out of character, in the Battle of Warsaw he tried to direct his troops from 300 miles in rear. Fortunately for Europe it was to cost him the victory, for he was a dangerous man with visions of becoming the militant standard-bearer of a pagan horde destined to sweep into limbo all Christian culture and Western civilization. His military reputation survived Warsaw, and he went on to become Chief of the General Staff, but in 1937 Stalin shot him, and had most of his immensely erudite books and treatises burnt.

It seems probable that Tukhachevsky's strategy underwent a major change when he found the Poles retreating precipitately before him. Believing Warsaw to be for the taking at any time, he abandoned a four-army frontal assault in favour of detaching two armies (the Fourth and the Fifteenth) to head west and south to attack strongpoints along the Vistula, and to cross that river. This would have the three-fold purpose of taking the Polish armies in flank and rear, cutting off their retreat across the Danzig corridor, and fulfilling Tukhachevsky's revolutionary ambition of striking west into Germany.

It was a costly miscalculation, which need not have occurred had Tukhachevsky been sufficiently far forward to take personal control of the battle and to see the position and condition of his troops. It lost him Warsaw, and by putting the Fourth Army with its back to the German border it meant that if things went wrong – as indeed they did – that army would have little chance of escape.

In 1923 Tukhachevsky gave a series of lectures to the Military Academy in Moscow in which he admitted that his failure to take Warsaw was due to the disposition of his forces, but he did not feel strong enough for a concerted punch at the centre, or for a simultaneous attack against both the Polish wings. The synchronizing and launching of two widely separated flank attacks would have taken time, and time was what Pilsudski needed – in the event he got just enough through Tukhachevsky's right hook – and it would have entailed an even more dangerous dispersion. But it is difficult to understand why a full-scale attack on the centre could not have succeeded with four armies available.

Concentration of force is an important principle of war, and both Tukhachevsky and Kamenev were guilty of disregarding it. Kamenev should have put the two Russian fronts under one commander who could have co-ordinated their endeavours. There were 200 miles between the two command headquarters, and to make matters worse Tukhachevsky and Yegorov disliked each other – it was a somewhat similar situation to that of Samsonov and Rennenkampf six years earlier. On 10 August Yegorov was ordered to safeguard Tukhachevsky's left flank by sending him Budienny's cavalry, but the latter preferred to take Lvov first and Yegorov did not overrule him. Had Yegorov obeyed the order he would probably have prevented Pilsudski's flank attack. But even without this assistance there was a good chance that Tukhachevsky's strategy might have succeeded had he been forward to control and co-ordinate the enveloping movement with a frontal assault. From his headquarters in Minsk, with communications as bad as they were, he could not successfully direct this intricate manoeuvre.

Tukhachevsky was too good a general not to appreciate the value of morale. Throughout his advance from the Beresina he had placed much importance on encirclement and the effect it would have on the enemy's morale. Indeed this was one reason for his attempt to cross the Vistula in rear of the Poles. And yet through bad administration he allowed his troops to outrun their supplies. There came a time when his armies had to go forward to victory or starve; they had hopelessly outstripped their supplies, and when counterattacked their morale – never very high – sank. This was only partly due to Tukhachevsky being out of touch with the forward troops; the principal fault lay in the inadequate transport arrangements and his failure to appreciate that on this occasion the troops could not live off the land. But again had he been forward the rate of advance might have been controlled to keep pace with the 33,000 rickety wagons on which the armies relied for food and ammunition.

The concatenation of these three blunders – loss of control, loss of support, and loss of supplies – was sufficient to destroy the chances of a Russian victory. Moreover, Tukhachevsky's armies were now dangerously extended, presenting a perfect opportunity for an enterprising counterstroke. Pilsudski was the right man to take such an opportunity.

In the course of a soul-searching night (5–6 August) in the Belvedere Palace, Pilsudski had formulated a plan of considerable daring, but it was not likely to commend itself to his generals, nor for that matter to the Council of National Defence or the Anglo–French mission, for it envisaged moving troops from the northern sector of the line to the south, in order to attack the extended and dislocated flank of the Soviet Sixteenth Army. The general feeling in Warsaw, however, was that the north was the weak sector and should be reinforced from the south for the defence of the Vistula and a counterattack, once morale had been built up, from that river.

Pilsudski's Chief-of-Staff, General Rozwadowski, had presented a plan to his chief on the morning of 6 August. In this he suggested concentrating the Fourth Army at Garwolin (some thirty miles southeast of Warsaw), and then attack north towards Warsaw. This was more in line with Pilsudski's thinking, but it involved even greater risks, and took no account of the morale factor which was an important component of his plan. In the end, armed with the authority of Head of State and possessing an unshaken confidence in his own judgement, Pilsudski persuaded the waverers that it needed desperate measures to be the catalyst of victory. And on 6 August he issued orders for the strategical distribution of the troops taking part.

Pilsudski's plan was a simple one, although the initial concentration would be difficult and dangerous. He aimed to hold the Russians before Warsaw and near Lvov for two or three days while he interposed five and a half divisions behind the river Wieprz facing the comparatively weak Mozyrz Group. Having smashed through this force he would hurl his troops as quickly as they could march – he had little cavalry – against the flank and rear of the Soviet Sixteenth Army causing, he predicted, chaos and confusion. Such an action should not only prevent that army from piercing the Warsaw defences, but create a good opportunity for a forceful counterattack to be launched from the centre. The essence of the plan, therefore, was a double counterstroke with his own priming the heavier one.

The shock troops (as Pilsudski described them) were to be the 14th, 16th, and 21st Divisions of the Fourth Army, and two of the best divisions, the 1st and 3rd Divisions of the Legion, then operating in the south. In both cases the disengagement and subsequent concentration of these troops presented grave problems, for they were all in contact with the enemy. The Fourth Army was fighting along the line of the Bug at this time, and while all three divisions had to carry out a flank march in the face of the enemy the 14th, operating in the Janow area, had over forty miles to march to the concentration area.

The task in the south was an even more difficult one, although the morale and fighting ability of the troops there was somewhat better than those in the north, and they had recently repelled and thrown back a strong attack of Budienny's Cossacks. However, that general was still an active threat, and in removing the two good divisions of the Legion there became a serious disparity in numbers and a gap was left open for Budienny to exploit. The withdrawal of the divisions was in the hands of General Rydz-Smigly, and by means of a vigorous offensive action, and helped by a brigade of cavalry, he extricated the troops with the greatest skill and against every prediction of failure.

The concentration area selected lay behind the Wieprz with the left lying on Deblin. Time was the essence of the operation, and great credit is due to the commanders concerned that the troops were fully assembled by 13 August. So much could, and nearly did, go wrong. When soldiers in close contact with the enemy are withdrawn (especially after a long retreat) for no apparent reason, morale is likely to suffer. But Pilsudski was pleasantly surprised to find on his arrival at Pulawy, which was to be his headquarters, that although equipment and clothing were in an atrocious state morale on the whole was good, and the troops seemed up to the task before them. In the south the withdrawal was only accomplished by some hard fighting, in the course of which an officer, carrying the operation order for the flank attack, was killed and the order fell into Russian hands. Such carelessness could have invalidated the whole plan, but fortunately the Russian General Staff, acting on wrong information received from their Twelfth Army, did not believe the paper to be authentic.

Pilsudski had planned his attack to go in on the 17th. He felt that divisions would need three or four days to sort themselves out, rest, improve or improvise equipment, and absorb the battle plan. But on pressure from Warsaw, where the bridgehead was under considerable strain, he agreed to advance the attack by a day to dawn on the 16th. The first objective was the Warsaw–Brest–Litovsk road, and the order of advance from left to right was the 14th, 16th, 21st, 1st, and 3rd Legionary Divisions. The attack was to be on a very wide front, the 14th Division advancing slightly west of north from Deblin and the 3rd Legionary Division marching almost due north and only slightly west of the Bug.

The Russians were taken completely by surprise, and there was virtually no opposition before the 18th, the day on which Tukhachevsky was first informed of the attack. This was partly due to the Mozyrz Group being quickly crushed without apparently being able to report back. Tukhachevsky was later to attribute Pilsudski's rapid progress to the fact that the heavy fighting in front of Warsaw had necessitated his withdrawing troops from his lines of communication and that Budienny, on whom he relied to operate against the Polish right, was engaged before Lvov. The Russian Twelfth Army had only come under Tukhachevsky's command on 13 August, and although it must have posed a threat to the 3rd Legionary Division it does not appear to have received any information or orders.

On the 17th the 14th Division was into and beyond Garwolin, and the 21st had reached Lukow. Neither of these divisions had met with any opposition and Pilsudski, who lunched with the headquarters staff of the 21st Division on that day, was told that what resistance there was had been firmly dealt with by an enthusiastic peasantry armed with every kind of agricultural implement. That night the 14th Division took Kolbiel, and on the next day it reached Novo Minsk. This same day the 21st Division was at Sokolow and the 1st Legionary was on the Bug near Drohiczyn. Reports from the forward troops all told of only slight Polish casualties, while the left flank of the Russian Sixteenth Army was in chaos and collapse. News also came in that, in accordance with orders, the 15th Division from the Warsaw garrison had attacked east along the Warsaw–Minsk road, and it was now ordered to join the Fourth Army.

On 18 August Pilsudski, who had commanded very much from the front, motoring from one flank to the other directing and animating his troops, left for Warsaw. It is a measure of his personal magnetism that on his departure some of the fire went out of his troops, and on that day the flank attack made little or no progress. Certainly he found no fiery spirit in Warsaw; there the General Staff, without proper knowledge of the battle picture, were looking over their shoulders still fearful of encirclement, while the population were preparing, with what courage they could muster, to face disaster. Pilsudski's orders for an immediate advance by the First, Second, and Fifth Armies went some way to restore confidence and morale, but it was not until news was received on the 22nd that the 15th Division had taken Sniadowo that the inhabitants of Warsaw began to grasp that not only deliverance from, but destruction of, the Russian armies had been accomplished. Even then it was difficult for them to realize the full magnitude of this achievement.

Warsaw had been saved, and with Warsaw all Central and Eastern Europe, from the menace of Bolshevism by the courage of her soldiers and the brilliant stratagem and manoeuvre devised and executed by her Head of State. But some credit must go to the Anglo–French mission as perhaps the crucible from which victory was shaped. The tireless efforts of its members on the diplomatic front, their help with supplies, their unapparent – although undeniable – moral support, and above all the steadying influence, advice, and encouragement, both on and off the field, of the military members cannot be discounted in any assessment of these stern but glorious days.

Tukhachevsky may have been a very unpleasant man, but he was an excellent general. Why therefore did he command his armies from so far in rear during the attack on Warsaw? It is a question not easily answered, for he knew that communications were bad, and that liaison with Yegorov's army group would be nearly impossible from Minsk. He may have been guilty of that battle-losing crime of underestimating the strength of the opposition, and he almost certainly had not paid proper attention to the qualities of Pilsudski, his rival commander. Whatever reason Tukhachevsky had for his distant headquarters it was responsible for his being out of touch with the battle at a critical time. Warsaw, like Tannenberg, was a battle lost and won largely through personalities: the courageous, and quite unexpected, counterstroke by Pilsudski, and the stalwart defence by Sikorski, caught Tukhachevsky off balance at a distance from which he found it impossible to stem the tide of lost initiative and lost morale.

There was one other factor that saved Warsaw. The Polish nation became united in the face of danger. Faction and intrigue were – at least temporarily – laid aside. Treachery, or even dissension, on the home front can seriously undermine the efficiency of the fighting troops and become a probable factor for defeat.

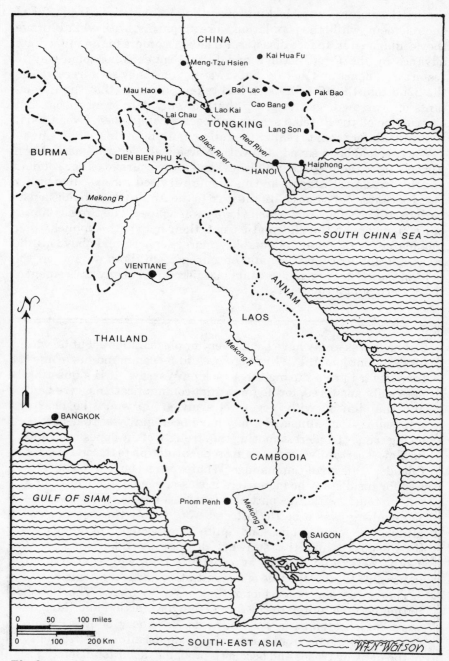

The Siege of Dien Bien Phu: 13 March–8 May 1954

23 The Siege of Dien Bien Phu
13 March – 8 May 1954

WHEN the Japanese surrendered in August 1945 the French, who had retained a presence in Indo-China throughout the war, hoped to revert to the *status quo ante* and resume the role of a colonial power. But this was not to be, for they immediately found themselves beset by internal and external problems that they were unable to overcome, and which were to lead them into a damaging and disastrous revolutionary war.

In 1930 a communist revolutionary, who was later to call himself Ho Chi Minh, formed the Indo-Chinese Communist Party. Banished by the French he established himself in Kwangsi province of China, where in 1941 he formed a political party called the Viet Minh. In Kwangsi he was joined by another revolutionary, a schoolteacher from Hanoi called Vo Nguyen Giap, who was to become his lieutenant and in due course the commander of his army.

The Japanese takeover of Indo-China in March 1945 was a considerable help to the Viet Minh. By the end of August of that year Ho Chi Minh, who had already formed a fairly efficient guerrilla force of some 5,000 men led by Giap, was established in Hanoi at the head of a puppet government, and in control of Tongking and northern Annam. For a short period he enjoyed the precarious protection of the Chinese Nationalists, who barred the way north at the 16th Parallel to General Le Clerc's French force that had landed at Saigon in November. But the Chinese (apart from some captured Japanese rifles) were a broken reed when it came to material assistance, and in May 1946 they left the country.

Ho Chi Minh knew very well that his guerrillas, although increasing in numbers daily, were in no position to take on the French, and so he decided to negotiate. Eventually an agreement, unsatisfactory to both sides and not likely to last long, was reached. Giap, who was busy training and expanding the guerrilla force at its base camp in the area of north-east Tongking known as the Viet Bac, was eager for armed resistance. But Ho Chi Minh, a calm, deep, and patient man, knew very well that peace, even an uneasy peace laced with cease-fires and truces, was important to him, and continued to attend conferences and negotiate.

However, in the autumn of 1946 the French lost patience and made demands which Ho Chi Minh considered quite unacceptable. Now the Viet Minh must obtain independence by force, and at the end of November their war of resistance, which was to last eight years, began. But time spent in negotiation had not been wasted, and the two Viet leaders immediately embarked upon an elaborate plan of guerrilla warfare with a force now expanded to 30,000 men operating in a number of zones each with an autonomous organization, but subordinate to Giap's overall command.

The advent of Communist China in 1949, with its material aid, was a catalyst in the shaping of the Viet Minh, and by 1950 Giap had raised a regular force of four infantry divisions in the Viet Bac. His divisions had four regiments, each of three battalions, and their strength was around 10,000 combatants. The commissariat depended upon a huge force of locally recruited peasant porters.

In the autumn of that year Giap felt himself strong enough to go over to the offensive against the French Expeditionary Force and their recently formed Viet Namese Nationalist army. At first, by skilful use of his superior numbers in a selected area, Giap met with great success. He swept the French clean out of northern Tongking and posed a serious threat to Hanoi and Haiphong. But with the arrival in December of their great soldier, General (later Marshal) de Lattre de Tassigny, French fortunes noticeably improved, and 1951 was a bad year for the Viets.

In January a large-scale attack in the Red River delta, where de Lattre took personal command of the French troops, was a hard-fought, close-run affair in which Giap, with a superiority of at least three to one, lost 6,000 men killed in a three-day battle. Two further and extremely costly defeats that year decided him to revert to guerrilla warfare. But at the end of the year de Lattre returned to France dying of cancer, and was succeeded in Vietnam by the much more cautious General Salan. Through this change in command Giap got the breathing space he needed to regain the initiative. He not only replaced his heavy losses, but expanded his army to six divisions, one of which was the 351st Heavy Division containing a regiment of engineers, two artillery regiments, a heavy weapons regiment, an anti-aircraft regiment, and later a field rocket unit.

The raising of this division, and much else, was indirectly the result of a visit to Peking by Ho Chi Minh in April 1950, where he entered into an agreement with Red China for the supply of a wide range of arms, and military instructors. Field guns, anti-aircraft guns, small arms, and quantities of ammunition poured over the Yunnan border that year and later, save only for a short period during the Korean War, and even that break proved beneficial, for when it ended the Chinese were able to supply the Viets with captured modern American weapons. To what extent the Chinese participated in the actual fighting is not clear; there was a large military mission present to ensure the proper use of the arms supplied, and during the siege of Dien Bien Phu there was almost certainly at least one Chinese anti-aircraft regiment in action. But it would appear that Giap, the self-trained military prodigy so underrated by the French, was in sole command of all the major battles.

General Salan was replaced by General Navarre in May 1953. Navarre was a cavalry officer who had held important staff positions (chiefly on the Intelligence side) and an armoured command. Normally self-confident, he was somewhat diffident in accepting the appointment, for he had no experience of high command and did not know Indo-China; but the politicians swept aside his disclaimers and sent him off with a directive to bring the war to a satisfactory stage from which the government could negotiate.

At the time of his arrival the French forces in Indo-China were given as 189,000, comprising 54,000 French troops, 20,000 Legionnaires of varying nationalities (many Germans), 30,000 North African troops (Moroccans and Algerians), 10,000 Air Force, 5,000 Navy and the Viet Namese Army of 70,000.* However, the greater part of these troops were required for garrison duties in such places as the chain of defensive positions in the Red River delta known as the de Lattre Line, and elsewhere throughout the command. Giap, with six divisions and three independent regiments, had at least 80,000 well-trained first-line troops, and a strong second-line militia of regional troops available for local operations. He also had a large reserve in varying stages of training. The Viet Minh were in control of the greater part of Tongking, held a commanding position in the 'waist' of Annam, and had a few strongpoints farther south.

It was not a very promising situation for Navarre, but he was quick to discern the weaknesses of his command, and prepared a long-term plan based on a more mobile army, reinforcements, and American aid. This he took back to Paris, where it was not particularly well received, and he returned with a promise of only ten more battalions, some American aid with strings attached, and an order to get a move on. This he did with a successful operation in the north, a less successful one in the waist of Annam, and the evacuation of the fortified camp at Na San.

Na San had been Salan's only successful operation. Three parachute battalions had been dropped well into enemy-held country to construct a strongly entrenched camp against which Viet Minh troops could (and did) destroy themselves in a series of costly and pointless attacks. The

*O'Ballance, p. 195.

successful evacuation of the garrison encouraged Navarre to think there was little danger in maintaining isolated bases in enemy territory. This, together with the obligation to protect the friendly kingdom of Laos, decided him to form a similar, but larger, fortified camp at Dien Bien Phu, which straddled the only invasion routes to Laos from the north.

The village of Dien Bien Phu, which lies some 180 miles west of Hanoi, had been in Viet Minh hands since November 1952, and was a likely forward base for any Viet invasion of Laos. It is situated almost in the middle of a rich, fertile valley that measures some twelve miles in length and eight in breadth. The valley forms a basin completely rimmed by a series of jungle-clad hills whose peaks in many places rise to over 3,000 feet. It was not the easiest of places to defend, or to supply by air.

Navarre selected Major-General René Cogny to be commander of the troops in Tongking, and from his base in Hanoi to direct the Dien Bien Phu operation. Cogny was a huge man physically with an excellent brain, he had been brought to Indo-China by de Lattre de Tassigny whom he greatly admired. Ambitious, outspoken, and prickly, he would argue orders if he disapproved of them, and in making the choice Navarre must have realized his worth, for there was no love lost between them. However, both were agreed that Colonel de Castries was the right man to take command of the garrison. Castries was a cavalryman and personally known to Navarre. He had recently commanded armour with success in the delta. Navarre anticipated mobile warfare in Dien Bien Phu, which was intended to be an offensive/defensive base, and felt that a cavalry officer in command would be most suitable.

On 20 November 1953 shortly after 10.30 a.m. the 6th Colonial Paratroop battalion and the 2nd Battalion of the 1st Paratroops were over the two dropping zones. Operation Castor had begun. The valley stretched itself placid in the sunshine, the peasants were at work in the fields and the Viet Minh troops were taken unawares. The battalions dropped some three miles apart. The 1st Paratroops landed unopposed, but the Colonials, who came down just north-west of the village, met with spirited resistance and suffered a few casualties. Early in the afternoon the 1st Battalion Colonial Paratroops, together with two batteries of 75mm guns, a company of mortars, and a surgical unit were dropped, and by 4 p.m. the Viet Minh troops had withdrawn from the valley leaving 96 dead.

On D2 heavy equipment, including a bulldozer, was dropped and engineers commenced repairing the main airstrip and strengthening the 'fortress'. The valley contained a number of tiny hamlets, and a few hillocks rose from the predominantly flat plain. The small river Nam Youm bisected the valley. The French in their previous occupation had constructed two airstrips; the main one with a runway of 16,000 yards was near the village, and there was a smaller one some three miles to the south.

The defence was to be based on a number of bastions, each of which received a lady's name, and each was ringed by a series of (in theory) inter-supporting strongpoints. Somewhat isolated to the north was Gabrielle, manned by the 5th Algerian *tirailleurs*; to its south-east was Beatrice, held by the 3rd battalion of the Foreign Legion's 13th Demi-Brigade; clustered round the principal airstrip was Huguette with the 1/2nd Foreign Legion and a 155mm-gun troop; north and west of Huguette was Anne Marie, manned by Thais, and to its south Claudine with the 1st Battalion Foreign Legion Demi-Brigade; east of the river were Dominique and Éliane, manned respectively by the 3/3rd Algerian *tirailleurs* and 4th Moroccan *tirailleurs*. Three miles to the south, and dangerously isolated, was Isabelle, strongly held by the 3/3rd Foreign

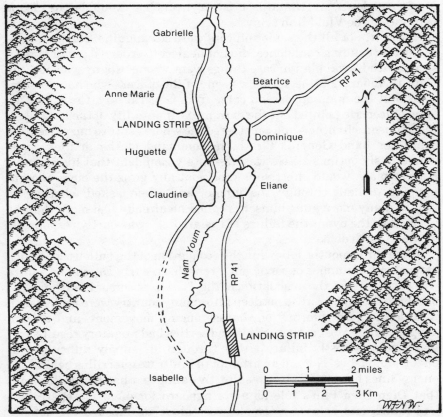

The Siege of Dien Bien Phu: 13 March–8 May 1954

Legion, 2/4th Algerian *tirailleurs*, a Moroccan *goum*, a battery of 105mm guns, and a troop of tanks. Command headquarters and the Field Hospital were situated underground just north of Claudine, and here was centred the mobile striking force of infantry tanks and guns. At this stage there were just under 5,000 troops in the valley.

During the following weeks aeroplanes were constantly arriving bringing senior service visitors and ministers from Paris to listen to what Generals Navarre and Cogny hoped to achieve, for it was widely believed that upon the paddy fields of Dien Bien Phu the destiny of French Indo-China turned. Most of these distinguished visitors were impressed by the position, which was being strengthened every day by entrenchments, wire, and mines. General Navarre estimated the enemy would require at least three full divisions to invest the perimeter, and if these could be tied down an operation (Atlante) planned for January in Annam would greatly benefit. Should the enemy attempt a large-scale offensive Navarre was confident that the garrison's fire power would mow them down, and that this 'bristling hedgehog' would be the means of blunting the Viet Minh army.

However, not all the senior officers were so sanguine. Navarre himself, while exuding confidence, did not neglect to order Cogny to make a secret withdrawal plan in case things went wrong. Cogny was nothing loath to undertake this, for he was one of the officers who had reservations, but the main opposition came from General Fay, the senior air force officer. He pointed out the extreme vulnerability of the airstrips – the garrison's lifeline – and considered the whole venture misplaced. On the other hand General Piroth, in command of the artillery, was dangerously optimistic. He was absolutely confident that his counter-battery plans would effectively knock out any guns the enemy might manage to haul through the jungle, and when asked whether he required any more guns himself, replied he already had more than he needed. In the event the failure of the artillery was partly responsible for the French defeat.

In the three months following the occupation of the valley the French carried out a number of sorties in strength. In early December a force was sent to assist the evacuation of the Thai garrison of Lai Chau, and other strong raids of all arms deep into enemy country were undertaken in order to gain information, harass enemy movement, and disrupt supply routes. Most of these raids and sorties had nugatory results, and many were a costly failure either through air supply difficulties or enemy ambushes. Nor did an attempt to infiltrate guerrillas behind the enemy lines have any better results. By January it had become obvious that Dien Bien Phu's role as a springboard for offensive operations had failed, and belated attempts were made to improve the defence by bringing in more troops, artillery, and tanks, for the enemy was closing the ring, and clearly intended to take the bait with an all-out offensive.

Navarre and Cogny had not only hopelessly underestimated the number of first-line troops Giap would be able to put into the field, but also his ability to bring up heavy equipment over appalling terrain, and at the same time to carry out mobile warfare in which he ran rings round the French attempts at similar tactics in the winter of 1953–54. Giap moved his divisions and regiments about without facing any serious resistance – he even succeeded in sending troops in and out of Laos. Marching long distances by day, and even longer ones by night to avoid enemy strafing, the winding divisional columns crept ever closer to the French camp. Each man besides his personal weapons carried his waterbottle, his ration of thirty pounds of rice, and a shovel with which he dug himself in at the end of a night's march.

By the time he was ready to open the attack on 13 March Giap had elements of four infantry divisions and the Heavy Division closely ringing the French bastions. A total of 49,000 combatants (and a further 10,000 would be thrown in as the siege went on) faced the French garrison, which although reinforced by 12 battalions still numbered only 13,200 of which no more than 7,000 were first-line troops.

The greatest surprise to the French was the performance of the 351st Heavy Division with its expertly handled fire power. The Viet Minh outgunned the French in heavy weapons by more than three to one. Moreover, through prodigious efforts the guns were hauled over steep jungle tracks, camouflaged when necessary by such ingenious methods as lashing tree tops together, and manhandled on to the forward slopes. Here they were dug in and sited to bring direct fire on to vulnerable parts of the French camp, and in particular the airstrip. The guns at Isabelle could not reach them, and the counterbattery of those in the centre proved ineffective. If the French could have seized and held the high ground the story would have been different.

The thunder of gunfire rolling down the valley was an ominous beginning to 13 March, and during the day it continued unabated – and unaffected by the French riposte. The principal concentration was on the strongpoint Beatrice, with neutralizing fire on the centre of the camp. Major Pégeaux, commanding the 3rd battalion of the Legion's 13th Demi-Brigade, was killed by a direct hit on his command post, and shortly afterwards Colonel Gaucher, in command of the central sub-sector, was also killed. But it was not until 5.30 p.m. that Beatrice was assailed by an avalanche of men, stern and unflinching, who hurled themselves upon the wire and died in hundreds. Fresh battalions were poured in and by midnight the Legionnaires, who had fought with the utmost gallantry, were completely swamped and Beatrice was in Viet

Minh hands. It was out on a limb and ripe for picking, but its loss meant that other parts of the camp now came under enemy fire.

The next evening it was the turn of the isolated northern post, Gabrielle. The pattern was much the same down to the consequences of a direct hit on the command post. Colonel Piroth was asked to silence the enemy batteries, but again his gunners were unable to do so. Once more clouds of men stormed the position, once more they were mown down on the wire, and once again numbers prevailed and the Algerians, having given a good account of themselves, fell back.

On 15 March Anne Marie was attacked in force and the 3rd Thai Battalion (holding numbers one and two strongpoints) had no stomach for the fight, and who can blame them, for it was not their war and they knew the country well enough for them to slip away quietly in the darkling, and disappear into the jungle or go over to the enemy. In the end only one strongpoint held fast, and that was withdrawn to Huguette. And so it was that within forty-eight hours of the first attack three of the main French bastions had fallen to the enemy, and furthermore they had lost their artillery commander. Sadly disillusioned, and shamed by the worthlessness of his boasts, Piroth had held a grenade to his chest and pulled out the pin.

After this initial onslaught there was a comparative lull in the fighting until the end of March, although there was always considerable activity both inside and outside the fortified camp. Giap needed this respite in order to bring up fresh troops to replace the enormous number he had lost in storming the three bastions, and he also needed time for his slow, but exceedingly sure, commissariat to replenish ammunition stocks. Thousands of porters* and bicycle men busied themselves like a horde of ants over winding trails. And during all of this time Giap was tightening the ring of steel round the camp, sapping forward with trenches from which he proposed to launch his next attack.

The French had got themselves into an unenviable position, and even after this short time it must have been obvious to their senior commanders that they could not win the battle. The supply situation alone could have told them that. The number of aircraft available was insufficient even with both airstrips in use, and already they were virtually out of action. This latter posed a serious problem for the evacuation of the wounded. The occasional ambulance aeroplane managed to land (often under fire) until the end of March, and helicopters continued to make dangerous and difficult descents for a few more weeks, but it proved impossible to evacuate all the seriously wounded from a field hospital quite unable to cope with the high number of casualties.

---

*At the beginning of the battle Giap had 31,500 in close support, and almost as many strung out over his long lines of communication.

Before the next round of serious fighting began there was more trouble at garrison headquarters. Colonel Piroth was already dead, and now Castries' chief-of-staff broke down and had to be evacuated. Castries himself was nearing the end of his tether, and Lieutenant-Colonel Langlais had to be brought into headquarters to assist in the command. General Cogny seriously considered dropping in to take charge of the battle, but was persuaded against it. It was a lost cause, and this was no time for a quixotic gesture by the commander of all the Tongking forces, even though it might have brought him fame immortal.

As both sides squared up for the coming second phase of the battle the morale of the French troops remained high despite their critical situation. The enemy batteries that ringed the heights became daily more deadly, but even so supplies continued to arrive – although some, dropped from too great a height, landed in enemy-held territory – and some guns and troops were also dropped. Among the latter were Major Bigeard's 6th Colonial Parachute Battalion, which had come in with the initial wave, and then been evacuated to fight elsewhere.

The second phase lasted from 30 March to 4 April. Langlais and Castries had done their best with the material available to strengthen the defence, and had placed a quota of reliable troops at all the vital strongpoints, concentrating on the defence of Dominque and Éliane east of the river. It was upon these two bastions that the Viet Minh barrage and assault was directed. Troops from the 312th Division, leaping from trenches pushed to within 300 yards of the forward Dominique strongpoints, surged forward seemingly indifferent to minefields and wire. The terrified Algerians bent before the storm and departed for the rear.

What was to be called the battle for the Five Hills had made an unpromising start with three of Dominique's six strongpoints soon captured. Two of these were briefly regained in a counterattack by Foreign Legion paratroopers, but by the end of the second day's fighting Giap's men were in possession of the north-east corner of the bastion, and were preparing to deepen their penetration.

While possession of Dominique was being fiercely contested Éliane came under heavy attack from the greater part of 316 Division. Here two companies of Moroccans positioned in one of the strongpoints followed the Algerian example and bolted, and every other position on this vital bastion had been softened up by concentrated artillery fire. But the defenders hung on grimly throughout the night, and by daybreak the fighting had subsided somewhat, and the French made determined, but unsuccessful, attempts to regain the lost Dominique positions.

On the night of 1 April one of Huguette's outlying strongpoints was attacked from the north-west by two regiments of 308 Division, and part of the airstrip was lost. The men of this bastion had to fend for themselves, because what troops were available for counterattacking were needed to save Dominique and Éliane. If they were lost what happened at Huguette was academic. On 2 April it was Isabelle's turn. A few days earlier the 3/3rd Foreign Legion had been ordered to join the battle at Dien Bien Phu, but they had been driven back and only their tanks averted a disaster. Then for the next three days the garrison was subjected to a series of fanatical attacks by the 57th Infantry Regiment of 304 Division, all of which they beat off.

During 2 and 3 April in all areas under attack savage fighting, much of it hand-to-hand, took place. Early on the 4th, men of 308 Division made a determined attempt to gain more of the airstrip, but when this failed with the customary heavy casualties the fighting died down. The hopelessly outnumbered and sternly embattled garrison had survived, although considerably dented, and Giap had lost literally thousands of men in an abortive attempt to break into the inner defences of the camp. His losses could be made good, but the French were not in the same enviable position. Early in the battle the 2nd Battalion 1st Parachute Light Infantry Regiment and other details jumped in, but it was a desperate business in the face of heavy flak, and only a small offering. The garrison had been down to less than 4,500 infantrymen before this drop (of which 1,600 were in Isabelle), and only one of the five paratroop battalions had more than 300 men. Tanks were reduced to four, and there had been serious artillery losses.

Giap's desperate and costly attacks on the Five Hills and northern Huguette positions had not brought him the victory he had wanted. The stubborn defence of the French had come as a surprise. However, the superb courage and utter disregard of death shown by Viet Minh troops had brought some reward. By the time the fighting died down in early April they had possession of part of the airstrip, two strongpoints on Dominique and one on Éliane. The loss to the French of the Dominique positions was particularly serious, for they barred the north-east entrance to the garrison's central position, which was now within a mile of Viet troops. The perimeter had become dangerously restricted, which narrowed the target for enemy artillery and seriously affected the dropping of supplies.

The decision to continue sending in reinforcements was not an easy one to take, for the battle was lost and the chances of a breakout were very slim. Nevertheless, Cogny felt that the losses suffered in the valiant defence of the Five Hills should be made good at least in part. The principal landings took place between 9 and 12 April with not particularly happy results. As well as the difficulties of restricted dropping zones the monsoon, which had recently begun, was exceptionally active on the night (9 April) that the 2nd Foreign Legion

Parachute Battalion was to be dropped. Two companies and head-quarters landed within the 'fortress', but they were more fortunate than some. On the night of 11–12 April 40 per cent of the 850 men dropped landed in Viet Minh hands. Most of those being dropped in this operation were volunteers from Legion infantry battalions, and some were making their first jump in these most inauspicious conditions, with inevitable casualties.

For a short while the fighting slackened, but conditions worsened. The monsoon, which the French had hoped would come as a friend, proved to be another enemy. Rain fell from leaden skies in sheets of water, turning the parched dust to rivers of mud. The Viets were well accustomed to such conditions, but the besieged floundered about in the slime and filth of unrevetted trenches, and the rain seeped through the flimsy roofs of the dug-outs. The plight of the wounded was appalling, operations were performed with the greatest difficulty, and in the foul conditions gangrene began to affect wounds. Low cloud and mist hampered the air supply but not the Viet ack-ack gunners. The garrison was reduced, but it still had to be fed, and so did its prisoners. The future was dark indeed, and over Saigon and Hanoi there hovered a miasma of despair. It was decided to organize a relief force.

Giap spent the middle weeks of April sapping steadily forward to within a short distance of Castries' headquarters and the main French defences. Isolated Isabelle was surrounded, but remained defiant. Viet Minh units were withdrawn from Laos and other places, and reserves from training camps were summoned to make up numbers for the next major offensive. The Chinese were asked to provide 720 tons of ammunition and another anti-aircraft regiment. Giap reckoned to bring into the field 35,000 infantrymen and 12,000 gunners, sappers, signallers, and details. The garrison of Dien Bien Phu dug themselves in and prepared to stem the tide as best they could.

The principal fighting in April, after the Viet's assault on the Five Hills had been largely resisted, was directed upon the three northern strongpoints of Huguette and what was still left of the airstrip (the chief dropping zone) in French hands. The initial attack had taken place during the Five Hills battle, and now after a comparative lull of nearly a month the fighting had flared up and become some of the fiercest seen so far. It was a desperate affair for the French against vastly superior odds, and although reinforcements arrived they were never enough; by 23 April the three small, but important, Huguette strongpoints had been lost and the Viets had gained a further lodgement on the airstrip. The French suffered 500 casualties in this fight, including some of their best Legionnaire paratroopers, but the Viets had paid even more dearly for their gains, losing a large proportion of three regiments. It was only a temporary setback for Giap, but he required a full week to replenish ammunition and bring up more troops for what he hoped would be the final push.

Operation Condor had been under consideration for some time. Originally designed as a pursuit of Viet Minh troops after they had been broken up by the stubborn and active defence of Dien Bien Phu, it had to be changed in April to a desperate attempt to rescue the garrison. Colonel de Crévecoeur, who commanded the French troops in Laos, was in charge of the operation under Navarre, but it quickly ran into trouble through the contumacy of senior officers.

At the beginning of April, Cogny had agreed its usefulness if the force made haste, but Navarre procrastinated, for he was hesitant about compounding the Dien Bien Phu disaster with more troops. Cogny, who by now was hardly on speaking terms with Navarre, informed Castries on 14 April that the relief force was on the way, but this was not strictly true, because although a part of Crévecoeur's force was moving, Navarre did not give his final orders until the 27th, and then the airborne element was cancelled. Crévecoeur made what speed he could, but his North African and Laos troops were untrained in jungle warfare, and could not achieve a breakthrough in time. The familiar story of too little and too late.

Meanwhile, Giap was anxious to bring the battle to a swift and victorious conclusion. Not only was it proving extremely costly in manpower and materials, but the forthcoming international conference in Geneva would be considering the Indo-China situation. Accordingly on 1 May he hurled his men once more against the strongpoints. Encroachment tactics were over, and he reverted to the mass attack. Because his trenches had been worked so close to the French perimeter there was no opening barrage, but the wire was blasted by plastic charges carried by men contemptuous of death, dug-outs were demolished, and the whole front came into close intense fire action, writhing under the effect of constant shot and shell. By the evening of 2 May the Viets had made some small gains on Éliane and Huguette, and the outposts of Isabelle but, counterattacking with the bayonet, the French drove them from some of these gains and showed there was plenty of fight in them yet.

But the end was near, not because the morale and courage of the defenders was giving way, for they upheld both splendidly to the end, but because ammunition was running out. All along supplies had been the key to this battle, and now the Viet Minh human chain was still standing up bravely to cannon, bomb, and napalm rained on it whenever the weather allowed the French air force to fly, but there was nothing more for the French. It is true that on the night of 2–3 May part of a battalion of Colonial Paratroops, who had only arrived from France a few days previous, were dropped. But they came far too late to be of any use and only added to the anguish, sacrifice, and futility of the dying days of Dien Bien Phu. Someone had the sense to turn the remainder of the battalion back in flight.

During the last few days of the battle the monsoon did its worst with low cloud and drenching rain. Conditions became appalling, but the French air force continued to drop supplies (196 tons was despatched on 6 May), but so small was the French perimeter by now that the Viets collected a great deal, and were soon rushing upon their enemy in an odd assortment of French uniforms and American helmets.

Gradually, inch by inch, the French in the Huguettes and Claudine were forced to give ground, the hand-to-hand fighting was being conducted by both sides with a savagery reminiscent of a more barbarous age; as a Viet Minh soldier fell on came another in a white heat of disciplined passion. The perimeter kept shrinking; in the last two days the fighting was concentrated on the vital strongpoints of Éliane. On the morning of 7 May the last of these was caved in by fresh hordes of Viet troops, and by that afternoon Dien Bien Phu was disintegrating, with only isolated pockets of resistance still maintaining the fight. So as to save further bloodshed by another night of useless fighting Castries announced that fighting would cease at 5.30 p.m. At that time only in Isabelle was there still some semblance of order.

Although at the receiving end of some very heavy bombardment the garrison of Isabelle, until the last few days, had not been subjected to the punishing fighting of the main position. However, in most other ways its situation was the least enviable of all the bastions. Its principal role was to give flanking fire for the main position with its 11 105mm howitzers, and to do this 1,166 men with guns and tanks were confined in a very small, rather boggy perimeter. Soon after the battle had commenced their small airstrip was out of action, the road to Dien Bien Phu was cut, and the Viets had the position encircled. The garrison did not even have the morale-boosting pleasure of the two brothels, which a thoughtful command had installed farther north. Survival depended on airborne supplies, and on account of the very restricted dropping zone Isabelle lost an even greater percentage than the main position.

On 1 May the Viets had turned their full attention on this isolated bastion, and the fighting for the next seven days was as fierce as any, and the artillery concentration on the small area devastating. Nevertheless, by the afternoon of 7 May although some strongpoints had been swamped the main position still held. About 4 p.m. Colonel Lalande, commanding the bastion, received a wireless communication from Castries to say that fighting would end that evening and that he (Lalande) was free to attempt Operation Albatross. This was a scheme for a fighting withdrawal worked out for the main garrison, which was to fall back through Isabelle, whose troops would act as rearguard. But events overtook the forward positions, and no breakout by them could be made. Lalande, for the sake of morale, had kept the scheme to himself and now attempted it without any rehearsal. At 10 p.m. two companies disappeared into the darkness, but they were quickly cut off, over-whelmed and split up. Some men got back to Isabelle, and a handful escaped to the jungle. Fighting continued for a while, but further resistance was pointless, and at 1 a.m. on 8 May Colonel Lalande surrendered. The battle of Dien Bien Phu was over.

It had been a victory for the Viet Minh, and there seems little doubt that it had been masterminded by Vo Nguyen Giap. It is true that he had the weight of numbers, and a nearly homogenous army comprised of men dedicated to the cause of freedom. Nevertheless, Giap's fire and spirit, no less than his rapidly acquired tactical prowess, was the motivation behind the incredible exertions and endurance of his troops. He had paid very heavily for the glory; it is estimated that the Viet Minh suffered 23,000 casualties of which 8,000 were killed. The smaller French garrison, of which the Foreign Legion with seven battalions provided more than half the fighting men, also suffered grievously. In round figures there were 9,000 casualties of which 2,000 were killed, and a further 7,000 were marched away as prisoners on 8 May.

Dien Bien Phu was not the end of the first Vietnamese war: it had another three months to run. Both governments, French and Viet Minh, were war weary, but the Viets were prepared to hang on grimly to get what they could by negotiation. Giap now had some 90,000 first-line troops with which to confront the French, who in June decided on a change of command, General Ely replacing Navarre. He conducted the last operation of the war, Auvergne, in which he brought in troops to hold an enclave south of the Hanoi–Haiphong road. He was faced with many difficulties, and had to fight a number of small inconclusive battles against defended localities. The operation soon petered out, and on 3 July French and Vietnamese representatives met at Trung Giao (just north of Hanoi) to discuss, among other things, an exchange of prisoners. It was the beginning of the end; on 23 July the delegates at the Geneva conference, where a representative of the Viet Minh govern-ment was present, agreed a cease-fire. The Viet Minh received all the country north of the 16th Parallel. Laos, Cambodia, and South Vietnam were to be independent. A period of relative peace and happiness would soon be forfeited under further blows of fortune.

It is possible, with the advantage of hindsight, to find many reasons for the French defeat at Dien Bien Phu, although lack of courage and endurance by those taking part is certainly not one of them. The whole concept of establishing an isolated offensive/defensive base deep in enemy country was probably wrong, and certainly needed much more thought. There were many errors of judgement, chief of which was the total misappreciation on the part of the French general staff of the strength, mobility, and fire power of the Viet Namese Army of Liberation, and the competence of its commander, while greatly overestimating the efficiency of its own counterbattery riposte. Air power might not have won the war, but it could have saved Dien Bien Phu.

The French government, perhaps due to its NATO commitment, found it difficult to supply Indo-China with sufficient aircraft, particularly with heavy bombers, and the United States turned down the opportunity of aerial supply which, without committing them to a dangerous involvement, might have tipped the scales. And finally there was no overall commander for the battle. Navarre, Cogny, Fay, Castries, and Langlais all stirred the tactical pot, and it did not help that Navarre and Cogny carried antipathy towards each other to the point of hatred.

These are mostly abstract reasons for defeat. The deciding factor in the battle itself was undoubtedly logistics, and in that field the Viet Minh showed a considerable superiority. With the exception of some food (a Viet Minh soldier subsisted on rice, lentils, and dried fish), and later French stores parachuted into their lines, all Viet Minh battle requirements came from China. It is difficult to be quite certain of the tracks used to bring supplies, for these are numerous and confused.* Before the second war there was a railway line running from Kunming to the Indo-China border town of Lao-Kai, but no account mentions any supplies coming in by rail. More likely the tracks from Meng-Tzu-Hsien to Man-hao and Kai-Hua-Fu to Pak-bao were used, entering Tongking in the Lao-Kai, Cao Bang, and possibly Lang Son areas, and thence to Dien Bien Phu by provincial roads. By March 1954 the Viets had completed a motor road of sorts from Lai Chau to Dien Bien Phu, which would have facilitated supplies coming through Lao-Kai.

Over these external and internal routes, and other tracks hacked through the jungle, long lines of porters trundled their loads, and divisions marched to the battle area. The French air force and navy pilots flew daring missions right up to the end of the siege in an attempt to disrupt these supply lines, but they had very little success. Every time roads or tracks were cut the Viet engineers were quick to repair them, or else to cut a bypass. Supply depots and bridges across the Red River were well protected, and to approach these and the principal routes pilots had to brave a corridor of deadly flak. Whenever possible supplies and troops were moved by night, but even in daylight they were a difficult target.

*The author has walked some of them, and knows the problems!

The Vietnamese needed no instruction in camouflage; depots, columns, and gun positions were well concealed amid the impenetrable foliage, and when there was anything to cook smokeless ovens betrayed no positions. These were just some of the factors that prevented successful interdiction.

The backbone of Giap's supply system was relays of porters, literally thousands were recruited from the peasantry, usually on a self-supplying basis. These men could not have supported an army manually; it was made possible by the use of converted bicycles. Ever since 1951 the Viet Minh had been using bicycles manufactured in the Peugeot factories. The seat was removed and wooden struts were used to strengthen the frame, and bamboo poles extended the handlebars for ease in guidance when heavily loaded. These converted machines could carry split loads totalling up to 450 pounds (as opposed to only 45 pounds per man), and in the dry weather they were easily manoeuvred along jungle tracks. Thus if Giap had, say, 50,000 bicylces he was bringing up somewhere around 10,000 tons of ammunition, spare weapons, petrol, food, etc.

During the last month of the siege the monsoon had broken and bicycle transport had become difficult if not impossible, but by then the Viets were operating about 600 two-and-a-half-ton Russian Molotova trucks over tracks and routes made possible for their use by another huge conscription of coolie labour. Navarre had hoped that these roads would become impassable in the rains and make Giap's supply position as difficult as his own, but this did not happen. Moreover, the low cloud gave the Viet columns considerable protection against French aircraft, while seriously affecting the accuracy of their own drops.

As has been shown, the success or failure of the Viet Minh supply system depended, to a great extent, on porters. On the other hand the French equivalent depended, entirely, on air support. Whereas the Viet Minh could recruit as many porters as they needed, at no time did the French have sufficient aircraft for their requirements. In its simplest form that is why they lost the battle.

Matters might have been made easier for Navarre had he organized an adequate build-up of supplies during the weeks preceding the siege. But Giap had shown high qualities of generalship in forcing him, against his declared policy, to dissipate his resources by establishing small airheads for his mobile columns that were endeavouring to outmanoeuvre Viet Minh raids into northern Laos and the Mekong valley. In accomplishing this Transport Command used up what reserves were available.

At the time of the siege there were at most 100 transport aeroplanes, and only half that number of bombers (B-26s) with a shortage of crews. Nevertheless, between the first and last days of the siege no fewer than

1,629 sorties were flown through very accurate flak from 37mm anti-aircraft guns, which caused severe damage and losses – the French admitted to losing twenty-three aircraft. There was also a shortage of ground staff, and the Americans were chary of providing more aircraft if they could not be maintained. In the end they did provide 1,200 maintenance men, which helped to shore up the supply situation, but was far from solving it.

In the very short time, after the siege had commenced, in which it was possible to land Dakotas the garrison's daily minimum food requirement of 150 tons could usually be met, but once it came to parachuting the problem became very acute. On two occasions in April record drops of 217 and 229 tons were achieved, but usually the figure was well below the minimum needed. There were two other complications to exercise the administrative staff. The allocation of priorities between medical requirements, munitions, reinforcements, and food usually resulted in food having to come last, which could mean that fighting efficiency suffered when men were sometimes existing on survival rations. And anyway food was a problem in itself, for what was acceptable pabulum for a European was not for a Mohammedan, nor for an African or a Vietnamese. Each had their own differing requirements.

It was remarkable how well the French air force and navy pilots coped in the face of appallingly difficult and dangerous conditions. Troops and supplies were dropped round the clock up to the very last days of the siege on to a perimeter that was shrinking daily. The inevitable losses of valuable stores to the enemy was very seldom the pilots' fault, but just an unavoidable risk that had to be taken in a desperate calculation, which from the earliest days of the battle could be seen to have gone wrong and become the one certain factor that ensured eventual defeat.

In the course of the battles described many of the factors that make for victory or defeat have been analysed. At Dien Bien Phu there were three, one of which – failure of supply – has not been previously encountered, although at Borodino and Warsaw it played an important, but not vital, part. The French simply had not got the means to keep the base supplied with reinforcements, ammunition, food and medical necessities. The Viet Minh, on the other hand, through clever organization and forced labour, managed well – with the exception of the medical side which did not trouble them greatly. Failure to pay proper attention to logistics is a fairly certain cause of defeat in battle.

The French committed two other errors that contributed to their downfall. Like the British at Isandhlwana they hopelessly underestimated the strength and ability of the native army opposing them, and they conducted the battle with no clearly defined chain of command. Either of these mistakes could prove fatal, but at Dien Bien Phu they were subsidiary to the overriding failure to keep the garrison properly supplied.

24   The Nature and Pattern
of War

WAR comes about, usually, as a prolongation of argument leading to
the decisive act of battle, which is the means of obtaining a political
object. Once it was invested with the glamour of chivalrous romantic-
ism, and even in modern times it brought forth much that was good as
well as bad. But with the invention of ever more destructive weapons, it
has become a particularly vicious crime against mankind and a sing-
ularly sterile means of resolving international dispute, or even of
extirpating evil. Nevertheless, it would be a rash man who predicted
there would never be another war, for in certain circumstances – such as
the complete removal of the nuclear deterrent – it could very well
happen, and nations have to be prepared.

The study of war is war and, as in so much else, first-hand experience
is invaluable, but there are many lessons to be learnt from past campaigns and the methods of the masters who fought them. The author's
fourth-uncle, Sir Charles Napier, himself a master of war, once wrote to
a young officer acquaintance of his, 'By reading you will be distinguished . . . A man cannot learn his profession without constant
study to prepare especially for the higher ranks. When in a post of
responsibility, he has no time to read; and if he comes to such a post with
an empty skull, it is then too late to fill it.'*

From the earliest days of fighting, military strategy has been the art
of bringing the enemy to battle on the most advantageous terms; it
decides the time, the place, and the numbers with which the battle will
be fought. Having committed the enemy to the fight, tactics have been
the ways and means of defeating him. But over the centuries the
increasing power of weapons has caused commanders to evolve new
systems of attack and defence to reflect the changing patterns of arms
and armaments. Tactics, therefore, and the science of war will change
with the times, but the underlying principles remain constant and were
as vital in battles fought in ancient days as those fought in the twentieth
century.

*Henderson, p. 185.

359

The pattern of war is more clearly seen through the study of methods by which battles were won and lost, and in the very first campaign described in this book will be found stratagems and principles that run through many of the succeeding ones. In the Second Punic War there are examples of the strategy of indirect approach. When Hannibal (himself an exponent of this strategy) was at bay in southern Italy various Roman generals failed conspicuously to dislodge him. But Scipio, who had previously used the indirect approach to strike a deathblow against Hannibal's base in Spain, now repeated the manoeuvre. Slipping away from Sicily in the face of considerable political opposition, and with a comparatively small force, he took the war to Cartagena behind Hannibal's back.

The strategy and tactics of the indirect approach are broadly based. They do not merely include the factors of time and space, but closely relate the psychological to the physical. The history of war shows that the direct approach along the expected lines of attack is often unsuccessful, but from the earliest days of fighting the great commanders have won many of their victories through a strategical or tactical indirect approach. However, in achieving this they have nearly always combined the psychological with the physical, for without some form of surprise or deception the enemy can block the manoeuvre. There are many forms of indirect approach, strategic and tactical, and besides Scipio's unexpected arrival at Hannibal's home base there are other examples in at least eight of the battles described.

Duke William on landing at Pevensey was not prepared to march north for a direct confrontation with Harold, but cleverly adopted a strategy that he knew would bring the English king many miles to give battle after a long march with an incomplete army. This important psychological advantage over his opponent before the battle began was also gained by Saladin at Hattin. He led a detachment to take Tiberias, a move well calculated to lure the Christian army from their safe base at Saffuriyah to cross a parched desert before giving battle to his troops strongly positioned on the Horns of Hattin.

Frederick the Great, who incidentally operating on interior lines in Silesia was a constant practitioner of the indirect approach, gives a clear tactical example at Leuthen. In the American Civil War McClellan and Grant, like Scipio at Zama, made use of naval power to achieve strategic surprise through the indirect approach in the Peninsula and Vicksburg campaigns. Ludendorff's attack on Samsonov's left wing at Tannenberg, and Pilsudski's counterstroke at Warsaw are further examples.

The strategy that conceived Scipio's defeat of Hannibal, and the skill with which he conducted the campaign, were one of the finest examples of the art of war, and brought out lessons which, *mutatis mutandis*, held good throughout the succeeding centuries. On arrival in Africa he cunningly lured Hanno's Carthaginian force into an ambush and then, in the face of vastly superior numbers, fell back to a defensive position. In the following spring he deceived and completely surprised the two investing armies, and in a night attack destroyed their camps and thousands of their soldiers. This left Scipio free for a direct assault on Carthage, but the city was strongly held, and with Hannibal expected in his rear and Syphax still at large, he could not risk a siege. He therefore determined to gain his objective by moral rather than physical means, and so he marched south-west into the Carthaginian granary where he defeated Hasdrubal, and plundered the city's supply line. He then split his army, sending a strong detachment to capture Syphax, while with the remainder he threatened Carthage.

The defeat of their armies, and the indirect pressure put upon them, eventually decided the Senate to seek peace terms from Scipio. But these were soon violated, and with the arrival of Hannibal at Leptis Minor the final act in the drama was ready to begin. But once again Scipio did the unexpected and completely surprised the enemy. He neither advanced to attack nor remained to defend his base. Instead he marched away from both Carthage and Hannibal into the Bagradas Valley, where he again ravaged the Carthaginian supplies, and drew closer to his important ally, Masinissa. In doing this he took a grave risk in exposing his line of communications and withdrawal. But the gamble came off. The Carthaginian Senate compelled Hannibal to march after him, and Zama was the last of Scipio's spectacular successes.

This brief recapitulation of the Carthaginian campaign is given because in it so many of the principles and patterns of war were enacted, most of which constantly recur. Surprise, the power of manoeuvre, supplies, communications, concentration of force, morale, political interference and good generalship all played their part in this African campaign.

Surprise, together with its two handmaidens, speed and deception, is more easily achieved tactically than strategically, although in neither case is it achieved easily. Every commander strives to outwit his opponent by attacking when and where he is least expected, and in so doing to gain a decisive tactical advantage. But, as Clausewitz points out, surprise is often at the mercy of chance and while it 'lies at the root of all operations' it can rarely be 'outstandingly successful'. That is to say surprise initially gained (particularly strategic surprise) may be nullified by subsequent events. In the campaigns here discussed Napoleon in June 1815 by the very boldness of his plan and the secrecy (another important ingredient of surprise) of his concentration completely surprised the Allies, but he did not achieve anything decisive. In our own time the landing at Anzio undoubtedly took the Germans by surprise, but probably their biggest surprise was the Allies' failure to take advantage of it.

On the other hand the history of war is littered with instances of outstanding tactical successes achieved by surprise. Frederick at Leuthen with his new form of attack, Magruder's deception before Richmond, the speed and secrecy of the Zulu attack at Isandhlwana and Rosecrans's misleading feint at Chickamauga were stratagems that gave initial advantage, and in two cases total success, through surprise.

Scipio forced the Carthaginians to sue for peace by lowering their morale through the systematic destruction of the city's supplies and the power of manoeuvre he displayed in defeating first one and then the other of their armies. The importance of morale needs no stressing. Napoleon, with his oft-quoted dictum 'the moral is to the physical as three to one', and all the great commanders were well aware that battles cannot be won by troops whose morale is low. Every soldier over the centuries – for human nature is the one unchanging factor – has come to the battle elevated or despondent according to the state of his morale, and some of the fundamentals that will uphold it are the justice of the cause for which he is fighting, the competence of the leadership, the efficiency of his weapons, the supply of food and clothing, and the security and well-being of his family. In one guise or another morale features in every battle, and it is the aim of the commander to bring it to the highest pitch in his own troops, and endeavour to lower it in those of his enemy. Ways of attempting to raise morale have varied from the use of elephants at Zama to the use of whores at Dien Bien Phu!

An integral component of high morale is an efficient supply system. Supply can also be a decisive factor in itself, as was the case at Hattin and Dien Bien Phu. Even in early days when armies lived off the country, lines of communication were important, for it was usually necessary to establish depots. Living off the land became more and more difficult as the size of armies increased, and indeed would limit the numbers that could operate efficiently, for although there are many examples of ragged, hungry armies triumphing over appalling conditions, that state of affairs can only be temporary if morale is not to suffer. A proper system of requisitioning was an undoubted improvement over the compulsory seizure of livestock, crops, etc., but there were always problems and anxieties in those early days. Matters did not really ease until the improvement of roads (bad roads in the days of ox-drawn transport greatly hindered mobility and manoeuvre) and the coming of the railways.

Lines of communication have a two-fold purpose as a link to the base, or in some cases (Borodino for example) with supply depots, and as a means of retreat. Operations against the enemy's lines of communication are best conducted by small specially trained units or guerrilla

bands; there were many successful examples of this in the last war –
especially in the Western Desert. A large-scale attack becomes a flanking operation, which is difficult to mount, for it involves denuding troops
from the forward positions and unless circumstances are absolutely
right, when it can succeed brilliantly, it will be at best ineffective and at
worst dangerous.

Scipio in Tunisia, Napoleon at Borodino, and Grant at Vicksburg had
their lines of communication wide open to attack. But of the three Scipio
was in the most danger, for had Hannibal been allowed his way Scipio's
retreat might have been blocked, and he could have been brought to
battle in unfavourable circumstances. The Russians had insufficient
strength to menace Napoleon's depots, which was fortunate for him
because it would have been better had these been echeloned upon
more than one line of communication. Grant was living off the land
and knew his opponent well enough to consider his retreat in small
jeopardy.

Linked to supply and communication is the presence of fortresses.
These have played an important part in war, and feature in some of the
campaigns described. At the time of Hattin, and earlier, the Crusaders
owed their survival in the Holy Land to their well-sited fortresses. They
not only facilitated their supply system and safeguarded their lines of
communication, but formed bases for offensive operations and were a
refuge in the case of retreat. They performed a similar service at the
time of the English Civil War when they defended well-provisioned
towns and blocked communications. They could usually be reduced in
the course of time, but meanwhile they seriously impeded operations.
Dien Bien Phu was a different type of fortress, but with much the same
purpose as a castle. Sited originally to block the invasion routes to Laos,
and to form a base for offensive operations, it failed in this latter role
because the garrison was never large enough to permit the sortie of a
worthwhile fighting force.

Scipio was very aware of the importance of manoeuvre, and of course
most wars are primarily a matter of movement. A commander tries so to
manoeuvre his force that he concentrates maximum power at the place
of his own choosing in the most favourable circumstances. Almost all the
great military writers lay it down unequivocally that concentration
must be the norm, and dividing an army or detaching a force the
exception. There are occasions when splitting is justified. Scipio detached Laelius to defeat Syphax; the risk was acceptable, for his ally,
Masinissa, had to be returned to power. At Manzikert, however, it is
difficult to justify Romanus's decision to split his army by a distance of
thirty miles, and at Chickamauga Rosecrans ran a grave risk by having
his flanks forty miles apart against Bragg's cleverly concentrated army.
Had Bragg's well-planned convergent attack taken place there could

have been a Federal disaster. A convergent attack, or an enveloping movement, can be on occasions a perfectly valid reason for splitting a force.

When Frederick at Leuthen, using his famous Oblique Order, hit the left wing of the Austrian army with a powerfully packed punch he not only gained a complete tactical surprise, but he also fully justified the splitting of his army. Napoleon might have succeeded when he split his at Quatre Bras and Ligny – as he had done many times before – but the main attack, through unfortunate circumstances, was not sufficiently loaded. This leads into economy of force, the close companion of concentration.

Economy of force means the use of all the troops that are on the battlefield, or in the vicinity. Clausewitz considered it better for troops to be wrongly used than not to be employed at all. There are many instances in the twenty battles described where commanders have made this error. At Bosworth Richard kept Northumberland in reserve. A force in reserve is being used, if only passively at first, but there are occasions – and Bosworth was surely one of them – when a reserve is unnecessary. Northumberland's somewhat unreliable men might have been better in the front line, and this would have allowed Richard to detach a force to turn Henry's left flank, which might have had a decisive effect on the Stanleys and the battle. As it was Northumberland's men took no part in the battle, like D'Erlon's 330 years later at Ligny. Wellington had 17,000 men and 30 guns doing nothing at Waterloo, the Russian cavalry took no part at the Alma, where they could perhaps have turned defeat into victory, and in the Seven Days campaign Jackson's entire corps was virtually unemployed, as was Rennenkampf's army at Tannenberg. It is easy to be critical and in some cases there may have been good reasons at the time, but economy of force is an important principle.

Any study of the pattern of war necessarily includes a brief review of the degree of political interference that generals have to suffer. This is in evidence in some of the battles described. The Carthaginians might have won at Zama had Hannibal, their greatest general, not been ordered to carry out a plan of which he did not approve by politicians without any military knowledge. At the time of Naseby, and indeed earlier, the Committee of Both Kingdoms was as much a marplot as was George III's minister a little over a hundred years later. In both instances interference with the conduct of the campaign hampered the commanders in the field, and in the case of Saratoga the interference came from a distance of 3,000 miles and was transmitted by sail. In the American Civil War President Lincoln was guilty on at least one occasion (the Peninsular campaign) of meddling with the command and thereby possibly losing the battle. President Davis was less of an amateur than Lincoln, nevertheless his direct orders to commanders in the field were not in the best interests of the Confederates.

War is a political act instigated and, in its wider spheres, controlled by the government. In modern times, when it has become global, a master strategist is required with the ability to balance the needs of one campaign against another in different parts of the world. If there is a politician with fighting experience and who has made a deep study of military history (Winston Churchill for instance – although such a man is very rare) he is admirably qualified to propound strategic plans for the general direction of the war, but once operations have begun the soldier in charge should not be distracted by political agitations.

There is one other operation worth looking at, and that is pursuit. At Zama there was no need for one – what happened to Hannibal's cavalry is not precisely known – and so one starts with Hastings, the second battle in the series. Here Norman knights appear to have carried out a somewhat uncontrolled pursuit that was limited to the few remaining daylight hours. According to some of the Chroniclers the house-carls rallied (probably at Oakwood Gyll) to cover what had become a rout, and in some way many knights perished in what became known as The Malfosse before William called off the pursuit.

The principal precept in a pursuit is that it should be undertaken swiftly, ruthlessly and for so long as possible, so as to take full advantage of the low moral condition of a beaten army. Its limitations are governed by fatigue in troops who may have had a long approach to battle followed by a stiff fight, by natural obstacles (which include night) and by enemy action.

In the days when cavalry was queen of the battlefield that was the arm which did the most damage in the pursuit. But over the centuries the cavalry pattern was constantly changing. The heavily armoured knight and his equally heavily armoured horse were of little use in a fast pursuit, and with the coming of the longbow and then gunpowder the knight tended to become an infantryman in battle. But through the perspicacity of such great commanders as Gustavus Adolphus, Cromwell, and Frederick the Great the horse regained its importance on the battlefield, and at Naseby the pursuit, which went on for eleven miles and ended only with night, was mainly a cavalry affair. Night usually put a stop to pursuit, although in three of the battles described – Leuthen, Waterloo, and Warsaw – there was no let-up for darkness.

But cavalry alone could deal only with a demoralized enemy on the run, and not with a well-conducted retreat. Jomini said that retreats 'are certainly the most difficult operations in war'. To be successful they should be carried out in a slow, orderly fashion and covered by a strong rearguard. In this case, or when the enemy is falling back on reserves, the pursuit still has to be rapid, well controlled and undertaken with all three arms. The most convincing victory can be sadly tarnished by the sort of losses the Normans are said to have suffered at Hastings in even a small rearguard action.

There are very few occasions when the immediate pursuit of a beaten enemy is not possible, but history relates many where a pursuit was possible but not undertaken. This occurred in three of the battles recounted – Borodino, Gettysburg, and Chickamauga. At Borodino the Russians were defeated, but in no hurry to leave the field. Had Napoleon hustled them they would have offered further resistance, and his army was already sadly diminished by sickness and casualties. He had set his sights on Moscow, and wanted to arrive in the capital as complete as possible. In the event he did so without further loss, but was unable to accomplish his purpose. With hindsight one could say it might have been better to have exerted extreme pressure on Kutuzov and destroyed his army, but there were other armies and Napoleon had greater designs than the defeat of just one of them.

If Napoleon was right not to pursue, Meade and Bragg were almost certainly wrong. Lee conducted a very orderly retreat from Seminary Ridge, but Meade made no attempt to follow until a day and a half later, and then the Union army marched at a very leisurely pace. Lee was unable to cross the swollen Potomac until ten days after the battle. Prior to that he had taken up a defensive position with the river behind him. Meade with a larger force, and a considerable moral advantage, allowed him to cross to safety unopposed. Lincoln was most annoyed. Bragg surrendered a similar chance to destroy his opponent's army when he failed to pursue Rosecrans after his victory at Chickamauga. Thomas's corps was totally exhausted, and the whole Federal army could have been caught off balance at Rossville Gap, and Chatanooga probably saved. Bragg said his casualties had been heavy and his men were tired. This was true, but morale was high and the effort should have been made.

These principles and patterns of war that emerged from one campaign fought more than two thousand years ago, and many of which occurred again in the succeeding battles described, are not exhaustive, but they are typical of those that will continue to emerge in any future war.

Bibliography

Chapter 1: BATTLE OF ZAMA

Caven, Brian, *The Punic Wars*, Weidenfeld & Nicolson, 1980
Hart, B. H. Liddell, *A Greater than Napoleon, Scipio Africanus*, William Blackwood & Sons, 1926
Lazenby, J. F., *Hannibal's War*, Avis & Phillips, 1978
Polybius, The Histories of, Vol. II, translated from text of F. Hultsch by Evelyn S. Shuckburgh, Macmillan & Co., 1889
Scullard, H. H., *Scipio Africanus in the Second Punic War*, Cambridge University Press, 1930
Scullard, H. H., *Scipio Africanus: Soldier and Politician*, Thames & Hudson, 1970
Titus Livius, *The History of Rome*, Book XXX, translated by Cyrus Edmonds, London, 1875

Chapter 2: BATTLE OF HASTINGS

Belloc, Hilaire, *William the Conqueror*, Peter Davies, 1933
Bryant, Arthur, *The Story of England*, Collins, 1953
Burne, A. H., *Battlefields of England*, Methuen, 1950
Burne, A. H., *More Battlefields of England*, Methuen, 1952
Churchill, Winston S., *A History of the English Speaking Peoples*, Vol. I, Cassell, 1956
Compton, Piers, *Harold the King*, Robert Hale, 1961
Douglas, D. C., *William the Conqueror*, Eyre & Spottiswoode, 1964
Freeman, E. A., *The Norman Conquest*, Clarendon Press, 1869
Fuller, J. F. C., *The Decisive Battles of the Western World*, Vol. I, Eyre & Spottiswoode, 1954
George, H. B., *Battles of English History*, Methuen, 1895
Lemmon, C. H., *The Field of Hastings*, Budd & Gillatt, 1957
Muntz, Hope, *The Golden Warrior*, Chatto & Windus, 1948
Oman, Charles, *A History of the Art of War in the Middle Ages*, Methuen, 2nd edition, 1924
Ramsay, James, *The Foundations of England*, Vol. II, Swan Sonnenschein, 1898
Schofield, Guy, 'The Third Battle of 1066', *History Today*, October 1966
Seymour, William, *Battles In Britain*, Vol. I, Sidgwick & Jackson, 1975
Stenton, F. M., *William the Conqueror and the Rule of the Normans*, Putnam, 1908
Stenton, F. M., *Anglo-Saxon England*, Clarendon Press, 1943

Chapter 3: BATTLE OF MANZIKERT

Attaleiates, Michael, *Histories*, Vol. 50, *Corpus Scriptorum Historiae Byzantinae*, Bonn, 1829–97

Bryennius, Nicephorus, *Histories*, Vol. 26, *Corpus Scriptorum Historiae Byzantinae*, Bonn, 1829–97
Cahen, Claude, *Pre-Ottoman Turkey*, Sidgwick & Jackson, 1968
Finlay, George, *A History of Greece: The Byzantine and Greek Empires*, Oxford University Press, 1877
Friendly, Alfred, *The Dreadful Day*, Hutchinson, 1981
Fuller, J. F. C., *The Decisive Battles of the Western World*, Vol. I, Eyre & Spottiswoode, 1954
Gibbon, Edward, *The Decline and Fall of the Roman Empire*, Vol. VI, Methuen, 1898
Husey, J. M., *The Later Macedonians, the Comneni and the Angeli*, Cambridge Medieval History, Vol. IV, *The Byzantine Empire*, Cambridge, 1966
Jenkins, R. J. H., *The Byzantine Empire On the Eve of the Crusades*, London, 1955
Lewis, Bernard, *The Emergence of Modern Turkey*, London, 1961
Matthew of Edessa, trans. Eduard Dulaurier, *Chronicles*, Paris, 1858
Oman, C. W. C., *The Byzantine Empire*, T. Fisher Unwin, 1892
Oman, C. W. C., *A History of the Art of War in the Middle Ages*, Vol. I, Methuen, 1924
Runciman, Steven, *Byzantine Civilization*, Methuen, 1961
Streater, Jasper, 'The Battle of Manzikert', *History Today*, Vol. XVII, April 1967

Chapters 4 and 5: BATTLE OF HATTIN

Beha ed-Din Abu El-Mehasan Yusuf, *Saladin*, Palestine Pilgrims' Text Society, London, 1897
Chronique Arabes des Croisades, texts collected and presented by Francisco Gabriell and translated from the Italian, Sindabad, Paris, 1977
Conder, C. R., *The Latin Kingdom of Jerusalem*, London, 1897
Finucane, Ronald C., *Soldiers of the Faith*, J. M. Dent & Sons Ltd, 1983
Fuller, J. F. C., *The Decisive Battles of the Western World*, Vol. I, Eyre & Spottiswoode, 1954
Hindley, Geoffrey, *Saladin*, Constable, 1975
Keightley, Thomas, *The Crusaders*, John W. Parker, 1847
Lane-Poole, Stanley, *Saladin and the Fall of the Kingdom of Jerusalem*, G. P. Putnam's Sons, 1898
Latrie, M. L. De Mas, *Chronique D'Ernoul*, published for La Société de L'Histoire de France, Paris, 1871
Oman, Charles, *A History of the Art of War in the Middle Ages*, Vol. I, Methuen & Co. Ltd, 1924
Peters, Edward, *The First Crusade: The Chronicle of Fulcher of Chartres*, University of Pennsylvania Press, 1971
Recueil des Historians des Croisades, Vols III and IV, Paris, 1841–1906
Richard, Jean, 'An Account of the Battle of Hattin', *Speculum*, Vol. XXVII, 1952
Runciman, Steven, *A History of the Crusades*, Vols I and II, Cambridge, 1951 and 1952
Runciman, Steven, *The First Crusade*, Cambridge University Press, 1980
Setton, Kenneth M., (ed. Marshall W. Baldwin), *A History of the Crusades*, Vol. I, *The First Hundred Years*, University of Pennsylvania Press, 1955
Smail, R. C., *Crusading Warfare, 1097–1193*, Cambridge University Press, 1956
Stevenson, W. B., *The Crusaders in the East*, Cambridge University Press, 1907
Treece, Henry, *The Crusades*, The Bodley Head, 1962
William of Tyre, *A History of the Deeds done beyond the sea*, 2 vols, Columbia, 1971

Chapter 6: BATTLE OF BOSWORTH

Bagley, J. J., *The Earls of Derby, 1485–1985*, Sidgwick & Jackson, 1985
Cheetham, Anthony, *Life and Times of Richard III*, Weidenfeld & Nicolson, 1977
Gairdner, James, 'The Battle of Bosworth', *Archaeologica*, LV, 1896

Kendall, P. M., *Richard III*, George Allen & Unwin Ltd, 1955
Rees, David, *The Son of Prophecy*, Black Raven Press, 1985
Richmond, Colin, 'The Battle of Bosworth', *History Today*, Vol. 35, August 1985
Seymour, William, *Battles in Britain*, Vol. I, Sidgwick & Jackson, 1975
Williams, D. T., *The Battle of Bosworth*, Bosworth Publications, 1984

Primary Sources:
Chronicle of the Abbey of Croyland (Third Continuation), translated from the Latin by
 Henry T. Riley, London, 1854
Three Books of Polydore Vergil's English History, edited by Sir Henry Ellis, Campden
 Society, 1844

Chapter 7: BATTLE OF NASEBY

Clarendon, Edward Earl of, *The History of the Rebellion and Civil Wars in England*, Vol.
 IV, Clarendon Press, 1888
Dore, R. Roger, *Sir William Brereton's Siege of Chester and the Campaign of Naseby*,
 Transactions of the Lancashire and Cheshire Antiquarian Society, Vol. LXVII, 1957
Douglas Hamilton, William, ed., *Calendar of State Papers, Domestic Series, 1644–1645*,
 London, 1890
Fraser, Antonia, *Cromwell: Our Chief of Men*, Weidenfeld & Nicolson, 1973
Fuller, J. F. C., *The Decisive Battles of the Western World*, Vol. II, Eyre & Spottiswoode,
 1955
Gardiner, Samuel R., *History of the Great Civil War, 1642–1649*, Vol. II, Longman, Green,
 & Co., 1889
Kishlansky, M. A., *The Rise of the New Model Army*, Cambridge University Press, 1979
Markham, C. R., *A Life of the Great Lord Fairfax*, Vol. I, Macmillan & Co., 1870
Morley, John, *Oliver Cromwell*, Macmillan, 1910
Rogers, H. C. B., *Battles and Generals of the Civil Wars, 1642–1651*, Seeley Service & Co.
 Ltd, 1968
Seymour, William, *Battles in Britain*, Vol. II, Sidgwick & Jackson, 1975
Slingsby, Sir Henry, (ed. D. Parsons), *Diary*, 1836
Thomson, G. M., *Warrior Prince*, Secker & Warburg, 1976
Walker, Sir Edward, *Historical Discourses*, London, 1705
Wedgwood, C. V., *The King's War, 1641–1647*, Collins, 1958
Woolrych, Austin, *Battles of the English Civil War*, B. T. Batsford Ltd, 1961
Young, Peter, *Naseby, 1645*, Century Publishing, 1985
Young, Peter and Holmes, Richard, *The English Civil War*, London, 1974

Primary Sources:
Ormonde Manuscript, Series II, Historical Manuscripts Commission, London, 1903
Portland Manuscripts, Vol. I, Historical Manuscripts Commission, London, 1891

Chapter 8: BATTLE OF LEUTHEN

Campbell, Thomas, *Frederick the Great: His Court and Times*, Vol. III, London, 1843
Carlyle, Thomas, *History of Frederick II of Prussia*, Vol. VII, London, 1888
Duffy, Christopher, *Frederick the Great: A Military Life*, Routledge & Kegan Paul, 1985
Fuller, J. F. C., *The Decisive Battles of the Western World*, Eyre & Spottiswoode, 1955
Goldsmith, Margaret, *Frederick the Great*, Victor Gollancz, 1929
Kitchen, Martin, *A Military History of Germany*, Weidenfeld & Nicolson, 1975
Lloyd and Templehoff, Generals; General Jomini observations; *The History of the Seven
 Years War*, Vol. I, London, 1808
Rosinski, Herbert, *The Germany Army*, Hogarth Press, 1939

Chapter 9: SARATOGA CAMPAIGN: THE BATTLES OF
FREEMAN'S FARM AND BEMIS HEIGHTS

Arnold, Isaac N., *The Life of Benedict Arnold: His Patriotism and His Treason*, J. C.
    Nimmo & Bain, 1880
Burgoyne, John, *A State of the Expedition from Canada, as Laid Before the House of
    Commons*, London, 1780
Decision on the Hudson, U.S. National Park Service, 1975
Digby, Lt William, (ed. J. P. Baxter), *The British Invasion from the North*, Albany, 1887
Fortescue, J. W., *The History of the British Army*, Vol. III, Macmillan & Co., 1902
Fuller, J. F. C., *The Decisive Battles of the United States*, Hutchinson, 1942
Fuller, J. F. C., *The Decisive Battles of the Western World*, Vol. II, Eyre & Spottiswoode,
    1955
Furneaux, Rupert, *Saratoga: The Decisive Battle*, George Allen & Unwin Ltd, 1971
Gentleman's Magazine, The, Vol. XLVII, 1777, London
Hudleston, F. J., *Gentlemen Johnny Burgoyne*, Bobbs-Merrill Co., 1927
Lunt, James, *John Burgoyne of Saratoga*, Harcourt Brace Jovanovich, New York, 1975
Mackesy, Piers, *The War for America, 1775–1783*, Harvard University Press, 1964
Nickerson, Hoffman, *The Turning Point of the Revolution*, New York, 1928
Seymour, William, *Yours to Reason Why*, Sidgwick & Jackson, 1982
Stedman, C., *The History of the Origin, Progress, and Termination of the American War*,
    Vol. I, London, 1794
Wilkinson, James, *Memoirs of My Own Times*, Vol. I, Philadelphia, 1816

Chapter 10: BATTLE OF BORODINO

Brett-James, Antony (ed.), *General Wilson's Journal, 1812–1814*, William Kimber, 1964
Chandler, D. G., *The Campaigns of Napoleon*, Weidenfeld & Nicolson, 1967
Duffy, Christopher, *Borodino*, Seeley, Service & Co. Ltd, 1972
Glover, Michael, *Warfare in the Age of Bonaparte*, London, 1980
Holmes, E. R., *Borodino, 1812*, Charles Knight & Co. Ltd, 1971
Tolstoy, Leo, *War and Peace*, New York, 1982
Wilson, General Sir Robert, (ed. The Rev H. Randolph), *Narrative of Events During the
    Invasion of Russia*, John Murray, 1860

Chapters 11 and 12: BATTLES OF LIGNY AND WATERLOO

Becke, A. F., *Napoleon and Waterloo*, Kegan Paul, 1936
Chalfont, the Lord (ed.), *Waterloo: Battle of Three Armies*, Sidgwick & Jackson, 1979
Chandler, D. G., 'Napoleon's Battle System', *History Today*, Vol. XV, February 1965
Chandler, D. G., *The Campaigns of Napoleon*, Weidenfeld & Nicolson, 1967
Cotton, Sergeant-Major Edward, *A Voice From Waterloo*, London, 1854
Gardner, Dorsey, *Quatre Bras, Ligny and Waterloo*, Kegan Paul, Trench, & Co., 1882
Glover, Michael, *Warfare in the Age of Bonaparte*, London, 1980
Gronow, Captain, The Reminiscences and Recollections of, The R. S. Surtees Society, 1984
Jomini, General Baron de (trans. S. V. Benet), *The Campaign of Waterloo*, New York,
    1853
King, Mackenzie (ed.), *With Napoleon at Waterloo*, Francis Griffiths, London, 1911
Lamb, Richard, 'Ligny: Napoleon's Final Victory', *War Monthly*, April 1981
Longford, Elizabeth, *Wellington: The Years of the Sword*, Weidenfeld & Nicolson, 1969
Manu, Michael, *And They Rode On*, Michael Russell, 1984
Mercer, Cavalié, *Journal of the Waterloo Campaign*, Vols I and II, William Blackwood &
    Sons, London, 1870
Siborne, W., *History of the War in France and Belgium*, Vols I and II, London, 1844
Sloane, W. M., *Life of Napoleon Bonaparte*, Vol. IV, Macmillan & Co, 1901

Chapter 13: BATTLE OF THE ALMA

Bryant, Arthur, *Jackets of Green*, Collins, 1972
Clifford, H. H., *Henry Clifford, VC*, London, 1956
Fenwick, K., *Voice from the Ranks*, London, 1954
Fortescue, J. W., *A History of the British Army*, Vol. XIII, Macmillan & Co., 1930
Gibbs, Peter, *The Battle of the Alma*, Weidenfeld & Nicolson, 1963
Gough Calthorpe, Lt-Colonel S. J., *Cadogan's Crimea*, Hamish Hamilton, 1979
Hibbert, Christopher, *The Destruction of Lord Raglan*, Longman, 1961
Holt, Elizabeth, *The Crimean War*, London, 1974
Hume, Major-General J. R., *Reminiscences of the Crimean Campaign*, London, 1894
Kinglake, A. W., *The Invasion of the Crimea*, Vols II and III, William Blackwood, 1877
Maurice, Major-General Sir F., *The History of the Scots Guards*, Vol. II, Chatto & Windus, 1934
Russell, W. H., *The British Expedition to the Crimea*, G. Routledge & Co., 1858
Seaton, Albert, *The Crimean War: A Russian Chronicle*, Batsford, 1977
Warner, Philip, *The Crimean War*, Arthur Baker Ltd, 1972
Wood, General Sir Evelyn, *The Crimea in 1854 and 1894*, Chapman & Hall, 1896
Woodham-Smith, Cecil, *The Reason Why*, Constable, 1953

Chapters 14 and 15: SEVEN DAYS' BATTLE

Alexander, E. P., *Military Memoirs of a Confederate*, Charles Scribner's Sons, New York, 1907
Catton, Bruce, *Mr Lincoln's Army*, Doubleday & Co. Inc., New York, 1951
Catton, Bruce, *This Hallowed Ground*, Victor Gollancz, 1957
Freeman, D. S., *R. E. Lee, A Biography*, Vol. II, Charles Scribner's Sons, New York, 1934
Freeman, D. S., *Lee's Lieutenants*, Vol. I, Charles Scribner's Sons, New York, 1943
Fuller, J. F. C., *The Decisive Battles of the United States*, Hutchinson & Co. Ltd, 1942
Henderson, G. F. R., *Stonewall Jackson and the American Civil War*, Vol. II, Longman, Green, & Co., 1904
Johnson, R. U. and Buel, C. C., (eds), *Battles and Leaders of the Civil War*, Vol. II, New York, 1888
McClellan, G. B., *McClellan's Own Story, The War for the Union*, London, 1887
Steele, M. F., *American Campaigns*, Vol. I, Washington, 1935
Webb, Alexander S., *The Peninsula*, Charles Scribner's Sons, New York, 1881
Wood, W. B. and Edmonds, J. E., *A History of the Civil War in the United States, 1861–5*, Methuen & Co., 1905

Chapter 16: BATTLE OF GETTYSBURG

Alexander, E. P., *Military Memoirs of a Confederate*, Charles Scribner's Sons, New York, 1907
Catton, Bruce, *This Hallowed Ground*, Victor Gollancz, 1957
Catton, Bruce, *Gettysburg: The Final Fury*, London, 1975
Civil War Times Illustrated Gettysburg Edition, Vol. 2, No. 4 July 1963
Coddington, Edwin, *The Gettysburg: A Study in Command*, New York, 1968
Fox, Charles K. (ed.), *Gettysburg*, A. S. Barnes, 1969
Freeman, D. S., *Lee's Lieutenants*, Vols II and III, Scribners, New York, 1943
Fuller, J. F. C., *The Decisive Battles of the United States*, Hutchinson & Co. Ltd, 1942
Gordon, J. B., *Reminiscences of the Civil War*, Archibald Constable & Co., 1904
Johnson, R. U. and Buel, C. C. (eds), *Battles and Leaders of the Civil War*, Vols I–IV, New York, 1888
Lee, G. C., *The True History of the Civil War*, Philadelphia and London, 1903
Mitchell, Joseph B., *Decisive Battles of the Civil War*, Putnams, New York, 1955

Paris, the Comte de, *History of the Civil War in America*, Vol. III, London, 1883
Stackpole, Edward J., *They Met at Gettysburg*, The Stackpole Company, 1951
Steele, M. F., *American Campaigns*, Vol. I, Washington, 1935
War of the Rebellion, U.S. War Department, Official Records
Wood, W. B. and Edmonds, J. E., *A History of the Civil War in the United States, 1861–5*, Methuen & Co., 1905

Chapter 17: VICKSBURG CAMPAIGN

Badeau, Adam, *Military History of Ulysses S. Grant*, Vol. I, London, 1881
Catton, Bruce, *This Hallowed Ground*, Victor Gollancz, 1957
Catton, Bruce, *Never Call Retreat*, Victor Gollancz, 1966
Churchill, Winston S., *The American Civil War*, Cassell, 1961
Everhart, William C., *Vicksburg*, National Park Service Handbook, 1961
Fuller, J. F. C., *The Decisive Battles of the United States*, Hutchinson & Co. Ltd, 1942
Grant, U. S., *Personal Memoirs of*, Vol. I, T. Fisher Unwin, 1895
Greene, F. V., *The Mississippi*, New York, 1882
Johnson, R. U. and Buel, C. C. (eds), *Battles and Leaders of the Civil War*, Vol. III, New York, 1884
Livermore, W. R., *The Story of the Civil War*, G. P. Putnam's Sons, 1913
Marshall, Charles, *An Aide-de-Camp of Lee*, Little, Brown & Co, Boston, 1927
Simon, John Y. (ed), *The Papers of Ulysses S. Grant*, Vol. 8, Southern Illinois University Press, 1979

Primary Source:
War of the Rebellion, Series I, Vol. XXIV, Parts 1, 2 and 3, 1860

Chapter 18: CHICKAMAUGA–CHATTANOOGA CAMPAIGN

Andrews, J. Cutler, *The South Reports the Civil War*, Princeton University Press, 1970
Badeau, Adam, *Military History of Ulysses S. Grant*, Vol. I, London, 1881
Catton, Bruce, *This Hallowed Ground*, Victor Gollancz, 1957
Catton, Bruce, *Never Call Retreat*, Victor Gollancz, 1966
Churchill, Winston S., *The American Civil War*, Cassell, 1961
Cist, Henry M., *The Army of the Cumberland*, New York, 1882
Fuller, J. F. C., *The Decisive Battles of the United States*, Hutchinson & Co. Ltd, 1942
Gracie, Archibald, *The Truth About Chickamauga*, New York, 1911
Grant, U. S., *Personal Memoirs of*, Vol. I, T. Fisher Unwin, 1895
Hattaway, Herman and Jones, Archer, *How the North Won: A Military History of the Civil War*, University of Illinois Press, 1983
Johnson, R. U. and Buel, C. C. (eds), *Battles and Leaders of the Civil War*, Vol. III, New York, 1884
Steele, M. F., *American Campaigns*, Vol. I, Washington, 1935
Sullivan, James R., *Chickamauga and Chattanooga Battlefields*, National Park Service Handbook, 1961
Wood, W. B. and Edmonds, J. E., *A History of the Civil War in the United States, 1861–5*, Methuen & Co., 1905

Chapters 19 and 20: BATTLE OF ISANDHLWANA

Clarke, Sonia, *The Invasion of Zululand 1879*, Brenthurst Press, 1979
Clements, W. H., *The Glamour and Tragedy of the Zulu War*, John Lane, The Bodley Head, 1936

Colenso, Frances E., *History of the Zulu War and its Origins*, Chapman and Hall Limited, 1880
Coupland, Sir Reginald, *Zulu Battle Piece, Isandhlwana*, Collins, 1948
Durnford, Lt-Colonel E., *A Soldier's Life and Work in South Africa*, London, 1882
Emery, Frank, *The Red Soldier*, Johannesburg, 1977
French, Major the Hon. Gerald, *Lord Chelmsford and the Zulu War*, John Lane, The Bodley Head, 1939
Furneaux, Rupert, *The Zulu War*, Weidenfeld & Nicolson, 1963
Harford, Colonel Henry, *Zulu War Journal*, (edited by Daphne Child), Shutter and Shooter, Pietermaritzburg, 1978
Morris, Donald R., *The Washing of the Spears*, The Chaucer Press, 1973
Rothwell, Captain J. S., RA, *Narrative of the Field Operations Connected with the Zulu War of 1879*, War Office, London, 1881

Chapter 21: BATTLE OF TANNENBERG

Evans, Geoffrey, *Tannenberg 1410:1914*, Hamish Hamilton, 1970
Frankland, Noble and Dowling, Christopher, (eds), *Decisive Battles of the Twentieth Century*, Sidgwick & Jackson, 1976
Fuller, J. F. C., *The Decisive Battles of the Western World*, Vol. III, Eyre & Spottiswoode, 1956
Hart, B. H. Liddell, *A History of the World War, 1914–1918*, Faber & Faber, 1934
Hindenburg, Marshal von, (trans. F. A. Holt), *Out of My Life*, Cassell, 1920
Hoffmann, Maj-General Max, (trans. Eric Sutton), *War Diaries and Other Papers*, Vol. II, Martin Secker, 1929
Ironside, Maj-General Sir Edmund, *Tannenberg: The First Thirty Days in East Prussia*, William Blackwood & Sons, 1925
Knox, Maj-General Sir Alfred, *With the Russian Army, 1914–1917*, Hutchinson & Co., 1921
Ludendorff, General Erich, *My War Memories, 1914–1918*, Vol. I, Hutchinson & Co.

Chapter 22: BATTLE OF WARSAW

D'Abernon, the Lord, *The Eighteenth Decisive Battle of the World: Warsaw, 1920*, Hodder & Stoughton, 1931
Davies, Norman, *God's Playground: A History of Poland*, Vol. II: *1795 to the Present*, Clarendon Press, Oxford, 1981
Fuller, J. F. C., *Decisive Battles, Vol II: From Napoleon the First to General Franco*, Eyre & Spottiswoode, 1940
Reddaway, W. F., *Marshal Pilsudski*, George Routledge & Sons Ltd, 1939
Roure, Rémy, *Le chef de l'armée rouge – Mikail Toukatchevski*, E. Fasquelle, Paris, 1928
Simpkin, Richard, *Deep Battle: The Brainchild of Marshal Tukhachevskii*, Brassey's Defence Publishers, 1987
Trotsky, Leon, (trans. Brian Pearce), *How the Revolution Armed*, Vol. III: *The Year 1920*, New Park Publications, 1981

Chapter 23: SIEGE OF DIEN BIEN PHU

Fall, Bernard B., *Hell In a Very Small Place: The Siege of Dien Bien Phu*, Pall Mall Press, 1967
Graham, Lt-Colonel Andrew, *Interval in Indo-China*, London, 1956
Hammer, Ellen J., *The Struggle for Indo-China*, Stanford University Press, 1954
Langlais, Colonel Pierre, *Dien Bien Phu*, Paris, 1963

O'Ballance, Edgar, *The Indo-China War, 1945–1954*, Faber & Faber, 1964
Roy, Jules, *The Battle of Dienbienphu*, Faber & Faber, 1965

Chapter 24: THE NATURE AND PATTERN OF WAR

Clausewitz, Carl von, ed. and trans. Howard, Michael and Paret, Peter, *On War*, Princeton University Press, 1984
Custance, Admiral Sir Reginald, *A Study of War*, Constable & Co. Ltd, 1927
Hart, B. H. Liddell, *The Decisive Wars of History*, G. Bell & Sons Ltd, 1929
Henderson, Colonel G. F. R., ed. Malcolm, Neill, *The Science of War*, Longman, Green, & Co., 1905
Jomini, Baron A. H. de, trans. Mendell, Captain G. H. and Craighill, Lieutenant W. P., *The Art of War*, Philadelphia, 1862
Oman, C. W. C., *The Art of War in the Middle Ages, AD378–1515*, London, 1885
Tuker, Lt-General Sir Francis, *The Pattern of War*, Cassell & Co. Ltd, 1948

Index